RECORDS OF
THE MEDIEVAL SWORD

For all swordsmen, past and present.

RECORDS OF
THE MEDIEVAL SWORD

Ewart Oakeshott

THE BOYDELL PRESS

First published 1991
The Boydell Press, Woodbridge

Reprinted 1998, 2002, 2004
Transferred to digital printing

ISBN 978 0 85115 566 1

The Boydell Press is an imprint of Boydell & Brewer Ltd
PO Box 9, Woodbridge, Suffolk IP12 3DF, UK
and of Boydell & Brewer Inc.
668 Mt Hope Avenue, Rochester, NY 14620, USA
website: www.boydellandbrewer.com

A CiP catalogue record for this book is available
from the British Library

This publication is printed on acid-free paper

Printed and bound in Great Britain by
TJ Books Limited, Padstow, Cornwall

CONTENTS

List of abbreviations

Behmer
Elis Behmer, *Das zweischneidige Schwert der Germanischen Völkerwanderungszeit* Stockholm 1939

Boccia & Coelho
Lionello G. Boccia & Edoardo T. Coelho, *Armi Bianche Italiane*, Milan 1970

Christensen & Hoffmeyer
E.A. Christensen and A.B. Hoffmeyer, *Gammelt Jern* Copenhagen 1968

Davidson
Hilda Ellis Davidson, *The Sword in Anglo-Saxon England*, Oxford 1961

Dufty
R. Dufty (ed.), *European Swords and Daggers in H.M. Tower of London* (London 1974)

EAA
Blair, Claude, *European and American Arms*, London

Gamber, Ortwin
Die mittelalterlichen Blankwaffen der Wiener Waffensammlung (Vienna 1962)

Gun Report
The Gun Report, Aledo, Illinois

Hayward
J.F. Hayward, *The Kretschmar von Kienbusch Collection of Armour and Arms*, Princeton 1965

Hoffmeyer
Ada Bruhn Hoffmeyer, *Middelalderens Tvaeeggede Svaerd*, Copenhagen 1954

Laking, Sir Guy
Laking, Francis *A Record of European Arms and Armour through Seven Ages* (London 1921)

Leppaaho
J. Leppaaho, *Spateisenzeitliche Waffen aus Finnland* (Helsinki 1964)

Mann & Norman
James G. Mann (rev. A.V.B. Norman) *European Arms and Armour in the Wallace Collection* (London 1962, 1986)

Oakeshott, *AOW*
Ewart Oakeshott, *The Archaeology of Weapons* London 1960

Oakeshott, *MS*
Ewart Oakeshott, *Medieval Swords*, 'Gun Report' 1987

Oakeshott, *SAC*
Ewart Oakeshott, *The Sword in the Age of Chivalry* (London 1964: 2nd edn London 1981)

Schneider & Stuber
Hugo Schneider & Karl Stuber, *Waffen im Schweizerischen Landesmuseum: Griffwaffen I* (Zurich 1980)

Seitz
Heribert Seitz, *Blankwaffen* Vol. 1, (Braunschweig 1968)

Stuber & Wetler
Karl Stuber & Hans Wetler (eds.), *Blankwaffen, Festschrift Hugo Schneider* (Zurich 1982)

Wegeli
R. Wegeli, 'Inschriften auf Mittelalterliche Schwertklingen', *Zeitschrift für historische Waffenkunde* III, 1903

Ypey, *Antiek*
'Een Romans Ceremoniel Zwaard, gevonden bij Rees aan den Nederrijn', *Antiek* June/July 1985

Ypey, *Offa*
Ypey, J. 'Einige Wikingerzeitliche Schwerter aus den Nederlanden', *Offa*, 41 (1984)

ZHWK
Zeitschrift für historische Waffen - und Kostumkunde, Vienna

PREFACE

This book marks the culmination of a lifetime of research into the origins, development, classification, usage and mystique of the knightly sword of medieval Europe. What is presented here is a selection from a very large body of photographs and notes amassed and collated over a period of over half a century – and, of course, only shows a tiny proportion of the surviving swords; for instance, I have not been able to include the splendid collections in Copenhagen, Stockholm and Zurich, not to mention countless others in provincial museums all over Europe. Its intention is to set before the reader my own comments and observations, all based upon intensive and (I hope) scholarly study of these magnificent and glamorous weapons. The notes, written down over this half-century originally in the heat of observation or revelation have been organised, clarified and extended as the years of study have passed. My first intention was merely to be able to bequeath them to the library of the Royal Armouries at the Tower of London in order to offer to the students of following generations the benefit of the work I have done. Thus there is a certain informality in presentation since I believed that I would be directly addressing, as from the grave, young students such as I myself once was. Now that a proportion of these notes are to be published, it has seemed proper and desirable to print them as they are, *ipsissima verba*, so that I may still seem in direct contact with the students who use this book.

I have to admit that my approach to this fascinating subject is a romantic one. I have been unable to avoid seeing, and celebrating, glamour as well as the academic niceties in all the books and articles I have written; and the enthusiasm which still burns in me is the outward expression of a love-affair with the sword which began when I was four, seventy years ago. However, the reader will find little romance in the pages which follow and he will have to supply the Glamour himself from what he finds there, for I present only bones – the elegant and stately bones of an ethos and a *Zeitgeist* which, in the late 20th century, is difficult to understand. Even so, as in pagan graves, along with the bones may sometimes be found a gem.

The framework which supports this study is a typology of the European two-edged sword of the High Middle Ages (c.AD1050-1520) which I worked out in careful detail thirty years ago and first published in *The Archaeology of Weapons* and elaborated four years later in *The Sword in the Age of Chivalry*.

In the heat of youthful enthusiasm I worked out this typological analysis during the 1950s, never dreaming that I might be requested and required to elaborate upon it, so when I came to make this elaboration as a definitive typology, I had to squeeze extensions into the rather sketchy framework I had developed. Now, another quarter-century on, I am faced with having to do it again, once more to press new knowledge, new ideas, above all new *finds* into what had become a typological strait-jacket which has become a standard reference. Now you will find not only swords which were unknown in 1960, but others, which I had put firmly into certain types, now moved (in the light of new information and clearer thought) into other types. Nor is that all. I have had to add three new sub-types – Xa, XIIa, and XIIIb – and two entirely new types, XXI and XXII. I doubt whether I shall live long enough to elaborate yet again, though I am sure someone will have to do so sooner or later. Space does not permit, nor the work require, that this typology should be repeated here in full though of course the basic typology (bones again) is set out and illustrated; and since inevitably much of what I wrote all those years ago has been outrun and outmoded by another thirty years of research, most of the many errors in those books can be corrected and some of the mass of new discovery included – and no doubt many fresh errors perpetrated which will in their turn be corrected by the uncovering of more evidence as the decades pass. It will fall then, maybe to you who read this, to take over where I have to leave off.

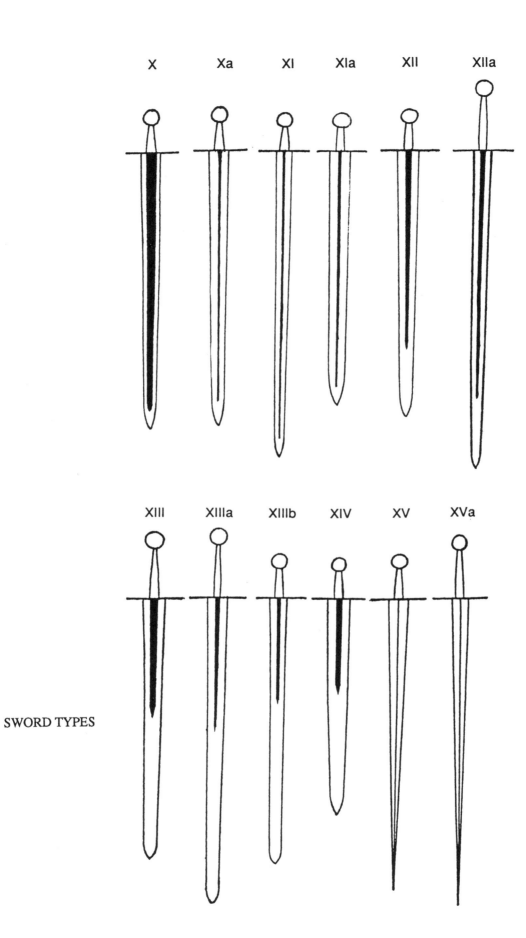

X Xa XI XIa XII XIIa

XIII XIIIa XIIIb XIV XV XVa

SWORD TYPES

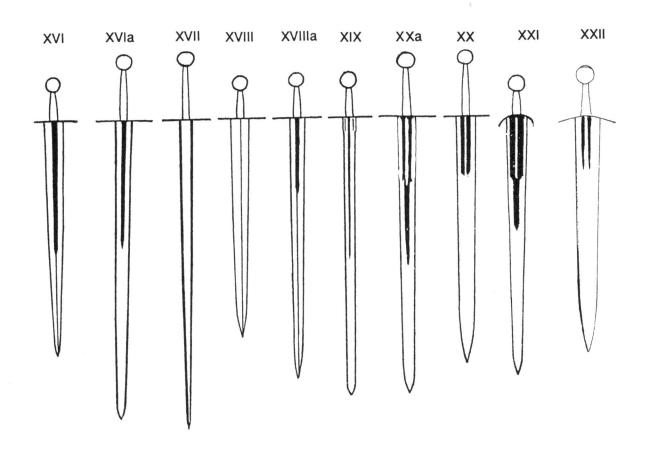

XVI XVIa XVII XVIII XVIIIa XIX XXa XX XXI XXII

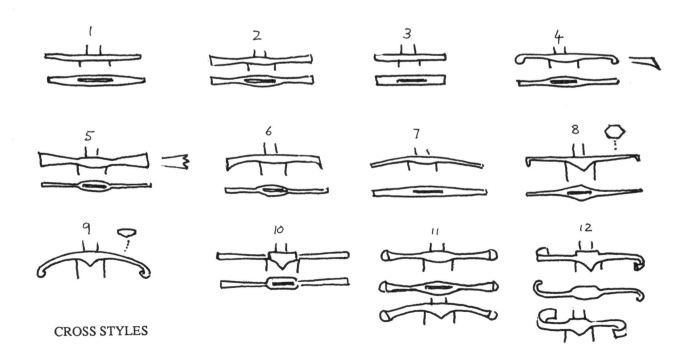

1   2   3   4

5   6   7   8

9   10   11   12

CROSS STYLES

ACKNOWLEDGEMENTS

To name everyone whose support and encouragement has been of such vital importance to me over the past sixty years would occupy far too much space, for in truth their name is legion; I must however, name just a few of them, beginning with four who have gone on before me. They are my old friends Russell Robinson and Evan Perry of The Tower of London, and John Hayward of The Victoria and Albert Museum: and that towering supremo of the armour world, Sir James Mann, KCVO, FBA, PPSA, a Grand Seigneur into whose presence I first crept in 1946 to be received with a warmth of approval that sent me away filled with determined zeal to do what in the end I have done. Without his continued support right up to the time of his death, and the friendship of the other three, I should have lacked the inspiration and drive in those early years so essential to me in my task.

There are obvious reasons why I must not name the many friends still engaged in the pursuit and study of arms and armour who have been so generous to me by giving me access to the collections, both public and private, in their care, and who have supplied many of the photographs in this book; but those who read this composite acknowledgement must know how extremely grateful I am to each and every one of them for all that they have done for me.

However, two outstanding personalities must be named, for they are old and valued friends of forty years standing, whose emminence in high office has never cooled that friendship. They are A.V.B. Norman, MA, FSA, and Claude Blair, MA, VPSA.

My thanks also are due to the present owner of the Sword of Edward III, discussed here in Appendix D, who has most generously supplied numerous photographs of the sword, some of which are reproduced; and to the Bundesanstalt für Materialprüfung of Berlin, in the person of Dr Christian Segebade, whose report is reproduced (in translation) in full.

Of course, every author who presents a book of this kind must acknowledge the long-suffering patience of his nearest and dearest, and this I do with all my heart; but there is one whose patience and long-suffering must have been stretched to the very limit – Mrs. Pat Tucker, who with unfailing good-humour has typed and retyped the whole thing over the period of several years, interrupted all the time by a spate of articles and notes all in my very small, cramped handwriting. I would crown her with many crowns. And lastly, as the principal functionaries of any procession always come at the end, I must especially make known the depth of my gratitude to The Worshipful Company of Cutlers and The British Academy, whose response to an appeal for funds to support the production of so large and so fully illustrated a work was given with instant and unstinted generosity.

So may this book, which is my monument, be also a lasting tribute to all those, wherever they may be, who have made it possible to turn what had long seemed only an impossible dream into a reality.

INTRODUCTION

I once wrote 'of all the weapons devised by Man in the long lapse of the centuries, the sword is the only one which combines effectiveness in defence with force in attack, and since its Bronze Age beginnings has gathered round itself a potent mystique which sets it above any other man-made object. Though the sword did not reach its peak of practical efficiency in combat until the 17th century with the development of the swift deadly little small-sword in the France of Louis XIV, the flowering of its mystical significance came at the end of the 11th century.'

Here, then, underlying the dry bones of archaeological study, is the concept of a most noble weapon which had high significance in the minds of men and fulfilled a most vital practical purpose in their hands. In spite of the deep knowledge of this within the race-memory, many scholars in the last century and a half, learnedly writing about arms and armour, have almost completely ignored the knightly sword of medieval Europe, dismissing it as a crude and brutish chopping instrument of dull and unvarying shape.

A glance through the following pages of photographs might seem to support this view but closer inspection will show how false, in fact, it is. These swords have an austere perfection of line and proportion – surely the very essence of beauty – which is comparable with, perhaps, the majestic pottery of the Chinese Sung dynasty; and though all these swords of the high middle ages in Europe are made upon the same basic design of blade, cross-guard and pommel, there is great diversity in all three elements. Each 'type' is different from any other, and across the types run what may be called 'Families' of swords, which, unlike the types themselves, reflect the passing changes of fashionable taste. And if they have beauty, they are also extremely efficiently designed for the work they were called upon to do, being as carefully balanced (for those purposes) as is a modern tennis-racket or fishing-rod, and contrary to popular belief are by no means heavy; from the time of the ancient Celts to the last days when they were actually used in battle (that is, within living memory) the average weight was around 2 lbs.

The 'knightly' sword is derived directly, via the swords of the Vikings, from the long two-edged iron swords of the prehistoric Celts. Very many of these splendid weapons from the first four centuries B.C. have been found in various parts of Europe, though the only ones so far found in the British Isles are small and of poor quality. Most of the Continental-found ones have blades of an average length of 30" (76cms) and are about 2" (5cms) wide at the hilt – dimensions which are of the same average as swords of the medieval centuries. There are of course exceptions – there is one of these swords in the British Museum found at Orton Meadows near Peterborough whose badly bent blade is over 45" (114cms) long, and as I have said there are many short ones, especially from Britain. Most of these iron-age blades are flat with edges running nearly parallel to a spatulate point, and some are of superb workmanship with shallow grooves or fullers running down the centre of the blades almost to their points; some of these fullers are double or treble, and many are decorated with a texture of tiny dots, which at first glance look like rust-pits but are not, for they are distributed to a controlled pattern and are all of much the same size, and they appear only in the fullers.

I mention these prehistoric blades in some detail because I want to point out that even in the pre-Roman iron-age in Europe there were bladesmiths whose work was as skilful as those of any later age before the 16th century. These swords, too, are light and well-balanced, admirably made for the work they had to do.

Among the finds of swords dating from these pre-Christian centuries are a few which at first sight would be taken to belong to the late 14th century AD for their long blades are acutely tapered and the two edges are separated by a ridge, giving to the blade the section of a flattened diamond. Most of these have been found in contexts such as the bog-deposits of Denmark, which rule out any possibility that they are not of the iron age. They are in fact the long swords of the Roman auxiliary cavalry of a distinct type called *spatha* to differentiate them from the short infantry *gladius*.

These long broadswords of the Celtic and Roman Iron-Age were used also by the Teutonic races of the North, who by about the third century AD were obtaining swords of a different kind from probably, sources within their own 'spheres of influence' in Germany and the Rhineland. These were made, as it were, to a different specification, for a very complex method was used in order to produce a good stiff blade, for the older types seem to have had a tendency to bend, and sometimes a warrior would have to straighten his blade under his foot in the heat of combat. The ownership of these 'pattern-welded' blades, which were so rich and rare that they were considered to be royal treasures, was confined to chieftains or especially favoured 'Hearthmen' of Kings, but by about the middle of the 9th century efficient blades of a far simpler style of manufacture were being produced where a much steelier iron was used, thus obviating the need for the elaborate pattern-welding of former times. This was partly because the use of the sword had become much more universal with the spread of the roving and raiding of the Vikings; and it was these swords, carried all over the known world by these far-travelled war-bands, which were the direct forerunners of the knightly sword.

These precursors of the later Iron Age – the period of the great folk-migrations – and of the Viking Age which was the culmination of those wanderings have been very definitely classified by O. Elis Behmer whose *Das Zweischneidige Schwert der Germanischen Völkerwanderungszeit* was published in Stockholm in 1939, and by Dr Jan Petersen, who published a complete typology of Viking swords in Oslo in 1919, *De Norske Vikingesvaerd*. Both of these typologies, however, were based upon the forms of sword-hilts alone, taking no account of the shapes of blades – which is not surprising, since during those centuries between c. AD250 and 900 there was very little, if any, variation in the actual outline of blades. They varied a little as to size and weight; most of the earlier ones (up to c.850) were pattern-welded while the later ones (c.850-1050) were not, and some had very shallow fullers or none, others had well-defined ones, a few had multiple ones (in a few cases blades have been found with a single fuller on one side and a double one on the other) but these variations were not taken into account in classifying the types.

I was able to follow Jan Petersen when in the late 1950s I worked out a typology of swords to go forward into the High Middle Ages, but in my case I had to take into account the form of the whole sword, not just the hilt, because the only way to make a workable typology of these very variable swords dating between c. AD1050-1510 was to use an aesthetic standard: the appearance, the silhouette if you like, of a sword was what determined its type and the fullering of blades was critical; any type might have a considerable variety of pommels or crosses in its members, but still remain in a particular type.

Petersen numbered his types and sub-types in Roman letters from A to X and Y, so, for the sake of sensible continuity, I made my first type X, ten, and numbered them off in Roman figures up to XX*. My Type X was the same, basically, as Petersen's swords in his X and Y categories, so I went straight on, only moving from letters to numerals. This typology (which, like Behmer's and Petersen's, has so far been regarded as standard and has not been superseded) has been set out in detail in another place, but in order to make this collection, this record, of medieval swords comprehensible I must describe the main characteristics of each type. In the typology of entire swords, I added another one for pommel-forms, and a third for the varying styles of cross-guard. (Until the later 16th century this feature of a sword's hilt, which the Norse called the lower hilt, was never called the 'quillons' but always the cross–*crux*, *croix*, *croisée*, *Kreuz*, *cruz*, *croce* etc). In order to clarify verbal description of the types, I append a diagram.

All the types have blades with two edges; backswords (single-edged blades) and the various forms of curved sword are studies in their own right, and are not included.

In describing the type, I shall add to each its average dimensions, and weight, but it must be understood that such an average will of necessity be vague, for there was in some types (such as XVI, XVII and XVIII) a great deal of variation. Some types have one or more sub-types, which are designated by the addition of a,b, or c.

Dating

The schematic drawing of the typology will show quite clearly the basic forms, while the photographs which follow, with their attendant notes, will show some of the varieties of hilt-forms which were used more or less indiscriminately across the types. When we come to consider the question of dating we are on much more difficult grounds, for with the exception of a very few surviving swords which can clearly be dated to within a span of a few years, most swords have nothing to offer but the internal evidence of their own form, condition, or in rare cases, of the inscriptions upon blade or hilt. Recent (i.e. during the past forty years) discoveries of archaeological material has given some precision, previously unsuspected, to the dating of inlaid calligraphic inscriptions, which I will have to treat as a separate section of this introduction.

In considering the possible date of a sword, we have to have some idea of what we mean by its 'date'. Is it the time at which the blade was made? Is it the time at which the blade was mounted in its hilt – a time which could well have been several years after the actual forging of the blade, just as that mounting could have taken place in a region far from the place of that forging? Also, in its time a good blade may have been re-hilted more than once, just as a hilt may have been mounted upon several blades. We know from the clear evidence of the Norse sagas that a good sword may have been in use over a long period, even across several generations, and though such documentation does not exist except in anecdotal form for the High Middle Ages, we have reason to believe that cherished swords were carried often by grandsons of the original owner. (Certainly we do know that many a fine old blade used by Scottish highlanders in the Jacobite risings was still being used, fitted in a regulation hilt, by officers in Highland regiments at least up to the end of the 19th century).

So the date of a sword's usage might span a century or two, which is of no use in dating it. Therefore we have to make some attempt to strike a mean, and try to assess the time at which blade and hilt came together to make a living sword.

Let me say at once that to put a sword into one of the types is by no means to give it a date. The typology is merely a scaffolding to bring some order into the otherwise amorphous and infinitely varied mass of medieval blade, cross and pommel forms. However, having said that, it is possible to assert that swords with flat broad cutting blades *should* date to a period before the introduction of plate armour in the mid-fourteenth century, were it not for the absolutely indisputable fact that such blades continued in use right through the Middle Ages, particularly in Southern Europe. The big war-swords of Type XIIIa are to be found quite often in unmistakeable contexts of the late 15th – early 16th centuries.

*It is a thought which I rather treasure in my old age that when I was at the start of my work on these swords, I corresponded with Jan Petersen in the same way as now young students correspond with me, thus spanning a period from before the Great War, when Petersen was doing his research for his thesis, to the 1990's.

This problem is made more complex, too, by the longevity of pommel forms. The so-called typical 'Viking' forms (lobated, or of a D-shaped elevation like a tea-cosy, or of a distinctive brazil-nut shape, or formed like an early 19th century Napoleon-style cocked-hat) are still seen in battle scenes in manuscript or upon sculptured monuments far up into the 13th century; the disc-form pommels (plain disc, or variations upon the so-called 'wheel' form) first appear in art, and in Viking grave contexts, in the 11th century, and continue to be popular until the time of Henry VIII, Charles V and Francis I. To ease this complexity, there are just a few types whose popularity does seem to have been confined to a reasonably short span of time. Late in the 14th century a form which has been dubbed variously of 'scent-stopper' or plummet form appears to have become very fashionable all over Western Europe, as well as variants of it, more comprehensively shown in all forms of art of the 1440s to the 1460s, a form likened to a fish-tail. All these forms will beeen clearly among the photographs below.

When these particular pommel forms are found upon swords, then it is reasonable to suggest a date with some exactitude; but it must always be remembered that it was (and still is) the easiest thing in the world to dismount a sword and alter its hilt, either in whole or in part, by replacing the pommel or the cross with one either more fashionable, more to one's personal taste, or to give the sword a better balance. So we might have a blade of a sword forged in Germany in the 1360s with a cross made in Italy in 1420 and a German or Burgundian pommel of 1475.

These desperate hazards which seem to attend any attempt to date a sword are real, but I have put the matter in the most severe form as an indication that any date any expert may assign to a medieval European sword can at best be speculative, and at worst is absurd.

Findings

Such hazards are of course extreme. The majority of medieval swords which survive have been recovered (from the earlier part of the period, say between c.300 and 1125), either from graves or from the beds of rivers or lakes, or in the Pagan North from the great deposits of arms recovered from peat-bogs in Denmark. Though the scope of the book is mostly concerned with the swords of the High Middle Ages, it is necessary here to make brief mention of these bog-deposits, for they have a distinct bearing upon the actual recovery in modern times of swords from water.

The archaeological fact of the deposits themselves is given force by the comments of Roman historians upon certain ceremonial habits of the barbarians of Gaul and Germany. Orosius, writing of a Roman defeat by the Gaulish tribe of the Cimbri at Aurausia in 105 BC says:

> When the enemy had taken posession of two camps and an immense booty, they destroyed under strange imprecations all that had fallen into their hands. The clothes were torn and thrown away, gold and silver thrown into the river, the ring-armour of the men cut to pieces, the accoutrements of the horses destroyed, the horses themselves thrown into the water, and the men with ropes round their neck hung from the trees, so that there was no more booty for the victors than there was mercy for the conquered.

Then Caesar, writing of similar customs among the Gauls, is even more to our purpose:

> When they have decided to fight a battle they generally vow to Mars the booty they hope to take, and after a victory they sacrifice the captured animals and collect the rest of the spoil in one spot. Among many of the tribes high piles of it can be seen on consecrated ground; and it is almost an unknown thing for anyone to dare, in defiance of religious law, to conceal his booty at home or to remove anything placed upon the piles.

It has now been established beyond reasonable doubt that some of the great deposits taken from the peat in Denmark were originally laid out as Caesar says, on open ground which over almost two millennia has has become bog; and that some deposits were under water, in meres which have become bog. This is shown by the fact that hollow vessels like buckets, which might have floated, were held down by having stones put inside them, and other floatable objects were firmly pegged down.

These great deposits – Nydam, Vimose, Kragehul and Thorsbjerg – contained very many swords. A large number of these were destroyed, as Orosius said, by being either broken, or bent – almost folded up, some of them – or having their edges so violently hacked about that they could never have been used again. Even so, there are plenty which came out in good enough condition to be taken straight into hand-to-hand combat, for peat is a splendid preservative of iron and steel.

It is also evident that weapons, swords in particular, were ceremonially thrown into rivers and lakes, for what reason (other than to conform to a religious ritual) we do not really know. That this practice was continued into the High Middle Ages is borne out by the large numbers of swords which have been found in such places. Only very few, by the nature of the rivers they were found in or the places upon those rivers where they came up, are likely to have been lost by being dropped by accident off bridges, or out of ferries or boats, or lost in fighting at fords. The fact that about 80 per cent of medieval swords which have survived have come out of rivers or lakes is, I believe, common-sense evidence that they were not casually dropped in, but deliberately thrown in, especially as most of them have come up in places where there never was a bridge or a ford, or in streams too small to accommodate boats.

There is little documentary evidence for this practice from the later Middle Ages except the persistent legend of Excalibur, magically rising from one lake to be given to Arthur, and being returned at his death to another. The 'Lady of the Lake' is clearly a romanticised re-characterisation of the guardian priest of the deposit of arms. The splendid story so well told by Malory and

Tennyson of how the dying Arthur orders Bedivere to throw Excalibur into the mere, ends in a way which may seem to be fanciful, a piece of poetic moonshine. I believe, however, that this is not so. If these lines from Tennyson are considered in the practical light of common-sense, sense may be found in the legend:

> So flashed and fell the brand Excalibur
> But ere he dipt the surface, rose an arm
> Clothed in white Samite, mystic, wonderful
> And caught him by the hilt, and brandished him
> Three times, and drew him under in the mere.

Imagine the scene: in the dim moonlight Bedivere, distraught and exhausted by a long day of battle with defeat at the end of it, stands dizzy at the mere's edge. The sword flashes in the faint light and hits the water with a splash which to his bemused and shattered mind might well seem to be a white arm coming out to receive it. Bedivere, here in Tennyson and in his predecessors, may be fictional, but it is reasonable to suppose that at some time, maybe quite often, when a sword was thrown into water by real people, especially in dim light, the splash its entry would make could well be taken, considering the powerful wishful thinking to which the medieval mind was so prone, to be a white-sleeved arm coming out to take the offering.

Why such offerings – for they were offerings – were made is a mystery. We do know that the Teutonic peoples wherever they were to be found put weapons into the graves of their warriors. We know from the sagas that often such weapons, swords in particular, were taken out of graves, often a generation or more after their burial, to be given to a favoured member of the family, or sometimes just stolen, as Skeggi of Midfirth in Iceland one day quite casually landed at Roskilde in Denmark and broke into the burial-mound of the chieftain Hrolf Kraki and stole the sword Skofnung.This was nearly four centuries after Hrolf's death, and Skofnung passed on from hand to hand for a further century and a half. There are many instances of such happenings in the Norse literature, too many to enumerate here. We also know, from the sagas as well as from actual finds, that swords were often broken before they were buried so that they could never be used again.

Even in these days of the late 20th century, it is possible to understand the distress it can cause when the time comes for a man to be parted from some piece of property which, for him, has very close emotive ties as well as, perhaps, great monetary value. He knows that it will pass from his loving care to someone to whom it means nothing but a quick means of raising money, and that it will go straight into the sale-room to be subjected to all the horrible indignities which inevitably await it there. Nowadays nobody would dream of throwing thousands of pounds worth of property into a river, or burying it in a grave or burning it in the crematorium; but in the age of the Vikings (and far beyond) such an action would be ritually correct. Unless there was some very worthy relative or especially close comrade into whose care a man's sword might legitimately and trustingly be passed, far the best thing would be for it to die with its owner, as Roland tried to ensure when he lay at the point of death in the pass of Roncesvalles. Maybe what he said and did with Durendal under the lonely pine-tree on the hillside (in the best-remembered episode of the whole great epic of the *Song of Roland*) is the true and simple answer to this question. Certainly he speaks for everyone who cares what happens to his sword when he can no longer keep and guard it.

> The Count struggles to his feet; he tries to break Durendal on a dark stone which stands there. Ten times he strikes, but the sword will not splinter nor break. 'Eh, good Durendal, you were set for sorrow; so long have you been wielded by a good vassal. Now I am lost and can care for you no longer. I have fought so many battles on the field with you, kept down so many countries which Charles holds, whose beard is white. Let no man have you who would run before another! 'Ah, good Durendal! How beautiful you are, how bright and white! How you gleam and flash in the sunlight!' Again Roland strikes the sword on the stone. The steel grates, but will not splinter nor break. When he sees that he cannot break it, he begins to mourn the sword to himself.

Thanks to these sentiments, we in this age are able to see and handle, study, appreciate, love and sometimes to own these splendid things which in fact did not die with their owners, but were preserved by the soil of the grave or the mud of the river-bed. So well has mud preserved many of them that, far from being dead, like the well-preserved mummies of the Pharaohs, they still live in one's hand, and would be as ready to serve as they ever were.

Find-Places

It is necessary to say a word about the places at which swords have been found. To be able to say that a certain sword was found on the site of a certain battle, thereby providing a firm *terminus post quem* date, is of no use at all. If half-a-dozen swords, an axe or two, dozens of arrow heads and many spears, were to be found on a battle-site, *this* would be evidence. But it never happens; it is only the isolated sword that is generally found in a stream or a pond near to a battle-site. After any battle, all the debris of value – and swords above all weapons were of great value, as well as being easily portable – was collected up; all the armour, clothes, jewellery or any other moveable property left upon the dead was stripped off before the bodies were put into pits. The only example so far discovered where there is some armour in grave-pits was found a century or so ago in Gotland, on the site of a battle which took place outside the town of Visby on a hot August afternoon in 1361. We know beyond doubt that the dead were left out in the hot sun for three full days. Before it became possible to bury them, they were in such a nasty condition

4

that they were bundled into the grave-pits as they were, with their armour on. But not a weapon (except some arrow-heads which were actually inside the bodies) was found in these pits when they were opened. Of course not: the rotted state of the bodies would not prevent all the loose weapons being gathered up.

Space will not allow me to give more than three examples of the risks attendant upon trying to date casual sword-finds near battlefields. Early in the last century a sword was found on the field of Bosworth (1485) and was published in a book in 1819, with a drawing, captioned 'sword found on the site of the battle'. Unfortunately it is an unmistakeable 'dish-hilt' rapier of the 1640s. Then there are a number of fine, well-preserved swords in the City Museum of Lincoln, found near that city in the River Witham. There were two famous and splendidly documented battles in Lincoln, one outside the walls, on the river-bank, in 1141 and another fought in 1216 in the town square up on the hill between the castle and the Cathedral, followed by a pursuit down the main street to the town gate. This battle didn't get beyond the gate and down to the river, for a frantic cow got stuck in the gate when the beaten French got to the bottom of the hill. This caused a jam in the gate which brought the whole thing to a standstill (except for some very satisfactory slaughter of the French army, which had been sent over by Philip I to remove King John).

Nobody knows now what part of the river this group of swords came out of (they were found in 1788). One is a Roman *gladius*, and one a broken basket-hilted backsword of the Civil War period – the 17th century Civil War, not King Stephen's or King John's. Certainly several of these swords might be relics of Stephen's battle, for a lot of knights did get thrown into the river, but that battle cannot account for the Roman sword or the 17th century one found at the same time.

Then, most significant of all because for over a century it has been held up by scholar after scholar (myself the latest of them) as being invaluable as a fixed dating point, is a sword now in the Moyses Hall Museum at Bury St Edmunds, said to have been found late in the last century in a ditch on the site of a battle fought nearby at Fornham, in 1171. It is a finely preserved sword of Type XI, with a beautifully executed calligraphic inscription inlaid in silver in the blade. So, here seemed to be a perfect *terminus post quem* for not only the sword-type, but for the style of the inscription too.

Unfortunately, there are several factors which cast the most serious doubts upon this assumption, and in the 1950s some important excavations in Finland gave very convincing evidence that the very 'handwriting' of this inscription was of a century earlier. Having said that, of course it must not be overlooked that there is no reason on earth why a sword dated (i.e. *made*) in the late 11th century should not have been lost in a battle of the late 12th. But consider the circumstances of the find-place. To begin with, since 1171 no-one recorded the exact site of the battle, and there has for centuries been no knowledge at all of where it was within an area of perhaps 16 or 20 square miles, especially as the topography of the whole place has changed completely. Secondly, there are two Fornhams, Fornham St Martin and Fornham All Saints, not very close together. This spreads the possible area still wider. And, of course, nobody knows (because the find was not properly recorded) just where the sword was found. 'A ditch near Fornham' (which Fornham?) is very vague identification indeed.

So must it be with so many medieval swords found on or near the places where a battle is known to have been fought; but on the sites of great well-known battles – Hastings, Evesham, Bouvines, Crécy, Mauron, Sempach, Agincourt, Beaugé, Patay, Mont'lhery, Nancy, Marignano – swords have not been found at all. I believe that any note that a sword was found 'near the site of the battle of X' has to be taken with rather more than a a pinch of salt.

Inscriptions

In a previous paragraph I used the word 'handwriting' in connection with calligraphic inscriptions inlaid on the blades of swords. This may seem a fanciful concept, but research which I have been pursuing during the last few years has shown, I believe without much doubt, that it is possible to say that, for example, the inscription upon a blade from a Viking grave in Finland is cut into the steel and inlaid with silver wire by the same hand as one from Switzerland and another from Whittlesea Mere in Cambridgeshire, and so on.

Such a statement calls for a clarification. From the earliest making of iron swords, various marks have been stamped or inlaid upon blades. Many of the swords of the La Tène III period (c.300 B.C.) found at the eponymous site in Switzerland bear stamped marks, presumably the trade-marks of smiths, many of which marks were still in use in exactly the same form in Europe in the 17th century; but it was not until the smiths of, possibly, a region near to modern Solingen in the Rhineland began in the later 9th century to produce fine blades of steel without using the cumbersome and complex technique of pattern welding that actual lettered inscriptions began to be inlaid upon blades. The earliest gave the name of the smith who forged the blades – or, more accurately, the family name of the workshops where they were made, for they seem to have been in production under the same name for perhaps more than two centuries. This name, a Frankish – Germanic one, was Ulfberht. It would, in a modern context, be Ulfberht Ltd, or Ulfberht Inc. A few swords, mostly single examples, have been found with other names (Leutfrit, Niso, Atalbald, Banto for example) but there are literally dozens of Ulfberhts. Another firm came into production a little later, perhaps c.950, called Ingelrii and this name gave the essential clue to what it was, for many scholars (even in the face of the fact that there were so many swords marked Ulfberht) believed that the name on the blade referred to the owner of the sword. Until, in a lake in Sweden, a fine Viking sword came up, with the legend INGELRII ME FECIT. That, of course settled it.

These inscriptions (and they were not all smith names: a Finnish grave-find has AMEN on each side of its blade and another in private hands has IESUS and MARIA) were crudely inlaid into the blade in rather wobbly letters made of strips of iron. Some were exceedingly crude and incorrectly spelt. It is even possible that, like the German bladesmiths of Solingen in the 17th century, workshops of inferior quality forged the names of the great firms. In 17th century Solingen, it was common practice for German smiths (whose blades were in fact excellent) to seek a more fashionable cachet for their products by putting the words EN TOLEDO or TOMAS AYALA and so on, spuriously using the name of the great sword-blade centre of the time, and adding (often mis-spelt) the names of some of the great, and fashionable, bladesmiths of Spain. There is only one piece of evidence, itself rather shaky, to support my statement that in the Viking age a smith may have done the same. In the little museum at Wisbech in Cambridgeshire is a Viking sword with the mis-spelt Ulberht name on one side, and a garbled Ingelrii on the other.

However that may be, these iron inlaid inscriptions were rather crude affairs, and were put into the blades by the smith. They had to be. The method was to cut the letters into the un-tempered blade with a cold chisel; then little strips of thick iron wire were cut; sometimes these were twisted so that they gave a sort of snake-skin effect, like pattern-welding, to each letter. Then the blade would be heated cherry-red, so would one by one the strips of wire, each one laboriously hammered into the chisel-cut letters. After that the blade would be tempered, for blade and letters would have now become welded together as one unit. Then, it would be finished off with files and burnished.

With such a method, it is of course totally impossible to identify a 'hand', or even the work of one shop. The smith himself would almost without doubt in those days have been totally illiterate, and would have worked his name in from a pattern given him by some clerkly person. Some of the later examples of this technique of inlay have more ambitious inscription, IN NOMINE DOMINI being the most usual – and the extraordinary muddle most smiths seem to have made in the arranging of those fourteen letters has to be seen to be believed.

However, there were other inscriptions. It was believed (until I began to work on it and put two and two together) that the fine, legible, literate and beautifully executed inlaid inscriptions were of necessity much later than the 'old' iron ones, being firmly placed into the later 13th and early 14th centuries. This was held as an absolute truth until in the 1950s Dr Jorma Leppaaho of Helsinki University opened a large group of graves of the late Viking period in Southern Finland. About a decade after these were taken from the graves, very careful x-ray photographs were taken of their blades, and some, which to the naked eye looked like nothing so much as short lengths of rusty iron strapping, were chemically treated (given, in effect, an archaeological barium meal) before being x-rayed. The results were astounding. In blade after blade, beautifully written inlays appeared; some were fragmentary (for most of the blades had been ritually broken before burial) but enough were complete to make it absolutely plain that these were Viking blades, and were (a) contemporary with the iron inlaid ones, many of which were found in the same cemeteries, and much more significant (b) that they were absolutely similar in style and content to the inscribed swords found mostly in Germany and Switzerland, (though at least two were from England – Fornham and Whittlesea Mere) which, since they were authoritatively given time and place in a great seminal thesis by Dr Rudolf Wegeli in 1903, have been held up as examples of late 13th and early 14th century work.

Dr Leppaaho's finds were published by Helsinki University after his death, in 1964, but the absolute importance of the publication, and of his work, was completely unnoticed until I got hold of it in 1983. Not only was it possible now to place these inscriptions side-by-side with others found hundreds of miles away, but to be able to see individual quirks and idiosyncracies in the form of the letters themselves which seemed very clearly to point in fact, to handwriting. So Dr Wegeli's work has now to be looked at again; so has everyone else's who followed him, myself included. So, many swords which have been confidently and didactically placed in the 14th century (by me as well as everyone else) have now to be re-dated to the late 11th or, at most, early 12th centuries.

I have published these findings in considerable detail elsewhere, and have reprinted some of them below as Appendix B, but much will be found in the notes to the photographs to explain what I mean.

The point about these finely lettered inscriptions inlaid with silver and occasionally gold and, later, in brass (latten) is that the method by which they were produced had to be totally different from the iron ones. There, an illiterate smith banged his mis-shapen letters into the fine steel of his blade while both blade and letters were at welding heat. The other style was far more sophisticated. For one thing, because the wires with which the letters were inlaid had a lower melting-point than the steel's welding heat, the whole inscription had to be applied to the blade after it was finished – tempered, filed and burnished. Then the letters were delicately cut in with a burin or a diamond, and this was clearly done not just by a craftsman who was literate, but by one who was in fact a skilled calligrapher as well. The wires of silver or whatever were lightly hammered in; whether this was done by the calligrapher, or the bladesmith, or a jeweller is impossible to know; but there can be no doubt that the whole process was totally different and opposite to the alternative technique of using iron.

The comparing of these Viking-age swords from Finland with their analogues from the rest of Europe, which have for so long been misdated to the 13th century, has at least provided fairly firm dating for those with silver inlaid inscriptions. To set against this, the fact that the hilts of many of these inscribed swords have pommels of a type hitherto regarded as belonging exclusively to the late 13th and the 14th and 15th centuries, and not by any means to as 'absurdly early' a date as the late 11th, has loosened many hitherto firmly accepted dates for many un-inscribed swords as well. A particular example of this is one of the finest medieval swords still in existence. This is in the Wallace Collection (A459) in London (noted here at No. Xa.1 below).

For the excellence of its proportions and the supreme quality of its blade (which bears no mark or inscription), as well as for its very nearly pristine condition beneath its hard blue-black patina of Goethite (Fe Ooh) and its living, vibrant force in one's hand, it is to my mind the supreme example of a knightly sword of the High Middle Ages in the age of mail. It is of Type Xa, and is always assumed to date in the first half of the 14th century. But does it? Most swords of this type, as shown by the silver inlaid legends and the finds of Dr Leppaaho, must date between 1075 and 1120; and there is no reason why this supreme specimen should not also. The form of its hilt (pommel and cross) are both matched exactly among Leppaaho's Viking finds, and the only excuse which might be found for its late dating would be in the quality of its blade. Yet it is unquestionably of Type Xa; its fine condition is no better than that of many Viking swords of the 9th and 10th centuries; and it is pointless to suggest, in face of the mountain of evidence supplied by blades right back to the Celtic iron age, that because of its quality the blade cannot be as early as the 11th century.

On the other hand, there is an equally large mountain of evidence, in contemporary 14th century art as well as surviving, fairly firmly dateable 14th century swords, that there is no very valid reason why it could not be of the later date, either. I give this example at length in order to stress the point that dating of any medieval sword, especially such as fall into the types in Group 1, is very chancy unless the sword has good internal evidence to date it, or was found in a context which at least can give it a *terminus post quem*.

Find-Contexts

The question of context, too, is fraught with uncertainties. A sword found in the tomb of a prince (like that of Sancho IV of Castile found in his coffin in Toledo Cathedral – No.XII.7 below) or of a simple knight gives a *terminus post quem*, but neither a *terminus ante quem*, nor a place of origin. For consider: a sword is dredged up from the Great Ouse River near to the village of Stretham, four miles upstream from Ely and the causeway from Stuntney along which the Conqueror's Normans finally broke into the defences of Ely itself in 1070. Ergo, says the enthusiastic antiquarian, here is the sword of one of those Norman knights of 1070. So it could be, were it not for the fact that it was found four miles (as the crow flies, perhaps six as the winding river flows) away from that battle-site; and those intervening miles, in 1070, were covered with impenetrable fen and marsh and thicket. How did one of those knights get there? And why? Besides, it has all the stylistic appearance of belonging to a period some century or more later than 1070. In the face of such speculations, it does not seem very safe to assign it to that particular conflict. Now consider further: it *is* reasonable to assume that the sword was deliberately thrown into the river; its find-place is indisputable, but if (as generally happens) it is labelled by experts as being 'probably English', this is absurd. Any sword, found anywhere, may have passed (and probably did pass) through many hands in places all over Europe and the Near East. For instance, a blade is forged at Passau, on the Danube, in 1258. It is hilted maybe in Milan; or maybe in Gloucester, or Norwich, or Gisors, or Caen or Montpellier, or Burgos, or Jerusalem, or Cracow. Then it is bought by a young knight in Antwerp, whence it has come in the baggage of one of the travelling salesmen who continually moved across the face of the nations. This knight is involved in a tournament at Beauvais, is unhorsed by a knight of Prussia who, in accordance with the rules of chivalry, takes the sword. *He* is killed in Lithuania, and the sword falls into the hands of a squire of Poland, who takes it home; he in turn goes to the Holy Land, where he strikes up a close friendship with a young knight from Cambridge. The Polish squire dies, and gives the sword to his friend, who goes home in 1272 and lives peacefully in his manor at Stretham until 1310. On his death, at his specific request, the sword is thrown into the Ouse. So what 19th or 20th century antiquarian can say it is probably English? The last person to have owned it might have been English – but then, in all those centuries of the High Middles Ages, any knightly person in England was just as likely to be Flemish, or French, or Spanish, or Bavarian . . .

Even a sword found in a coffin may have been passed around in this way. And since, until perhaps the turn of the 13th – 14th centuries there was hardly any stylistic difference in the form of swords found from Finland to Spain and from Wales to the Caucasus, there is neither point nor profit in trying to give any sword a local habitation and a name. We can say it is Western European; there are occasions when it may be reasonable to suggest that it is Southern European, or Eastern European, but these occasions are rare. There are a few hilt-forms – I can only think of three – which seem to have a locality – one in Scandinavia generally; one in Denmark specifically (but this is late, of the 15th century) and one in the Levant, a characteristic, crude, home-made iron hilt generally associated with a blade of very poor quality.

The typologies of Petersen and Behmer do suggest that certain forms of hilt or scabbard-mount originated in certain localities. Petersen in particular is able to place his hilt-types according to their distribution in graves or in casual finds; even so, thickly as various forms are found together in various places, this takes no account of the widespread roving of their owners. Take a specific example, his Type K. Several have been found in France. There are some from graves in Ireland, and one from a grave at Knin in Jugoslavia. Could one say then that Type K is Frankish, or Irish (Norse-Irish, of course) or Slavic?

Conservation

What *is* significant and interesting, if not actually important, about any sword's find-place is the physical conditions in which it has been lying. Most finds, as I have said, are from the beds of rivers, which generally preseve them very well. The whole point about such preservation revolves around the amount of oxygen which is able to get at and corrode the metal. A sword falling into deep mud, free from stones or organic debris which might trap oxygen or allow it to penetrate the close covering of mud, will initially become covered all over with a coating of rust, but as time passes the chemical interaction of this rust with the chemical constituents of the surrounding mud covers all the surface of the metal with a flint-hard coat of Goethite (FeOoh) which, once formed, prevents any further corrosion and so yields up to the archaeologist (or treasure-hunter with his metal-detector) a well preserved weapon, sometimes in almost pristine condition. This coating or patina can be removed either by long and arduous work with abrasives, which must get progressively milder as the goethite is rubbed off, or by submitting to electrolysis the dismounted blade, or the whole sword if there is no organic material surviving on it, such as its grip. It can be done with acid, but this leaves the sword in a nasty condition looking like lead; it seems to take all the life out of it.

Some river-mud has better preservative qualities than others. The Danube is splendid, so is the Great Ouse; and so can be the Thames in London, but this has strange characteristics. Many swords have been taken from this river between Richmond and Limehouse, some in almost perfect condition, some so rotted away as to be almost unrecognisable. Their age has nothing to do with their condition; for instance, a sword of c.1470 is only a tatty rotted fragment while a Viking sword of c.900, found in the same part of the river, is still perfectly usable with hardly a rust-pit in it.

Many swords, (but only a small percentage of the whole mass of present-day survivors) have been found in the ground while digging foundations, or ploughing. Even some of these are still in remarkably good condition. A few have been found in ancient houses, like a superb XIIIa illustrated and annotated at No.XIIIa.5 below, which was found behind 14th century panelling of a house at Linz. We know from evidence in the Norse literature that sometimes a sword would be buried, deliberately, in a stone cist, which they called a *stanfaet*. I only know of two actually found thus buried, but both are of outstanding interest. One (see No.XII.10 below) was found near Oslo in 1880 when a railway-cutting was being driven through farm-land at Korsoygaden near Oslo. It was in a stone box – not big enough for a coffin, just big enough for the sword, its scabbard and an iron-bound wooden shield. The other is a Roman *gladius*-type sword, found in a cist at Klinten in Gotland with its rich scabbard and belt-fittings. It is notable, incidentally, that all the Roman swords of this type which have been found in rivers, or ritually buried, have been richly decorated ones, the swords of officers, for the *gladius* of the rank-and-file legionary was shorter (about an average of 16" as against 21" of the officer's type) and, since these 'issue' *gladii* were handed in to be re-worked when they were too worn to be useful, they did not often get a chance to be ritually destroyed in order to be found by modern archaeologists.

Design

The question of the design, manufacture and distribution of swords is almost as impossible to answer with any certainty as is the question of date. That hilt styles – that is the form of pommel and the style of cross – were made to confirm to certain more or less set patterns in various regions at different times is self-evident, but it is not possible, ever, to say that such-and-such a pommel form 'went with' such and such a cross-style. It seems that any form of pommel might be used at any time, in any cutler's workshop, matched with any style of cross in a purely arbitrary way. This is not at all to say that forms of pommel and styles of cross were not deliberately designed, maybe even on the drawing-board, but it is natural to assume that the practical considerations of the using of the swords should have been paramount in any such designing. It probably was, yet there are several pommel forms, for instance, which make a sword uncomfortable in the hand. Those Viking styles which have straight lower edges with a sharpish corner at each end are diabolically uncomfortable – if one holds the sword in a natural way and tries to flex one's wrist, the corner of the pommel digs violently into the junction of hand and wrist. With a straight arm and a stiff wrist it is not too bad. If, however, the lower edge is curved upwards, or if the pommel is a thick disc, this does not happen and in fact the pommel is enormously helpful as a fulcrum to bring the sword back into position after making a blow, using the wrist as a lever against it. If the pommel of No. XI.5 below is examined, and then that of No.X.3 and imagination applied to both, you will see what I mean. I say this with confidence because I have wielded these swords, and speak from practical experience.

Manufacture

We do find that by the end of the 13th century and onward into the 16th more and more swords fall into what I would call 'families' which tend to cut across the types, and are pretty obviously the result of recognisable trends in fashion. This matter will be discussed later, for the question of deliberate designing is much more relevant to these families; now we need to look a little at the actual methods of manufacture – about which, I have to say, we know very little except for the complexities of pattern welding. This technique – or these techniques, I should say – have been exhaustively examined and much practical experiment has taken place. Even so, the findings remain rather confused because there are still differing schools of thought as to how it was done.

This experimentation has been very thoroughly documented in great detail, and since the period in which the method was in use is outside the scope of this survey, I have not described it. We have to begin here to look at the matter of manufacture with the rise of the Ulfberht factory in the 9th – 10th centuries. It has been established, I think beyond doubt, that this factory was situated in the Rhineland near to – or actually at the site of – the place where the great blade making and steel town of Solingen arose, a town which has always been associated with the making of blades, and where there is now a splendid *Klingenmuseum* which is devoted to all the arts of the sword. There is of course no doubt either that there were many other centres of production, though none perhaps so well documented.

Throughout the great chronicle of Jean Froissart there is constant mention of Bordeaux as a place from which all worthy blades come – blades of spears, axes and arrows as well as swords – but there is nothing, except what Froissart and his contemporaries have written, to substantiate this. It is now thought to be much more probable that they did not mean Bordeaux in Gascony, but another quite obscure centre in Haute Savoie called Bordeau – without the final x. This is within the region of ancient Noricum, from whence the Celts and the Romans after them got all (or most of) their steel weapons. Probably most of the European cities which became famous for sword-blades were producing them as early as the 12th century – Passau on the Danube, Cologne, Milan and Brescia and perhaps Toledo, though there is scant evidence before the very end of the medieval period that swords were made there. But lack of documentation especially for such early times, is not be considered as evidence of non-existence

I can quote one piece of documentary evidence as to the making of swords in Milan late in the 13th century and onward. In a work by one Galvano Fiamma, called the *Chronicon Extravagans*, the author writes (of Milan), 'In our territory immense numbers of workmen are to be found who make every manner of armour – hauberks, breastplates, plates, helms, helmets, steel skull-caps, gorgets, gauntlets, greaves, cuishes, knee-pieces, and lances, javelins swords and so on.'*

To go in detail into the actual technical methods of making blades would occupy too much space and would interrupt the sequence of what needs to be set down in this introduction – besides, let me admit that very little is known about it. At present (in 1990) there are several craftsmen in Europe and America who are making swords; these are not copies of medieval swords, made just to present an appearance. They are swords, every bit as powerful, well-balanced and effective as their prototypes. It just happens that they are made in the medieval manner, using as far as possible the tools which would have been available in a 12th century forge, and following the very form and pattern of chosen ancient swords. Notes from the experiences of some of these modern craftsmen is given below at Appendix A.

Supply

Until quite recently I held firmly to the view that the medieval knight chose, purchased, used and cherished his sword – or swords, because he would need several; one or two short, light 'riding swords' for going about his daily concerns, a few bigger ones, called in 15th-century England 'arming swords' which would be effectively used in battle, but were best for skirmish or single combat, and a war sword, this being a big one of Types XIIIa, XVIa or XVa or XVIIIb, according to his period in history.

This belief, which must have some truth in it, is not the whole truth, for it is becoming very clear in the light of recent discoveries, one in particular, that swords were 'issued' on a commisariat basis, even in Viking times. To set against the oft-repeated celebration in the sagas of the intense emotive personal bond between a warrior and his sword, here is one example of something which seems to be the direct opposite.

An episode in the last battle of King Olaf Tryggvason of Norway makes it clear that one of the duties of a king, or any war-leader, was to keep a stock of swords in readiness in case of need. In the account of this battle in *Olaf's Saga Tryggvasonar* in the *Heimskringla* we find that when he noticed that his men's swords were not cutting well, he called out 'Hey! are you being lazy with your swords? They don't bite for you!' A man replied 'Our swords are all blunt and badly nicked'. Then the king went down into the forehold (the battle was one of ships) and opened the High-Seat chest, and out of it he took many sharp swords and gave them to his men.'

An explicit example of swords being part of an army's commissariat is in the Bayeux Tapestry, where swords are seen being

*It is interesting to note here that plate armour is specified, before the mid-14th century.

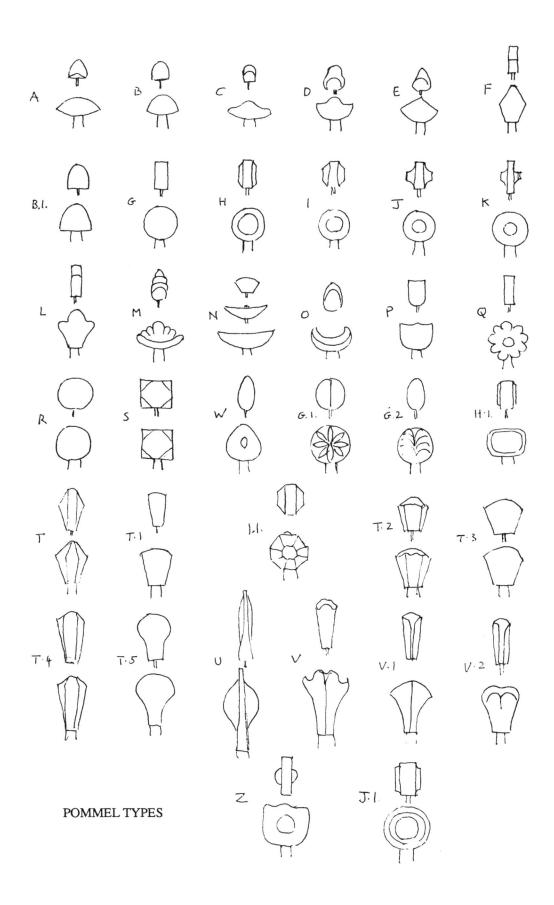

POMMEL TYPES

taken ashore from the ships with all sorts of other gear. All through the Middle Ages there are to be found, in chronicles and records, inventories of materiel as part of the supply of an army or an expedition; these generally tend only to specify so many hundreds of thousands of arrow-heads, shafts, bow-staves, gun-stones, spears, helmets, mail-shirts and so on, but now and again in these lists large numbers of swords are mentioned; and though this is not specified there can be little doubt that complete swords are meant, not simply blades. An interesting point arises here: it seems, from all of this evidence from Olaf Tryggvason onwards, that such 'issue' swords were not furnished with scabbards. They are naked in the Tapestry, no mention of scabbards is made in the inventories – and I cannot stress too emphatically that any sword would not go into any scabbard. Even when blades were made to a 'standard' pattern, as we know now that they were, particularly in the 14th – 15th centuries, each blade must differ from every other one in small dimensional, or proportional measures, for each was forged by hand. Therefore each blade had to be used as a mandril for its own scabbard to be made round it, or it would not fit well.

This documentary evidence for the supply of swords in bulk has been very comprehensively reinforced in recent years by the discovery in the River Dordogne near Castillon of a hoard of eighty swords, which by their style seem to date to the first half of the 15th century. A dredger brought them up, in a tangled clump. Some are in astonishingly good condition but some naturally enough were bent and broken. It was later established that the swords (no sign of scabbards or metal scabbard – mounts was found) were in a chest, and that the chest was in a barge. None of these things was at all surprising, for a clump of swords all mixed together like that could not have been casually lost, or ritually deposited. That part of the Dordogne was the principal supply-route from the great English base at Bordeaux to the up-river castles which in the 1420s and 1440s were still precariously held by the English during the closing years of the Hundred Years' War. They were evidently (or at least, presumably) in a barge, which in some way was sunk, going up to Bergerac or Castillon with supplies.

These were all fine-quality swords, but they were not new when they reached the mud of the river. All the good ones (most of which I have seen and handled) show unmistakeable signs of wear – considerable wear, nicks in the edges and the irregularities caused by honing. The only assumption one can make upon the evidence so far examined is that they were used blades re-hilted by a contractor, maybe in England or perhaps in the Burgundian low countries.

This statement calls for explanation. The hilts of these swords fall into three very distinct patterns, and the blades into two. The first group (the largest) all have deep wheel pommels, most with a recessed central boss (Nos.XV.5 and XV.8) and short, straight crosses turned abruptly downward at the tips. The blades are not very long (about 32" (81.2cms)) but broad at the hilt and having a very strong flattened diamond section, in many cases with the four faces strongly hollowed leaving a prominent ridge running down the middle of the blade from hilt to point. The blades of Group II are of similar section, but are longer (about 38" – 40" (99cms) and narrower. The pommels are mostly of a fish-tail form, and the crosses are straight, thickened in the middle and swelling to hemispherical knobs at the ends. (No. XVa.3). The third group so far has only three examples that I know of, and has a quite different form of blade, such as I have put into Type XXa. There is a ricasso just below the hilt, the section is of a flat hexagon, there is a shallow fuller running for approximately half the length of the blade, and this, on the ricasso which is about 1" (4cms) long, is flanked by a short fuller on each side. The cross is the same as in Group II, but the pommel is different from almost any other so-far known sword in that it is of a pear-shape with the narrow part upward (No.XXa.2).

The fact that so many similar hilts on so many swords all found together does very strongly suggest a common source for all of them – i.e. a contractor.

Sword Families

These groups of swords are very good examples of what I have called 'families' of swords. Those of Group I of the Castillon find are either of Type XV or XVIII; those of Group II are of Type XVa or XVIII, while those of III are of Type XXa. As I mentioned earlier, the families ran across the Types, because they are recognisable by their hilt forms which I am sure indicate the positive influence of trends in fashion, so these three groups of these Dordogne swords are in fact distinct families.

In this case again a schematic diagram is much more effective than words to describe sword-hilts, so on page 12, I have drawn the principal families which span the period. To support the diagram, I have made a list giving the principal characteristics of each family. This is really only a brief sketch, and an interim one at that, for as time passes more swords will emerge from the care of Mother Earth (and no doubt from obscurity in private collections as well) either to swell the numbers of existing examples of these families or to suggest fresh ones. While some of these families span a considerable length of the whole period under consideration, others seem only to have enjoyed a brief popularity; and it will be noticed that between c.1275 and 1425 no less than nine families arose and then vanished again, as the dictates of fashion (at that period more potent than ever before) decreed.

Naturally, I have set these 'family' notes in the chronological order in which the families first appeared; and I would emphasise that this list only shows the more prominent families. There were many smaller groupings, of which only one or two actual swords have so far survived, and only one or two representations in art, or none. The sword shown at No. XIV.2 is a case in point: it is a typical XIV, but the odd form of its pommel and the unusual style of its cross can only (so far) be matched by one other sword, but its 'fashionable' date is well confirmed by the appearance in art of three almost identical oddities, one on the Great Seal of Edward I, another on the seal of Charles of Anjou, and a third on the great seal of John Balliol of Scots, (c.1275 in each case). So I have not included these as a family, yet three of the odd swords (Group III) of the Castillon find, I have. This is because I have not yet seen all eighty of the swords in the find, and I believe others do exist.

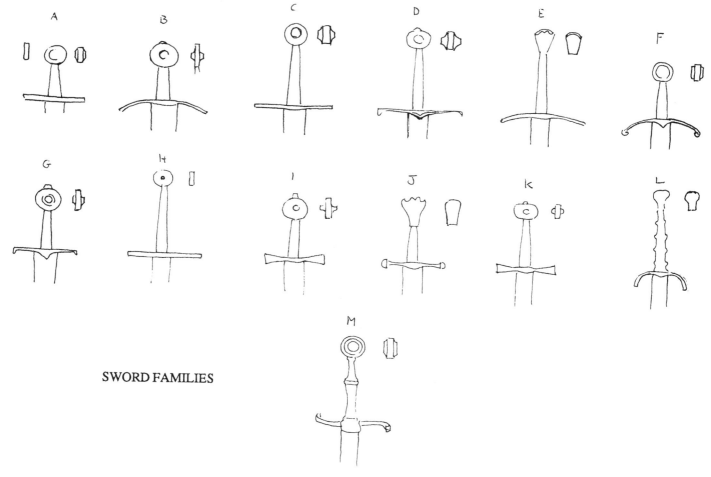

SWORD FAMILIES

FAMILY A
Very widely in use from as early as c.950 until c.1550, though far more popular c.1050-1300. A short hilt with a disc – or wheel-shaped pommel and a straight cross, often rather thick in its earlier manifestations.

FAMILY B
Most if not all of this family are of Type XIV; and it had a short life from c.1280-1325 – by which I mean it is between those dates that the majority of its representations in art are to be found. A short hilt, with a very wide, flat wheel-pommel with very prominent central bosses, and a fairly thin cross arched toward the blade, with plain ends. (No. XIV.7).

FAMILY C
Nearly all swords of Type XIIIA come into this family, though there are examples which can be dated as early as c.1100, and they are occasionally represented in art between c.1100-1250. After c.1250, though, they are to be found everywhere in manuscript pictures and sculpture of all kinds, but particularly monumental sculpture and brasses between c.1290 and 1360. A long hilt, with a very deep wheel pommel and a straight, plain cross (No. XIIIa.7, for example).

FAMILY D
This follows C, being popularly represented between c.1360-1410. A long hilt, with a deep wheel pommel often with recessed hollows in the central bosses such as are seldom found in pommels of Family C. The cross here is the distinctive feature. It is straight, rather long, generally of a neat rhomboidal section (though this is occasionally circular); it widens strongly at its mid-point to form an eccuson over the rib of the blade in its most elegant mannifestations, though this (in Poor Relations) is not always the case. The arms taper elegantly to the tips which turn abruptly downward through a right-angle. (Nos. XVa.6, for example).

FAMILY E
These swords, of the same proportions as those of D, have pommels made in the rather complicated shape of a truncated wedge, the upper, broad, end of which is arched and filed into four or six hollow 'scallops'. The grip is long, as is the cross. This arches towards the blade, and is generally of square section, rather thin, with no taper or widening toward the tips and no swelling at mid-point. Because two notable examples of this family were found in the graves of Austrian knights who fell in the battle of Sempach near Zurich in 1386, they are always called by collectors and other experts 'the Sempach type'. (No.XVII.1, for example.)

FAMILY F
Ask almost anybody to describe or draw a medieval sword, and they will turn to this family, which for a couple of centuries perhaps has been considered to be the epitome of the sword. Justly, too, for handsome specimens are the handsomest of all swords. The great-grandfather of the family is the sword of Henry V in Westminster Abbey (No. XVIII.1 below) which, though a very plain weapon (fully compatible with the character of such a down-to-earth and practical warrior) is extremely good-looking and is a dream to handle. The family's span of historical time seems to have been between c.1410 and – what? – 1550. There are many splendid examples surviving, and many are shown in art. Characteristic is the shape of the cross. The hilt is short, with a big wheel-pommel, and the cross, generally quite long (see No.XVIII.1 below) is of flat ribbon-like section with its width at right-angles to the plane of the blade. In most cases this ribbon-section is elegantly complex, for, though flat on the top, the underside is triangular. It is arched towards the blade, has a well-marked cusped ecusson at mid-point, and the tips are rolled, or scrolled, over.

FAMILY G
This has much in common with F; a short hilt, and a heavy wheel pommel, but the cross is a short version of that of Family D, being generally of rhomboidal section, well cusped at mid-point over the ridge of the blade, and with the tips abruptly turned down. Much represented in all kinds of contemporary art between c.1380-1440. (No. XV.8 for example).

FAMILY H
It is difficult to know quite where to place this in a chronological sequence, for there are not many surivors (though one may be found in nearly every great collection) and it is, unusually for medieval swords, an ugly beast. The hilt (and the blade) are long, made without delicacy or finesse. The blade is weak in section, its edges nearly parallel and its point rounded. The pommel is a flat disc, generally with a small circular recess in its centre; the cross is long, a shapeless bar of metal of round or square section. I regret having to write in a dismissive way of any sword, but most of the members of this family are dull, lifeless and undistinguished. Even so, they must have been popular, for as far as I can make out, they were in use from the early 13th century to the early 16th.

FAMILY I
Here we return to a handsome family. Most of its survivors so far have been found in the arsenals of Alexandria and Constantinople, where they have been preserved since the late 14th century as trophies of war. One must because of this assume that the family was a Southern European one. Its form is quite unmistakeable, and there are many examples of it. The pommels are of bronze, of wide, flat disc form with upstanding central bosses like nipples. The grip is short, and the cross is very much like a rather narrow bow-tie – flat in section, with the width on the same plane as the blade, widening somewhat at mid-point and spreading out strongly to the tips, which are cut off straight. The blades of all of them are very broad, flat, with narrow central fullers running about two-thirds of the length and with nearly parallel edges and very rounded points. (No XIIIb.4.) I know, at present, of no representation in art of these swords.

FAMILY J
These swords have a very distinctive shape. Most of them are quite big weapons, though not so large as the war-swords. The grips themselves are quite short – 4" or so – but the pommels are long and seem as it were to grow out of the tops of the grips. These pommels are best described as of fish-tail form, and are in many ways very like the truncated wedges of Family E, except that the sides are concave. The crosses are short, of circular section, widening at the mid-point and each arm is 'waisted', ending at the tips in hemispherical knobs. (No. XVIII.8 for example) Most surviving examples are from the Castillon find, and they are often seen in contemporary art from c.1420-1470.

FAMILY K
This is a Danish style. The hilt is generally of hand-and-a-half length; the pommel is of a very flat wheel-form with a prominent central boss of each face, and the cross is of the 'bow-tie' style of Family I. There are few examples, but it seems to be a definite family all the same.

FAMILY L
This is, as far as can be ascertained at present, almost exclusively a Danish variant of the long-gripped war-sword of the second half of the 15th century. The pommel is small and pear-shaped; the grip is extremely long – about 12" – 14" (30.5 – 35.6cms) and has four or five transverse ridges at intervals from top to bottom. The cross is short, of flat section with the wider dimension in the same plane as the blade, and it is very strongly arched towards the point.

FAMILY M
This is perhaps the most common family of swords in use in the Northern parts of Europe during the second half of the 15th century and the first quarter of the 16th. The pommel is of wheel-form – or perhaps it is better described as being a thick disc with raised rims set just inside the outer rim of the disc, enclosing a hollowed circular recess. The grip is long, formed in two distinct parts; it is narrow below the pommel, swelling gracefully to a transverse rib nearly half-way down, from which a thicker part tapers towards the cross, which is generally quite long and often has the tips turned, at right angles to the plane of the blade, in a horizontal re-curve. (Nos. XVIIIa.5 below) is a supreme example of this family).

The intriguing question of a sword's ownership is generally quite impossible to answer. There are a very few swords known at present which can firmly be attributed to historical personages in whose coffins they have been found, and a few more where painstaking research based on internal evidence can at least present a firm probability of ownership, but the majority have no known provenance, let alone anything more specific -besides, as I have pointed out above, in the high Middle Ages swords must have changed hands continually owing to the laws of war and the conventions of chivalry: the horse, armour, arms and equipment of a defeated knight became by all the rules the property of his captor, or his successful opponent. There is one perhaps stabilising factor in this – defeated in single combat, a knight (or person of knightly rank) was often given the option of buying his gear back for cash. Even so, taking everything into account, it seems we have to assume that any sword surviving today probably had several owners.

In the period we are chiefly concerned with here, the sword was a much more common weapon than it had been during the ages of the migrations and of the Vikings, so there are few references to the 'wanderings' of specific swords in the poetry of the chronicler, unlike those which we find in the Norse literature, where there are several well-documented tales of the wanderings and adventures of particular swords.

Space will permit only mention of a few, concerning historical characters. The first concerns the sword Skofnung, which originally belonged to a 7th century king of Denmark called Hrolf, with the added nick-name Kraki. He was a very tall, thin and knobbly man, so he was likened to a pole-ladder, which is a tall pole with foot-rests sticking out each side all the way up. He was buried in a mound in the royal cemetery at Roskilde, and Skofnung was buried with him. This sword was said in *Hrolfs Saga Kraka* to be 'the best of all swords which have been carried in the northern lands.' Then, generations later as we are told in 'Landnamabok', Skeggi of Midfirth one of the early settlers in Iceland '..... was chosen by lot to break into the mound of King Hrolf Kraki, and out of it he took Skofnung, the sword of Hrolf.' This was towards the end of the 10th century. Later, early in the 11th, according to *Laxdaela Saga*, the sword was in the possession of Skeggi's son Eid. When Eid was an old man he lent Skofnung to Thorkel Egjolfsson, who undertook to kill the outlaw Grim, who had killed Eid's son. Thorkel and Grim met and fought, but Thorkel made friends with him, and never gave Skofnung back to Eid. Thorkel still had the sword when he sailed over Broadfirth on his last voyage, but his ship sank; but one of its timbers, with Skofnung stuck into it, was washed ashore on an island (called afterwards Skofnungsey) from which it was recovered and borne by Thorkel's son Gellir; and when he was an old man he took it with him on a pilgrimage to Rome. However, he died on the way home, in Denmark, and (*Laxdaela Saga* again) was buried at Roskilde: 'He died and rests at Roskilde. Gellir had taken Skofnung with him, and it was not recovered afterwards.' So it went back almost to where Skeggi had taken it from generations back – and it must have been three centuries old then.

There is also, of course, the sword Aettartangi, the sword, among many other owners, of Grettir the Strong. Its very name means 'Sword (or tang) of Generations'.

A third is an even stranger story, and a little later in time and concerns historical characters who are authenticated in poem and chronicle outside the Sagas. It concerns Hneitir, the sword of King Olaf the Holy (later St. Olaf) of Norway. According to tradition this also was taken from the burial mound of an earlier King Olaf, and had been given to the second Olaf at birth when he received his name. The Christian king had it all his life until he was killed in 1030 at the battle of Stiklestad. As he fell, he dropped Hneitir on the ground, and it was picked up by a Swedish warrior who had just been disarmed: 'He had broken his sword, and he took up the sword Hneitir and fought with it .... He went back to Sweden and went home. He kept the sword all his life, and his son after him, and so one after another of his kinsmen took it, and always it followed that as each possessed the sword he told the next the sword's name and also whence it came.'

A descendant of this man went to Constantinople and joined the Emperor's Varangian guard, but he found that every night the sword disappeared from under his pillow and was found some distance away. The Emperor heard of this, and heard whose sword it had been; so he bought it from his guardsman for three times its worth in gold, and had it placed over the altar of St Olaf's church in Constantinople. This story was told by Einarr Skulason in his poem 'Gesr' and was recited in 1153 in the Cathedral at Trondjeim.

These are only three of the innumerable swords which are mentioned in the Sagas and the annals and chronicles of the early medieval period – like the sword of Edmund Ironside (who was killed in 1017) which Henry II (1154-89) is recorded as handling; the sword of King Offa (died 796) which was mentioned in an 11th century will as a bequest from the ætheling Aethelstan to his brother, and so on.

There does not appear to be this sort of reference to the longevity of swords in the poems and chronicles of the later Middle Ages, but this does not necessarily mean that there really is none. What it does mean is that nobody has looked for it. We do find it again in modern publication of research into the inventories of armouries (like those of Henry VIII at the Tower) where sometimes swords of former times are specified.

A very few swords survive today which have been taken from tombs; and in these cases we can safely say that here were at least, their last owners, however many others may have owned them before they were entombed. These examples are so few that I will enumerate them – and I will leave out legendary ones, or even probably legendary ones like the sword of Charlemagne in the Louvre, and stick to those actually found in coffins.

(1) Perhaps the earliest of these is the sword, seen but not removed, in the coffin of King John when it was opened in 1742. This was not described, except that it was corroded into four pieces and that its scabbard was much better preserved. 1217.

(2) A beautifully preserved sword (No.XII.5 below), probably of Type XII, found in the coffin of one of the sons of Alfonso el Sabio of Castile. This was the Infante Fernando de la Cerda, who died in 1270. It is as well preserved as the prince's fully, ceremonially clothed mummified body. This was in the Convent of Las Huelgas in Burgos, in the funerary chapel of the princes of Castile.

(3) An even finer sword (No. XII.7) was in the coffin of Fernando's elder brother, King Sancho IV of Castile who died in 1298 and was buried in the Capella Mayor of Toledo Cathedral. Here caution is needed: it is now known that the crown upon the head of the King's body had been that of his father Alfonso, and so *ipso facto* it has been very reasonably suggested that the sword may also have belonged to that earlier monarch. 1293.

(4) A sword found in the tomb of the emperor Albrecht I in the Cathedral at Speier. 1308.

(5) A once perfectly preserved sword in the coffin of Can Grande della Scala, Lord of Verona, who died in 1326. When the coffin was opened in 1923, the sword and all the other gear was taken from the body, and kept in the Museo Archaeologico of Verona. Now the sword is so perished, never having been properly treated to ensure its conservation, that only a few fragments of the scabbarded blade remain, and the hilt (No.XII.6 below). 1326.

(6) A sword found in the tomb – in the coffin – of the Gonfaloniere Giovanni dei Medici, in the church of Santa Reparata in Florence. He died in 1353. This when found was in a worse condition that that of Can Grande at Verona, but has been properly preserved. 1353.

(7) A perfectly preserved sword, never out of the possession of one family, of Buonarotto Buonarotti, leader of the Guelph party in Florence, who died in 1392. This is still in the Casa Buonarotti in that city. 1392.

(8) One of the most handsome of all these swords, found in 1698 in the coffin of Estore Visconti, along with his body preserved by the action of the soil, in the Basilica of Monza. The body was identified by reason of a gunshot wound in the left leg. Estore Visconti was killed on January 17th, 1413, during the siege of Monza, by a gun-stone. He was a bastard son of Bernabo Visconti, Lord of Milan, and after a chequered and valiant military life he became at the age of 56 for a few months, from May 1412 until his death, lord of Milan in his turn. In recesses on the four sides of the pommel are four enamelled plaques, two with the Viper of Milan and two with a cross. It has been suggested that this sword must have been made only after Estore became Lord of Milan in 1412, on account of these plaques, but it is not necessarily so, for arms of this kind could very easily be applied to an existing sword, or put in to replace older ones, so such arms are not a reliable dating criterion. However, there can be no doubt as to this sword's ownership, nor that its date must be before 1413.

There are, of course, certain swords (mostly of the High Renaissance and therefore not strictly within the purview of this sketch) to which attribution of ownership can be given by reason of arms or legends etched or inscribed upon them. There is for instance in the Musée de Cluny in Paris a beautiful sword with a bronze-gilt cross and a pommel which is of fish-tail form; and etched arms on the forte of blade which are those of Lodovico Sforza, il Moro, Lord of Milan in the 1490s. Here again, we are not compelled to believe either that the arms were put on the blade at the time of it making, or indeed that it really belonged to Lodovico. It is as easy to apply etchings to a blade as it is to change the elements of a hilt.

In the same way, in the Waffensammlung in Vienna, there is an exquisite sword attributed to one of Louis XII's marshals, Gian Giacomo Trivulzio of c.1500. The etched decoration suggests that it was his sword but .....

However, there is one sword, perhaps the most beautiful late medieval sword still extant – indeed, it must be one of the most beautiful ever made, for not only are its proportions excellent, of High Renaissance style, but its great blade is as powerful as a Viking's. The delicate decoration, etched upon the blade and engraved upon the gilt-bronze hilt is of the finest Italian renaissance workmanship – and under the arch of the cross is an inscription which reads CAES: BORG: CAR: VALEN: and the arms of the Borgias. This not only places the sword firmly in the possession of that superbly romantic and much maligned character Cesare Borgia, but dates it as well. He was only Cardinal of Valentino between 1493 and 1498. This is in the Casa Caetani in Rome.

There are of course many swords of this period of the end of the Middle Ages whose owners are positively known: the Emperor Maximilian I, and his father Frederic III; Carlos I of Spain (the Emperor Charles V), and his father Philip the Handsome, and so on but these are all highly decorated swords owned by the most potent and best-known monarchs of Europe, not simple knights. As it is the swords of these simple knights we are concerned with, rather than the captains and the kings, I will end this introduction to my Record by elaborating a little upon what I said at the beginning about the mystique of the sword and its powerful significance to the life and work of the fighting man both in its practical and spiritual aspects.

You will have noticed that where particular swords of the Migration and Viking periods have been mentioned, they have names. These names as you can see are celebrated in poem and saga, while in the literature of the later Middle Ages this is not so. However, there can be no doubt that favoured swords were given names just as their predecessors were, though we do not have the same documentary evidence. The practise of naming things is a very natural, human one – for instance, in a 15th century will in which the few belongings of a merchant's family are itemised, a wooden drinking cup named Edward is specifically mentioned; and in an inventory of some of the personal property of King Charles VI of France is the entry of 'A little sword called Victoire.' A sword was a living thing, and was named for this. It is a pity that we cannot know, now, what the surviving swords of princes were called; no doubt their owners named them, but it was often all a very personal matter (it still is: one gives one's pipe or one's bicycle a name, but it isn't generally written down in one's will). The average life-span of the owners of these swords was not much more than 40 years, and they reckoned to be fully-fledged warriors by the time they were seventeen; so we have to remember that swords belonged to and would be named by young rather simple-minded and unlettered fighting men, not middle-aged erudite 20th century academics. If to the modern scholar it may seem silly for a man to name his pipe Herbert (or a wooden drinking-cup Edward) he might have done so when he was young, romantic and foolish. It is the same with inscriptions on blades: most of the medieval inscriptions were religious invocations, but many consisted of strings of seemingly meaningless initial letters. It has (by 20th century middle-aged and erudite academics) been assumed that they, too, were invocations of Our Lady or the Deity. No doubt many were; but perhaps not all? An inscription containing the letters NED could be construed as containing the initials of the words NOMINE ETERNI DEI, and so on. Again, one has to accept that there could be other, now to us utterly hidden, meanings of either a personal nature, or at least a secular one. There can now be few people living who remember the cryptograms which members of the armed forces in World War II put on the backs of the envelopes of their letters home: SWALK, ITALY, HOLLAND. To you, the young student who reads this, perhaps in the 21st century, these cryptograms are as obscure as would be DICNLACDICLAE upon a 12th century sword-blade; but to us old men who put them on our letters home, they meant Sealed With a Loving Kiss; I Trust and Love You; Hope our Love Lasts and Never Dies. Cryptic, but full of intense personal meaning. Silly? Yes. But we were young, and scared and homesick. So may it have been with those who caused inscriptions to be placed upon swords. In short, we cannot assume anything; we have to admit that although we can make guesses, erudite and informed guesses, we may still be hopelessly wrong.

In the Viking age a chieftain would often give gold rings to his followers as a reward for valorous service (just as the Pharaohs did three thousand years earlier) presenting them sometimes on the point of his sword. In some German poems of the 11th and 12th centuries we read of swords also being used this way in the ceremony of marriage. The priest blesses the ring, taking it from the flat of the bridegroom's sword. In one of these poems in particular we find that the essential and binding act of the ceremony was the placing of the bride's thumb upon the pommel of the groom's sword. In this particular poem, which concerns a girl who was forced into marriage, her parents got her to the altar all right, but when it came to it by no means could they get her clenched hands open and a thumb placed on the groom's pommel. Unfortunately, the end of the poem is lost, but enough survives to indicate that the girl eventually got away with it.

There is another example of a similar function of a chieftain, or a king's, sword. This is from an account from Norwegian court law of the 13th century which is based upon a 12th century version, though it is likely to go back to earlier tradition. This is the ceremony when a king appoints 'hearthmen' – personal bodyguards who once would have been called 'huscarles' – and the new recruit takes his oath of allegiance:

> At the time when the King appoints Hearthmen, no table shall stand before the King. The King shall have his sword on his knee, the sword he had for his crowning; and he shall turn it so that the chape (of the scabbard) goes under his right arm, and the hilt is placed forward on his right knee. Then he shall the move the buckle of the belt over the hilt, and grasp the hilt so that his right hand comes over everything. Then he who is to become a Hearthman shall fall on both knees before the King on the floor. . . and shall put his right hand under the hilt while he keeps his left arm down in front of him in the most comfortable position, and then shall he kiss the King's hand.

In the same way, when the king receives a man as a 'Gestr', or member of a band of warriors of lesser rank than the hearthman, he is directed to put his hand forward over the sword 'where the hilt meets the guard'. The new man puts his under the hilt, kissing the king's hand at the same time, and thus swears the oath.

All through the Middle Ages and far beyond, the sword has been regarded as the embodiment of power and lordship, and what was essential to both – valour and force. With the burgeoning in the second half of the 11th century of the renaissance of art and culture came also the institution of chivalry. This brought the sword to its full glory. It attained a complete symbolism, and to all its ancient attributes was now added the touch of sanctity. Its very shape was that of the cross; it was a specific against evil and fear, a reminder that the sword was to be used in the defence of all that was good and noble in society and the Christian faith, and to the confusion of all that threatened these things. Its two-edged blade stood for truth and justice, one edge for rich oppressors of the poor and the other for the strong who persecute the weak.

Chivalry adapted and modified the time-honoured tribal ritual by which a youth was invested formally with arms, thereby becoming a man and a warrior and a full member of the tribe. In the complete, elaborate ceremonial of the making of a knight, the sword was the central ritual object. Laid upon the altar and blessed by a priest (or by a bishop, where possible) the sword, sanctified now, was handed to the aspirant and the words '*Accipe gladium istum in nomine Patris et Filii et Spiritus Sancti, et utaris eo in defensam tuam et Sancti Dei Ecclesiae, et ad confusionem inimicorum Crucis Christi ac Fidei christianiae.*' ('Receive this sword in the name of the Father and of the Son and of the Holy Spirit, and use it in your own defence and that of the Holy Church of God, and to the confusion of the enemies of the Cross of Christ and of the Christian faith').

Virtue has passed into it, and from it to its new owner. He brandishes it three times, sheaths it, and hands it to his sponsor who completes the ceremony with the final, primeval act. While the new knight's friends fasten the gilt spurs to his heels, his sponsor girds the sword to his waist. So, the original pagan act of investment with the arms was adopted by the might of the Church.

Thus, it is very probable that any medieval knightly sword which may come into a collector's hands was once given this mystical aura of virtue and power at the begining of its 'life', and was offered to the mystical forces of water at its end. It should be regarded as more than just a piece of ancient steel; some of the magic remains, if one knows where to look for it.

16

MEDIEVAL SWORDS

Precursors 1-3

These eight swords from some of the Danish bog-deposits are a minute selection of the great mass of swords from the Celtic Iron Age (c.400 BC – AD 100) and the Migration Period (c.250 – 600 AD) which are the ancestors of the knightly swords of the High Middle Ages. I have included them because they show this, and also because they show, right at the start of the 'Record', how well-preserved some swords may be, even from remote periods, provided the conditions of their burial have been conducive to good preservation. The student of arms should never be put off on the grounds that a sword appears to be 'too good to be true'. This is a trap into which the compilers of sales catalogues have resoundingly fallen in the past. Any object of antiquity has to be assessed on its own merits if it has no well-authenticated provenance, like so many of the swords shown here. If you meet a fine, beautifully preserved medieval sword in the sale room, or offered by a dealer, don't jib at it if it looks smooth and black without rust-pits – or even if it has been cleaned and the patina of ferrite or goethite cleaned off. Because it is smart and in good condition doesn't necessarily mean that it is a modern fake. On the other hand, there are superb modern fakes.... One has to use one's 'nose' and one's common-sense. But to reject a sword as a dud either because it looks too good, or because somebody tells you that he/she has 'never seen one like it' is absurd. If one considers the hundreds of thousands of swords which must have been made between c.400 BC and AD 1525 – probably *millions* – unless one can honestly say one has seen *all* of them, it is *not* honest to damn something because 'I have never seen one like this'. There were infinite variations of detail in the style of pommels, crosses, blades and inscriptions, most of them according to some medieval person's own particular fancy. One has to remember what a tiny percentage of these thousands of swords are available for study now. The number grows all the time, but it is still an incredibly small percentage.

1. Type: La Tène II.
Find-place: a bog at Lindholmgard, Denmark
Collection: Nationalmuseet, Copenhagen
Blade length: 26½" (67.4 cms)
Pommel-type: Unclassified.
Cross-style: Unclassified.
Date: c.300 B.C.
Condition: Very nearly perfect. The bone/wood/ivory grip missing.
Marks: None
Publication: Oakeshott, *AOW*; Behmer; Seitz.

This sword is perhaps the finest example of the long swords of the Celtic Iron Age, or the period of the La Tène culture. There are many of these big iron swords (a number of superb ones are in the British Museum) but this is perhaps the best preserved of them all. As you can see by its shape, it is meant purely as a slashing weapon, having no point. The delicate pattern in the double fullers of the blade – and how sophisticated, and how carefully forged, these are – is not an indication of Pattern Welding, but is made by a multitude of little etched pits.

The arched element at the top of the blade and below the lower ferrule of the hilt belongs properly to the top of the scabbard, from which it has become detached. The straight ferrule immediately above the lower one would once have been half-way (or thereabouts) up the grip. The little spherical pommel is of silver, capped with a pyramidal block of iron to take the rivetted turn-over at the top of the tang, as in all swords (European ones, that is) up to the present time.

It is not only the superb quality of this sword, which is of forged steel, not cast bronze, but its almost incredibly fine state of preservation which makes it so outstanding. The peat in which it was found has preserved the steel of the blade, and the thin iron plates of the scabbard in pristine condition so that the blade could be drawn out of the scabbard. Only the grip, of wood or bone or ivory, has perished.

If this sword, with a restored grip, were to come up for sale in one of the great London sale-rooms, it would be catalogued as '. . .in the style of La Tène III' – i.e., as a fake.

These La Tène period swords were the grandfathers of all medieval 'knightly' swords. I have put this first in this 'Record' for that reason, and as an indication to the student *never* to be led into the belief that because a blade is (a) well-preserved and (b) beautifully made in a highly sophisticated form, that it cannot be 'old'. Bladesmiths were as capable of making a fine blade of steel in 300 BC as they were in 1500 AD.

This ought to prove that many others to be shown below in as good a state of preservation are as honest and genuine as this one.

2-3. Type: Elis Behmer's Type V.
Find-place: Kragehul bog-deposit.
Collection: Copenhagen, National Museum.
Blade-length: 30" (76.2 cms) approx.
Date: Both c. AD 400.
Condition: 2. Very considerably perished blade. Bronze hilt and mounts, good. 3. Rusted into wood, leather-covered scabbard. Good, bronze hilt and mounts perfect.

Publication: Behmer; Oakeshott, *AOW*; Oakeshott, *MS*, part II; *Gun Report* 1986; Seitz.

These two swords from the Kragehul bog-deposit show in an interesting and unmistakeable way what was meant in the Norse literature by the distinction between what was called a 'SVAERD' and a 'MAEKIR'. 2) here is a Maekir, a narrow, pointed sword, while 3) is a Svaerd, a broad slashing one. That this distinction is not by any means made by these two having more or less corrosion, the complete preservation of the bronze scabbard-mounts, particularly the chapes at the point end, makes it clear beyond any possibility of argument that 2) had an acutely-pointed blade, and 3) had a broad one with a more spatulate point. Otherwise, as you can see, these two swords are of exactly the same type according to the forms of hilt and scabbard-mounts. (Elis Behmer's Type V.)

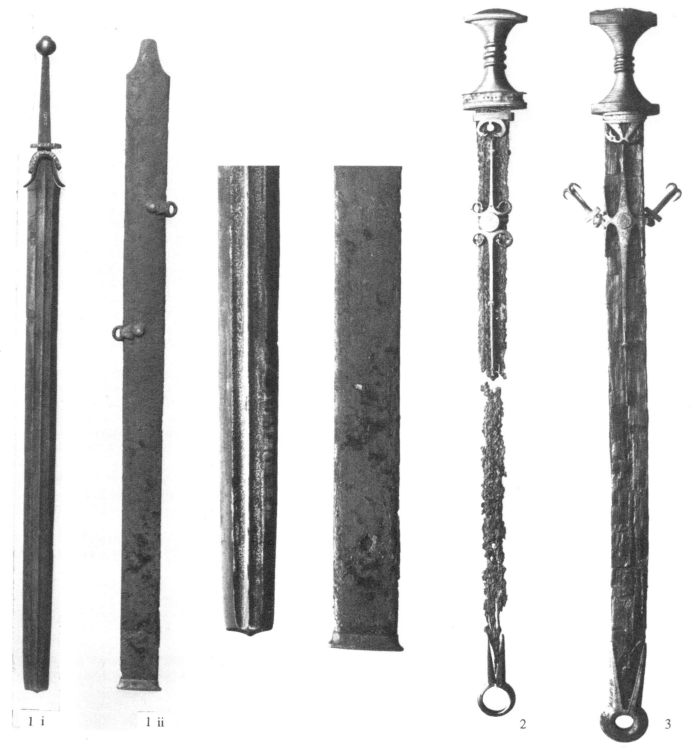

1 i   1 ii   2   3

Precursors 4-8

Type: 4. Unclassified. Roman Cavalry Spatha
5. Behmer's Type IV
6. Unclassified. Roman Cavalry Spatha
7. Behmer's Type V
8. ' '
Find-place: 4. Vimose (Bog-find)
5. Kragehul
6. Nydam
7. Kragehul
8. Nydam
Collection: National Museum, Copenhagen
Blade-length: All 30" (76.2 cms) approx.

Date: 4. c. AD 250 – 350
5. c. AD 400
6. c. AD 350
7. c. AD 400
8. c. AD 250 – 350
Condition: 4. Very good. No severe pitting.
5. Very considerable corrosion.
6. Good. Some deep pits.
7. Poor. Very fragile.
8. Very good. Some breakage of edges.
Publication: Behmer; Oakeshott, *AOW*; *Gun Report*, Dec. 1985; Seitz.

4 5 6 7 8

Type X

Most swords of the Viking Age come into this category, and X (ten) has been chosen to define the type, rather than 1 (one) because in the definitive analytical study of the swords of the Viking Period presented by Dr Jan Petersen in 1919. He classified the latest of the Viking hilt-styles (those with brazil-nut shaped pommels) as Type X (letter X). Since most of these Viking swords with brazil-nut pommels, as well as those which are rather vaguely called 'Pilzformige (mushroom-shaped)' by German archaeologists, all fall neatly into the first category of the typology of swords which I presented in 1960. I began my typology where Petersen left off, with X - number Ten. At the same time I, perhaps unwisely, re-named the 'Pilzformige' or mushroom pommel (which it wasn't, being D shaped in elevation and flat in plan, not like any mushroom or toadstool known to botany) as 'of tea-cosy form'. This, to non-tea-orientated continental students must have made little sense. However, in an English context it is perfect. The laid-down 'lazy D' is just like a tea-cosy. Those which are flat in plan are like one empty, those of a stouter and more rotund shape are like a tea-cosy with a teapot inside it. In the quarter-century which has lapsed since I named, or mis-named, this pommel form it is pleasant (to me) to find that in fact the name has been very generally adopted.

So, Type X is the 'typical', if there is such a thing, Viking sword with its great variety of hilt-forms and styles: and it goes on into the 12th century. Indeed, one may say it goes on into the 18th century as far as blade-shape goes, but there is no doubt that it is seldom found as a blade-shape in any blade made new later than c.1200. Of course, many very old blades continued in use, re-hilted according to changes of fashion, as long as the sword was used.

Four typical Viking swords, dating between c.750-1050

1. Type X
   Find-place: Unknown
   Collection: Private
   Blade-length: 80.2 cms (31⅝")
   Pommel-type: Behmer's Type VIII
   Date: c. AD 650-750
   Condition: Excavated, but very good. Some very large pits.

2. Type X
   Find-place: Unknown
   Collection: Private
   Blade-length: 80.5 cms (31¾")
   Pommel-type: Wheeler's Type VII
   Date: 9th century
   Condition: Excavated, but excellent. More corrosion near point.

3. Type X
   Find-place: Unknown
   Collection: Private
   Blade length: 76 cms (29½")
   Pommel-type: Petersen's Type A
   Date: 9th - 10th century
   Condition: Excavated. Considerable corrosion, especially near to point.

4. Type X
   Find-place: Unknown
   Collection: Private
   Blade length: 80 cms (31")
   Pommel-type: Petersen's Type X
   Date: c. 950-1050
   Condition: Good, excavated. Considerable pitting.
   Publication: Catalogue, Sotheby's, Nov. 1, 1983, London
   These four Viking swords were sold at Sotheby's in London on November 1st 1983. Lots 100, 101, 102 and 103.

1. A fine pattern welded blade with a hilt of very early Viking form, if not late Migration Period, decorated with closely-set vertical silver wires inlaid in the iron.

2. This is a most interesting and unusual sword. The fine pattern-welded blade patterns are, alternating, the 'BLODI-DA' (Blood-Eddy) and 'ANN' (like rows of mown hay) of the Norse poetry, very clearly defined. One side (shown in the photograph) has a conventional broad shallow fuller, but the other has no fuller, but close alongside the edge (right side of this photograph) runs a very narrow groove, from the hilt almost to the point. The tang of the blade, as you can see, is offset towards this edge of the sword. The offset tang and groove near the edge are characteristics of back-edged swords, from the Norse Saxes to 19th century sabres, yet this is an otherwise conventional double-edged blade. About 1 cm of the point is missing. The cross and pommel are decorated with strips of gold ribbon, engraved with tiny chevrons, inlaid in the iron of the very well-preserved hilt.

3. This has a pattern-welded blade with the 'ANN' pattern all the way down the fuller. The pommel is extremely flat in profile.

4. A much plainer sword with an undecorated iron hilt. There seem to be traces of iron-inlaid letters in the blade, but it also looks as if it is pattern-welded. Since, as far as we know from surviving examples, pattern-welded blades were never inlaid in iron, so it is difficult to reconcile these two possibilities. The blade is rather heavily corroded, and I found it difficult to make out whether it was pattern-welded or inlaid. But it did seem to be both. This is a good example of an aberrant specimen; but when one considers that though some hundreds of surviving pattern-welded blades have been examined, very many thousands, which are not available for study, were made in the centuries between say AD 250 and 850. So who shall say with honesty that 'no PW blade was ever inlaid in iron lettering, because I have never seen one?"

1 2 3 4

X. 5-6

5. Type X
   Find-place: ? Denmark
   Collection: The late Mr E A Christensen, Copenhagen
   Blade-length: 28" (71 cms) approx.
   Pommel-type: Petersen's Type X
   Date: c.950-1000
   Condition: Excavated, much corroded blade. Hilt not so bad.
   Iron inlays preserved.

6. Type X
   Find-place: Italy, somewhere unrecorded
   Collection: Philadelphia Art Museum, ex C.O. Von Kien-
   busch Collection.
   Pommel-type: Unclassified
   Date: c.950-1000
   Condition: Excavated. Considerable corrosion, only faint
   traces left of iron inlaid inscription.

5. Is a very good typical example of a sword of Petersen's
Type X coinciding with my own Type X. I have never been
able to examine this sword, so I don't know what inlaid pattern
is on the reverse side, but it would certainly be one of the
more-or-less standard patterns used by the ULFBEHRT firm
of bladesmiths, as in the example at 5.ii below.
6. This is a more-or-less conventional X, but the pommel is
unusual, though examples like it are shown in Italian and
Spanish art of the 10th-11th centuries.
Publication: Christensen and Hoffmeyer; Hayward.

5i

6

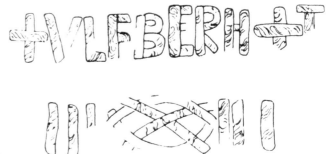

5ii

7. Type: X

Find-place: The River Thames, in King's Reach off the Temple in London.

Collection: British Museum (AS.20.23)

Blade-length: 29" (73.7 cms)

Pommel-type: Wheeler's Type VI

Cross-style: Too early for classification

Date: c.900-950

Condition: Excellent for a river-found sword. There is a little pitting under the hard brown patina. The blade bears on one side the name INGELRII in large letters inlaid in iron, on the other a sequence of three upright strokes, a diagonal cross, and three more uprights, also inlaid in iron. Both these inscriptions are exactly paralleled by those on the sword once in my care, now in the Glasgow Museum (see No. X.9 in this series).

Until I was able to examine this sword in 1950, nobody had noticed the inscriptions lurking below the patina. Once I had identified them, they were cleaned and brought to light by Dr Herbert Maryon in the Research laboratory at the Museum.

Publication: I think it would be safe to say every book, almost every article, in English dealing with arms and armour from the late 19th century until the latest one - David Edge's *The Arms and Armour of the Medieval Knight*, London, 1988.

A note was published in *The Antiquaries' Journal* in 1951, Vol. XXXI, Jan-Apr 1941, Nos. 1 and 2 'An Ingelri Sword in the British Museum' by me.

8. Type: X

Find-place: The River Witham near Lincoln

Collection: The British Museum

Blade-length: 32" (81.2 cms)

Pommel-type: Wheeler's Type VI

Cross-style: Not in the typology

Date: c.900-950

Condition: A nearly perfect example of the unblemished river-find. There are a few pits, and some erosion of the edges, but otherwise its surface, under the patina of Goethite (Fe.Ooh) is nearly perfect. The name LEUTFRIT (with the first T placed upside-down) is inlaid in iron on one side, and the single letter S on the other. These inscriptions I was able to discern in 1950 at the same time as I noticed those on the INGELRI sword from the Thames, both subsequently being cleaned in the Research Laboratory of the museum.

There is a similar sword (in the same condition) with this name (probably a version of LEOFRIC) in Russia.

Publication: The list would be too long, for it has appeared (like the Thames one) in almost every publication where the Vikings or their swords appear, since it was taken from the water in the 1840s.

7

8

X. 9

Type: X
Find-place: Unknown, probably in Germany
Collection: Ex. D'Acre Edwards, ex. Oakeshott. Now Glasgow Museum
Blade-length: 30⅝" (77.7 cms)
Pommel-type: B
Cross-style: 1
Date: c.950
Condition: Very good. River-found. There is a little light pitting overall, with deeper and more concentrated corrosion at the point.

When this came into my care in 1960, there was no visible trace of inlaid inscriptions. However, very careful examination in strong sunlight showed that there were iron inlays on each side of the blade. I thought I could make out the 'ULF-BEHRT' name, so I tried etching the blade, first with lemon juice with no result, then with vinegar with equal lack of success. So I tried Worcester Sauce – and the name INGELRII fairly leapt into view. Now (as the photograph shows) after a decade or more in the Museum, the name has dimmed considerably. On the reverse was a fairly common sequence of marks, – three upright strokes, a diagonal cross, followed by three more uprights. This is also found upon the reverse side of the INGELRII sword from the Thames in the British Museum (No. X.7 above).

This sword, safely enough dateable within the Viking period (950 is a sort of dead-centre, give or take a couple of decades either way) and because of the form of its long, narrow cross is an excellent example of a sword of a kind which the Vikings called 'GADDHJALT', Spike-Hilt.

Publications: Oakeshott, *SAC* Plate 1.c. (This shows the sword with a grip which I put on it, which the Museum removed, and before the Worcester Sauce treatment revealed the inscriptions.) Scott, J.G. *European Arms and Armour at Kelvingrove*, Glasgow, 1980.

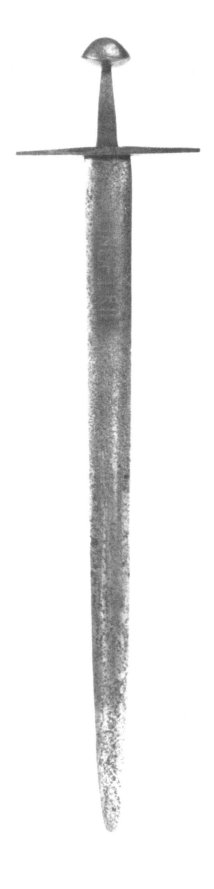

X. 10

Type: X
Find-place: Unknown
Collection: Ex. Harold Petersen, now private
Blade-length: 32" (81 cms)
Pommel-type: J
Cross-style: 1 (restored)
Date: Blade, pattern-welded, perhaps c.1000. Hilt and inlays c.1050-1100.
Condition: Excavated. Good. The original patination of Goethite once cleaned off with acid, giving the blade a nasty leaden look. Since coming into my care, it has been rehabilitated and looks as an excavated, cleaned blade should.
(i) shows the sword-only blade and pommel - as it was in Harold Peterson's collection.
(ii) shows it as now, with the cross very well restored.
Publication: *Gun Report*, 1986; Oakeshott, *MS* Pt. VIII.

The engraved and inlaid inscriptions on this sword are very interesting for several reasons. The blade is pattern-welded, and so is unlikely to be of a date later than c.1000 but the inlaid (in silver) patterns are very characteristic of a date in the second half of the 11th century, as shown in (iii). The meaning of this mark, on the obverse of the blade, is fairly obviously intended as a schema for a church, or indeed The Church, for the arch at the end of the two parallel lines (the walls of the church) is of exactly the same character as that shown, for example, at (iv), a panel from an ivory reliquary of San Millan de la Cogolla, c.1050. Arches of this particcular form are shown in very many manuscript pictures dating between c.750 and 1100. The sun, or star, figures are common Christian symbols; the meaning of the pairs of upright rectangles is obscure, as is the strange conjoined pair of crosses (Crosses Potent) at the point end of the design. Right up near the point on this side is a cross fleury, like a Bishop's processional cross. On the obverse are three circular motifs, a marigold (symbol of Christ) between two Greek crosses. This form of Greek Cross, with the equal arms very much splayed out at the tips, is found very frequently in art at the same periods as the 'arches' mentioned above, i.e. between c.750-1100. A very good example is on the Ardagh Chalice, in Dublin (c.850). But as a Christian symbol it appears everywhere during these years in this form.

A very similar inscribed and inlaid-in-silver pattern was found by Dr. Leppaaho in a late Viking grave in Finland (v). This is so similar in style (particularly the Cross Potent) though not in content, to the sword under discussion, that it must have originated in the same workshop, if not actually done by the same hand.

At the point on the obverse is a small hand, two fingers raised in blessing. This is parallelled again in art (i.e. The Bayeux Tapestry) very frequently in the period c.1000-1200.

The blade may have been an old one when these designs were inlaid in its surfaces, for pattern welding (as far as we know at present) ceased to be used after, let us say AD 1000, but the designs were absolutely typical of the later period of c.1050-

1100. The continuous usage of a good blade over a period of many centuries is well attested in the Norse literature as well as in later medieval poetry, inventory, chronicle, and romance. It continued very nearly up to the present, e.g. a number of fine old 16th and 17th century broadsword blades mounted in 'Regulation' Highland Scottish Military hilts from c.1850 to 1914 - as well as fine old medieval ones mounted in Scottish hilts during the 18th century.

i   ii   iii

iv

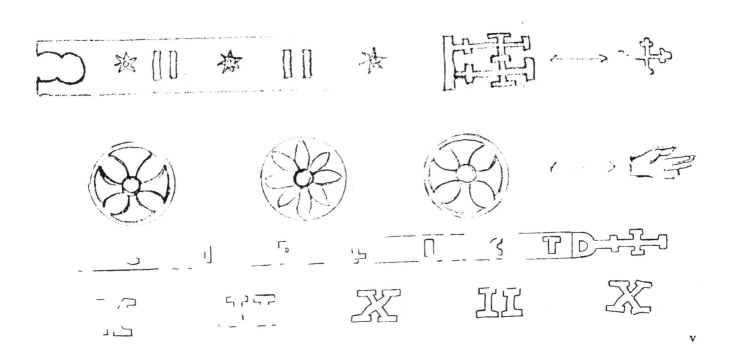

v

29

X. 11

Type: X
Collection: Museum & Art Gallery, Glasgow (A.631)
Find-place: Unknown
Blade-length: 31" (78.8 cms)
Pommel-type: F
Cross-style: 1
Date: ? c.1100-1150
Condition: Excavated, not very good. The edges are considerably perished, but the surfaces are not too bad except down near the point; there may be about 2 cms of this point missing. Once in my own collection, bought at Christies at the D'Acre Edwards sale in 1960, I parted with it to Glasgow in 1964. A very neat, light, and well-balanced sword. There is a mark on the blade which corresponds interestingly with similar symbols forming part of longer inscriptions on the blades of other swords shown here below, particularly in Appendix A.

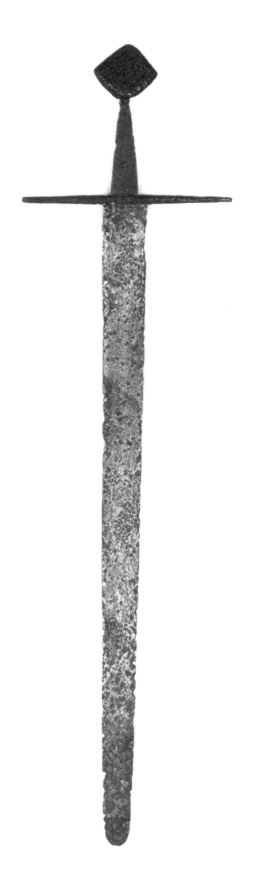

30

X. 12

Type: X
Find-place: Northumberland, England
Collection: Ex E.J. Pocock, E. Oakeshott, D. Oliver. Now
Glasgow Museum
Blade-length: 26" (66 cms)
Pommel-type: 1
Cross-style: 1
Condition: Quite good on one side, but very perished on the
reverse. Each side inlaid with letters and patterns in gold.
Cross and pommel (which is very flat, like a biscuit) in good
condition with some deep pitting.
Publication: see Appendix B.

This little sword was offered for sale in Carlisle in 1946,
having been found by the seller (unknown to me) hanging in
a farm kitchen in Northumberland. How long it had been there
is not recorded, but its presence on that wall does suggest that
it was a local find. This does not suggest that it is of English
(or British) origin, which it most certainly is not. Though
swords with these beautifully executed inlaid inscriptions
have been found all over Europe, it is now thought to be most
probable that they were made in Central Europe, possibly in
the area of the ancient Noricum, where most of the weapons
used by the Romans were made - and, indeed, those used by
the iron age Celts of the La Tène period. By analogy with
swords found in Viking graves in Finland during the late
1940's, many of whose blades bear these inscriptions and
inlays, these finely inscribed blades can all be dated firmly to
the period 1050-1125. It is possible to be fairly positive about
this because it is clear that most of the varied forms of
inscription and design were made by only a very few trained
calligraphers, whose 'handwriting' can be identified and isolated.

The fact that this sword's blade is very short was once considered to be because it had been broken or cut down; but this
seems unlikely as the sword as it is, is perfectly balanced, and
is surely one of a particular kind of short sword very popular
from the Migration period to the Industrial Revolution. There
is much mention of such short swords in the Norse Sagas - the
poet-warrior Grettir the Strong, for instance, always preferred
a short-bladed sword for serious fighting, keeping his beautiful 'family' sword (a rich heirloom) 'Aettartangi' for social
or ceremonial occasions. All through the Middle Ages such
short swords are depicted in art or described in literature,
though actual specimens dating before the 15th century are
very rare.

This one was bought in 1946 by a collector I knew well, Mr.
J. Pocock; he told me of it in 1947 and sent me a photograph,
but I never saw or handled it until it was offered to me (I
bought it) in 1983. In 1985 I exchanged it with Mr David
Oliver, who has since deposited it in the Museum in Glasgow.
It has been fully described in an article in the *Catalogue of
The Third Park Lane Arms Fair*, where I postulated a possible
meaning for the enigmatic series of the letters B O' A C
repeated four times on each side of the blade. The mark like
a large inverted comma between the O and the A is a Latin
abbreviation mark for the word 'que' (and): I suggest that the
meaning might be 'BEATI OMNIPOTENSQUE ANGELI
CHRISTI' - Blessed and omnipotent (are) the Angels of
Christ. This article is reprinted in Appendix B below.

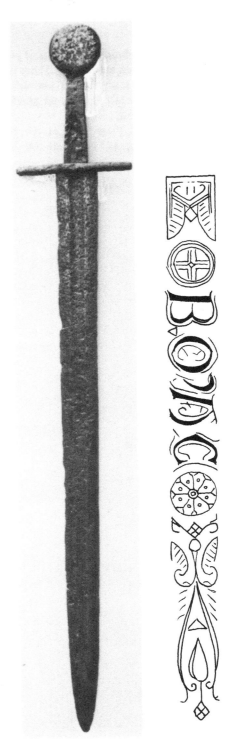

31

X. 13

Type: X
Find-place: Unknown
Collection: Ex Wilczec Collection, Landesmuseum. Zurich.
16203
Blade-length: 34" (86.5 cms)
Pommel-type: A
Cross-style: 1
Date: c.1100 or earlier
Condition: Good on the whole; some areas of pitting, but the
edges have not suffered, nor has the hilt. There is a very large
and straggling INGELRII inscription on one side of the blade,
unusually close up to the hilt. This is an absolutely classic
example of a Type X sword.
Publication: Hoffmeyer II, Plate IXa, Cat. p.9, No.26.
Oakeshott, *SAC*, p.140, fig. 127 and Plate 2A.

X. 14

Type: X (short)
Find-place: Unknown
Collection: Ex D'Acre Edwards. Now private
Blade-length: 23" (58.5 cms)
Pommel-type: H
Cross-style: 5
Date: c.1250
Condition: Excavated (probably a river-find). The blade is good with a little corrosion under the patina. The pommel and cross are of copper, maybe once gilt; but when I handled it in 1961 I couldn't see any traces. There is a cross patée engraved in the faces of the pommel, and each broadly-splayed end of the cross guard is engraved with a little grotesque figure, a large round head with little legs coming from under its chin, enclosed within a circle with tendrils going back towards the écusson. This figure is so strongly akin to the 'Babewyns' in English manuscripts of the period c.1250-1320 that it is inevitable that one should suggest an English origin for the hilt. The blade may of course be a lot older. There is in the fuller on each side an inscription of three minute letters, o s o. Comparison with other swords (i.e. No. XI.1 here) which have to be dated to the 12th century points clearly to a date c.1125-75 for the blade - a good example of an old blade re-hilted c.1270 plus or minus a decade or so.

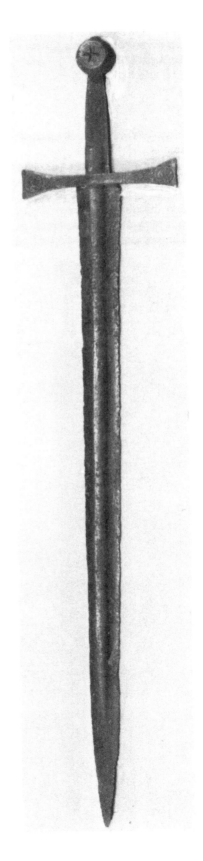

X. 15

Type: X
Find-place: The River Witham near Lincoln
Collection: The British Museum
Blade-length: 31" (78.8 cms)
Pommel-type: 1
Cross-style: 2
Date: c.1100-50
Condition: Perfect; one or two small areas of pitting under the very black patina.

This is a particularly interesting and important sword, for its blade has double-fullers running nearly to the point (like some fine Viking swords) and has a very beautiful lettered inscription on one side, running right across both fullers, and an interesting series of symbols on the other; on each side, near the point, is a little crescent-moon-shaped figure. All are inlaid in yellow metal, possibly (because of the very high quality of the blade) this is gold. There is a blade in Helsinki among Dr Leppaaho's Viking grave finds with a lettered inscription of strikingly similar character and form, which shows that this sword is of the same date - i.e. c.1100 - instead of c.1340 as it is labelled in the Museum and has always been so dated in the countless publications in which it has appeared. The form of the hilt, too, is exactly parallelled in several of Leppaaho's Viking grave-finds. In the face of such evidence, the very late dating cannot be sustained.

Publications: Laking, Vol.I; Oakeshott, *AOW*, Plate 7B (where it is wrongly dated, Dr. Leppaaho's work not having been published when I wrote the book).

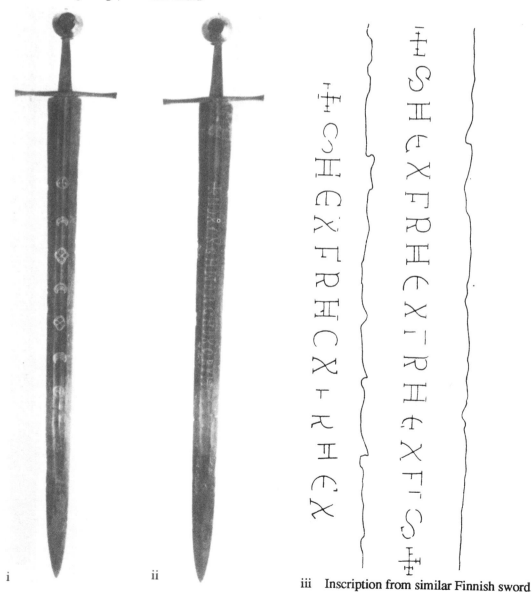

i   ii   iii Inscription from similar Finnish sword

X. 16

Type: X
Find-place: The River Great Ouse
Collection: The Museum of Archaeology and Ethnology, Downing College, Cambridge
Blade-length: 30½" (77.5 cms)
Pommel-type: A
Cross-style: 1
Date: c.950-1000
Condition: Excellent, except for a large hole just below the cross, which must have been caused by a piece of stone or some organic material in the peaty mud of the river-bed, which allowed oxygen to reach the blade, and corrode it at that spot. The iron inlays are intact, and show up clearly.
Publication: Oakeshott, pl. 2c *SAC*
This is an excellent sword, quite light and well-balanced, but I have only held it very gingerly because that great hole must have weakened the blade. On the iron inlay on one side is the name CONSTAININUS, on the other
+ INOMINEDOMINI +

Type Xa

Characteristic of this type is a long fuller, like a X, only narrower - but not so narrow as an XI. This is a very fine distinction, and may seem unnecessary. In fact, in my original typology of 1960, I had not isolated it; I put all Xa's into Type XI. It was only when *The Sword in the Age of Chivalry* was reprinted in 1980 that I decided that there was a clear distinction, and so in a new preface to the book I added my new Type Xa. It may seem a silly distinction, depending only upon the breadth of the fuller, but I think it is better that such a distinction should be made. There is no real difference in dating X's and Xa's, for both types were in use together from c.1000 on. This is proven beyond any reasonable doubt by a series of swords found in the early 1950s by Dr Jorma Leppaaho, of Helsinki University, in a large group of late Viking graves in southern Finland. These are all clearly dateable to the second half of the 11th century, give or take a decade each way; and the information as to reliable dating, not by the form of blades and hilts but by the style and 'handwriting' of inlaid inscriptions, which subsequent x-ray photography of the blades provided, is absolutely crucial to the segregation of types of sword and sword-inscriptions, and their dating. Among these finds, the incidence of X types and Xa's was about equal.

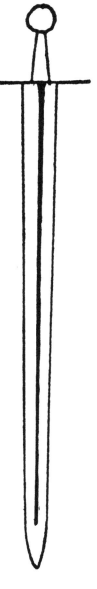

Xa. 1-2

1. Type: Xa
   Find-place: Unknown
   Collection: Wallace Collection, London (A.459)
   Blade-length: 33¾" (85.7cms)
   Pommel-type: J
   Cross-style: 2
   Date: ? 1100 ? 1300
   Condition: ? Excavated. Maybe a river-find, but could be out of a tomb. Its condition is as near perfect as it is possible for such a weapon to be. There is no pitting beneath the hard blue-black purplish patina, only here and there (particularly near the point) a slight roughness like groups of tiny pustules under the patina.

2. Type: Xa
   Find-place: S. Finland
   Collection: Helsinki University
   Blade-length: (Broken)
   Pommel-type: J
   Cross-style: 2
   Date: 1050-1150
   Condition: Excavated, but very good. The blade was ceremonially broken before burial.

This magnificent weapon is, I believe, the very finest medieval sword in existence at present. If there is a finer one, I don't know of it; and this is so special that it cannot be very likely that a better should, or could, be found. It is not just its perfect preservation - the edges are as sharp as a well-honed carving knife - or the beautiful rich colour of its patina, but the shape of the blade and its perfect setting in the simple hilt whose proportions are exactly and aesthetically right. It is clearly of Type Xa, with its finely tapering edges and long, well-marked fuller; but the section of the blade is very complex and sophisticated, for each edge of the fuller forms a strong ridge or rib, from which the surface of the blade sweeps down to each cutting edge in a strong concave curve.

This sword has always been dated, upon its form alone for there is neither mark nor inscription, to the first half of the 14th century. This may be so; but it is of a type which by analogy seems not to have been in use as late as that; more particularly, the form of both hilt and blade are parallelled exactly by some swords in those graves cleared by Dr Leppaaho. The photograph of one of these, (Xa.2), shows how exactly similar one of these hilts is; the fact that the blade is of such fine and sophisticated workmanship is no argument at all for a 14th century date, for even as early as the La Tène II period blades of equal or even superior quality were being made.

Because of long tradition and the scholarly insistence of museum authorities, this lovely sword will continue to be labelled, and catalogued, as of the early 14th century; but it isn't necessarily so. A very much more credible date for it would be between - yes! - 1050 and 1150.

Publications: Mann & Norman; Oakeshott, *SAC* Pl.19a; Leppaaho; Seitz, Pl.89c.

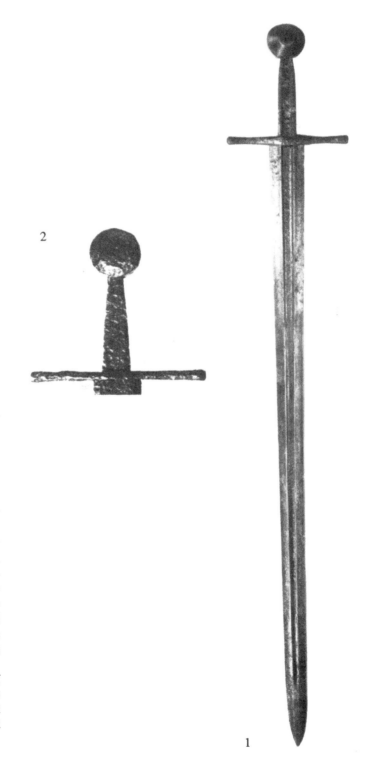

2

1

Xa. 3

Type: Xa
Find-place: Unknown
Collection: Private. Once my own.
Blade-length: 34½" (87.6 cms)
Pommel-type: A
Cross-style: 1
Date: c.1050-1100
Condition: Excavated, and properly (non-acid) cleaned. Some rust stains, no real pitting except on the iron of pommel and cross. Grip restored in 1978 by me.

This sword is of the same form as to its blade as the preceding example, and is in very much the same excellent condition. I saw it at Sotheby's in 1946, when it retained its patina of Goethite. I wanted badly to buy it, but I could only manage £10 and it went for £26. Whoever bought it, very skilfully cleaned it, not by acid but by the use of gentle abrasives and elbow grease.

I bought it, finally, at Sotheby's in 1977 where it was catalogued as 'a sword in 14th century style, the blade Sudanese'. Thus, I was able to get it for the price of a good dinner. Once I was able to examine it properly (I chanced my arm, and my certainty that it was no more a Sudanese blade than I was a Fuzzy-Wuzzy, when I got it) it was plain that in that fine 'Sudanese' blade there was a well-made inscription inlaid in iron - see ii, opposite. On the obverse, + NINOMINEDO-MIINI + and on the reverse a large Cross Potent. I was able to enhance and clarify this inscription by the same homely methods described above for my INGELRII sword, only this time the vinegar etched the letters clearly enough.

As for the hilt 'In 14th Century Style', this is, again, exactly matched by several of the Finnish Viking swords, as for instance iii below. Also the slight amount of corrosion and patination of Goethite which had not been cleaned off could never have been reproduced by a forger*. It was certainly considered, by Sotheby's, to be genuine in 1946. I suppose it was because the blade was cleaned that it was, so casually, consigned to the category of a fake. Even if it had been a fake, to say 'in 14th century style' was two centuries and more wide of the mark. Thus a superb 11th century sword was saved from the rubbish heap to which expert opinion would have consigned it.

*In the 1970's. It can be now, almost perfectly (1989).

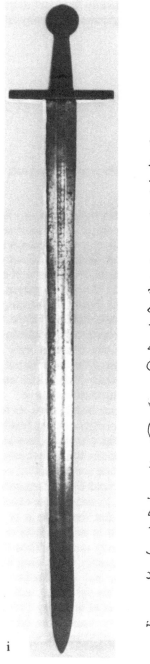

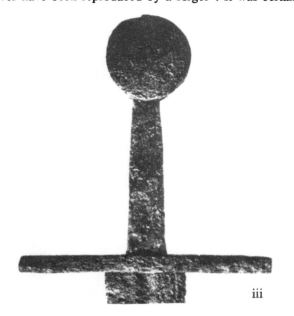

iii

i

ii

Xa. 4

Type: Xa
Find-place: Whittlesea Mere, Cambridgeshire
Collection: Private. On loan to the Victoria & Albert Museum
Blade-length: 34¾" (88 cms)
Pommel-type: I
Cross-style: 2
Date: c.1050-1120
Condition: Excavated. Upper part of blade's surface fairly well preserved along with much of the ? gold ? latten inlaid inscription.
Publication: North, Anthony, *European Swords*, p.6.1
Oakeshott, *SAC* Plate 6B

(i). The photograph shows the general appearance of the sword. Its colour is a fine brownish-purple.

(ii). This shows the inscription on one side quite clearly. It runs actually about half-way down the blade, but its lower half has vanished all but for an occasional gleam of the yellow metal. However, the well-preserved upper part shows very clearly the distinctive style of the well-formed letters, which can be seen to be of the same clear 'Handwriting' as

(iii). which is a photograph taken by x-ray of a silver-inlaid inscription in a sword-blade from a grave (Viking) in S. Finland, dating c.1050-1125. This seems to give a clear and unequivocal date to the Whittlesea Sword, which is labelled by the authorities of the Victoria & Albert Museum as of the early 14th century, clearly wrong by two centuries. The form of the hilt of the Whittlesea Sword, like the one in the Wallace Collection in London (No. Xa.1 in this series, above) is matched exactly as to the form of its pommel, and very closely by the style of the cross, by the hilt of a similar sword from Finland from the same group of graves. Note the facetted 'wheel' pommel, of a form, generally, previously, only attributed to the late 14th/early 15th centuries. (iv)
Publication: (iii) & (iv) Leppaaho, pl.28.i.

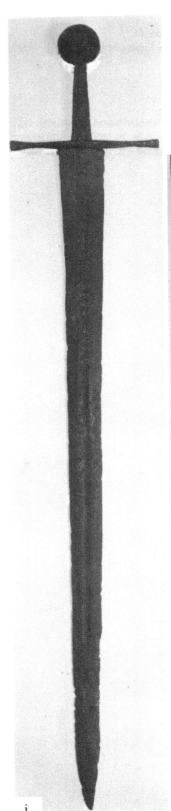

i

ii

iii

iii Inscription from similar
Finnish sword

iv Hilt of Finnish sword

39

Xa. 5

Type: Xa
Find-place: Near Newbury, Berkshire
Collection: H.M. Royal Armoury, Tower of London. IX, 1027
Blade-length: 33" (85cms)
Pommel-type: G
Cross-style: 1
Date: c.1100
Condition: Excavated. Good. Some corrosion of smooth surface in patches particularly on one side. Indecipherable traces of iron inlaid inscription (all the inlay lost).
Publication: Dufty, Plate 2b.
Oakeshott, *SAC* Plate 4.D.

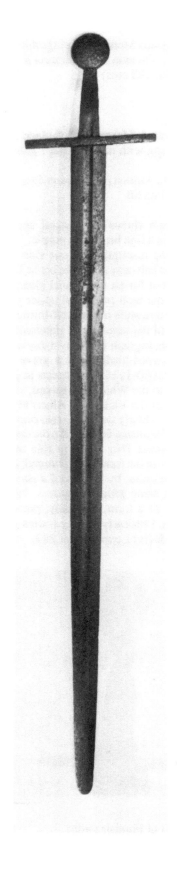

Xa. 6

Type: Xa
Find-place: Unknown
Collection: Private (ex. Harold Peterson)
Blade-length: 34" (87.7cms)
Pommel-type: B
Cross-style: 1
Date: c.1050-1125
Condition: Excavated. Good, most of surface surviving with considerable pitting. No visible trace of inlaid inscription.

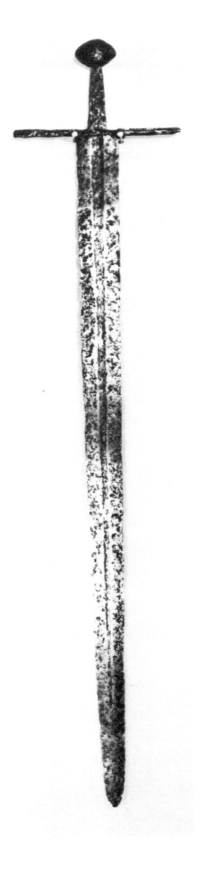

Xa. 7

Type Xa
Find-place: Unknown
Collection: Glasgow Museum & Art Gallery 11.29.g
Blade-length: 33" (85cms)
Pommel-type: A squashed-up variety of Type I
Cross-style: 1
Date: c.1050-1125
Condition: Excavated; heavily pitted, particularly near to the
point, some 1" (2cms approx.) missing, corroded away.
Publication: None

Xa. 8

Type: Xa
Find-place: Unknown (Continental)
Collection: H.M. Royal Armoury, Tower of London. IX, 1081
Blade-length: 32" (81.2 cms)
Pommel-Type: B.1.
Cross-Style: 1
Date: c.1100-50
Condition: Excavated. Good, but surface mostly corroded away. No trace of inscriptions. The hilt is better preserved than the blade, which is very far gone near the point.
Publication: Dufty, Plate 1c.

There is a sword of similar form in the Bernisches Historisches Museum in Bern (No.134 in the 1929 inventory), the grip of which is minimally shorter; otherwise the two are identical. The Bern one has remains of a silver-inlaid inscription (see (ii) below). The Tower sword was in the D'Acre Edwards collection sold at Christies in 1960. I tried to get it, but Sir James Mann for the Tower beat me, though I ran him up nicely. A very fine, well-balanced sword whose very thin, flat and flexible blade makes it handle well.

ii Inscription on Bern sword

i

43

Xa. 9

Type: Xa
Find-place: Unknown
Collection: Glasgow Museum & Art Gallery (Ex.coll. Sir Edward Barry) A.6533
Blade-length: 36" (91cms)
Pommel-type: R
Cross-style: A slender form of Style 5
Date: c.1050-1100 (give or take a couple of decades each way)
Condition: Excavated, very good. The surface is lightly corroded in a curious mottled way, looking like some kinds of pattern-welding; but since this mottling goes over to the edges, it is most likely to be a rather unusual corrosion pattern produced by whatever organic stuff surrounded it.

The remains of the iron-inlaid inscriptions (the inlaid strips have gone) is still decipherable. The spherical pommel is very small, which gives the sword an awkward, unbalanced look.

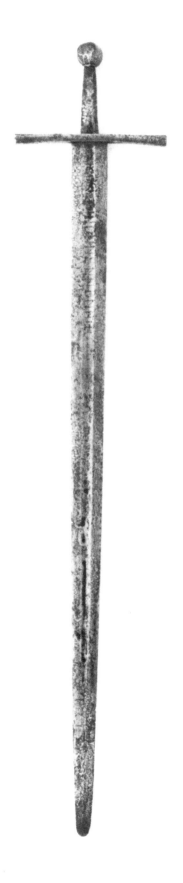

Xa. 10

Type: Xa
Find-place: Within a tomb in a church in S. Germany or Austria
Collection: Private
Blade-length: 37" (94cms)
Pommel-type: N
Cross-style: 1 – a very long, slender version
Date: c.1100-1150
Condition: Indoor preservation, either above or in a tomb. Very good in the upper two-thirds but considerably perished near to the point. The hilt is in excellent condition. There is no trace of an inscription.

These photographs show very clearly the actual form of this rather unusual pommel. If seen only from the front, it looks as if it was a simple boat-shape. There is a sword of very similar profile and appearance in the Schweizerisches Museum in Zurich (Inv. No. AG2465). I once had a tracing of a very similar sword, with this wide flat pommel, brought me from Romania by an American diplomat. Unfortunately (this was over thirty years ago) this drawing is lost, but I can't help thinking that this is the same sword. The present owner (Dec. 1987) sent me a very full set of photographs, with the statement that the sword was found in a knight's tomb. Unfortunately what knight this was, or when he died, or where the tomb was, has not been revealed. I assume that it was in Austria or South Germany.

The one in Zurich has a nearly identical pommel, but the cross is shorter and is slightly arched toward the point. There are remains of marks inlaid in the blade, only the engraved lines of which remain, none of the ? gold ? silver or latten inlay surviving. However, the style of the inlays matches some of Dr Leppaaho's Finnish Viking blades, so the date must be around 1100 – not, as the Zurich publication (Schneider & Stuber, I, 24, no.19) states, c.1200-1275.

The Finnish Viking sword is illustrated, with its x-ray-revealed inlays, in Leppaaho Plate 28.2. The Swiss sword is about the same size, 108 cms as compared with 111 of the one illustrated here.

Xa. 11-12

11. Type: Xa
   Find-place: Unknown
   Collection: Fitzwilliam Museum, Cambridge (Reserve Collection)
   Blade-length: 33" (83.8 cms)
   Pommel-type: B
   Cross-style: 1
   Date: c.1100
   Condition: Poor. The blade is very heavily pitted on both sides, but the edges are not much worn away. It is a fine, bold well-proportioned sword whose hilt exactly matches a sword from a Viking grave at Tryvaa in Finland.

12. Type: Xa
   Find-place: Hauko, Hakiala, Finland
   Blade-length: Fragment
   Pommel-type: B
   Cross-style: 1
   Date: c.1100
   Condition: Excellent. Inscription +INNIOINNEDINI on one side, +INNIMIDOINNI+ on the other.

12

11

The next three swords to be shown, together with drawings of the blade-inlays of four others form a group all clearly designed and executed in the same workshop, perhaps by the same hand. The inlays are in silver or yellow metal, perhaps gold (as in many other cases) or maybe latten; and one is in copper. Fully to discuss the conjectural meanings of these assorted symbols is not possible here, but a good deal of attention has been given to them in at least three important publications.

Only two of these blades were known when Rudolf Wegeli published his great doctoral thesis on blade-inscriptions in 1903 (*ZHWK* III). Both are of Type X, and were found in Switzerland, one at Yverdon and the other in the Neuenburg Lake, shown here at Nos. Xa.14 and 15. The most significant of them comes out of one of Dr Leppaaho's late Viking graves in Finland. (shown here at No. Xa.16). There is another complete sword from this atelier in the Musée de l'Armée in Paris, another from the River Bann in Ireland, and three broken and hilt-less blades in Holland, one from the Waal near Nyjmegen, one from the lower Rhine at Rees and one from Lummada on the Island of Osel.

This group of eight blades (with a ninth fragment from Finland) present the researcher with a series of problems as to the reason for adding these strange and seemingly meaningful symbols to sword-blades – even more baffling perhaps than the lettered inlays are. However, common-sense and perhaps a hard-headed approach can equate these symbols (particular-ly those on the blade from Lummada) with the engraved and gilded decorations on the blades of 18th century small-swords and 19th century sabres, which are not only very similar in design and content but except in a few cases where specific events or persons are commemorated (or of course where arms or heraldic badges are present), seem to make about as much sense. Using this bleak unromantic (and most un-Christian) approach, one can say that here is the work of an individual, or a group of craftsmen, with ideas of their own, doodling on the blades they are given to decorate; or of course, putting on assorted symbols to the requirements of a probably princely customer.

This heretical suggestion has perhaps as much validity as the rather earnest Christian approach to the problem as Wegeli's, or Eberle's or Ypey's, but what is uncompromisingly sure is that the dating of all of them (to the period 1150-1250) is too late, for the well preserved sword from Kokemaki in S. Finland gives a firm date by its find-context and the decoration of its perfectly-preserved silver plated hilt of at least a century earlier; and since the decoration of its blade with symbols of the same kind as all seven others, it seems that they, too, must be dated back at least to before 1100.

Publications: Wegeli; Eberle, M. *Ein Schwert mit Trans-chierte Klinge von Lummada auf Osel*, Riga, 1914. Ferguson, G. *Signs and Symbols in Christian Art*, New York, 1961; Ypey, *Offa*, 218, pl.3.3, 219-220.

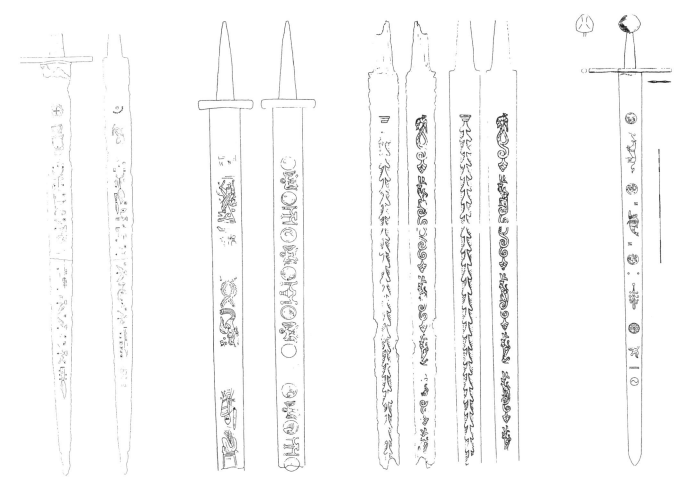

Xa. 13

Type: Xa (a borderline case: it could be an XI)
Find-place: In the River Aa, near St. Omer
Collection: Ex. Victor Gay. Now Berlin, Museum fur Deut-
sche Geschichte
Blade-length: 37¾" (96 cms)
Pommel-type: D
Cross-style: 1a
Date: c.1100
Condition: Perfect, under the patina. A nice silver-inlaid
inscription + NREDAREDX+ on one side and
+ N R A D N R A D N R A D N R A D N R A D R+ on the
other. clearly matched by a similarly written one on a sword
from a grave at Kangasala in S.Finland. A very similar hilt,
with only a fragment of a blade attached to it is also shown
here. This, in the Nationalmuseet in Copenhagen, is generally
dated c.1250+, but the blade is a pattern-welded one which is
unlikely to be later than c.900, and may well be two or more
centuries earlier – an excellent example of a good ancient
blade being re-mounted and used generations after it was
forged.

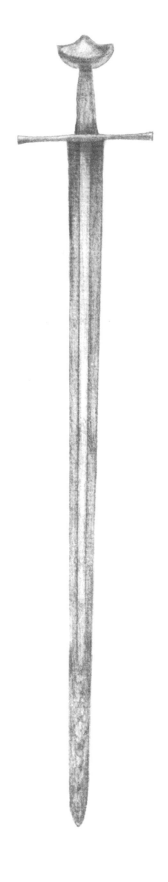

Xa.14

Type: Xa
Find-place: Yverdon, Switzerland
Collection: Schweizerisches Landesmuseum (LM 10116)
Blade length: 31½" (80 cms)
Pommel-type: A
Cross-style: 1
Date: c.1000+
Condition: Good. There is a lot of fairly deep corrosion all over, but the important silver-inlaid series of pictograms is perfectly preserved on one side, though much damaged on the other. These inlays are illustrated here.
Publication: Wegeli, fig. 12.
Ypey, *Antiek*, fig.6, p.8

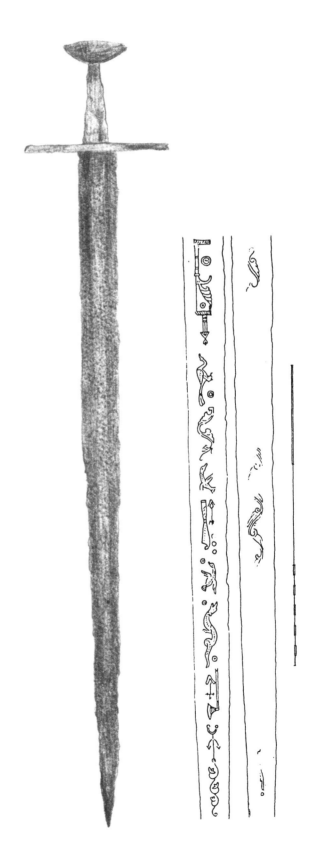

Xa. 15

Type: Xa
Find-place: The Neuenburg Lake, Switzerland
Collection: Schweizerisches Landesmuseum (In 7002)
Blade-length: 31" (80 cms)
Pommel-type: A
Cross-style: 1
Date: c.1000+
Condition: Good. There is a certain amount of deep overall pitting on the hilt, and patches of deep corrosion here and there upon the otherwise quite smooth surfaces of the blade. There are symbolic pictograms inlaid in silver on each side of the blade, illustrated herewith. These are similar to, and from the same atelier as, the sword from Finland shown here below at Xa.16, and the sword in Zurich from Yverdon, shown here above at Xa.14.
Publication: Wegeli, fig.13

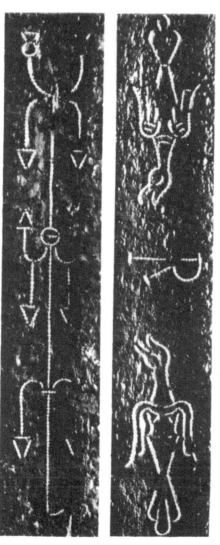

Xa. 16

Type: Xa
Find-place: Kokemaki, S. Finland
Collection: Helsinki University
Blade-length: 34½" (87.6 cms)
Pommel-type: (not classified) late Viking style
Cross-style: (not classified) late Viking style
Date: c.950-1000
Condition: Fairly good. There is a lot of corrosion on the blade surfaces, especially near the hilt, but the silver-inlaid marks and symbols have survived well. The silver-plated hilt is in particularly good condition, showing the engraved decoration in the 'Ringerike' style, dating it clearly to c.950-1000.

The blade is particularly long for a Viking sword, and near to the tip are other small silver-inlaid symbols, a crozier on one side and a Hand of God figure on the other. I know of only two other swords (at present) with similar marks near the point, one in the Moyses Hall Museum at Bury St. Edmunds in Suffolk, and the other once in the Harold Peterson Collection (see No. X.10 in this series).

Publication: Leppaaho, pl.36.

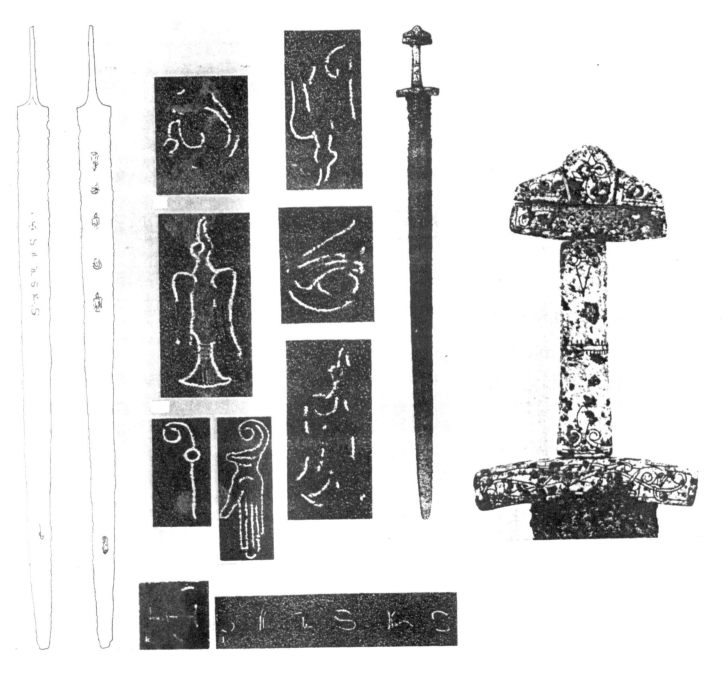

51

Xa. 17

Type: Xa
Find-place: Unknown
Collection: Private
Blade-length: 34½" (87.6 cms)
Pommel-type: J
Cross-style: 9
Date: Blade c.1100, hilt, c.1450
Condition: Excellent. The long blade is hardly corroded at all, its surface being covered only with patches of shallow staining. There are a few marks of usage on the edges, but not significant. The hilt is of latten, once gilded (a tiny trace only seems to survive on one side of the elegantly modelled rivet-block. The central boss of the pommel is longitudinally ridged. The original grip of ?lime-wood survives, with a narrow Turk's head of brass wire (contemporary with the hilt) below the pommel. In the narrow fuller in the blade, inlaid in iron, are the names + IESUS + on one side and MARIA on the other. Following the second letter A in this name is an inlaid symbol (also in iron) which though extremely hard to see may perhaps be a rather naturalistic representation of the lily-flower always associated with Our Lady. At some time, an over-enthusiastic owner of the sword tried to enhance, or to make more visible, the letters of these inscriptions and began to engrave round their outlines. He ruined the I, E and S of the IESUS inlays, but fortunately gave up, and left the remainder alone. Had he done all ten letters, it would not have been possible to see that they were in fact inlaid in iron. This sword was examined in the Royal Armouries on 27 April, 1989, when the metal of the hilt was definitely proved to be 15th century latten.

This fine sword provides an absolutely classic example of an old blade being still in use, or re-used, three centuries after its making and mounted in a handsome, new, fashionable hilt. The sword is also important by reason of the (so far as I know at present) uniquely used holy names, inlaid in iron. There are INNOMINEDOMINI inscriptions, in iron, in plenty; there is one Viking blade inlaid on each side with the word AMEN, but this is in silver.

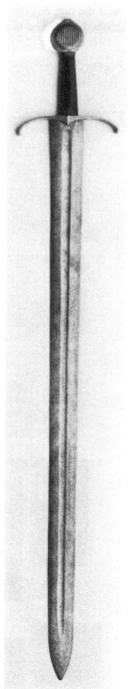

Type XI-XIa

This type is distinguished by having a slender blade, generally long in proportion to the hilt, with a very narrow fuller running to within a few inches of the point. In classic examples there is very little taper to the edges, though in well-preserved examples the point is quite acute. However, since so many river-found and earth-found swords have much heavy corrosion at the point, in such survivors the point appears to be spatulate and rounded. In my *Sword in the Age of Chivalry* I mistakenly added a Type XIb, thinking erroneously that such corroded blades constituted a sub-type. There is, however, a positive sub-type in XIa, where the blade is broad, but the fuller remains very narrow. Examples of these are rare, one of the best being shown here at XIa.1.

As with all of the other types, the form of pommel and style of cross varies a good deal within the limits of custom and availability during the period of usage – which in the case of Type XI seems to be between c.1100-1175. This statement, however, needs to be accepted only with caution. We don't know what hitherto unknown survivor may rise from earth or river or tomb with a reliable dating context to confound my typology. Or from somebody's collection, for that matter. So far as I know at present, XI's have inscriptions either in iron (as in XI.1 here) or in silver or latten or gold where the 'handwriting' matches Leppaaho's 11th and early 12th century Viking blades.

The beautiful Xa, in the Wallace Collection (No. Xa.1 in this series, above) is a perfect example where, having only the form of the sword (not its perfect preservation) to go by, it cannot be pin-pointed at all to any certain period between 1050 and 1350. All that can be said is that it is a classic Xa, whose hilt is matched exactly by (a) some of Leppaaho's Viking hilts and (b) hilts shown in monumental art between c.1250 and 1350. So it may be with Type XI, though at present (October 1990) I would not date any XI beyond c.1125.

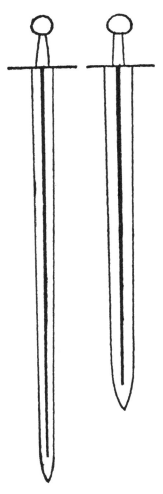

XI. 1-2

1. Type: XI
   Find-place: Unknown
   Collection: Private. Formerly R.T. Gwynn, Morgan Williams
   Blade-length: 34" (86.4 cms)
   Pommel-type: B
   Cross-style: 1. Long and thin
   Date: 1050-1125
   Condition: Excavated (near-perfect, fine blue-black patina. Iron inlaid inscription NISOMEFECIT on one side and a garbled version, not very clear, of INNOMINEDOMINI on the other.

2. Type: XI (Borderline Xa, but put in here to compare with 1)
   Find-place: Tyrvaa, Finland
   Collection: Helsinki University
   Blade-length: 32½" (82.5 cms)
   Pommel-type: B
   Date: c.1100
   Condition: Excavated , near perfect
   Publications: XI.1 An article in *The Ancestor* in 1903; Victoria and Albert Museum, *The Art of the Armourer*, 1953; XI.2 Leppaaho, pl.5.

This beautiful sword has been published and illustrated several times; the first I know of was in a very select and aristocratic magazine, *The Ancestor*, in 1903. Laking featured it in his *Record of European Armour and Arms. . .* in 1921, and it appeared again in the catalogue of the sale at Christies in 1921 of the Morgan Williams collection from St Donat's Castle. It was exhibited in the Victoria and Albert Museum in the 'Art of the Armourer' exhibition; however, for some reason in none of these publications was any mention made of the nature of the inscription.
There are two other swords inscribed NISOMEFECIT, one in the Museum at Stade, the other in Helsinki – illustrated in Leppaaho, Fig. 5.2.
This is a perfect example of the type, with its long blade and narrow fuller.

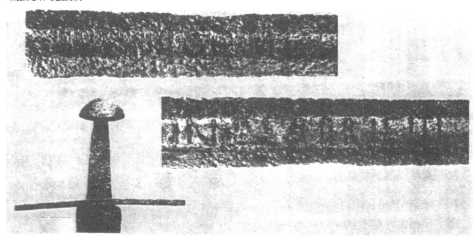

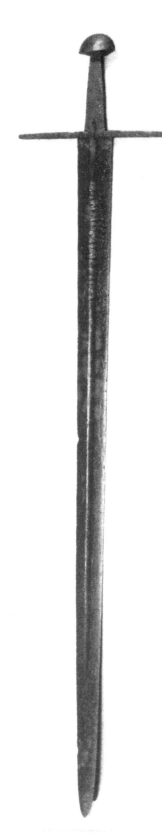

XI. 3

Type: XI
Find-place: Unknown, but in Denmark
Collection: Nationalmuseet, Copenhagen
Blade-length: 37" (94 cms)
Pommel-type: A
Cross-style: 1
Date: c.1100-50. Perhaps c.1075?
Condition: Excavated. Good. Some areas of deep pitting, surface gone near to the point; edges corroded away there, too. Hilt in excellent condition, very little pitting or eruptions.
Publication: Oakeshott, *SAC*

There are well-written silver-inlaid inscriptions on this blade (iii) which can be compared with one of Leppaaho's blades; the style of the lettering is very similar, though because the content of the inscriptions are quite different, the same letters do not occur in both. The exception is a number of S's; in both swords these are the sort of 'Lazy S' lying down which seems to occur frequently in blade-inscriptions of this period, e.g. a very fine Type XI sword found fairly recently in the R. Scheldt, now in a private collection, where the silver-inlaid letters, fairly widely spread, and only five of them. I shall refer to this style of inscription later, under Type XVI) are S, D, S, I, S., the S's lying back at an angle of 45 degrees to the edges of the narrow fuller. Unfortunately at the time of writing this I do not know what is on the reverse of this blade.

(i), shows the whole sword; (ii) the hilt – note the excellent condition of it; (iii) shows the letters of the inscriptions, enlarged.
The inscriptions read: Obverse: S S P E T R N U S
Reverse: + B E N E D I C A T N T N S E T M A T +
Note: the second 'letter' on the obverse is a mark of abbreviation for S (ANCTU)S.

iii

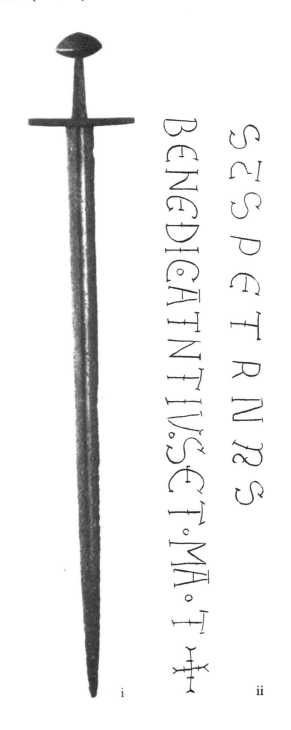

i

ii

XI. 4

Type: XI
Find-place: ?
Collection: Vienna, Weltliches Schatzkammer
Blade-length: 37½" (95.3 cms)
Pommel-type: B
Cross-style: 1, long and slender
Date: c.1050-1120
Condition: A state of perfect preservation. Indoor conditions, probably since it was first made in the 11th century. The iron hilt is gold-plated, and the gold plate is engraved (see notes). The grip is probably 'modern' – i.e. it is not medieval, though there is no earthly reason why it should not be, since the preservation of the sword is so perfect. However, being the Coronation Sword of the Holy Roman Empire, it is possible (why?) that, like the Charlemagne sword in the Louvre in Paris (which was 'improved' for Napoleon's Coronation), it has been done up at some time. The gilding was perhaps added to the iron hilt later than the date of the sword's making.
The scabbard is of olive-wood, made in the 11th century to be an exact fit for the blade, overlaid with panels of gold decorated with repoussé figures of kings. These are of a definitively 11th century style, but between each pair of panels is a band of enamel, done in tiny squares of red, white and blue set in a diaper pattern. These are as distinctively of the 13th century as the figures are stylistically of the 11th.
Publications: Laking, vol.1; Oakeshott, *SAC*, Plate 5,B and pp.32-3; Seitz, p.140, 141. Blair, Claude *EAA* 1962, No.18

This sword, though in form and balance it is a plain fighting sword, was none-the-less probably never used for anything but the function it performed until the dissolution of the Austro-Hungarian Empire in 1918, as a ceremonial sword used in the coronations of Emperors. It has always been known as The Sword of St. Maurice, not to be confused with another 11th century sword of the same spurious provenance in Turin. The figures in repoussé on the gold panels of the scabbard are placed so that they are right way up if the sword is held point upwards, an indication that as early as the time of the scabbard's making – second half of the 11th century, which by inference is that of the making of the sword itself – it had only a ceremonial function.
The gold plating upon cross and pommel is engraved; arms upon the pommel and religious invocations on the cross. On one side of the pommel are the Arms of the Empire, on the other the personal arms of Otto IV (1198-1218), a demi-eagle impaling three leopards. On the cross are the words in Gothic miniscules:
'CHRISTUS VINCIT, CHRISTUS REINAT. CHRISTUS INPERAT.' (sic)
These words were used as the Antiphon to the Coronation anthem 'Laudes Regine' as well as a war-cry used in the Third Crusade. Because of these things, it has been inferred that the sword dates from Otto IV's time early in the 13th century. This was before the unmistakeable style of the figures on the

scabbard was clearly identified as being of the earlier date. Because the panels are a perfect (and unaltered) fit for the olive-wood slats of the scabbard, and the slats are a perfect fit for the blade, it has to be inferred that the blade is as early as the scabbard which (like all medieval scabbards) was shaped and formed round the blade, using it as a mandril. Because the shape and proportions of the hilt are so closely akin to several other surviving swords clearly dateable to the 11th century (e.g. the one in the preceding note, XI.3 in Copenhagen) it has to be assumed that the hilt is of the same date as the blade and the scabbard. It is possible that the gold plating was put on rather later; it is certain that the engraved decoration was put on for the benefit of Otto IV, perhaps when it was to be used at his coronation in 1198. There is (and was) nothing easier, and nothing more often done, than to add the embellishment of arms, badges or inscriptions to existing hilts, just as is often done very skilfully by the 20th century faker.

A Note on the CICELIN Swords

The technique of iron inlay is too crude and uncertain to be able to say that 'handwriting' can be identified; there are obvious similarities in the inscriptions in the blades from this workshop, but these are more because of the nature of the technique than any individual character. The question, anyway, is irrelevant since all of them bear the same name, followed lest there be any doubt about the matter, by the words ME FECIT. A few swords bearing this legend have been identified; doubtless there are others covered in black patination whose inscriptions are still invisible; and very probably there are others still resting in earth or river-bed. The few which had been identified at the beginning of this century have been published in the *Zeitschrift für Historische Waffen-und Kostümkunde*, VII, part 8, and in Hoffmeyer, plate XII, h and i, and on p.21. One of these, which used to be in Hamburg, has a plain disc pommel, but the others – two in Berlin (formerly) and one in Helsinki (see XI.6 in this series) have 'profiled' or 'wheel' pommels of a form which was once believed – still is, by some – to have come into being only in the mid 13th century, instead of the mid-11th. The one in Hamburg and one of those in Berlin have straight, quite long crosses of Style 3, but the second Berlin one has a 'bow-tie' cross in Style 5 – the earliest example I know of, so far. The Shaftesbury one, as you can see by the illustration, has a decorated style 4, cross (also a very early example) and the Helsinki one another unusually early example of a style associated more with the 14th-15th century than the 11th-12th (Style 7).

+GICELINME!ECII
+HHOR DOIHHI+
+GICELIN ME FECIT
+INNOMINE DOMINI+

+GICELINHEFECIT+
+NNOMINIDOMINI+

XI. 5-6

5. Type: XI
Find-place: Unknown. (Found by a modern collector, in a bookshop in Shaftesbury in Dorset)
Collection: Private
Blade-length: 32" (81.2 cms)
Pommel-type: B
Cross-style: 4
Date: c.1100? Could be 1050, or 1175
Condition: Excavated, obviously a river find by the beautiful blue-black patina which is hardly pitted at all. There are traces of gold plating on the pommel but not on the cross. Iron inlaid inscriptions on both sides of the blade. The grip modern.
Publication: Oakeshott, *AOW* and *SAC*, pl.8b, pl.3a

6. Type XI
Find-place: Rovaniemi, Marikovaara, Finland
Collection: Helsinki University
Blade-length: 32" (83.1 cms)
Pommel-type: I
Cross-style: 7 – a very early example – Dateable – of this style
Date: c.1050-1100
Condition: Very good. Hardly any corrosion on the pommel and cross, and only a little on the blade.

This is an absolutely magnificent sword, in perfect condition. It was bought by a collector – one of the very well-known collectors of the 1930s to the 1960s who had better not be named, among the bundle of 19th century swords in an umbrella stand in a bookshop in Shaftesbury, in Dorset. It was covered all over with aluminium paint, and looked like a wooden dummy; but the Eye of the Collector was not de-ceived. When the paint had been taken off, the sword was brought to me to see if there was an inscription. I could see that there was, an iron-inlaid one. The owner left it in my care for several months, during which time I gently rubbed away at the blade – not with abrasives, but cloth, newspaper (which cleans well, apart from leaving ink) and my thumb. It become clear that on one side were the words INNOMINEDOMINI and on the other GICELINMEFECIT. This was subsequently proved by having an x-ray photograph taken in the Research Laboratory of what was then (in the 1950s) the Ministry of Works. There were unmistakeable marks of wear and usage on the edges – a few nicks, and unevenness made by honing, and the point was quite thinned and rounded by wear and sharpening. There were enough small traces of gold plating on the iron of the pommel to show that it had indeed been plated; but there was none on the cross. This is not unusual, for in nearly every case of swords of the Middle Ages shown in art, where colour has survived, pommels are shown gilded or coloured, but very, very seldom crosses which are shown to be grey or silver. Curiously, where pommels were silvered, crosses were also. This suggests a reasonable assumption that crosses, like grips and scabbards, quite often broke, or were cut up by opposing swords, or were replaced because an owner wanted a change, and so did not match an original pommel.

The cross of this sword terminates in little beasts' heads. These are made in a masterly way, with the minimum of carving but the maximum of effect.

One is shown here in close-up below.

I should add that this beautiful sword is light and flexible and is balanced like a fishing-rod.

XI. 7

Type: XI
Find-place: Unknown
Collection: Glasgow Museum Reserve Collection
Blade-length: 32" (81.4 cms)
Pommel-type: I
Cross-style: 2
Date: c.1100
Condition: Excavated. Poor. A great deal of corrosion and
deep pitting on the blade, and the hilt as well. The cross has
one arm nearly taken off by a very deep piece of corrosion.

XI. 8

Type: XI

Find-place: Unknown. Probably in Germany

Collectio: Ex. D'Acre Edwards, then Ewart Oakeshott. Now Glasgow Museum

Blade-length: 36½" (92.7 cms)

Pommel-type: A

Cross-style: 1

Date: c.900-950

Condition: Excavated. Poor. The blade is considerably corroded especially on the edges. However, the sword is of the utmost importance and rarity, for upon the tang are incised runic characters, and in the fuller of the blade on one side is a short lattice pattern inlaid in silver, and on the other an inscription in runic characters. The form of the pommel, and the length and slenderness of the blade, is exactly matched by a drawing in an Anglo-Saxon MS. of c.950-1000. (BL. MS Nero C.IV) (see XII.10 below)

The characters on the tang are three in number, the middle one now illegible, but the leading and trailing ones are O and O. These runes are of a distinctly Anglo-Saxon character, and cannot date later than c.950. The proportions of this sword are almost exactly the same as those of the 'Sword of St. Maurice' in Vienna. (See No. XI.4, in this series).

Publication: Oakeshott, *SAC* Plate 4a and p.32.

61

XI. 9

Type: XI
Find-place: In a ditch near one of the Fornhams, in Suffolk
Collection: Moyses Hall Museum, Bury St. Edmunds, Suffolk
Blade-length: 36" (91.4 cms)
Pommel-type: 1
Cross-style: 2
Date: c.1100
Condition: Not very good. There is a lot of deep pitting, with only a few patches of clean black surface – enough, however, to show the silver-inlaid letters of the blade inscription to show up clearly. Since this photograph was taken about 40 years ago, the blade has got broken into two pieces. The lettering of the inscription (shown here at (iii)) is matched for 'handwriting' by an inscription on a Viking Age blade from Finland (iv), which does seem to date the sword squarely to the early 12th century if not the late 11th. There was a battle fought somewhere (nobody now knows where within an area of perhaps 20 – 30 square miles) near Fornham in 1171. It has always been assumed that this sword is a survivor of that battle, but since there are two villages called Fornham next to each other, and the site of the find-place of the sword (it was found over a century ago) is as unknown as the precise site of that battle, one can't take it as a certainty that here is 'The Fornham Sword' with a *terminus post quem* of 1171. There is, however, no reason why it should not have still been in use about 70 years after it was made; and it may be a relic of the battle; but one should not say that it is so. This sword also has a little 'Hand of God' in silver near to the point.
Publication: Laking; Hoffmeyer, II, Plate Xd and p.12, No.6; Davidson, pp.49 and 120.1; Oakeshott, *AOW* Plate 6.d.

i   ii   iii   iv

XIa. 1

Type: XI.a
Find-place: Unknown
Collection: Ex. D'Acre Edward coll. Royal Armouries.
IX.1082
Blade-length: 29" (73.8 cms)
Pommel-type: E
Cross-style: 1
Date: c.1100-25
Condition: Excavated. Quite good. Surfaces of blade good except for the last 10" (25 cms) or so near the point, where it is very heavily corroded. The pommel and cross are well preserved. The grip is modern. There is a tiny inscription in the blade on one side, the letters S O S. It has been suggested that this unlikely-looking combination of letters is in fact the initial letters of the words SANCTA, O SANCTA.
Publication: Dufty, Plate 2c

Type XII

This is one of the most difficult sword-types to identify, because so many swords which might seem (perhaps by the forms of their hilts) to be of the type are in fact Xs, or even XVIs. In isolating the type, I laid down two totally arbitrary criteria: (1) that the blade should have noticeable taper, and an acute point, and the grip should be quite short, never of hand-and-a-half length, and (2) that the fuller should not extend beyond two-thirds of the length of the blade. This is all very well where these features are obvious; identification is easy enough as the illustrations below will show, but there are so many examples where the fuller is nearly (or quite) three-quarter length, making it nearly an X, or where there is none, as in No. XII.16 below, or where the hilt is of a clearly early form, as in XII.2 below, or where the taper is very slight and the point rounded, or when the grip is longer than the 'standard' 4" to 4½" single-hand length. So many swords have one or other, or even all, of these difficult characteristics that one has difficulty in pinning them down to any of the types.

I mentioned the 'early form' of the hilt of XII.2. I must reiterate my firm belief that you cannot *date* a sword by its *type*, for most of the types – not all, as you will see – can span the whole of the medieval period. Nor can you use the forms of cross and pommel to date a sword – hardly ever. There are a few, mostly in use in the 15th century, which are dateable to a few decades, and can be identified with a region; but most of the pommel-types and cross-styles span the whole period; besides, within those types and styles there must be an infinity of variation – personal, regional and in some cases plain careless on the part of the cutler who made them. A sword's cross is a most difficult object to make by forging, and distortion is difficult to avoid.

XII.1

Type: XII
Find-place: Unknown, but I believe in England
Collection: Private (as far as I know)
Blade-length: 32" (81.2 cms)
Pommel-type: H
Cross-style: 1
Condition: Excellent. Covered in a fine purple-brown patina, a few pits near the point and one or two nicks in the edges. I saw this sword when it came up for sale at Christie's in the 1970s, I believe in 1972. It is an absolutely classic, or standard Type XII sword, beautifully proportioned and very finely balanced, not very heavy. Its weight (I could of course only estimate this, but I think pretty accurately) is around 2 lbs. I could see no marks, but there may have been something under the patina. I understood from Christie's that it was a very recent river-find. The bronze pommel retains much of its gilding. The cross is of plain iron.
Publication: Christie's sale catalogue.

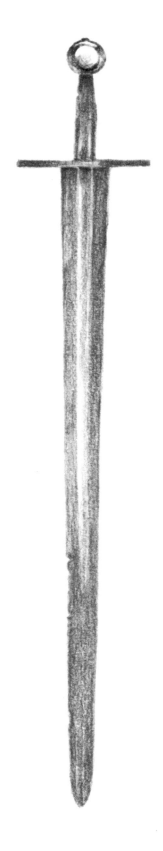

XII. 2-3

2. Type: XII
   Find-place: Unknown
   Collection: Schweizerisches National Museum, Zurich, LM15672
   Blade-length: 30" (76.1 cms)
   Pommel-type: B.1
   Cross-style: Unclassified, Viking. (Petersen's Type X)
   Date: c.950-1000
   Condition: Excavated, but good except for a very pitted surface.

3. Type: X or XII ??
   Find-place: Tryvanto, Leppaa, Hinnonmaki, Finland
   Collection: Helsinki University
   Blade-length: Blade ritually broken, probably about 30" (76 cms)
   Pommel-type: B.1
   Cross-style: Unclassified, Viking (Petersen's Type X)
   Date: c.950-1000
   Condition: Excavated, but very good, the iron inlays being complete and the surface good.
   Publication: Schneider; Oakeshott, *SAC*; Leppaaho.

This, by the shape of its blade, is definitely a Type XII; but by the same token, its hilt is of as definite a Viking form – Petersen's Type X. Since there is no value in using the type as a dating criterion, we must assume that here is a late Viking sword, and there are two others, extremely similar, among Dr. Leppaaho's finds all dating betwenn c.950-1100. There is another one in the museum in Zurich, too, with an identical hilt, though there is only a ragged fragment of the blade below the cross surviving. This was found in the Rhine at Stein-Sackingen, Aargau.

This well preserved Viking-Age sword (XII.2 here) is proof that blades of Type XII's distinctive form can be dated to the 10th century and not confined as they have been hitherto to the later 13th and the 14th.

The group of Type XII swords which follows demonstrates this early usage of the short-fullered blade even better.

3

2

XII. 4

Type: XII

Find-Place: Palermo Cathedral, to Saragossa Cathedral in 1399

Collection: Paris, Musée de l'Armée. Ex Pauilhac, ex Estruch collections.

Blade-Length: I can find no record. At a guess, 30"

Pommel-Type: Indefinable. A cross between a flattened spherical R, and an I

Cross-Style: 1

Date: Probably c.1170

Condition: Interesting. See notes.

Publication: J. de Blaneas. *Coronaciones de los Serenissimas Reyes de Aragon.* Saragossa, 1641; Zurita, *Annales* X chap. LXIX; Riquer, Martí de, *L'Arnes del Cavaller*, Barcelona 1968.

The sword – or a sword in this one's context – is also mentioned in 'Annales' in 1135, 1154 and 1217.

This is one of those rare swords whose history can be traced back to its origins, or nearly so. Well attested legend has it that it was given by San Olegario to Count Raymon Berengar III of Barcelona, by order of Pope Calixtus III. In a paper read to the Society of Antiquaries on April 7th 1932, Sir James Mann said that the gift was by order of Pope Calixtus II; but since that pope reigned between 1119 and 1123, and Ramon Berengar III was Count of Barcelona in the 1160s, clearly something is wrong. Maybe an uncorrected typing error. It must have been Calixtus III, who was on St Peter's throne in Ramon Berengar III's time. This Count on his death gave his horse and arms to the order of the Knights of St John of Jerusalem, and the sword was deposited in the Treasury of the Cathedral of Palermo. It was taken out two centuries later to be sent to Saragossa for the coronation of Martí I of Aragon, which took place on 13th April 1399. By that time a myth had grown around it that it was the sword of Constantine. Sir James cast doubt upon the validity of its history before 1399 on the sole grounds that 'the form of the hilt is of the 13th rather than the 12th century'. This is not so, though in 1932 the evidence was not available to prove that its form is entirely compatible with a 12th century date. The photographs (v) and (vi) show the hilts of two swords from those Viking graves cleared in 1950 by Dr Jorma Leppaaho. In (v), you can see a sword of c.1100 with precisely the same form of cross as this one, while (vi), shows an identical pommel, and a hilt of the same proportions. Here then is proof – proof, dear critic, not just evidence – that this form of hilt was actually in use in the late 11th century, let alone the 12th. I must add, of course, that similar hilts were popular in the 15th century, too, all of which goes to show yet again how risky it is to attempt to date a medieval sword by its form alone, without the supporting evidence of a find-context, or identifiable (or at least dateable) marks.

The sword was given new scabbard-mounts, presumably for that coronation, the upper locket (the only surviving mount) showing a figure of St Martin of Tours. Upon this rather flimsy evidence the sword has become known, since the 15th century, as the sword of St Martin. (i)

It was kept in the treasury of the Cathedral of Saragossa until 1888 when somehow it got into the vast arms collection of Josef Estruch, which in turn was acquired in 1899 by M. Georges Pauilhac. That superb collection passed to the Musée de l'Armée in Paris in the 1950s, where this sword now rests. The photographs of the sword reproduced here are instructive. (iv) shows it as it is now in the Musée de l'Armée, with its scabbard-locket; (iii) taken in 1896 when it was still in the Estruch collection, shows what might almost be a different sword. Most of the scabbard is present (it is here viewed from the back, so only the plain back of the St Martin locket of 1399 shows), the cross is bent, but the blade is clean and bright and except for about 2cms of the point being broken away, seems to be in very good condition. What a contrast to the 1960s photograph! In those seventy-odd years, the blade has deteriorated badly. It is heavily pitted all over, even more of the point is quite corroded away, and in the fuller half-way down there is a slit where it has worn right through. The hilt has been cared for – the cross straightened and the surviving cord and leather covering of the grip tidied up and preserved. So why has the blade become so bad? Not, I am sure, for lack of care. If, during its time in Saragossa and the Estruch and Pauilhac collections it had been kept in dry conditions in the scabbard, one of two things would have happened. One is that because of some amount of damp air having got in, the blade would have become heavily rusted, even immoveably bonded by corrosion to the fabric of the scabbard; or, as the 1896 photograph suggests, it would have remained bright. This, of course, it obviously did, but maybe when it was taken permanently out of the protection afforded by the scabbard latent oxidation got to work on it and produced the state it is in now – or as we hope it is. This photograph is now over two decades old, and a lot may happen to a sword in a museum in that time – witness the dreadful destruction of Can Grande della Scala's sword. (XII.5 below)

Two things are plainly shown. One, that a medieval blade, sheathed in dry conditions survives the centuries and two, that though it cannot possibly be the Sword of Constantine, or of Martin of Tours, it very probably is the sword of Ramon Berengar III, Count of Barcelona.

It has been published many times, mostly in Spain; but in England there has at least been one very brief (and not very accurate) publication in James Mann's paper in *Archaeologia*, LXXXIII, 1932, 'Some Notes on the Armour Worn in Spain from the 11th to the 15th Centuries'. There is much more (rather inconclusive too, with no mention of its condition or probable origin), in *L'Arnes del Cavaller* by Martí de Riquer, 1968, Barcelona.

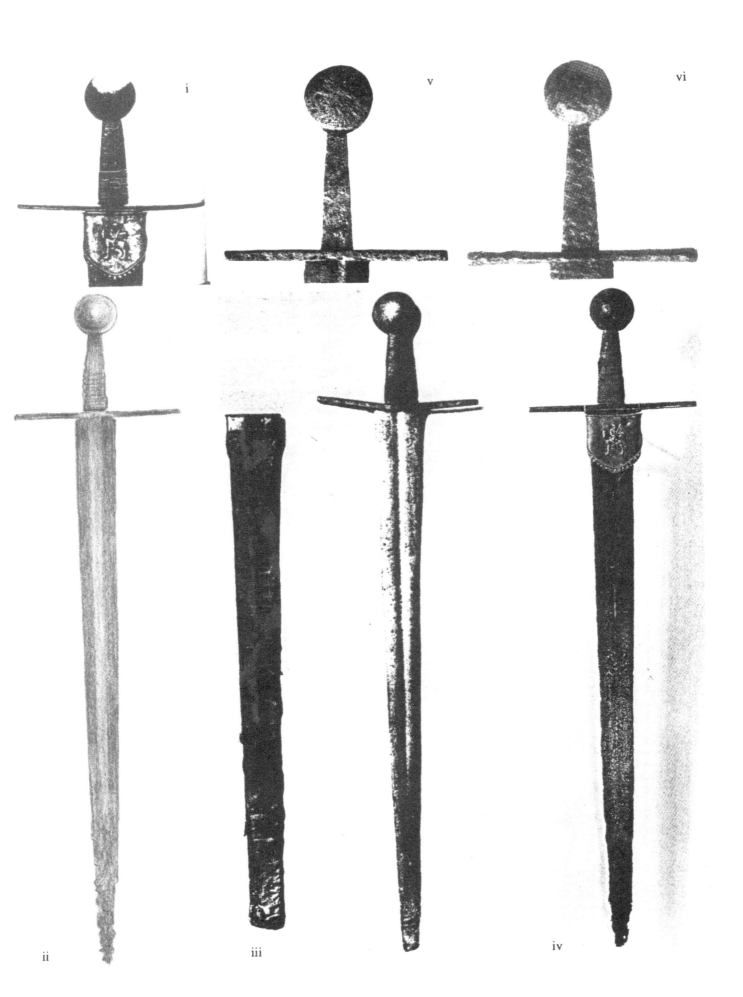

i

v

vi

ii

iii

iv

XII. 5

Type: ?XII
Find-Place: Convent of Las Huelgas, Burgos
Collection: "   "
Blade-length: Unknown. Approximately 32½" (82.5 cms)
Pommel-Type: 1
Cross-Style: 2
Date: Before 1270
Condition: The sword was found in the coffin of the Infante Fernando de la Cerda, son of King Alfonso el Sabio of Castile, upon his mummified body when his tomb was opened in 1943. The condition of the sword is uncertain, for the scabbarded blade may be severely corroded, or may be in fine condition. As far as I know, it has never been taken out of the scabbard. Perhaps it is rusted immoveably in? I have been told that it has been seen out of the scabbard, in fine condition, but I can't be certain. The pommel of bronze is perfectly preserved, with a blue-green patina, but the iron cross, which since the Infante's burial in 1270 lay under the prince's dead hand, is greatly corroded. However the grip with its bindings of yellow silk, with a criss-cross overbinding of red silk cord, with the remains of a circular tassel of red silk at the top – the lower one rotted under the hand – is in almost perfect condition, as is the scabbard of wood covered with leather, with the belt-fittings of buckskin. The belt itself, the long belt to the right of the (pictured) scabbard and the short tab to the left, for some reason were cut off at the time (?) of burial. (Compare the drawing of the belt and scabbard of Dietrich von Brehna, one of the figures of benefactors from the West Choir of Naumburg Cathedral). c.1260 at ii.
Publication: Oakeshott, *AOW*; Oakeshott, *SAC*; Gomez-Moreno, Manuel. *El Panteon Real de las Huelgas de Burgos*, 1946.

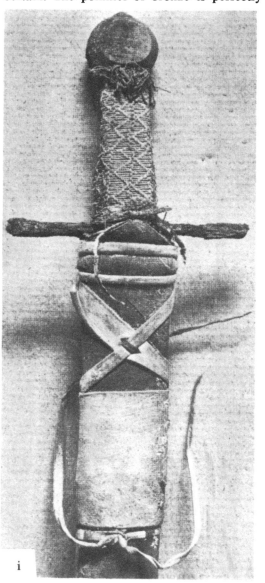

i

ii

XII. 6

Type: XII
Find-Place: The tomb of Can Grande della Scala, in Verona
Collection: Verona, Castelvecchio
Blade-Length: 30" approximately (76.1 cms)
Pommel-Type: 1
Cross-Style: 2
Date: Before 1329
Condition: Terrible. The photograph here was taken in 1921. Now, never having been properly cared for, its blade and scabbard have almost entirely rotted away. The mounts of the scabbard – upper and lower locket, chape, and belt-clasps, being of silver have survived, and the hilt with its grips of wood bound with fine silver wire with an overbinding of green silk cord is still much as it was, but as Can Grande's dead hand lay upon it from 1329 until 1921, the silk cord has mostly perished. The pommel and cross look as if they were covered in fabric, but this is some sort of organic growth from the mummified hand. The thickening at the mid-point of the cross is the remains of a fabric chappe or rain-guard. The scabbard is of wood, covered in red velvet.
Publication: Oakeshott *AOW*, pl.17; Blair, C. *EAA* No. 24

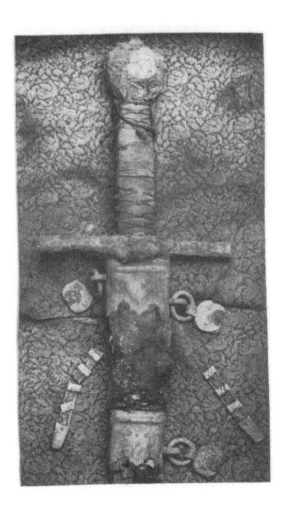

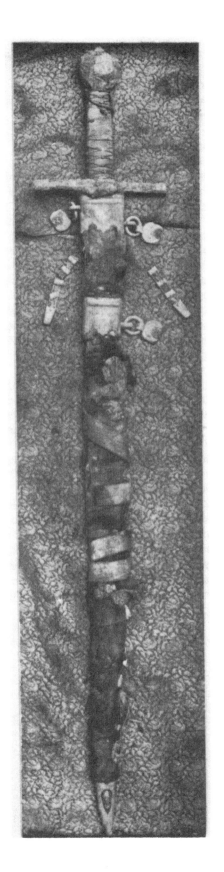

XII. 7

Type: XII
Find-Place: The tomb of King Sancho IV of Castile, Toledo Cathedral + 1298.
Collection: Cathedral Treasury, Toledo
Blade-Length: 36" approximately
Pommel-Type: 1
Cross-Style: 6
Date: Before 1298
Condition: Excellent, though worse now than when these photographs were taken in 1946, for the remaining coloured glass heraldic discs (with the arms of Castile and Leon) glued into the hardwood grip have now fallen out. The cross and pommel of gilded iron, decorated with engraved Mudejar ornament, are in perfect condition. The blade is perished almost to destruction in some parts, but is in mint, mirror-bright condition in others. The decoration on the blade is so perished that it is not possible to elucidate the content, let alone the meaning, of the exquisitely etched lettering.
Publication: Blair, Claude, 'Medieval Swords and Spurs preserved in Toledo Cathedral', *Journal of the Arms and Armour Society*, London, 1959; Oakeshott, *AOW*; Oakeshott, *SAC*. pl.7 & 9

These photographs were taken in 1946, when the tomb was opened. Upon the king's body were also a crown and a splendid pair of gilt-bronze prick spurs, as well as all his clothes (as was the case with his brother, Fernando de la Cerda, who died in 1270). The crown belonged to Sancho's father, Alfonso el Sabio, and it is believed that the sword, too, belonged to that monarch, so it may date over 20 years earlier than the time of Sancho's death in 1298.

The scabbard is of wood, covered with rose-coloured leather with a chape of silver. The belt is of green galoon with borders of red silk decorated with a cable pattern. This is secured to the scabbard by being sewn on to bands of black leather, with a single diagonal strip to prevent then from sliding apart. The buckle and strap-end have been cut off before the burial. Why, one wonders. At least the belt (now wound round the scabbard) is left, unlike Fernando's.

(Since this note was written, the armorial discs have been restored to the grip, as is shown in the cover illustration.)

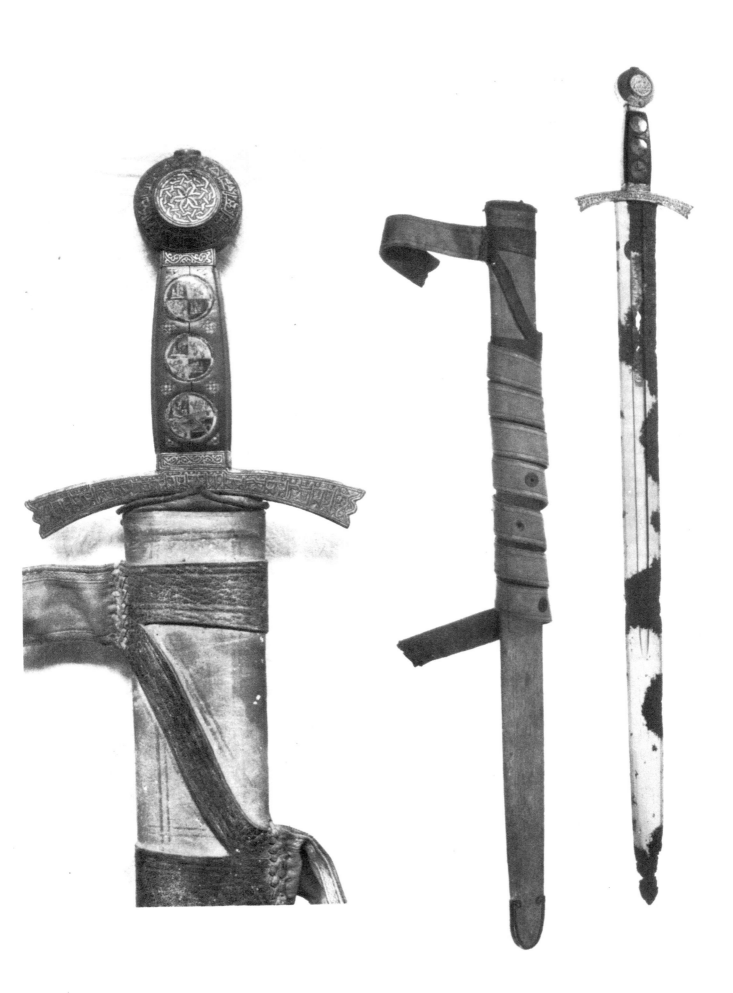

Type: XII
Find-Place: River Great Ouse, Stretham, Nr Ely
Collection: Museum of Archaeology and Ethnology, Downing College, Cambridge
Blade-Length: 36" (91.4 cms)
Pommel-Type: F
Cross-style: 2
Date: c.1150-1250
Condition: River-found, very good. Considerable pitting, especially the last 15" or so towards the point.
Publication: Oakeshott, *SAC*

Considering this sword's find-place, in the Great Ouse about four miles away to the south of Ely, it could be tempting to think of it as a relic of the fighting around Ely in 1070 when the Conqueror finally took the Isle by crossing the Marsh over the causeway from Stuntney, one-and-a-half miles to the east of the city; but as far as is known it is unlikely that any knight of that army would have been four miles off across the swampy fen to lose his sword at the point where it was found. It is much more probably one of the (so far, in 1988) seven swords from this river, in a twelve or so mile stretch between Southery to the north of Ely and Upware to the south which (varying in date from c.950-1400) were thrown in deliberately as 'sacrifices'.

It is very difficult to date this rather important sword; its blade is almost, if not quite, of Xa form, yet I have categorised it as a XII because of it rather long grip. Taking only the form of blade and cross, one would date it, via Leppaaho's finds, at c.1100, yet the form of the pommel is generally (though rarely) to be seen in works of art dating between c.1260 and 1320. Therefore it can only be suggested that it could be dated, because we don't yet know of a reliably dated example of the pommel-form as early as 1100, to a period of usage somewhere between 1250 and 1350.

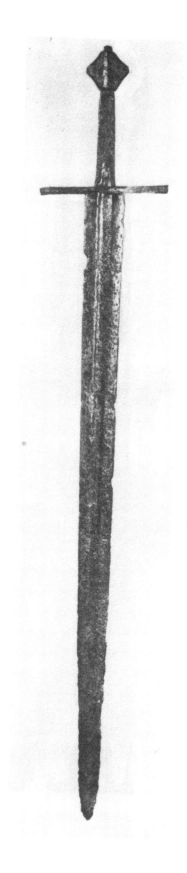

XII. 9

Type: XII
Find-Place: Unknown
Collection: Private. Ex.Collection Harold Peterson
Blade-Length: 34" (86.3 cms)
Pommel-Type: G
Cross-Style: 1
Date: Anywhere between c.1050-1200
Condition: Excavated. Poor. Very considerable pitting
Publication: Oakeshott, *SAC* pl.6a

This was formerly in the collection of Mr Harold S. Peterson of Arlington, Virginia.

The blade has a ricasso, an early example. This shows to some extent in the photograph, but Mr Peterson told me (I have not seen the sword myself) that it is a definite ricasso.

The tang is very weak, almost broken (by now it has probably broken off, or been sensibly repaired) below the pommel. Very many tangs are thin and weak at this point, not only on excavated swords, which would account for the numbers of blades without pommels which survive, sometimes with the cross still in situ.

This is of positive type XII form, but the forms of pommel and cross suggest a fairly early date; by analogy with some of the Leppaaho Viking swords, as early as c.1050, but it could be as late as c.1250. A classic example of the impossibility of making a firm dating based upon form alone.

XII. 10

Type: XII
Find-place: Korsoygaden, Stange in Hedmark, Norway
Collection: Oslo Museum
Blade-length: 34⅞" (88.5 cms)
Pommel-type: Unclassified
Cross-style: Unclassified
Date: c.1100 + or -25.
Condition: Not excavated in the true sense, having been buried in a stone chest. Apart from overall fine surface pitting, very good.

This sword was found in 1888 when a railway-cutting was being driven across farmland at Korsoygaden in the Hedmark district of Norway. It was in a stone 'cist' – not a coffin; it was too small for a body; with it were found its scabbard and the remains of a wooden shield. It is a sword of absolutely outstanding importance, not only to the dating of a pommel-type and an unusual cross-style, but as being a true archaeological proof of what seems to have been a not uncommon practise in the Migration Period and the Viking Age – even into the high Middle Ages – of burying swords, armour or both in stone boxes on chests – called for archaeological convenience 'cists'. This is often mentioned in the Norse literature, but I believe at present this is the only actual example recorded.

It has previously been stated (mostly by me, in my *Archaeology of Weapons* and again in *The Sword in the Age of Chivalry*) that, because of its pommel type (not one of the 'true' Viking forms) that this sword must be of the later 13th century. This is because some very eminent antiquarian scholars of the mid-20th century stated firmly (on no really sound grounds) that this 'developed' form of the lobated Viking pommel must of necessity be of late date, (a) because it was *developed* and (b) because they had never seen one like it in

ii   i

76

a Viking context (having not noticed this particular sword at all) and (c) because there are many effigies and grave-slabs and manuscript pictures, all of a date c.1270-1320, where various forms of lobated pommel *are* shown. Certainly, the old Viking form did persist. I believe this was partly because old and treasured swords continued in use, as they always had in previous ages and indeed as they did even into the 19th century, and partly because probably for purely un-scholarly sentimental reasons, an old (perhaps ancestral) Viking pommel was adapted some three or four centuries after it was actually made.

Why, then, can this sword from Korsoygaden be dated, firmly and uncontrovertably, to the late Viking Age? The fact of its burial in a cist, significant though it is, is not proof, since it is known that such burials were made after the Viking age. However, proof is supplied by the runes inscribed upon the bronze collars which once held the grip at top and bottom – features which in the Norse literature are called respectively *Vettrim* (for the upper one?) and *Valbost* (for the lower?). These runic characters, rather roughly incised in a rather 'home-made' style, have been positively dated as being no later than 1150 and unlikely to be much earlier than 1100. These datings have been made by two extremely eminent Runologists, Eric Moltke and O. Rygh, each independently corroborating the other's finding. On stylistic grounds and on the circumstances of its burial, Jan Petersen dated the sword to c.1050, as also has Dr Ada Bruhn Hoffmeyer.

Therefore this proof of date is sound, and (as you will see) causes a most interesting re-dating of the next sword to be shown in this series, which obviously came from the same workshop. Corroboration of the date can be found, too, in at least two pictorial representations, one dating from c.950-1000 and the other a couple of decades later. The first (iii), a drawing from an Anglo-Saxon manuscript. (BM MS Cotton Nero C.IV) shows a sword very like a Type XI, such as No. XI.8 above; but its unusually long, arched cross is remarkably similar to both of these actual hilts, this Korsoygaden one and the one over the page. The other artefact is a late Viking Age (c.1100) grave-slab which used to be in the churchyard at Ebberston in Northumberland (iv). Here the *pommel* is of the same form; so indeed, as far as form goes – arched shape, and clubbed ends – except that it is short, is the cross. So, to add to the evidence of the runes which is proof enough in itself, we have sound contemporary pictorial evidence as well.

The runes read: *Asmundr gerosi mik, Asleikr a mik* – Asmund made me; Asleik owns me. *That's* interesting in its own right, too. I only wish we could know the sword's name as well.

There is, most unusually for this period (but *not* for the later Iron Age which preceded it) a stamped maker's mark (or what seems to be one) on one side of the tang just below the pommel, which is hidden unless (as in photograph i) the *Vettrim* has slipped down to show it. This seems to be just a plain hexagonal shape.

It has been published now several times, but I will only give the most accessible publications here:

Hoffmeyer, I, p.33, and for the Ebberston slab, II, plate III; Davidson; p.63, fig.89, p.80

Oakeshott, *AOW*; Oakeshott, *SAC*; herein is false and out-dated information, which must be rejected.

Oakeshott, E. *The Third Park Lane Arms Fair, Catalogue* 1986. A very full discussion of the sword and its congener, reprinted here as Appendix B.

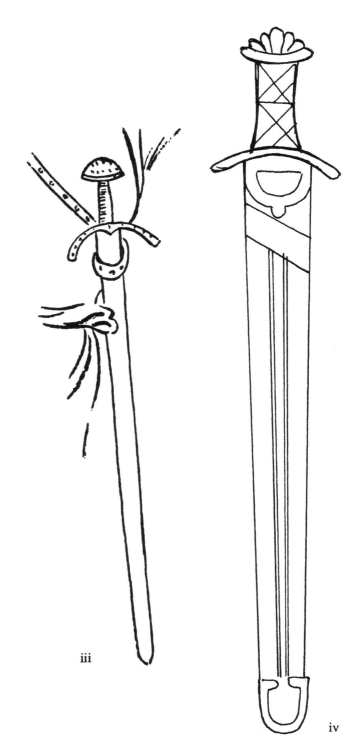

iii

iv

XII. 11-14

The following group of eight swords, four of which are described in full, all with pommels of the same lobed late Viking style, are of extreme importance in the dating of swords and blade-inscriptions. Two of them (one firmly dateable to c.1050) are twins; two others have blade-inscriptions of the same character (though of different content) clearly by the same hand, one of which is identifiable and, within half-a-century or so, is dateable to c.1050 the other four, from different find-places but all within a Viking context (one from a dateable 11th century grave), are by their forms of hilt closely akin, and one, which is one of the finest surviving swords of this period, has long and complete silver-inlaid inscriptions on its blade. This sword, with four of the others, is always dated by authorities as being of a period c.1300-20. Its clear and unmistakeable relationship (both sword-form and inscription) to the seven others of this group makes this dating absurd. All eight must now be placed firmly within a date-band of c.1000-1120. They may not all be by definition Viking swords, but all are within the Viking period.

The matter of some of these inscriptions is more fully dealt with in Appendix B.

Type XII
Find-place: The River Ouse, near Cawood Castle.
Collection: Private. Once on loan to the Tower Armouries.
Blade-length: 32" (81.2 cms).
Pommel-Type: Unclassified, lobated Viking form not classified by Jan Petersen.
Cross-style: Unclassified
Date: c.1100-50.
Condition: Excavated, but very good except for a lot of corrosion near to point. Inscriptions (iii and iv) inlaid in ? pewter, well-preserved. Hilt in good condition, plentiful trace of ?pewter ? tin – even, perhaps? silver.
Publication: Oakeshott, *AOW*; *SAC*; Blair, C., *EAA*, No.23

This sword was found early in this century in the river Ouse near Cawood Castle, south of York. For many years its owner had it on loan to the Armouries at the Tower of London; then in the late 1950s it came up for sale at Sotheby's. I tried hard to get it, but was outbid by its present owner (who must remain anonymous). It is a weapon of outstanding importance, not only for its condition but for its so very close similarity to its brother sword (No. XII.10 here) from Korsoygaden. It has been so authoritatively dated to the late 13th – early 14th century by many eminent scholars – following whom, I also insisted that it must be of that date – that it may now be very difficult to establish in the minds of arms and armour students that, in fact, it *must* date two full centuries earlier. (See Appendix B below). It is – you must admit – so exactly like the Korsoygaden sword that it can't, in all honesty, be two hundred years later. It is from the same workshop, if not from the same hand.

It may be a good idea to put forward a thought as to what I mean here by 'workshop'. We know, and can know, nothing whatever about the methods or organisation of the 'cutlers' who made hilts in these early times of the 11th and 12th centuries. Were they sort of one-man front-parlour workshops like those of the 'Little Mesters' (as they were called) who made beautiful knives and blades in Sheffield up to the 1950s, or were they well-organised 'ateliers' where a master craftsman employed several journeymen and apprentices? We don't know. What we do know, however, and have to admit, is that whoever made the hilt of the Korsoygaden sword must have made this one, too.

The inscriptions on the blade are interesting, because each side shows a totally different style of lettering – each of these styles, however, being closely matched with other 11th-12th century inscriptions. All this is fully discussed below in Appendix B.

If you compare these two hilts in detail, you will see how close the kinship is. Each pommel is of the same form; the Cawood one has its central lobe a little taller than the Korsoygaden one; each lobe on the Cawood pommel is decorated with an incised line, and it is plated with a dull, grey metal which looks like pewter (as do the inlaid letters of the inscription) but may

be tin or silver affected by chemicals in the mud of the river. The crosses are virtually the same – circular section, clubbed ends, small cusp at mid-point, and one arm bent more strongly than the other. If it wasn't that the cross of the Cawood sword is a little longer than that of the Korsoygaden one, it would be necessary to say that they are identical. As you can see, each of these sword's crosses are the same form and style as those shown in the Ebberston grave-slab and the drawing in BL MS. Cotton Nero C.IV. It is thus no longer possible to attribute a 13th/14th century date to these swords. Their date must be c.1080-1120.

This sword was exhibited in London in *The Age of Chivalry* exhibition at Burlington House in 1987 – labelled with the wrong date, as also in the catalogue of that exhibition.

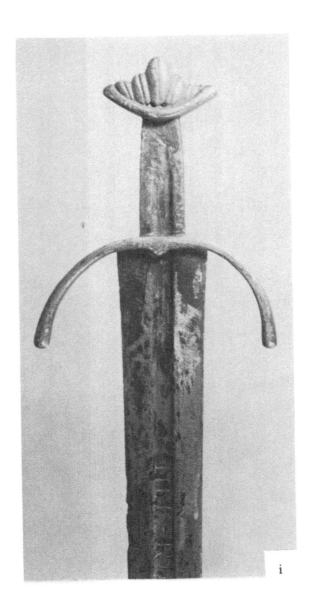

i

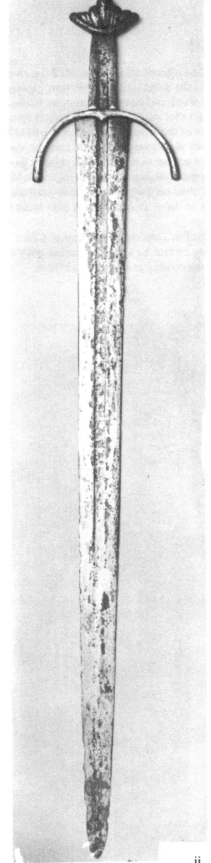

ii

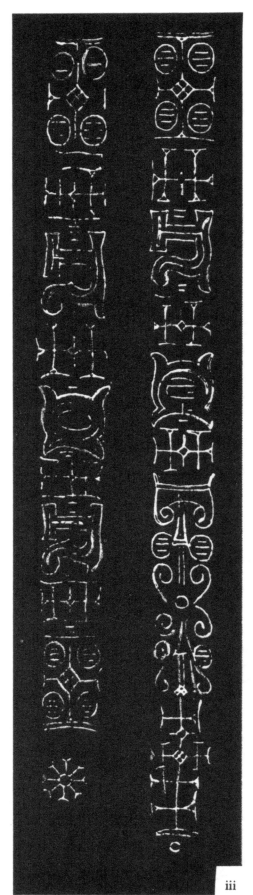

iii

iv

XII. 12

Type: XII
Find-place: Canwick Common, in Norfolk
Collection: British Museum (64738)
Blade-length: 28" (71.1 cms)
Pommel-type: Viking. In the same group as Nos. XII.9 and XII.10
Cross-style: not classified
Date: c.1050-1100

Condition: Not very good. The blade is broken half-way down, the point is corroded away and there is much surface pitting. This extends to the elements of the hilt, though it in no way obscures the shape or quality of the sword, nor has it greatly damaged the long inscriptions inlaid in silver which are of the very greatest importance.

This inscription consists of a repetitive series of letters, A N T A N A N T A N... which extend for 8" (20.3 cms) along the rather narrow fuller. Unusually, they are the right way up when the sword is held in the right hand with the blade pointing across to the left, instead of vice versa, as is the general rule with such inscriptions. However, the most significant thing about this inscription is that in the Kunstgewerbermuseum in Dusseldorf there is a sword whose blade bears a long, literate inscription in Latin on both sides, clearly made by the same hand. The letters run similarly from point to hilt, and their form, and their very small size, is identical.

(This sword in Dusseldorf is featured in full below at XII.13). The hilt of XII.12 is of the same type as those shown here at No. XII.14, from Russia and Finland, and as the swords from Korsoygaden in Norway (No.XII.10) and from Cawood (No.XII.11).

In the Fitzwilliam Museum in Cambridge is a fine Western European hanger, dating c.1600, whose short back-edged blade is engraved with the letters A N T A N, not repeated. There must be some definite significance in this as an acronym.

A similar hilt-form on a sword from a grave in S. Finland, c.1050

XII. 13

Type: XII
Find-place: Unknown, probably in Germany
Collection: Dusseldorf, Kunstgewebermuseum
Blade-length: 30½" (77.4 cms)
Pommel-type: G
Cross-style: 1
Date: After 1028, probably c.1040-60
Condition: Quite good, but a considerable amount of overall pitting, which does not obscure the extremely well-made, literate, lettered latin inscription, inlaid in silver, on each side of the blade.

These inscriptions consist of two rhyming moralising precepts, one on each side: + QUI FALSITATE VIVIT, ANIMAM OCCIDIT. FALSUS IN ORE, CARET HONORE + on one side and + QUI EST HILARIS DATOR, HUNC AMAT SALVATOR. OMNIS AVARUS, NULLI EST CARUS +. 'Who lives in falsehood slays his soul, whose speech is false, his honour' and 'The Saviour loves a cheerful giver, a miser's dear to no-one.' These are taken from a long series of moral precepts written in 1027 or 1028 by Wipo of Burgundy, a royal chaplain, for the edification of the ten year-old son of the Emperor Konrad II (1024-39) who became the Emperor Heinrich III in 1039. Therefore the date of the blade cannot be before 1027, and is unlikely to be much later than, say, 1060. It is clear from the shape of the tiny letters – the 'handwriting' – that this inscription was made by the same calligrapher who made the ANTANANTAN inscription upon the Canwick Common sword in the British Museum (No.XII.12 in this series, above.) That sword, by comparison of its hilt-form with a sword of late Viking style and positive date from one of Dr Leppaaho's graves, and an almost identical one from Russia, can be dated to the mid-eleventh century. The hilt form (disc pommel and long straight cross) is also parallelled exactly by others among those 11th century grave-finds (ii below).

Publication: Hoffmeyer, II, p.13, No.25 and Plate X,e
ZHWK VIII, p.132-3, fig.4; Erben, W. 'Schwertleite und Ritterschlag'; *ZHWK* III, p.294, fig.4, Wegeli, op.cit.

ii

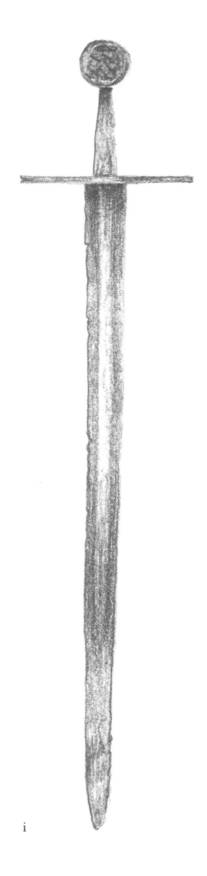

i

XII. 14

Type: XII
Find-place: Unknown
Collection: Museum für Deutsche Geschichte, Berlin
Blade-length: 30½" (77.4 cms)
Pommel-type: Not classified
Cross-style: 2
Date: c.1050-1120

Condition: Very good for an excavated (river-found?) sword. There are areas of considerable pitting, but the beautifully executed calligraphic inscriptions, inlaid in silver, survive remarkably well as is shown here at (ii). The quality of each of these inscriptions, which are of quite different styles, shows beyond doubting that here is the work of a master. Each is a work of art in its own right.

This sword has been dated at c.1250, but there can be little doubt that this is about a century too late. This dating has been based mostly upon the style of the inscription, giving the typically Viking style of pommel as a late survival. However, it is in direct parallel with the pommels of the Korsoygaden and Cawood swords, and the Ebberston grave-slab, and the Canwick Common sword, so I think one can place it into the first half of the 12th century.

There is a sword in Poland, found at Goclowo, (iii) of definite IX century date with an extremely similar hilt, both cross and pommel being like this one, and another with an Ulfberht blade with a similar pommel from Finland (iv).

These two swords are published:

Nadolski, Andrzej, *Studia nad uzbrojeniem polskim w. X, XI and XII, Wieku*, 1954, Lodz, Tab. II,2., p.242.

Nadolski, Andrzej, *Polskabron*, 1984, illus.5.

There is no doubt that these lobated 'Viking' style pommels appear in art up to the late 13th century, but I think this does not necessarily indicate that they were being made new at that time. We know that such things had very long lives in medieval times – as indeed they often still do. I still smoke a pipe which my uncle, who was a war correspondent, smoked in the trenches in Flanders in 1916. There is a fine bronze pommel in the British Museum very similar in shape to those on the Korsoygaden and Trent swords, which of course is labelled as of the 13th century, though it need not necessarily be so.

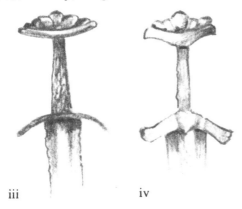

iii   iv

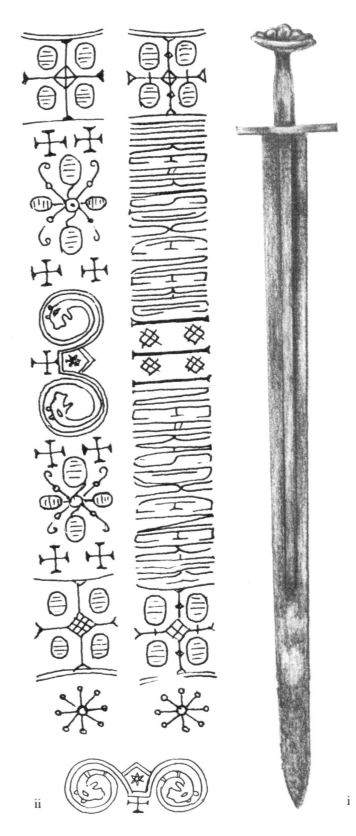

ii   i

XII. 15

Type: XII
Find-place: Convent of San Vicente, nr Logrono, Spain
Collection: Madrid, Instituto del Conde de Valencia de Don Juan
Blade-length: 30" approximately (76.2 cms)
Pommel-type: G
Cross-Style: 6
Date: c.1200-50
Condition: Preserved indoors, with care, therefore extremely good.
Publications: Blair, Claude, *EAA*; Oakeshott, *AOW*; Oakeshott, *SAC*, pl.19c. Hoffmeyer, II, pl.11b & p.14,7.

When it was preserved in the convent of San Vicente, this sword was known as 'The Sword of Santa Casilda'. I don't know why, nor do I know anyone who does. The colours of the enamelled shield of arms in the pommel have faded to pale grey and dark grey, so they can't be identified – all we have is a Barry Wavy of Eight. The legend in Lombardic capitals engraved round the edges of the pommel is in Latin: 'AVE MARIA PLENA GRATIA', while that on the cross is in Spanish 'DIOS ES VINCENTOR EN TOD' and 'O DIOS ES VINCENTOR EN TODO A' (God is the conqueror of all. The final A perhaps stands for the word AMEN. The pommel and cross are recorded as being made of gilded iron and gilded bronze respectively (see Hoffmeyer).

The fact that the inscription on the cross is in Spanish is a very strong piece of evidence that the hilt was made in Spain – or at least for a Spanish customer. The grip of wood is covered with red (now pink) leather, with a criss-cross overbinding of narrow leather strips secured by gilt pins. Laking says that it is a 19th century replacement, but when I examined the sword in 1949 I felt sure that it was original.

It is a supreme example of a Type XII sword – indeed, a supreme specimen of a knightly medieval sword. It is as sweet and well-balanced in the hand as it is beautifully proportioned, too. I shall never forget the feel of it, nor the privilege of having it in my own hand forty years ago.

In other publications (notably Laking and Hoffmeyer) it is dated c.1300, but I think, on the evidence of its shape and style of decoration it must be nearly a century earlier than that.

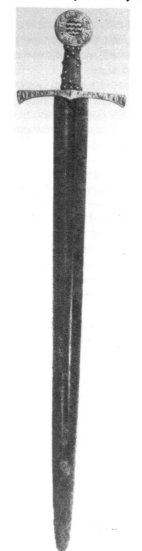

XII. 16

Type: XII
Find-place: A town in N. Italy
Collection: Private, USA
Blade-length: 29½" (75 cms)
Pommel-type: J
Cross-style: 5 – or a variant of it
Date: c.1250-1300
Condition: Good. This was found with two other swords in a house being demolished in an Italian town. The swords were hidden between two walls, so had been preserved in dry conditions. The gilt-bronze pommel and cross have been severely cleaned, but are in very good condition, the iron under the gilding not having corroded at all. The blade and tang are covered in a rather thick brown patina – though to call it a patina when it is more in the nature of the thick brown deposit is perhaps too polite to it. Beneath this crust, however, the blade seems to be perfectly preserved.
Publications: None
It is difficult to categorise this sword with certainty, for there is no clearly defined fuller in the blade, and its grip is rather long for a Type XII, the whole thing being in the proportions of a Type XIII. Compare it, for instance, with No.XIII.1 in this sequence. However, the taper of the blade and the acuteness of its point is more in the nature of a XII, so I have put it under that type. It is a good example of one of those many cases where it seems quite impossible to put certain swords into a typological straight-jacket.

The cross is unusual, too, rather heavy, made (like the pommel) of bronze gilded. It has been bent, and though it shows a strong transverse ridge along the middle of both arms on the 'outside', on the reverse it is quite plain and flat. This feature of half-decorated crosses is very common, particularly in 15th century hilts.

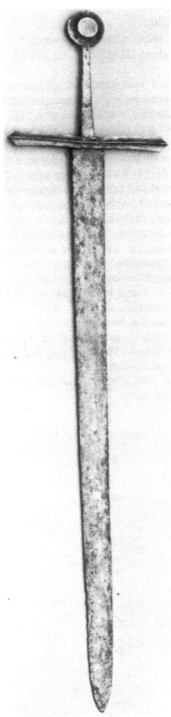

XII. 17

Type: XII
Find-Place: Unknown
Collection: Unknown. Probably private. Formerly Whawell Collection
Blade-Length: 30" approximately (76.2 cms)
Pommel-Type: J
Cross-Style: 6
Date: c.1275-1340
Condition: Excellent. Carefully preserved.
Publication: Laking III, p.207-8, fig.1014A

Since this sword was illustrated and described by Laking doubts have been cast upon its age, the hilt having been, on the highest authority, condemned as a 19th century fake. It came up for sale at Sotheby's in 1951 where I had a chance to examine it myself. The blade is unquestionably genuine, a very fine XII with inlaid-in-silver designs suggesting a date (for the blade) of c.1150-1200 (cf designs in fig.12 of Appendix B). The beautiful hilt of gilt copper (which is the part condemned) looked perfectly good to me, but until a further examination, and, preferably, scientific testing can be made, the doubts cast upon it by Sir James Mann, Russell Robinson, Charles Beard etc. in the 1950s must carry considerable weight. When I examined it, and believed it to be good, I had only then acquired the first 20 years of the 55 years' experience of medieval swords which I have now. I hope my opinion would still be the same.

The hilt is decorated on the cross with a chiselled foliate design at the tips; the grip is bound with fine copper-gilt wire with two broad collars. These collars, and the cross, bear the inscription in Gothic characters:
COLLIGE PER ME REGE SUM (MUM) MEDIO REGE PUNGE PER IMUM

The pommel, decorated with the same conventional foliage as the cross, has inset on one side a shield of arms, checky Or and Azure, the arms of the Counts of Dreux. The enameller, as fairly often happened, has by mistake reversed the order of the metal and the tincture. On the reverse, a relic (a knucklebone) is inset behind a disc of crystal.

This family became extinct in the male line on the death of Count Pierre de Dreux in 1345; therefore this hilt is not likely to have been made after that date. The shape of the escutcheon containing the arms suggests the last quarter of the 13th century. The blade may well be a century earlier, but this does not by any means indicate that blade and hilt must be a 19th century association, since it is by no means improbable that a good 12th century blade should, in the 14th century be mounted in a new hilt. See, for a perfect example, No. XA.17 above.

XII. 18

Type: XII
Find-place: A river or lake in Denmark
Collection: Nationalmuseet, Copenhagen
Blade-length: 32" (81.2cms) approximately
Pommel-type: J
Cross-style: 2
Date: c.1225-75
Condition: River-found. Very good. Little serious pitting. The blade shows a distinct bend, in the plane of the blade, towards the left (in the photograph). This is a fairly common condition in such flat blades caused not by any conditions of burial, but in the forging of the blade.
Publications: None

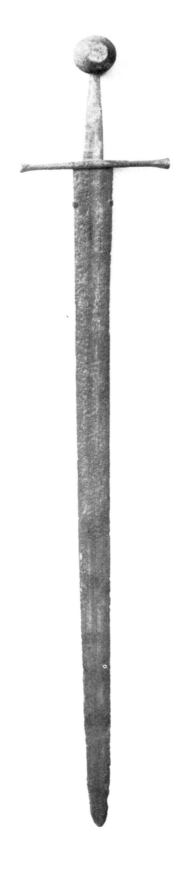

XII.19

Type: XII
Find-place: The Collegiate Church of St George, Cologne
Collection: The Schnütgen Museum, Cologne
Blade-length: 33½" (85.3 cms)
Pommel-type: J.1.
Cross-style: 2
Date: c.1320-50
Condition: Extremely good. Known as 'The Sword of St George' this has been kept since 1929 in the Schnütgen Museum, before which from time immemorial it has been in the Church of St George. The covering of the grip has been restored, in the 18th century, with morocco leather (perhaps by a bookbinder) and unfortunately put back on the wrong way up, with the wider end under the pommel instead of above the cross. Also there has been a little round tang-button, as on a small-sword, added. The scabbard has been similarly restored with the same red morocco leather, but the beautiful 'architectural Gothic' chape and locket, in silver gilt, survive. The central recesses in the pommel are filled with designs in translucent enamels. One would expect more or less conventional heraldry, or a religious device, but on the one side where all the enamel survives is a butterfly, its wings spread across the disc. This is in the unusual colours of white, purple and yellow enamel, all on a dark blue ground, the whole surrounded by a border of little cusped 'architectural' features. The other side has a similar border, but most of the enamel of the device has come away. In the well-marked fuller of the blade is a mark made with a punch – another early example of such a punched mark.

(i) shows only the back of the scabbard, where the chape and locket are simply plain silver-gilt. The two suspension-rings may be compared with those on the scabbard-mounts of the swords of Juan 'el de Tarifa' (1317), Can Grande della Scala (1329) and the Westminster Bridge sword in the Museum of London (c.1325).

Publication: Hans Ulrich Haedeke, 'Das Schwert des Heiligen Georg.' Stuber and Wetler, p.9.

iii

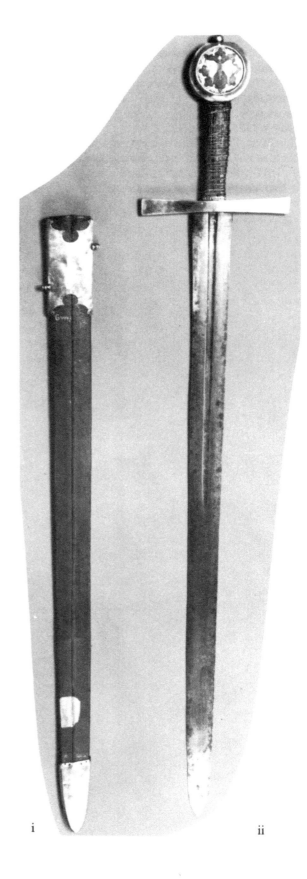

i   ii

Type XIIa

The swords illustrated below I once put into Type XIIIa, but this was a mistake; they have to go into a new sub-type of XIIa, because the blades taper too strongly for a XIIIa style, and are too acutely pointed.

When I worked out my typology in 1958, I did not know of the first of these (XIIa.1), and because I had then come across no others which would be made into a 'Great Sword' subtype of XII, I forced it into Type XIIIa.

Thirty years and many publications later, it may seem strange to admit a careless mistake and to correct it; but it's never too late to improve one's work and I believe absolutely essential to admit, and correct, one's own errors. So here, thirty years on, I present Sub-Type XIIa.

XIIa. 1

Type: XIIa
Find-place: Unknown
Collection: The Burrell Collection, Glasgow
Blade-length: 36" (91.4 cms)
Pommel-type: J
Cross-style: 2
Date: ? c.1300-50
Condition: Excavated. Good. Some scattered deep pitting.

XIIa. 2

Type: XIIa
Find-place: Unknown
Collection: Private
Blade-length: 35" (88.9 cms)
Pommel-type: 1 (recessed)
Cross-style: 1
Date: c.1300-1350
Condition: Almost pristine. It has obviously been preserved
with care in an armoury, for there is no corrosion and only a
little staining; and the grip of wood, bound with cord and
covered with leather, survives intact. There is a little latten-
inlaid dagger mark on each face of the blade a few inches
below the cross. The form and size and 'drawing' of this mark
matches precisely with similar dagger marks on (1) the Great
Sword of Edward III in St. George's Chapel, Windsor and the
very large war-sword (see No.XIIIa.2 below) in the Museum
of London, which was found in the Thames opposite the
Temple in London. These three blades are obviously from the
same workshop. The present owner bought this outstanding
sword at Sotheby's in London in 1940, during the 'Blitz' when
with bombs falling all around sales were held in the basement.
He told me he got it for £1.10.0d – the equivalent of £1.50.
Publication: *Connoisseur Year Book*, 1951

Oakeshott, *SAC*, p.49, not illustrated, and wrongly described
as a Type XVIa!

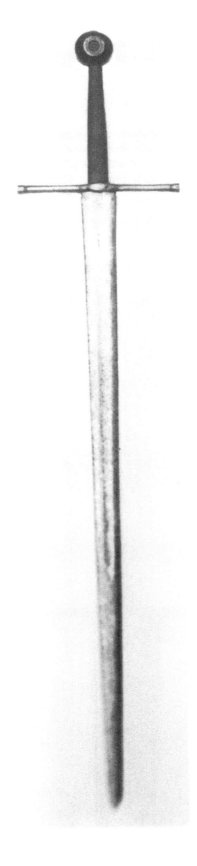

XIIa. 3

Type: XIIa
Find-place: Alexandria, the Arsenal
Collection: The Royal Armouries, H.M. Tower of London. IX.915
Blade-length: 35½" (90 cms)
Pommel-type: A variant of Type K
Date: c.1350-1400
Condition: Almost perfect, except that the grip is lacking. There is an Arabic inscription incised in the fuller just below the hilt, which has been translated as 'Inalienable property of the treasury of the marsh province of Alexandria, may it be protected'. There is a smith's mark on the tang.
This was sold in 1960 in the D'Acre Edwards sale at Christies, where I tried for it myself, and ran Sir James Mann up a good deal, but of course he beat me.
Publication: Dufty, Plate 4d
Oakeshott *SAC*, Plate 29, where it is erroneously classified as of Type XVIa, instead of XIIa.

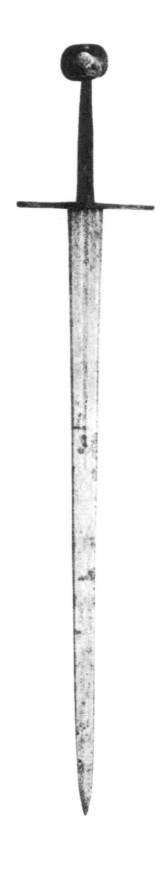

XIIa. 4

Type: XIIa
Find-place: Unknown
Collection: Private
Blade-length: 43¼" (110 cms)
Pommel-type: 11
Cross-style: 1
Date: c.1250-1350
Condition: Excavated? River found? Considerable pitting on all surfaces, below the patination. Five nice brass inlaid marks on the blade on one side, just below the cross, a little heart; below this an S within a circle, and below that a rather badly executed cross patée in a circle. On the other side a cross patée (which looks like an equal-armed cross) within a circle with an S within a circle below it. The pommel is interesting, for the decoration is unusual, a series of stamped rosettes on the flat rims of the central boss which surround the hollowed insets, one of which (on the same side of the sword as the heart mark) has a neat cross patée in it.

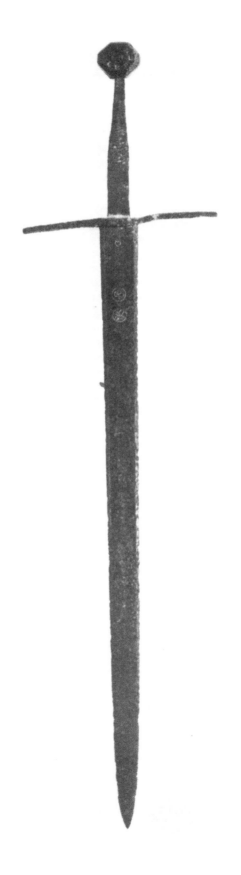

XIIa. 5

Type: XIIa
Find-place: Unknown
Collection: Museum für Deutsche Geschichte, Berlin
Blade-length: 37" (94 cms)
Pommel-type: I.1.
Cross-style: 1, curved
Date: Before 1240
Condition: Generally good, but considerable pitting on the blade and cross. The decorated pommel, being of bronze (probably once gilded) is perfect. The arms on the central parts of the pommel, on one side an Eagle Displayed and on the other four rampant lions. These arms are of a landgraf of Thuringen and Hesse, and the sword belonged to Konrad, Grand-Master of the German Order, 1239-41. This gives a fairly positive *terminus post quem* for dating one of these big war-swords of Type XIIa (and of course, XIIIa as well) and for an early use of this form of facetted 'wheel pommel' – as if the one from Finland's Viking graves cleared by Dr Leppaaho Xa.4 (iv) wasn't enough proof for a date before the 14th century.
Publication: Mulles/Koelling Platow, *Europaeische Hieb-und-Stichwaffen*, Berlin, 1981, No.9.

Type XIII-XIIIb

Characteristic of this type (whose sub-type contains the majority of surviving examples) is a blade whose edges run very nearly parallel to a rounded point, and whose tang is noticeably longer than the usual 3"–4" (8.2cms or 11.1cms) of single-hand sword of the preceding types. The sub-type, XIIIa, is the 'Grete War Sword' par excellence with its very large blade 32"–40" (81.2 and 101.7cms) average length and long grip, of between 6" and 10" (15cms and 25.5cms). Pommel forms on survivors vary, though the 'wheel' shape of pommel-types I to K predominate. Crosses both on surviving examples and those shown in art are nearly always straight, generally of Style 2.

They are often mentioned in inventory, poem and chronicle as 'Swerdes of Werre', 'Grans Espées d'Allemagne', 'Schlacht-schwerte', 'Grete Swords', 'Espées de Guerre', 'Grete War Swords' and so on, always indicating large size and specific purpose.

They are generally referred to as of German origin, too, an attribution borne out by the frequency with which they appear on German tomb effigies of the 14th century; they are found nearly as often upon Spanish effigies of the same period, and occasionally on English ones. There are so few French knightly tomb effigies left since the destructive efforts of the Revolutionaries of 1789 that it is not possible to quote a single French example. The very fact, I believe, that the French in the 13th and 14th centuries always referred to them as 'big German swords' is proof enough that Germany was their area of origin and greatest use.

Those shown in art are generally dateable between say c.1250 and 1370; the German and Spanish effigies between 1320-1370. There is, however, archaeological evidence to suggest very strongly that these big, hand-and-a-half gripped swords were not uncommon as early as the 12th century. (See Appendix B).

The XIIIa's vary greatly in size, some being true two-hand swords. A prime example of such an outsize one is the sword of Edward III in St George's Chapel in Windsor Castle, which has been there since the Order of the Garter – or at least, St George's Chapel – was founded in the mid-14th century. This sword is overall more than six feet long, yet its proportions are such that it must be classified as an XIIIa. By contrast, a more modest one is shown here at XIIIa.2, though it is still a very big sword.

I know of a few good examples of Type XIII, all shown here. One of the best (XIII.1) used to be in the Harold Peterson Collection in Virginia; a second is in the Royal Armouries (shown here in Multiple Miscellaneous 1 below) a third in the Royal Scottish Museum in Edinburgh. and a fourth, a very big sword with an enormously broad blade, which I saw, and drew, at Sotheby's in the days of my youth, in 1935. There is a fifth in a private collection in Italy. These are shown below.

Sub-type XIIIb has been isolated, though its variation from Type XIII itself is so slight that much isolation seems to be splitting hairs; but I have made it so, therefore I am committed to allowing it to stand. The only real different from Type XIII is that the grip is shorter; the form of the blade remains the same.

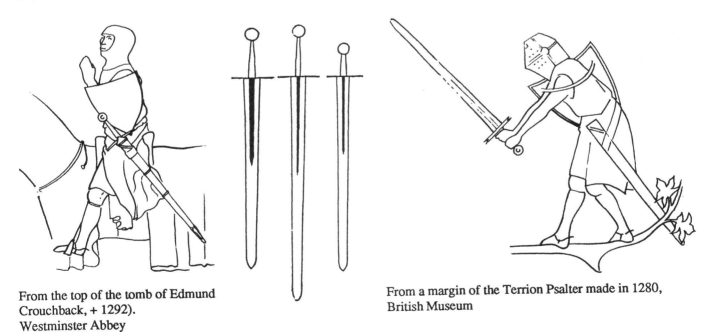

From the top of the tomb of Edmund
Crouchback, + 1292).
Westminster Abbey

From a margin of the Terrion Psalter made in 1280,
British Museum

XIII. 1

Type: XIII
Find-place: Unknown
Collection: Ex Harold Peterson, ex D'Acre Edwards, now private
Blade-length: 31" (78.7 cms)
Pommel-type: J
Cross-style: 2
Date: ?1200-1300
Condition: Excavated (?river-found?). Excellent. Very little pitting. When I saw it at the D'Acre Edwards sale in 1960, it had a curiously greenish patination. Since it was sold at Harold Peterson's sale at Christies on July 5th, 1978, I have lost track of it.

This is an absolutely classic example of a Type XIII sword with its parallel-edged blade, rounded point and long grip. The three fullers in the blade are rather uncommon, but by no means unusual in swords dating from the fourth century to the 18th. There is a mark on the blade which I noted in 1960, but unfortunately cannot now find to include here! The sword handles well, but as may be expected of a slashing-sword, the point of balance is well down toward the point. Its weight is just over 3 lbs.

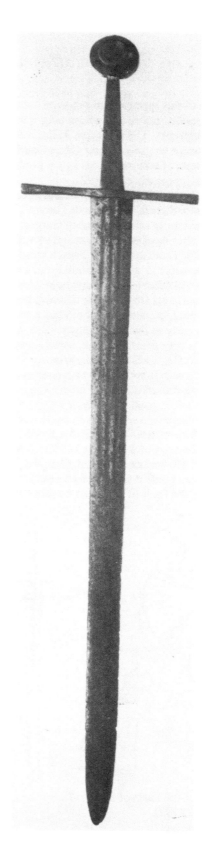

XIII. 2-4

2. Type: XIII
   Find-place: Unknown
   Collection: Royal Scottish Museum, Edinburgh
   Blade-length: 31½" (80 cms)
   Pommel-type: E
   Cross-style: 2
   Date: c.1250 + or – 20
   Condition: Excavated. River? Good. Some pitting
   Publication: J.G. Scott, *European Arms & Armour at Kelvin-grove.* (Glasgow, 1980.)

3. Type: XIII
   Find-Place: Unknown
   Collection: Unknown
   Blade-length: 32" (81.2cms)
   Pommel-type: G
   Cross-style: 1
   Date: c.1200-50 (The hilt form suggests a century earlier)
   Condition: Excavated. River. Good. Some pitting, quite deep.

4. Type: XIII
   Find-place: Unknown
   Collection: Private
   Blade-length: 33" (83.8cms)
   Pommel-type: B.1
   Cross-style: 1
   Date: c.1150-1200
   Condition: Excavated. River. Good

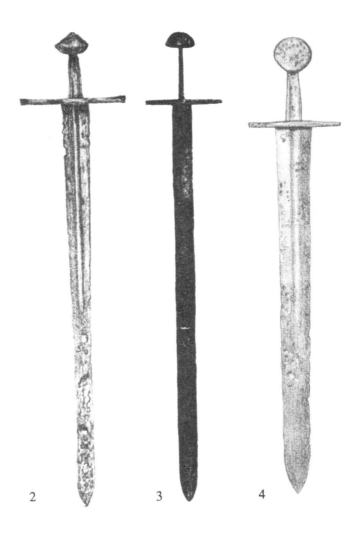

These three Type XIII swords are shown together, to a constant scale, to show the great size of No.4. This I saw, handled, and drew at Sotheby's in 1935. It isn't as heavy as it looks, but it is quite remarkable in the breadth of its blade, and the diameter of its flat, thin pommel to match. I did not note any marks.

No.2 in Edinburgh is a less handsome sword; if it wasn't for the nearly parallel edges of this blade, it would have to be categorised as a Type XII, not a XIII, especially as the grip is short. There is a tiny inlaid three-letter inscription – O S O – in silver. There is no parallel for this among Leppaaho's grave-finds, though it is a common enough inscription, sometimes written S O S, on XIIth century blades. The pommel is very massive, being very broad in profile. Rather a clumsy sword.

No.3 is a classic XIII, interesting for its purely Viking form of pommel and its very thin, stalk-like tang. Tangs like this are not very common, though by no means rare. They look, seen face-on, as if they were thin and weak in contrast to the very broad flat tangs more often seen. However, the section of these stalk-like tangs is square; there is as much solid metal as in the broad, flat ones.

XIIIa. 1

Type: XIIIa
Find-place: Unknown to me
Collection: Kunsthistorisches Museum, Vienna. Wien A8W
Blade-length: 40" approximately (101.2cms)
Pommel-type: J in an extremely deep form
Cross-style: 2
Date: c.1300-50
Condition: Can only be called 'mint'. The blade bears no rust-pits and looks as if it had never been used. Pommel and cross are unstained – not, I think, overcleaned – but the small escutcheon of ?silver or enamel in the central boss of the pommel is missing. The grip,(with its circular tassels top and bottom of cut leather) is an early 16th century refurbishment.
Publication: Gamber, p.22, no.17.

This is perhaps the supreme example of a Type XIIIa sword, its perfect preservation indicates its centuries-long sojourn, probably unused, in an armoury. It is known as 'The Sword of Dietrich von Bern'. This name has been given in Germanic legend to the Ostrogoth 5th century Emperor Theodoric, Thidrek in the Volsungasaga, and in the Nibelungenlied. The sword must, I think, date in the first half of the 14th century for (a) it is so typical of those big 'Riesenschwerte' which are to be so clearly seen on tomb effigies of this period and (b) because the very distinctively-shaped 'wheel' pommel of Type J in an exaggerated form doesn't seem to have been used before c.1300: but this can only be said with a strong reservation. I don't know of an example, actual or pictured, which can be positively said to predate 1300. That, however, does not at all mean, or even suggest, that some day we shall not find proof that such a pommel-form was in fact in use many decades earlier. I can only present what is known now.
There is a beautifully executed inscription in the fuller of the blade. This does not seem to be etched, nor is it inlaid in silver or latten; it just seems to be lightly engraved, and was added, like the grip, in the 16th century. It reads *Gennant Herr Dietrich von Berns Schwert*, the letters being characteristic of the time of the Emperor Maximillian 1.

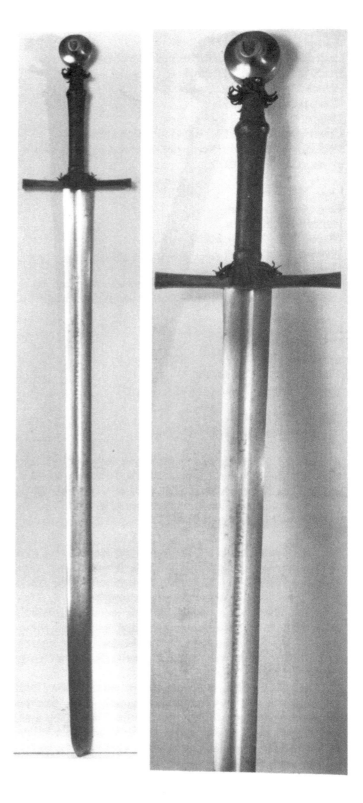

XIIIa. 2

Type: XIIIa
Find-Place: The River Thames in London, opposite the Temple
Collection: Museum of London
Blade-Length: 39½" (100.4cms)
Pommel-Type: J, in an extremely deep form
Cross-Style: 2
Date: c.1300-50
Condition: River-found. Good. Shiny brown patina. Considerable pitting in large patches.
Publication: Laking; Oakeshott, E., 'A War-Sword of the XIVth century in the Guildhall Museum', *Journal of the Arms and Armour Society*, London, 1954; Oakeshott, *SAC*; Blair, C., *EAA*, 26

This is an enormous sword, very nearly of two-hand proportions, and rather heavy. The point of balance is well down towards the point, ideal for a weapon designed to deal slow, powerful slashing blows. There are little crosses inlaid in copper on the central bosses of the pommel, which is of exactly the same form, very deep, as that of the 2-hand sword of Edward III at Windsor and the 'sword of Dietrich von Bern' in Vienna. Since it was found in the river at the point where in the 14th century the gardens of the Temple in London ran down to the river's edge, and since it has crosses in the pommel, it is tempting to suggest that it is a Templar knight's sword thrown into the river when the Order of the Temple was dissolved by Edward II in 1314. That it was thrown deliberately into the river is far more likely than that it was lost overboard; the suggestion that the crosses indicate a Templar is more suspect, for when these knights embellished things with crosses, they tended to be crosses in a form heraldically known as 'cross-crosslets' – i.e. each arm of the cross has a short transverse bar at right angles across it, just below the tip of the arm.

The really interesting point about this one is the mark of a little dagger inlaid in latten in the fuller about 1.5cms below the hilt. This is exactly matched (a) by the same mark in the Edward III two-hander and (b) the same again in the beautiful XIIa shown here at XIIa.2 above. Rather similar dagger marks are to be seen on swords of Type XVII below; but these three are different in shape, and each is identical with the others.

XIIIa. 3-4

3. Type: XIIIa
   Find-place: Unknown
   Collection: Glasgow Museum and Art Gallery
   Blade-length: 33" (83.8cms)
   Pommel-type: A distorted variant of Type 1
   Cross-style: 1
   Date: Anything between 1100 and 1350
   Condition: Excavated. Poor. Heavy overall deep pitting.

4. Type: XIIIa
   Find-place: Unknown
   Collection: Glasgow Museum Art Gallery 139.65 Hg
   Blade-length: 36" (91.5cms)
   Pommel-Type: K
   Cross-Style: 2
   Date: c.1250-1325
   Condition: Excavated. Middling. Considerable pitting on the
   blade, pommel seriously corroded.
   Publication: None.

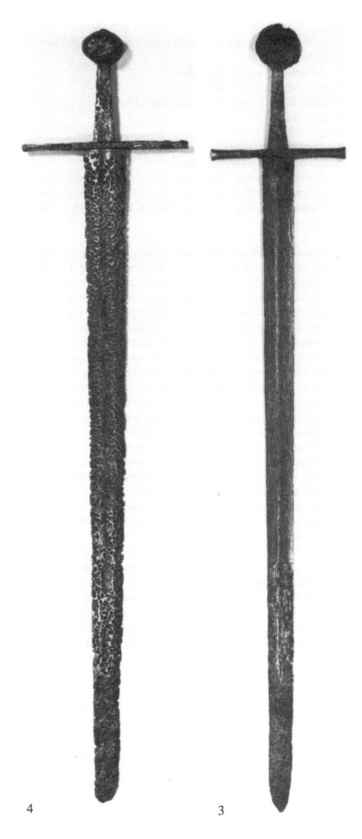

4   3

XIIIa. 5-6

5. Type: XIIIa
   Find-Place: Behind ancient panelling in a medieval house in Linz, Austria.
   Collection: Private, in Germany
   Blade-length: 34" (83.8 cms)
   Pommel-type: 1
   Cross-style: 2
   Date: 1300-50
   Condition: Almost perfect. Original wood-leather grip survives.

6. Type: XIIIa
   Find-Place: Unknown, in Bohemia
   Collection: Private
   Blade-length: 36½" (92.7cms)
   Pommel-type: An unusual 'writhen' variant of T
   Cross-style: 2
   Date: c.1480-1510
   Condition: Almost perfect, superficial pitting, original wood-cord-leather grip survives.
   Publication: None? I believe a Museum Director in Prague has published a paper on it, or will soon do so (1988).

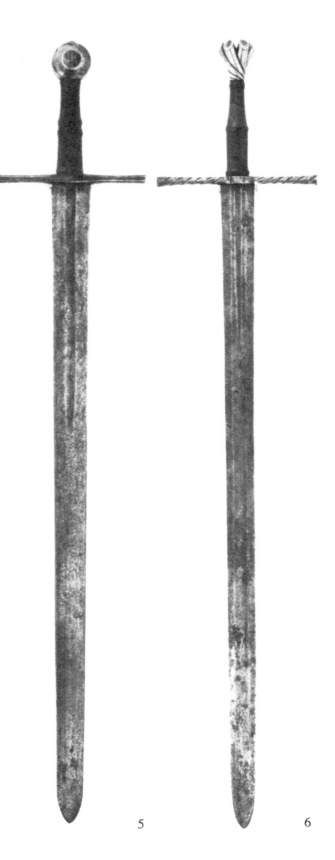

5   6

I have kept these two photographs together, for though both swords are of the same type, they are widely different in date. When the photographs were taken, both swords were in the same collection, but have now been transferred. No.5 is a perfect, and nearly perfectly preserved, example of the type. The house in which it was found in Linz is known to have been in existence before 1307, when it was in the possession of Heinrich and his son Wernbart an dem Urfahr. This house was demolished in 1938, when the sword came to light and into the possession of a boy. Forty-seven years later he parted with it to a friend of mine in Germany. He sent me a very comprehensive series of photographs in colour, for which there is not space here, but they show in detail the extraordinarily good preservation of the grip, only a little of its thin leather covering having broken away.
There is a mark, a Cross Fourché, inlaid in latten on the blade. No.6 is in the same sort of condition (though not found in that house in Linz) and is a very good example of the revival in popular usage of XIIIa's at the very end of the 15th century. This blade has a stamped 'twig' mark, very commonly found on blades from the late 13th century till the late 16th.

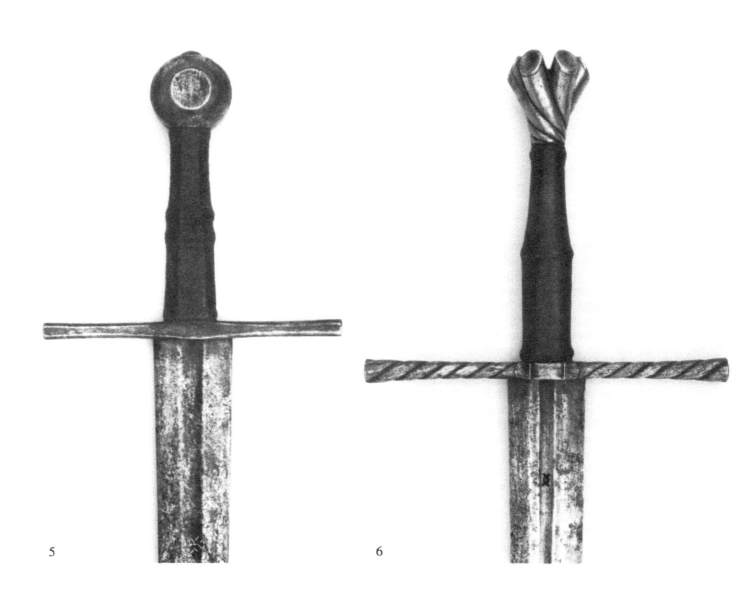

5   6

XIIIa. 7-8

7. **Type:** XIIIa
   Find-place: The Hall of Victories, Alexandria
   Collection: Glasgow Museum and Art Gallery, A7627i
   Blade length: 34" (83.8cms)
   Pommel-type: 1
   Cross-style: 2
   Date: c.1350+
   Condition: Good. Preserved in an armoury. Some rust-staining but few serious pits.
   Publication: Scott, J.G., *European Arms & Armour at Kelvingrove*, 1980, p.12

8. **Type:** XIIIa
   Find-place: Unknown, probably Alexandria
   Collection: Private
   Blade-length: 33½" (83cms)
   Pommel-type: 1
   Cross-style: 2
   Date: c.1350+
   Condition: Good. Preserved in an armoury

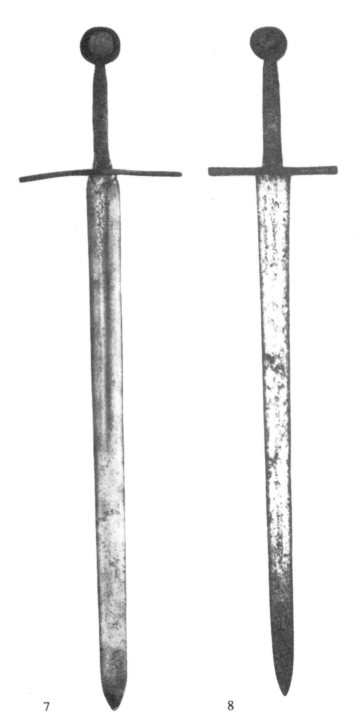

7   8

Both of these swords bear inscriptions in a Nashki Arabic script. That on No. 7 reads: 'Inalienable bequest to the Armoury of the frontier city of Alexandria in the time of Alsaifi Faris, the Commissary, A.H. 840 (AD 1430-31). On No.8 it reads 'Inalienably bequeathed to the frontier city of Alexandria the well-guarded during the days of our master, chief of the Emirs Al Saifi Al Nasiri Aristai'. This emir was Governor of Alexandria in AD 1400-1. This same inscription appears on a sword of Type XIIIb (q.v. below) in the Art Museum of Philadelphia. The late dates in the 15th century do not give a making date for the swords, which were probably old when given to or acquired by the Arsenal. There is one, an identical twin with the Philadelphia one, in Toronto, dated AD 1368. No. 8 here was found recently in a junk-shop in New Zealand, painted all over with aluminium paint, presumably having been used in a play or a pageant. The owner brought it to England, where it was sold at Christies and where I saw and handled it. Though (like most of the XIIIa's), it looks clumsy, it handles well so long as one swings it in the manner for which it was designed, that is to deal, great slow slashing blows with a straight arm and swung from the shoulder using the strength of the back to supplement the weight of the sword -nearly 4lbs – which is centred at a percussion-point about one-third of the way up from the point.

XIIIa. 9

Type: XIIIa
Find-Place: Perhaps the Danube
Collection: Burrell Collection Glasgow. Ex Martineau Collection
Blade-length: 36" (91.5cms)
Pommel-Type: I
Cross-Style: 2
Date: 1200-1250
Condition: Excellent. River-found. The dark red-brown colour of the patination, according to what Sir James Mann told me, suggests the Danube mud, which is a superb preserver of swords. In the fuller on each side, widely spaced, engraved and inlaid in latten, are the letters A.C.L.I. The leather-covered wooden grip survives in very good condition. This again is a heavy sword (about 3¾ lbs) but, if handled correctly, handles well.
Publication: Oakeshott, *SAC*, pl.14B.

XIIIa. 10-12

0. Type: XIII.a
   Find-place: Unknown
   Collection: Burrell Collection, Glasgow
   Blade-length: 36½" (92.1 cms)
   Pommel-type: K
   Cross-style: 2
   Date: c.1270-1330
   Condition: River-found. Excellent. No serious pitting.

1. Type: XIII.a
   Find-place: Unknown
   Collection: Museum and Art Gallery, Glasgow
   Blade-length: 35" (88.9 cms)
   Pommel-type: 1.1
   Cross-style: 1
   Date: ? Early for this type c.1200-50 – or 1100-50, more likely.
   Excavated. Rather ragged and heavily pitted.
   The long, narrow fuller is like a Type XI blade and the

pommel, of facetted wheel form, is of a shape found among the Leppaaho Viking swords. The cross is of an early style, also in use (called Gaddhjalt-Spike-Hilt) by the Vikings. This could be an XIa, if I had isolated such a sub-type. As I have not, it has to go into XIIIa.

12. Type: XIII.a
    Find-place: Unknown
    Collection: Private
    Blade-length: 34" (86.4 cms)
    Pommel-type: J
    Cross-style: 2
    Date: c.1250-1300
    Condition: Excavated, very good. Some very deep nicks, made in use, on the edges. Note the double fuller and compare this with XIII.1 in this series.
    Publication: Oakeshott, E. 'Medieval Swords: X', *Gun Report* 1986

10   11   12

XIIIa. 13

Type: XIII.a
Find-place: Unknown
Collection: Museum für Deutsche Geschichte. Berlin, No.25
Blade-length: 33½" (85.4 cms)
Pommel-type: 1
Cross-style: A variant of 2
Date: c.1120-50
Condition: Very good indeed. The blade is bright, hardly
pitted at all. There is a certain amount of light staining on the
pommel and cross. The elaborate, complex silver-inlaid inscriptions give the key to a date far earlier than is generally
allowed – c.1120 instead of c.1300. This is fully considered
and explained below in Appendix B. The blade is quite short
for an XIIIa, but the length of the grip puts it firmly into that
type. The inscriptions in full, (when the extremely close-set
letters are spaced out) is as follows: on one side
ENRICS DX NERICS (i.e. ENRICUS DUX NERICUS)
and on the other a very complex series of designs reminicent
of folk-art – and of the Hex signs upon houses in present-day
Amish country in Pennsylvania.
Publication: Hiltl, G., *Die Waffensammlung der Museum für
deutschen Geschichte*, p.44. No.256.; Wegeli, Plates 24-26.;
Post, Paul, 'Enricus Dux'. *ZHWK* 247. Plate 1c.; Oakeshott,
E. *Catalogue of the Third Park Lane Arms Fair*, 1986.

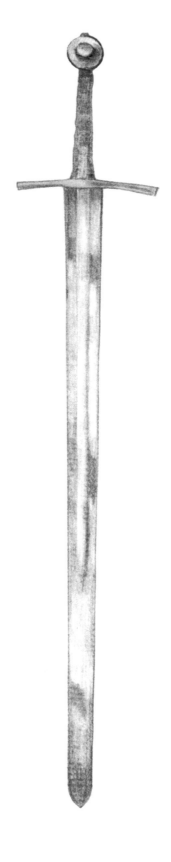

XIIIa. 14

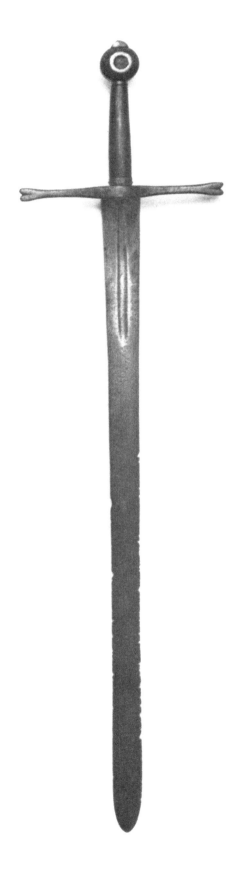

Type: XIIIa
Find-place: A church in Austria (town or village unspecified)
Collection: Private. Ex. author's, ex. Col. MacNaghten, ex.Austrian Collector.
Blade-length: 38" (96.5 cms)
Pommel-type: 1, recessed
Cross-style: 5
Date: c.1250-1300
Condition: Preserved in a church. Good. Overall small pitting. Overcleaned. Original grip.
Publication: Oakeshott, *AOW*; pl.9a Oakeshott *SAC* pl.13

This is one of the few surviving swords which is definitely known to have been preserved in a a church. It was bought in a lot of four swords by my uncle at Sotheby's in November 1939, and given to me. It formed part of the collection of a Col. MacNaghten, of Chew Magna in Somerset. I was able to trace its provenance. Col. MacNaghten bought it, also at Sotheby's, in a collection in 1935 catalogued as 'The property of an Austrian Collector'. Further enquiry showed that he had obtained it 'from a church in Austria'.

When I got it, forty-nine years ago, it was covered with a thick layer of red rust, very hard, below which was a dark blue-brown (i.e almost purple) flint-hard patina covering the small rust-pits which show up clearly in the photograph. Being young (23) and totally inexperienced (I had never even handled a medieval sword before) I wanted it to be all shiny, so with immense labour I cleaned it all off, surface rust, patina and all, from each side of the blade and all of the hilt, thereby destroying valuable, irreplaceable evidence. Seldom have I regretted any act of mine so much. This sword remained with me from 1939 until I sold it to Peter Dale Ltd. in 1975; where it is now, I have no idea.

The posession of this, my first medieval sword, led me first to begin research to find out what it was, its origins, date and so on, this in turn sparking off my lifelong interest in the Sword in the Age of Chivalry. Everything I have written collected or enthused over ever since springs from that November evening when, after the MacNaghten sale, my uncle gave me this sword. Neither of us knew then what he had started.

I, together with the Research Laboratory at the British Museum did so much work on this sword in a practical archaeological way, and I and others did so much historical research based upon its condition, that to note it all here would break up the even sequences of this book. Therefore all this has been put together and presented below as Appendix C.

XIIIa. 15

Type: XIII.a
Find-place: Unknown
Collection: Collection Malacrida, Milan
Blade-length: 33" (84 cms)
Pommel-type: S
Cross-style: 2
Date: c.1210-1320
Condition: Excellent. Does not seem to be earth-found; there is a certain amount of staining on the otherwise bright metal of the pommel and cross, as on the bright, and slightly pitted, blade. There seem to be no marks.

An exactly similar hilt is shown on an English effigy of c.1300 at Halton Holgate in Lincolnshire, and there are at least three swords of the same type, with similar Type S pommels, in Stockholm. The grip is probably a restoration.
Publication: Puricelli-Guerra, Arturo, *Armi in Occidente*, Milano, 1966, No. 22 and p.54.
Boissonas, Charles, *Collection Ch.Boissonas. Epées.* X, shows a similar sword, a little longer and narrower in the blade.

XIIIb. 1

Type: XIII.b
Find-place: Toledo Cathedral
Collection: Toledo Cathedral Treasury
Blade-length: 28" (71.1 cms) approximately
Pommel-type: 1
Cross-style: 2
Date: Before 1319
Condition: Almost as new except that the red velvet covering of scabbard is rather worn. There is a good deal of light rust-staining of the blade just below the hilt, where a certain amount of damp air would have got into the scabbard, but lower down the surfaces are clean and bright, except for a few stains near to the point.
Publication: Blair, Claude, 'Medieval Swords and Spurs Preserved in Toledo Cathedral'. *Journal of the Arms and Armour Society*, London, 1959; Oakeshott, *AOW*; Oakeshott *SAC* and several Spanish publications which I cannot at present trace; Blair, C. *EAA* 27.

This sword is quite small – not, I feel sure, a boy's sword but one of those light 'riding swords'. The enamelled arms on the pommel, repeated on all six of the scabbard mounts, are of Leon and Castile in a form similar to that on the seal of Don Juan, a younger brother of Fernando de la Cerda and Sancho IV of Castile. he was nicknamed 'El de Tarifa' and was killed fighting against the Moors in 1319.
The hilt is plated with silver, and seems to be not 'plated' in the true sense but overlaid with thin plates of silver, once gilt. The grip is bound with a single strand of twisted silver wire. The scabbard is of wood covered with red velvet, and its mounts are of silver gilt, bearing the enamelled shields of arms only on the outside. The opening of the scabbard has emerging from it a semi-circular flap which hangs down the back, as you can see in the photograph here at (iii). The silver-gilt belt-ends are here wrongly mounted on a single ring, whereas they should be one in each ring on either side of the locket.
There are no marks on the sword, but most interestingly there is a mark made with a punch in the silver on the back of the upper locket of the scabbard. This consists of crossed keys with a star impaled with another charge which is unidentified, within an escutcheon. The crossed keys seem to have a strong papal identity, suggesting that the sword was perhaps a papal gift. The use of such a poincon at such an early date is noteworthy. Here is an unmistakeable sort of 'By Appointment' mark of a heraldic charge placed neatly within an escutcheon. This mark has a positive bearing upon the identification of other marks of a similar kind.
I was able to handle and examine this delightful little sword in the Armouries at the Tower of London when it was part of the exhibition there of 'The Armours of Kings and Captains' in 1949. It is beautifully balanced, and still as sharp as a carving knife. This is a shining example (literally!) of a sword which has been preserved in a scabbard and has not rotted away, maybe because it has since the 14th century been preserved in the treasury of Toledo Cathedral, and not hung over a tomb?
The system of suspension is a very early example of its kind, for one does not expect to find locket-hangers like this until c.1330-40. Here it is, before 1319!

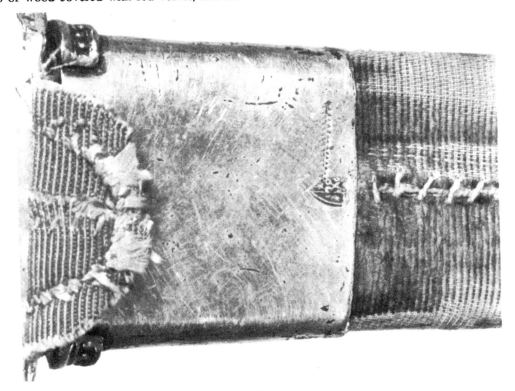

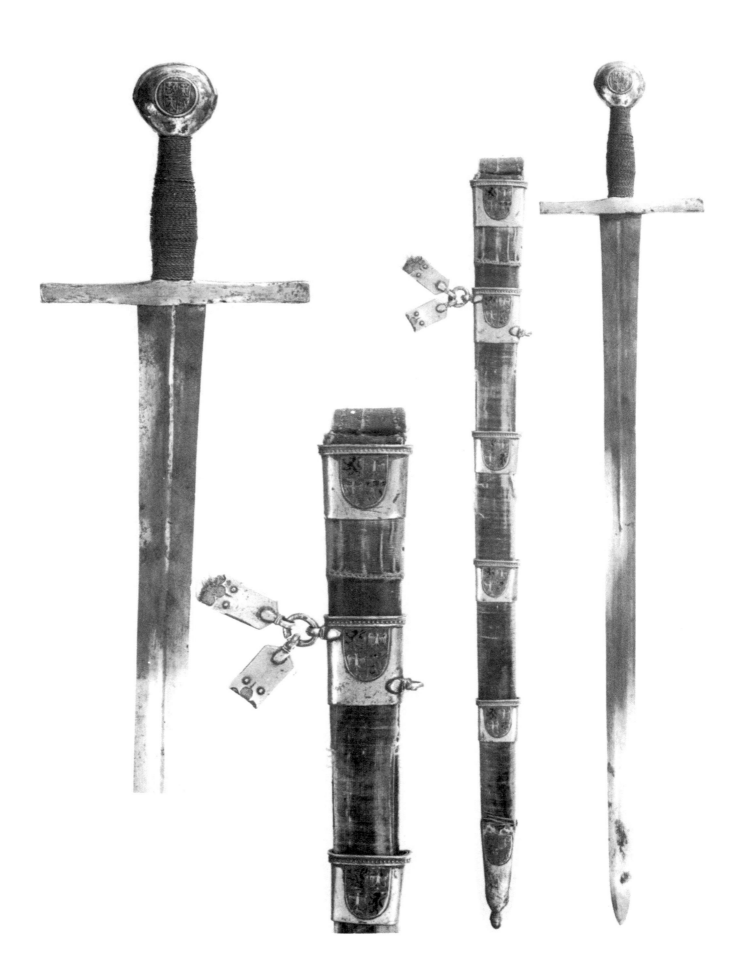

XIIIb. 2

Type: XIIIb
Find-place: Unknown, but in Scandinavia
Collection: Private, ex. Peter Dale Ltd.
Blade-length: 30½" (77.5 cms)
Pommel-Type: 1
Date: c.1250-80
Condition: Excellent. Not excavated. There is a certain amount of pitting in the lower part of the blade and on the cross, but little on the pommel. The grip may be original. On each side of the pommel, inset into the recess, is a ? Roman copper coin. On the outside of the pommel (ii) a Maltese Cross has been incised right across the face of the inset coin.

This is a remarkably fine sword, a perfect example of that rather rare sub-type, XIIIb. There seem to be no marks on the blade. I have not been able to see and handle this sword for myself, but I am told that it is fairly heavy, say 3lbs, with the point of balance about one-third of the way down from the hilt.

There is a very similar blade, unmounted, in a private collection in Norway, and a superb one in mint condition, also unmounted, in the Kunsthistorisches Museum in Vienna, with engraved arms upon it giving a sure attribution to Ottokar II, King of Bohemia, who died in 1258.

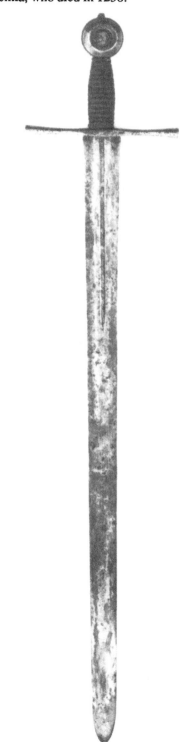

XIIIb. 3

Type: XIII.b
Find-place: Unknown
Collection: Severance Collection, Cleveland Museum, Ohio
Blade-length: 32" (81.2 cms) approximately
Pommel-type: 1
Cross-style: 2
Date: c.1240-80
Condition: Very good. It looks as if it had been preserved in a church. There is hardly any deep pitting anywhere. The grip is a modern replacement, and being rather too fat and bulgy, I think it detracts from the appearance of a very nicely proportioned sword. The shallow fuller comes to an end just short of the cross – rather an unusual feature (cf. No. XIIIa.14 and Appendix C).
Publication: Oakeshott, *SAC*, Plate 8A.

XIIIb. 4

Type: XIII.b
Find-place: Alexandria, Arsenal
Collection: Philadelphia Art Museum (Kienbusch Collection)
Blade-length: 34½" (87.6 cms)
Pommel-type: An exaggerated Type K
Cross-style: 5
Date: c.1350-60
Condition: Very good. Indoor preservation, the grip lost. The pommel is of latten. The inscription on the blade, in Arabic Nashki script tells that it was deposited in the Hall of Victories in 1367 (A.H.769). This suggests that it might be spoil from an abortive attack upon Cairo in 1365 by Pierre de Lusignan, titular king of Jerusalem, based in Cyprus. However, like so many of these European swords deposited in the Mamluk arsenal at Alexandria, it may have been simply a gift. There is a whole group of these swords, of this precise type and form; nine of them are now in the Askeri Museum at Istanbul, one is in the Royal Ontario Museum in Toronto, and one came up for sale at Christie's in March 1988.
Publication: Oakeshott, *SAC*, Plate 12A; Alexander, D.G. 'European Swords in the Collections at Istanbul' *ZHWK*, 1985. (This deals with the nine in Istanbul); Blair, C. *EAA* 29.

XIIIb. 5

Type: Probably XIIIb, but might have been XIII
Find-place: Unknown
Collection: Kunsthistorisches Museum, Vienna
Blade-length: 38½" (98 cms)
Pommel-type: There is no pommel
Cross-style: Nor any cross
Date: Between 1253 and 1278
Condition: Pristine. This beautiful blade has clearly never been mounted, nor used. This accounts for the extremely long tang, for it is obviously how the blade came from the blade-smith, so that it could be hilted as a XIII, or a long-gripped war sword of XIIIa, or a single hand XIIIb. There are engraved designs and letters on the blade which give it a positive attribution to King Ottokar II of Bohemia (1253-1278), when he was killed crossing a river during an attack upon Durnkrut. These marks are not inlaid in metal, simply cut into the blade, and (considering the royal insignia) very poorly executed. This is an absolutely untouched example of the Type XIII style of blade, and the extreme length of the tang suggests that very possibly most blades came to the cutler in this way, so that the hilt could be made to a length to suit the customer.
Publication: Laking, 1; Gamber, O. p.20, No.12 and p.16.

The inscriptions give quite clear attribution to Ottokar II. On one side a small cross, followed by the Austrian arms of the *Bindenschild* with a great helm above, crested with a pair of wings, then the letters TEVPDLS: on the other side a small heart, the double-tailed crowned lion of Bohemia the letters R G F B R, followed by a cross crosslet with, on either side of the fuller, a star.

The opposition of the Austrian *Bindenschild* with the winged crest of Bohemia points unmistakeably to King Przemysl Ottokar II of Bohemia (crowned in 1253) who by marriage to the Babenbergerin Margrethe became Archduke of Austria; on his great seal of 1269 he put the combined Bohemian crest and the Austrian shield. The Bohemian lion is another sign.

In 1278 Ottokar fell in battle at Durnkrut against Rudolf I of Hapsburg, so this blade must date between 1253 and 1278, which gives a very good date-base for the big Type XIIIa *espées de guerre*, which by its size this would almost certainly have been.

Type XIV

This is a very distinctive sword-type which by its incidence in works of art can be given a more than usually precise life-span between c.1275-1340. Its characteristics are a short grip and comparatively short blade which is broad at the hilt and tapers strongly to a sometimes very acute point with a generally flat section fullered in its upper half. Crosses tend to be generally quite long and slightly arched, while the pommel-type most commonly found allied to these other elements is of Type K, broad and flat with small raised bosses.

Naturally, like all swords, their sizes vary; and we do not have very much hard archaeological evidence to go on, for, in spite of the type's obvious popularity in the period of its usage, very few examples are so far avaialble for study. Not so their appearance in works of art – sculpture, tomb-effigies, MS miniatures and early Italian paintings. When they are depicted in their scabbards, it is not possible to be certain that they are not of Type XV (q.v. below) but enough are shown naked to make dating secure. They appear once or twice along with the more usual XII's in the Maciejowski Bible (c.1260) as well as in the Oxford *Romance of Alexander*, an English MS dated c.1333, where XIV's are shown along with XIIIa's, XII's and XV's.

XIV.1

Type: XIV
Find-place: Unknown
Collection: Metropolitan Museum of Art, New York
Blade-length: 32" (81.3 cms)
Pommel-type: J.1
Cross-style: 7
Date: c.1325-50
Condition: Almost pristine – obviously preserved in an armoury of a house where it has been constantly cared for, not hung up in a church where centuries of dust and probably neglect produce a lot of rust and patination, as in No.XIIIa 14 above.
Publication: Oakeshott, *SAC*; pl.16 Oakeshott, 'Medieval Swords: XII' in *Gun Report*, 1986

This is an absolutely outstanding sword, not only because of its condition but by reason of its splendid proportions and great size. It is dated, by the Museum, as belonging to the 15th century, but everything about it proclaims its age as being of the first quarter of the 14th. The (now indecipherable) etched lettering in the fullers is remarkably akin to that in the blade of the sword in Toledo Cathedral of Sancho IV el Bravo of Castile, who died in 1298, and whose sword, found on his body, probably belonged to his father Alfonso el Sabio; so that etched blade must date before 1298 and is very probably a couple of decades earlier. (See XII.7 in this series).

The pommel of this Type XIV sword is of bronze, with applied rings (the shape of Sikh quoits) of silver on which are engraved the words SUNT HIC (sic) ETIAM SUA PRE-CUNE LAUDI (Here also are the heralds of His praise). The cross is of bronze decorated – like a Viking sword – with vertical strips of silver wire. The grip is of wood, bound with leather thongs with a covering of thin leather over all.
The point-end of the blade is of a pronounced flat diamond section, which according to the criteria I have set out for arranging my typology, ought to make this sword a Type XVI, not a XIV; but the general shape is so typical of a XIV that I have given it the benefit of the doubt.

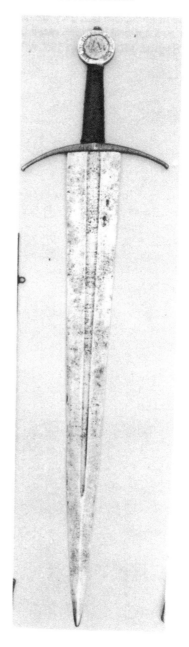

XIV. 2

Type: XIV
Find-place: Unknown
Collection: Royal Armouries, H.M. Tower of London. Formerly Sir Edward Barry. IX.1107
Blade-length: 27" (68.6 cms)
Pommel-type: Unclassified. I don't know of another, but see notes below.
Cross-style: unclassified
Date: c.1250-80
Condition: Excavated (River-found). Good, but considerable all-over pitting below the patina of goethite.
Publication: Dufty; Oakeshott, 'Medieval Swords: XII', *Gun Report*, 1986

This is a sword of absolutely classic XIV shape, but the hilt is, as far as I know at present, unique in a surviving specimen. However, three Royal seals, in excellent condition, all dateable between c.1260-80, show clear representation of this kind of sword – i.e., a typical XIV. One is the Great Seal of Charles of Anjou, King of Sicily, where blade, cross and pommel are exactly like this one (ii); another is the Great Seal of Edward I. Here blade and cross are the same, but the pommel is a kind of 3-lobed one, which by some lapse of attention I did not include in my pommel-typology of 1958. Certainly it is a rare type; I know of no actual survivors, and only two representations in art which are unmistakeable. One is on Edward I's seal, the other on the sword hilt of the statue on the S. porch of Chartres Cathedral showing Roland receiving the sacrament from archbishop Turpin. There are many photographs of this figure – see (i) here – but recent ones show the sword without a pommel, which has fallen off during the past decade. There are, however, a few pommels shown in the magnificent illustrations in the Maciezowski Bible which may be of this type (c.1260).

The two seals, shown here at (ii) and (iii) are very valuable as setting an early date for the usage of Type XIV swords, just as the figures in St Denis and Marburg (all c.1310-1340) give a late date for them. The Great Seal of the abortive King of Scots, John Balliol, shows this style of cross with a typical 'Viking' lobed pommel. The Scots called John 'Toon Tabard' - i.e. stuffed shirt. (iii)

i

ii

iii

117

XIV. 3

Type: XIV
Find-place: Somewhere in Denmark
Collection: Nationalmuseet, Copenhagen
Blade-length: 28" (71.1 cms)
Pommel-type: R
Cross-style: 1, curved
Date: c.1300+ or – 20
Condition: Excavated, probably from a bog. Poor, very cor-
roded. Interesting double fuller.

XIV. 4

Type: XIV
Find-place: Unknown
Collection: ? private. Ex collection Jack Pocock
Blade-length: 30" (76.2 cms)
Pommel-type: 1
Cross-style: Indeterminate. Perhaps a slender 6
Date: c.1300
Condition: Excavated, probably river-found. Poor. The lower part of the blade is so far gone that it is now quite flat, but there is a possibility that before it was rusted away this lower one-third may have been ridged, in which case it would be a XVI, not a XIV.

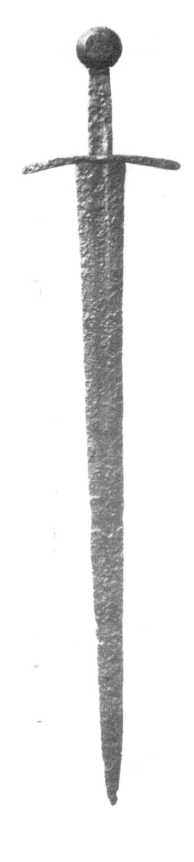

XIV. 5

Type: XIV
Find-place: A peat-bog in N.Italy
Collection: Royal Armouries, H.M. Tower of London. Ex. de Cosson, John Wallace, Ralph Parr
Blade-length: 32½" (81.9 cms)
Pommel-type: W
Cross-style: A vague Style 4
Date: c.1275-1325
Condition: Nearly perfect, below a beautiful, smooth, almost unblemished purple-black patina. The grip is a modern replacement.
Publication: Oakeshott, *SAC*. pl.20a

This is undoubtedly one of the finest – i.e. the most handsome – medieval swords to survive, in such perfect condition, too. Its broad blade gives the impression that it is a massive, rather heavy weapon, but it is in fact beautifully light – just about 2lbs – and very well balanced, like a good tennis racquet. The clearly-defined fuller (which doesn't show up at all in the photograph) is quite long, as in the blade of No. XIV.1. above here, and on each side 7" or so below the cross is engraved a pair of concentric circles, in between which appear the letters TOTOTOTO. This is a motto found quite often on 13th and 14th century rings, meant as an affirmation of loyalty and fidelity.

This type of pommel is rare. I know of only three others – one on a sword taken out of the River Witham at Lincoln, now in the museum there; one – a very small boy's sword (which really is a boy's sword) in the museum at Glasgow, and a third in a private collection in the North of England. In this sword, and the Lincoln one, the small central eminence has a little silver plate in it. There is a freestone effigy, too, at Gosberton in Lincolnshire which shows very clearly one of these pommels. Stothard's drawing of this effigy shows the hilt of the sword very well, but gives only the impression of a vaguely spherical pommel. However, when I had a close look at the effigy itself, it was very plain to see that the sculptor had made a very clean and well-cut representation of one of these Type X pommels. The cross of this Gosberton effigy's sword, too, is very similar to that of the sword discussed here. The effigy's date, stylistically, is c.1320-40.

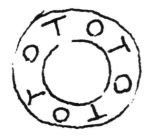

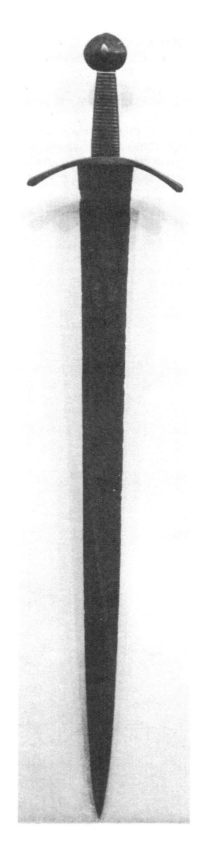

XIV. 6

Type: XIV
Find-place: Unknown
Collection: Nationalmuseet, Copenhagen. Ex collection E.A. Christensen
Blade-length: 33" (83.9cms)
Pommel-type: K, facetted
Cross-style: A curved, sophisticated and elegant form of 1
Date: c.1300
Condition: Perfect. Must have been preserved in a house or an armoury and well-cared for. The grip is probably original.
Publication: Christensen & Hoffmeyer

This is one of those perfectly preserved, sharp and shining medieval swords which are too easily condemned as being 'too good to be true'. Considering that it was acquired about thirty years ago by a collector and connoisseur as astute and experienced as Mr Christensen, there can't be much validity in any doubts about its authenticity. It's a big sword, as you can see from the dimensions upon the elaborate series of drawing Mr Christensen sent me just after he had acquired the sword.

In the catalogue of his collection, made before it went on his death to the Danish nation, he dates it at c.1475. ('Gammelt Jern', No.66, p.88), but I believe this is nearly two centuries too late. its whole form – pommel, cross and blade – are so strongly fitted into the classic XIV shape that I am sure it has to be dated between c.1275-1325. It is an absolutely outstanding sword, and I think the sketches he sent me give a very clear idea of its size, and the rather unusual form of its long, beautifully made double fullers. Unfortunately, the only photographs I have are not very good.

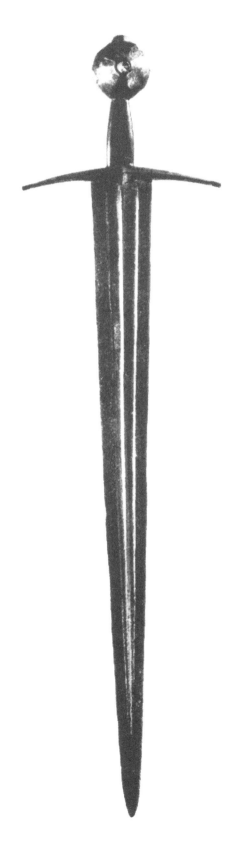

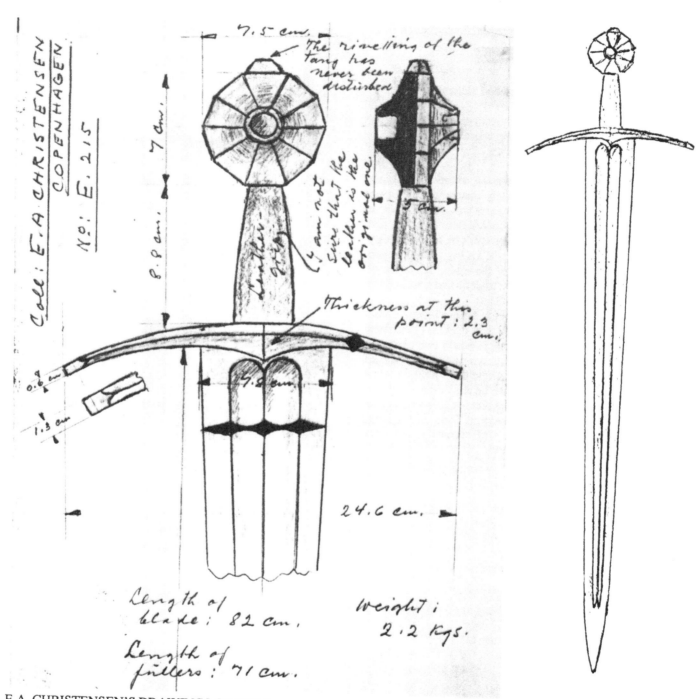

Coll: E.A. CHRISTENSEN
COPENHAGEN

No: E. 215

7.5 cm.

The rivetting of the tang has never been disturbed

I am not sure that the leather is the original one.

Leather-grip

Thickness at this point: 2.3 cm.

7 cm.

8.8 cm.

0.6

1.3 cm.

7.9 cm.

5 cm.

24.6 cm.

Length of blade: 82 cm.

Length of fullers: 71 cm.

Weight: 2.2 Kgs.

E.A. CHRISTENSEN'S DRAWINGS OF XIV.6

XIV. 7

Type: XIV
Find-place: Unknown
Collection: Mine. Formerly Gerald Gardiner and Baron de Cosson
Blade-length: 29" (73.7 cms)
Pommel-type: K
Cross-style: Curved 1
Date: 1270-1320
Condition: River-found, the blade cleaned by electrolysis. Very good. The hilt, of iron plated with silver, has been cleaned (by me) on one side, leaving the brown patination of the mud in which it lay on the other. The original grip survives in good condition – lime wood covered with thin leather, once red now black.
Publication: Oakeshott, *AOW*; Pl.7d Oakeshott, *SAC* Pl.19b & 46b

I have illustrated and described this sword before (in *The Archaeology of Weapons* and *The Sword in the Age of Chivalry*) but I make no excuses for publishing it yet again, for it is the very model of a Type XIV, as you can see by its photographs. One of the prime characteristics of this Type is that blade, cross and pommel tend to be broad, producing a bold kite-shape. There are four well-marked fullers on each face of the blade, running just short of half-way to the point. There are marks in these fullers, punched twice on each side, which seem to have been in common use until the 17th century. There are sword-blades, too, of the La Tène III period of the Iron Age which are stamped with the same mark as the one in the middle here. The same marks appear on some of the swords now in the Askeri Museum in Istanbul, taken by the Turks from the Arsenal of Alexandria. These swords c.1380, are illustrated and described in an article by D.G. Alexander (*ZHWK*, 1985, Heft 2).

This sword has been in my care now since 1952, so I know the 'feel' of it very well indeed. It is very light, the blade very thin in section from about half-way down stiff yet flexible and still very sharp. The very flat pommel is heavy and gives it an extremely good balance; it moves very quickly and lightly.

There is plentiful evidence of a good deal of wear, in the shape of undulations in the edges caused by honing, and at the point there is a large nick, which was never honed out. It is to this nick that I owe my long association with the sword. I first heard of it from Sir James Mann, who told me of a very fine sword which Sir Edward Burrell was after, but that when he saw it, and saw the nick, he decided against it. So it came up at Sotheby's in 1946, where I couldn't afford it. Dr Gardiner got it, and after his death it came to me. So, had that nick not been there, it would be in Glasgow now, in the Burrell Collection, instead of on my wall; and when I am gone, it will find itself safely in the Fitzwilliam Museum in Cambridge.

It owes its present clean appearance to some previous owner's decision to dismount it, and clean the blade by electrolysis. The tang was found to be very thin and weak just below the pommel (as so very many tangs on medieval swords are seen to be) so it was reinforced, badly, with two small rivets. The sword has travelled with me extensively when I was lecturing, and during these excursions and adventures – it very nearly fell off a porter's trolley under a train on the station at Montreal in 1966 – which caused the badly made reinforcement to weaken until ultimately, in rather disastrous circumstances, it fell apart in New York. That in a way was a good thing, because I had it properly restored and now it is as strong and secure as it should be.

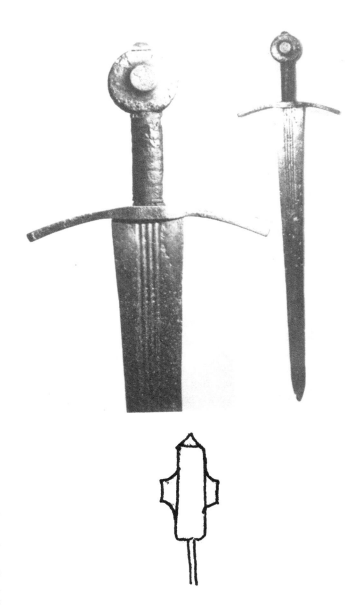

Type: XIV
Find-place: Unknown, perhaps Chartres Cathedral
Collection: Musée de l' Armée, Paris. Ex Pauilhac collection
Blade-length: 26¼" (66.5 cms)
Pommel-type: K
Cross-style: 7
Date: c.1300-50

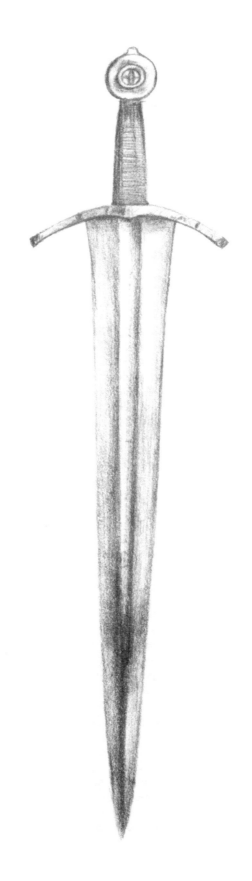

Condition: Nearly perfect. Obviously preserved in a church or an armoury. The hilt of iron (pommel and cross) is plated with gold, all of which survives except for a few patches where it has flaked off. In the central recess of the pommel, below a thin plate of rock crystal, is a brown fragment of ancient woven fabric, in the form of a cross. The original leather covering of the grip survives. On the blade is a finely lettered inscription: 'NULLA DE VIRTUTIBUS TUIS MAJOR CLEMENTIA EST' ("Nothing of your virtues is greater than clemency"). The famous 'archaeologue des armes' of the last part of the 19th century, M. Charles Buttin, averred that because only a king could truly exercise clemency, the sword must have belonged to one of the French monarchs of the first half of the 14th century. This seems a little far-fetched in view of the enormous power exercised by the great nobles which their control in their regions of the 'High Justice, the Middle and the Low'. They, like the Counts of Coucy, were almost autonomous. Indeed, the legend carved in the 12th century over the lintel of the main gate of the vast chateau de Coucy suggests a power and an arrogance far above that of the mere King of France.

> *Roi je ne suis*
> *Ne Duc, ne Comte aussi*
> *Je suis le Sieur de Coucy*

Such magnates surely must have been in a position to exercise clemency. However that may be, this is a kingly sword, and the form and construction of its hilt exactly matches that of a sword made c.1340 for Edward III, even to the piece of ancient fabric in the pommel. Since that sword came out of Spain in the 1890s, controversy has dogged it, one school of antiquarian thought believing that it was indeed (with its companion dagger) made for Edward III, another school asserting with passion that it is a fake. Because of this, a great national treasure has been lost to the country of its origin, for it was believed in by a private collector in Germany, who bought it in 1984. (See Appendix D)

To return to the French sword. It is known that Philippe IV, le Bel, deposited one of his swords in Chartres Cathedral in 1308 together with his armour in gratitude for his victory in battle at Mons en Pouille. It was last recorded in that cathedral in the 18th century. It is probable that this is that sword.

XIV. 9

Type: XIV

Find-place: The Neuenburg lake, Switzerland

Collection: Schweizerisches Landesmuseum, Zurich (IN6982)

Blade-length: 27⅜" (69.5 cms)

Pommel-type: 1

Cross-style: 6

Date: c.1300

Condition: Very good. There is an inlay of well-formed marks on each side, in the fullers, a cross potent followed by a combined letter, either an n joined with an l, or a form of N alone, then a clear N S D followed by another cross potent. In various publications of this sword three separate variants of this inscription are given. Wegeli gives it correctly in his 'Inschriften' but in the small booklet issued by the Museum in 1957 it is wrongly given as N E S D, and in *Griffwaffen* of 1980 it is given as N S . I have used a photograph of Wegeli's interpretation, which accurately matches the actual figures on the sword. Wegeli dates it far too late, at the end of the 14th century instead of the more likely end of the 13th.

This inscription, by its style (four letters widely spaced) and the form of the letters, is extremely like the inscription on a type XVI sword (No. XVI.3 in this series) in Copenhagen, which must date at around the same time.

Publication: Wegeli; Haupt, Paul, *Schwerter und Degen* Bern, 1957; Schneider & Stuber, p.32, no.34.

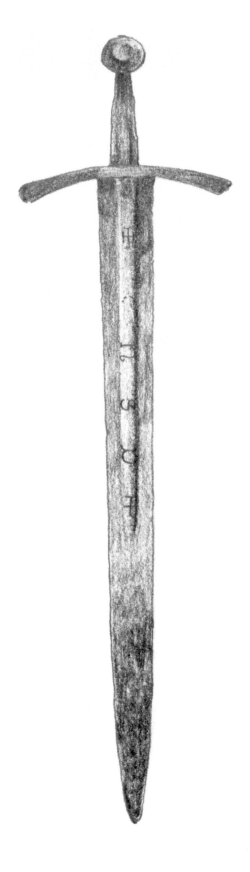

Type XV-XVa

he general outline, or silhouette, of this type is very much like that of Type XIV, but the section of the blade is totally different,
s is the prime function of the sword. The XIV's were made and used when most defensive armour was still mail, with or without
etal or leather of quilted reinforcement. The function of a XIV, like all it predecessors, was to be a slashing and hewing weapon.
. XV was meant to be able to deliver a lethal thrust, even though armour was largely of plate. It seems to have developed along
ith the development of plate armour. Here, however, I must add a rider. Many of the blades of swords in the period of the Celtic
on Age, particularly le Tène III, are of this same stiff, flattened diamond section with a prime function of thrusting. The long
oman Spatha, used by the anciliary cavalry, is of a form which, if found or seen out of context, could well be taken to be the
lade of a sword of Type XV or XVIII of the 14th or 15th century A.D., instead of between 200 B.C. and 400 A.D..

The illustrations and notes which follow will demonstrate the form and general appearance of the type and its long-gripped,
and-and-a-half subtype, which by the 15th century would be called an *espée bâtarde*, or Bastard Sword. With this type, unlike
ome of its predecessors, dating becomes impossible without some kind of firm evidence, preferably external or contextual, for
e type was popular from the late 13th century to the late 15th – indeed, the blade-form continued in use into the 19th century.
onsidering that we find it first in 3rd-century BC contexts, it must be the most long-lived blade form in the Western world.

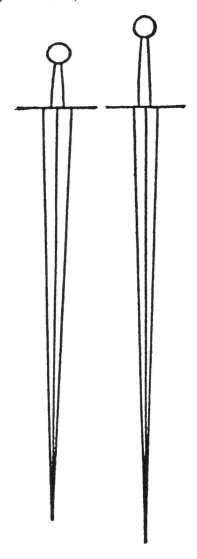

XV. 1

Type: XV
Find-place: Northern France
Collection: Wallace Collection, London (A.462)
Blade-length: 29 3⁄16" (74.5 cms)
Pommel-type: 1
Cross-style: 7
Date: This could be as early as c.1275, or as late as 1450.
Condition: River-found. Very good indeed. Very little pitting under the patina.
Publication: Mann & Norman; Oakeshott, *SAC*, pl.22a

This is a perfect example of a Type XV. In nearly perfect condition, it is a very handy and well-balance weapon. The form, of its hilt in particular, is one which is often seen in art as early as the mid-13th century (if not in fact before that) but was also obviously popular all through the 15th. It is akin – very clearly akin in a brotherly way – to some of the swords from the great hoard of 80 swords found in 1973 crated in the remains of a barge sunk in the River Dordogne near Castillon. Since these, by the marks upon some of them and by the distinctively dateable form of others and the context of their find-place cannot date to any period other than between c.1425-1460, it is very uncertain that this sword shown here is not of the same period. Yet it could be a century or more earlier. However, the boldly-struck smith's mark on the blade is almost identical with that on one of the Castillon swords, so the balance of probability has to swing towards the later date.

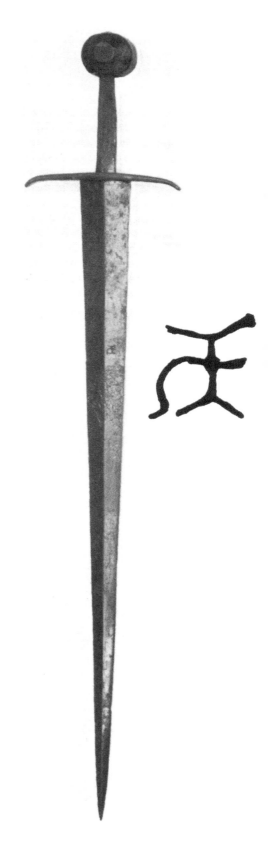

XV. 2-3

Type: XV
Find-place: The River Dordogne, near Castillon
Collection: Unknown ? Private
Blade-length: 36" (91.5 cms)
Pommel-type: V.2
Cross-style: 11, straight
Date: c.1410-50
Condition: River-found. The blade is badly corroded, but the hilt, particularly the pommel, is good.

Type: XV
Find-place: The Great Ouse, at Southery
Collection: Downing College, Cambridge, Museum of Archaeology and Ethnology
Blade-length: 35" (88.9 cms)
Pommel-type: J.1
Cross-style: 2
Date: c.1400-25
Condition: River-found. Good. Rather a heavy sword, about lbs.
Publication: Oakeshott in Stuber & Wertler; Oakeshott, *SAC* I.25

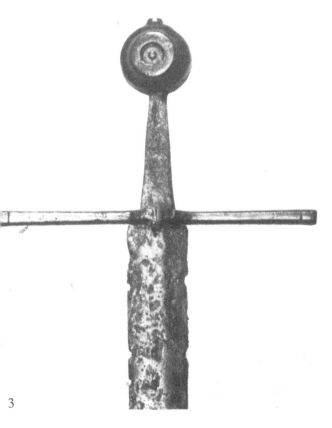

3

2   3

Type: XV
Find-place: Unknown
Collection: Private. Ex. author, ex Douglas Ash
Blade-length: 27" (68.5 cms)
Pommel-type: G.1
Cross-style: 10
Date: c.1470-1500
Condition: Excellent. Must have been preserved in an armoury or in a house, and cared for. The hilt retains most of its original blue colour, as well as its grip of ? lime wood covered with red velvet and bound with silver wire. This grip shows interesting marks of wear, the velvet covering being worn away where the heel of a hand has rubbed it and there is a good deal of hand-grease where it was gripped. There is a mark of a small cross inlaid in copper on the blade, which is of extremely thick section. Rather a heavy sword, well balanced for thrusting.
Publication: Oakeshott, *AOW* pl.19; Oakeshott, *SAC* pl.27b

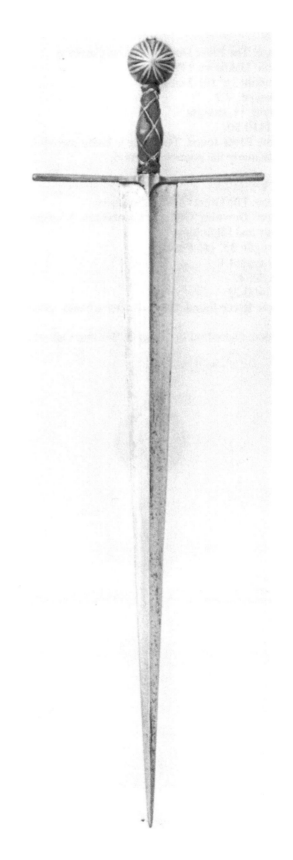

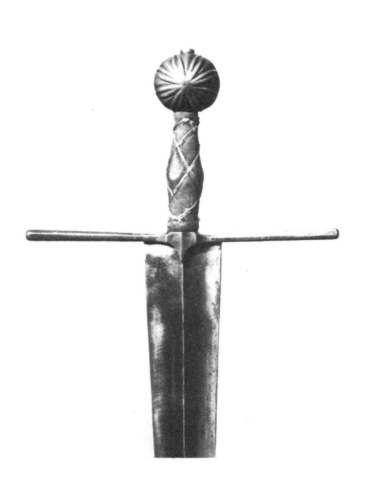

XV. 5

Type: XV
Find-place: The River Dordogne near Castillon
Collection: Private
Blade-length: 32" (81.2 cms)
Pommel-type: K, recessed
Cross-style: 8
Date: c.1420-50
Condition: River-found. Good. Some pitting on blade and erosion of edges near the hilt. There is a mark on the blade very similar indeed to the mark on the Type XV sword in the Wallace Collection, shown here at XV.1. Another of these Castillon swords, too, bears the same mark. This suggests a 15th, not a 13th century date for XV.1.
Publication: None

XV. 6

Type: XV
Find-place: The River Thames, when the foundations of West-minster Bridge were being prepared in 1742.
Collection: The Museum of London
Blade-length: 30" (76.2 cms)
Pommel-type: J
Cross-style: A rare style which I have not categorised, like a Style 9 with the ends turned up instead of down.
Date: Before c.1330
Condition: River-found. Good, but some deep pits in the blade; the hilt hardly pitted at all. All three silver scabbard-mounts survive, with inside them fragments of leather.
Publications: Too numerous to give all of them. Notably: Laking, Mann, J.G. 'Arms and Armour in England' (London, 1960). *The London Museum Medieval Catalogue* (1924), a small publication by The United Services Museum, 1921; and (of course) Oakeshott, *AOW* p.308, fig.149; Oakeshott, *SAC* p.138, fig.125

This important sword has been published and illustrated in nearly every book or article dealing with medieval arms, but because it is so important as a dating criterion and because of its marks and scabbard-mounts I make no apology for bringing it out yet again. The cross is unusual: there is another contemporary sword, found in France and illustrated in Laking (Vol.1) which has a similar one, and another appears on a sculptured Italian grave slab of 1397, to Tiberto Brandolini in the church of San Francesco at Bagnacavallo (illustrated in *Armi Bianche Italiane*, Boccia and Coelho, Nos. 80, 81, 82 and p.334). There are several others of this form shown in Italian paintings of the first half of the 15th century.

The silver mounts, the upper locket of which is engraved on the outside with a Stag's Head Caboshed and the motto 'Wist I, Wist I' give a firm date between say c.1320 and 1340, for it is clear from representations in art of all kinds, which can be firmly dated to these two decades, that this mode of suspension of the sword was fashionable in Europe, but not before and not after. Good examples are the sword of Can Grande della Scala (No. XII.6 here) who died, and had his sword buried with him, in 1329, and the tomb effigy of Sir Maurice Berkeley who died c.1330, in Bristol Cathedral. There is a mark on the blade which is repeated (clearly made by the same punch) on one of the central bosses of the pommel. Until recently, it would have been assumed that the presence of the same mark on blade and pommel indicated that the bladesmith made the hilt (an unlikely and I believe quite improper assumption) but recent research, presented in a doctoral thesis by a graduate of Nuremburg University, has shown that the marks stamped upon blades are the marks of the cutler who made the hilt and mounted the blade in it.

This sword seems to provide a very useful piece of hard evidence to support this thesis.

XV. 7

Type: XV
Find-place: Unknown
Collection: Wallace, Collection, London. A.460
Blade-length: 30" (76.2 cms)
Pommel-type: K, recessed
Cross-style: 7
Date: c.1350-1400
Condition: Very good, though severely cleaned and perhaps somewhat restored. The blade seems to have been cleaned by electrolysis, though it bears a large number of extremely long, deep and severe scratches, as though the patination had been posed by a chisel. The well-preserved cross and pommel are covered with a shiny black substance which looks like paint, but may be varnish over blueing (re-blueing). The grip, bound with cord, is covered with the same stuff, and may have been added when the sword was cleaned when it was in the collection of the Comte de Nieuwekerke.

have put it under Type XV, for that is its present shape, but the blade has obviously been severely honed, so it may originally have been a Type XVIII.
Publications: Mann & Norman; Seitz; Oakeshott, *SAC* pl.35a; Hoffmeyer. pl.25b and p.26, no.23

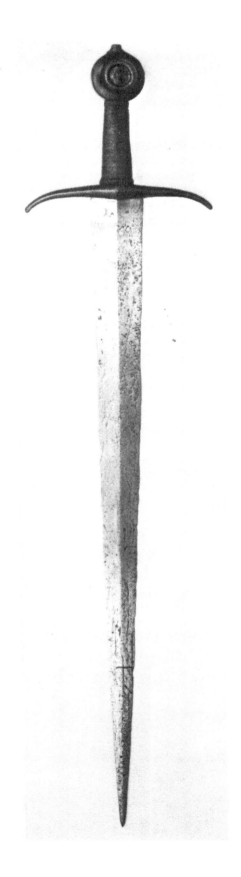

XV. 8

Type: XV
Find-place: River Dordogne near Castillon
Collection: Private
Blade-length: 30¼" (76.7 cms)
Pommel-type: K, recessed
Cross-style: 8
Date: c.1420-50
Condition: River-found. Excellent. Some pitting on the blade surfaces, large nick on one edge has been filled. The pommel and cross are in particularly good condition.
Publication: Oakeshott, in Stuber & Wetler

This sword, like others in this Castillon find, is very much like No.XV.1 in this series. In silhouette they are hardly distinguishable one from the other. However, I have included this because I am far more closely acquainted with it, with the look and feel of it, than any of the other though I handled most of them. This one is a perfect cut-and-thrust weapon, light and quick in the hand and beautifully balanced. In the centre of the recesses in the pommel are what look for all the world like the well-formed heads of rivets, as if a rivet had been driven transversely through from one side to the other, through the top of the tang as a sort of belt-and-braces means of securing the pommel. However, long and minute examination of this has led me to reject the rivet theory. I believe these well-formed, truly circular domed features are simply particularly well-made examples of the small raised lumps, often very roughly shaped, which were left inside these recesses to form a key for the glue or mastic which held any decorative disc of silver or enamel in place. There is a long note about the use of glue in the securing of such decorative plaques in these recessed pommels under Type XVIII.1 below, so I won't go into it here except to say that there is absolutely overwhelming evidence that glue, and/or a good force fit, was all that was used in these 14th and early 15th century recessed pommels not, as has so often been insisted upon by experts in the teeth of all the contrary evidence, that such decorative discs were held in by the burring-over of the edges of the rims of these recesses. There are no surviving recessed iron pommels of this form that show any sign at all of undercutting or turning-over but there is considerable concrete evidence – proof, in some cases – for the use of glue, for in a few swords (i.e. Nos. XV.1 and XV.12 below) the actual glue survives and can be clearly seen, in the case of XV.12 where on one side of the pommel the glue remains in the recess, with the imprint of the decorative disc still upon it and where on the other side the glue can be seen around the edges of the surviving disc (in this case a copper coin of the Duke of Urbino).

XV.9

Type: XV
Find-place: Unknown
Collection: Metropolitan Museum of Art, New York
Blade-length: 29" (73.7 cms)
Pommel-type: K
Cross-style: 8, curved
Date: c.1400-50
Condition: Not excavated, but preserved indoors. The blade shows a lot of quite deep overall surface pitting as if it had been allowed to get very rusty; but the hilt of gilt-bronze with horn grip is in near perfect condition.

The very elegant grip of dark greenish-black horn is held by long vertical fillets of gilt-bronze along each edge. It is a most elegant, useful sword which has had doubts cast upon its authentic age, being held by some authorities to be a 19th century fake.

Publication: New York, Metropolitan Museum Bulletin
Oakeshott, *SAC*, pl.23 and 24

Type: XV
Find-place: Unknown
Collection: Philadelphia Art Museum, ex. Kienbusch, Londesborough and Bernal Collections.
Blade-length: 30" (76.2 cms)
Pommel-type: V.1
Cross-style: A slender 5
Date: c.1480-1510
Condition: Perfect. This superb sword, which the Earl of Londesborough bought at the Bernal sale in 1859, came into Mr K.O. von Kienbusch's hand in the 1950s. He wrote to me, sending these photographs, when he had got it, and said he had never gone overboard to the same extent over any other sword. There is some fine etching, incorporating a heraldic rose (ii) and a hunting-horn, on the forte of the blade, and a very handsome stamped smiths/cutlers mark which shows well in the photograph at (iii). So does the very lightly-stained surface of the blade. The grip survives. Since it was in position just as it is shown here in 1859 (for it is carefully described in the Bernal Catalogue) it is unlikely to be a modern replacement. It is bound with red cord, overlaid with a rather complicated sort of net of a slightly thicker cord.

There is a painting of St George by Piero della Francesca dated 1424, which shows an identical (and I mean identical, not similar) hilt, so maybe the sword itself should be dated to the first quarter of the 15th century, not to the last. The etched decoration might very well have been added (as such decoration so often was) late in the century to an earlier sword. Certainly it is a weapon of such grace, beauty and efficiency that it would very naturally be cherished, embellished and used long after the time of its making.
Publication: Laking, Vol.1.

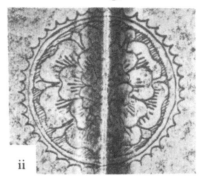

ii

iii

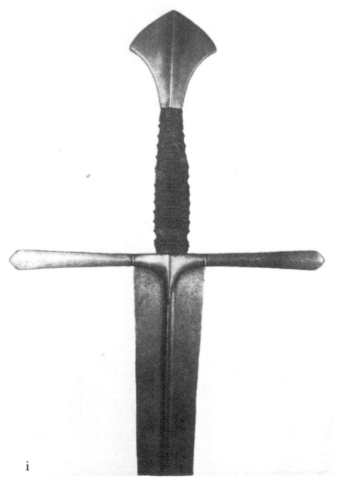

i

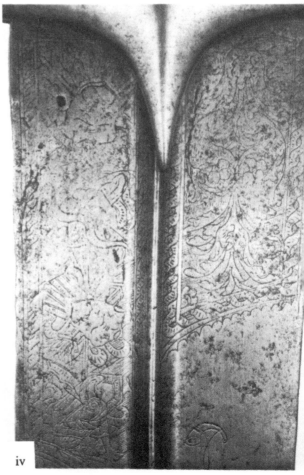

iv

XV. 11

Type: XV
Find-place: The River Dordogne near Castillon
Collection: Private
Blade-length: 28" (71 cms)
Pommel-type: A form of J.1
Cross-style: 8
Date: c.1400
Condition: Good, but a number of very deep nicks on the edges, caused I think by corrosion, not wear. The blade is a fine, well-formed and stout one with a strong midrib and flat faces. One side is well-preserved, but on the other are large areas of deep and serious corrosion. At some time, maybe in the blade's working life, it has been broken and re-welded – this shows up in the photograph as a light band across the blade just half-way down. There are no blade-marks. The pommel is unusual (see sketch at (ii) of its profile) and it has a rather ornate rivet-block at the top made integrally with the pommel. It is in the shape of a golf tee, or perhaps more nearly, a ludo piece. Rivet blocks of this kind are to be seen on Scottish swords and in Spanish MS illustrations of the period c.1380-1425.
The cross is particularly well-made, of bold and elegant form, almost in perfect condition on one side (as shown in the photograph) but rather corroded on the other. There are considerable remains of the wooden core of the grip left sticking to the tang, together with some sort of mastic up under the pommel and into the aperture where the tang goes in.

XV. 12

Type: XV
Find-place: Unknown. Probably in Italy.
Collection: Private.
Blade-length: 31" (78.8 cms)
Pommel-type: J, recessed
Cross-style: 8
Date: c.1380-1410
Condition: Very good. Obviously cared for in an armoury. There is a scattering of light, small circular rust-pits all over the blade, with rather larger patches on the pommel. The wood core of the old grip, now treated with hardener, survives and there is a copper coin of the Duke of Urbino glued into the recess on one side of the pommel. This is not a modern replacement; there can be no question that it is not contemporary with the making of the pommel. There used to be a similar insert on the other side. Here you can see plainly the ancient glue or mastic which secured it, still bearing the circular impression where the coin or enamelled disc was fixed. This pommel provides absolutely incontrovertible evidence that such inserts were glued into these pommels. There is a neat mark engraved and once inlaid in silver, a trace of which remains, on each side of the blade, a cross patée within a circle.

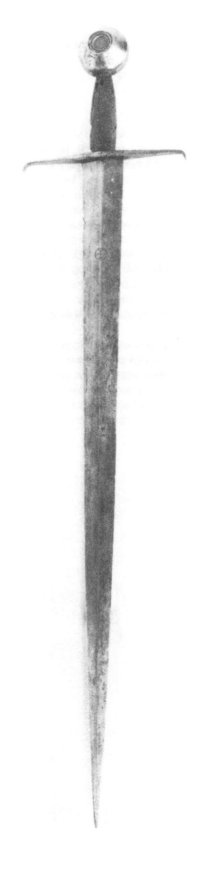

XV. 13

Type: XV

Find-place: The Cathedral, Monza

Collection: The Treasury of the Basilica of San Giovanni Battista, Monza

Blade-length: 27⅞" (71 cms)

Pommel-type: T.3

Cross-Style: 8

Date: Before 1413

Condition: Very well preserved. It was found in or before 1698 in the coffin of Estorre Visconti (Lord of Milan 1412-13). The metal of the hilt is very well preserved, covered only with a smooth brown patina; the grip of wood is bound with a single strand of twisted copper wire which retains traces of gilding. Over the mid-point of the cross is a rain-guard of silver, one side of which has been lost since it was recorded in 1915. This rain-guard is decorated with floral designs with a border formed by two plaited tresses of hair each with a tassel at its end. This indicates that Estorre was a member of the Fellowship of the Tress (Zopfgesellschaft), a knightly association founded by the Archduke Albrecht III of Austria (1365-95) who was popularly known as 'Albrecht with the Tress'. The blade is covered with an evenly distributed patina of very small pits under a smooth brown film as on the hilt. The sword is light and very well balanced.

Publication: Blair, C. *EAA*; *ZHWK* January, 1963; Boccia & Coelho, No.85; Oakeshott, *SAC* pl.21 and 22b

XVa. 1

Type: XVa
Find-place: Lake of Lucerne
Collection: The Royal Armouries. Ex collection Sir Edward Barry
Blade-length: 32" (81.2 cms) approximately
Pommel-type: J
Cross-style: 8
Date: c.1350-70
Condition: Poor. There is a lot of deep pitting underneath the patina, but the old grip survives though the metal of the hilt is badly corroded, as is the lower one-third of the blade. An extremely similar sword, in the same kind of condition though lacking the grip was found in the Thames in London, and is now in the collection of the Society of Antiquaries at Burlington House in London. This form of sword seems to have been fashionable in the 14th century, judging by the number of survivors, all as alike as peas in a pod.
Publication: Laking, *Connoisseur*, February, 1905. Dufty.

XVa. 2

Type: XVa
Find-place: Unknown, but almost certainly a tomb
Collection: Glasgow Museum A recent acquisition
Blade-length: 31" (79 cms)
Pommel-type: J. recessed
Cross-style: 8
Date: c.1320-40

Condition: Very good. It is clear from the patination of its surfaces that it came from a tomb, very probably from the coffin. If you compare its patination with that of the sword of Estorre Visconti, (No.XV.13 above) the similarity is plain to see. There is a little rust-staining, with a few patches of light pitting. The wooden core of the orginal grip survives as well as the outside part of the iron rain-guard, round the edges of which is a delicate design inlaid in gold, much of which survives. On the other side, where the down-turned flap has gone, there is an area of the top of the blade from which the dark patina of the coffin's atmosphere has, very wisely, not been cleaned away as it has on all the rest of the metal surfaces (except the surviving flap of the rain-guard). On the upper part of the blade, more prominent on the side where the rain-guard survives, there are very clear 'ghost' or 'negative' marks of differential corrosion where the metal mounts of the scabbard (which, by inference, was too perished to retain when the sword was brought out) used to be. This can be seen plainly here in photograph (i).

These marks are of outstanding importance, for they show a style of sword-suspension – i.e. of an upper and lower metal socket some 6" (15 cms) apart, with a ring on the forward side of the upper one and the rear side of the lower – which seems only to have been in use between, at extremes, c.1310 and 1350. This gives a sword which otherwise by its style would be dated c.1360-1400 the more certainly established earlier date of c.1310-50. A very close parallel to this sword in a work of art is the sword shown on the brass of Sir John de Creke in the church at Westley Waterless in Cambridgeshire. This is dated stylistically at c.1340-45. The two swords, the real one and the represented one, are extremely alike except that Sir John's sword's cross is shorter and plain at the ends. The definite cusp at the mid-point of this cross is more than likely a representation of a rain-guard as on this survivor. Datable examples of this form of suspension are to be seen on the little sword of Don Juan, el de Tarifa, who was killed in 1317, and the one in the coffin of Can Grande della Scala of Verona, who was buried in 1329 (Nos. XII.6 and XIIIb.1 above.)

In every way this is a sword not only of outstanding quality and beauty, but of great value as a dating-point by reason of the indications of the scabbard-mounts; but also because the marks on the blade (shown here at v) are made by the same punch as those on the blade of a sword in the Bayerische Nationalmuseum (XXa.1 below) – a sword in very nearly a pristine condition with very interesting inscriptions on its blade, and literally no rust-marks to mar its gleaming surface. This is of a style which is always confidently dated, by comparison with representations in art of similar sword-hilts, at around 1380-1410.

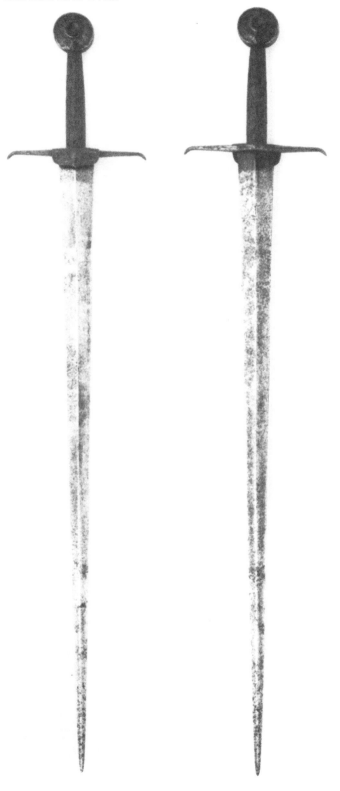

141

XVa. 3-5

Type: XVa
Find-place: The River Dordogne near Castillon
Collection: The Royal Armouries, H.M. Tower of London
Blade-length: 37" (94 cms)
Pommel-type: T.5
Cross-style: 11, straight
Date: c.1420-60
Condition: Good in parts. The hilt and upper blade are comparatively free from serious pitting, but the lower quarter of the blade is very seriously perished. This sword is considerably larger than the others in this hoard.

Type: XVa
Find-place: Castillon
Collection: Private
Blade-length: 34" (86.4 cms)
Pommel-type: A variant of V

Cross-style: 11, straight and short
Date: c.1420-60
Condition: Quite good. A few deep pits, but a number of very deep nicks in the edges of the blade. There is considerable corrosion on one side of the cross. There are remains of a leather rain-guard at the mid-point of the cross.

5. Type: XVa
Find-place: Castillon
Collection: ? Private
Blade-length: 33" (83.9 cms)
Pommel-type: V.2
Cross-style: 11, straight, short
Date: c.1420-60
Condition: Good, except for some extremely large nicks in the edges.
Publication: Oakeshott, in Stuber & Wetler

3

4

5

143

XVa. 6

Type: XVa
Find-place: In 1946, in a house sale, place unknown.
Collection: Private
Blade-length: 34" (86.2 cms)
Cross-style: 8
Date: c.1370
Condition: Poor. Considerably restored, for some two-thirds of the blade was broken off and rotted when it was found in a very distressed condition on the floor with a bundle of walking-sticks in a house-sale in 1945 or 1946. The hilt and the upper one-third of the blade was in good condition, with the wooden core of the original grip, but the broken piece of the blade was far too gone to be welded back on to the stump. So a completely new piece was made, using the old bit as a template. The cross and pommel have been blackened, and a new grip put on. This is most unfortunate. The then owner of the sword was unhappy with the rather tatty old grip, and caused it to be replaced in the workshop of the Armouries at the Tower of London. Sadly, the old, original grip was thrown away. However, there was a photograph taken before this unhappy event – not a good one, but at least it shows the rather unusual shape of the grip. (iv). Very careful and deep research leads inexorably to the possibility, even probability, that this is the sword which until the time of the Commonwealth (1649-1660) hung above the tomb of Edward, Prince of Wales, The Black Prince, in Canterbury Cathedral. It will never be possible to prove that it really is this sword, but the very powerful evidence makes it totally impossible to prove that it is not. It is of the right date; it is in the right sort of condition to have been hanging in the Cathedral from the time of the Prince's funeral in 1376 until, some time in the 1650s, it was stolen. The corrosion on the upper part of the blade exactly matches that on the surface of the helm, which still survives there; the blade, restored though it is, fits the remains of the scabbard and on the blade is stamped a cutler's mark of a fleur-de-lys crowned within an escutcheon. This figure was used as a royal badge by the later Plantagenets and all the Tudor monarchs, and up to the early 17th century was a mark used upon sword-blades to indicate that the cutler had a 'By Appointment' privilege to a Royal House, in the same way as in 16th century Spain the words *Espadero de Rey* (Sword maker to the King) had the same significance. There can be little doubt that this sword is the one lost from the Cathedral – legend has it that Cromwell himself took it away – but since it cannot be proved positively to be so, it has not been possible to restore it to its proper place. Although, it being in my possession, I made sincere efforts to present it – or rather, to return it, to the Cathedral; the Dean and Chapter preferred not to accept it. So it remains with me.

ii

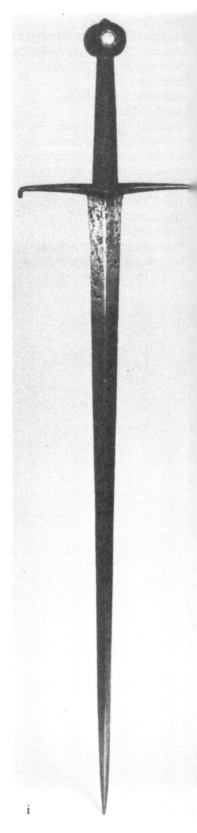

i

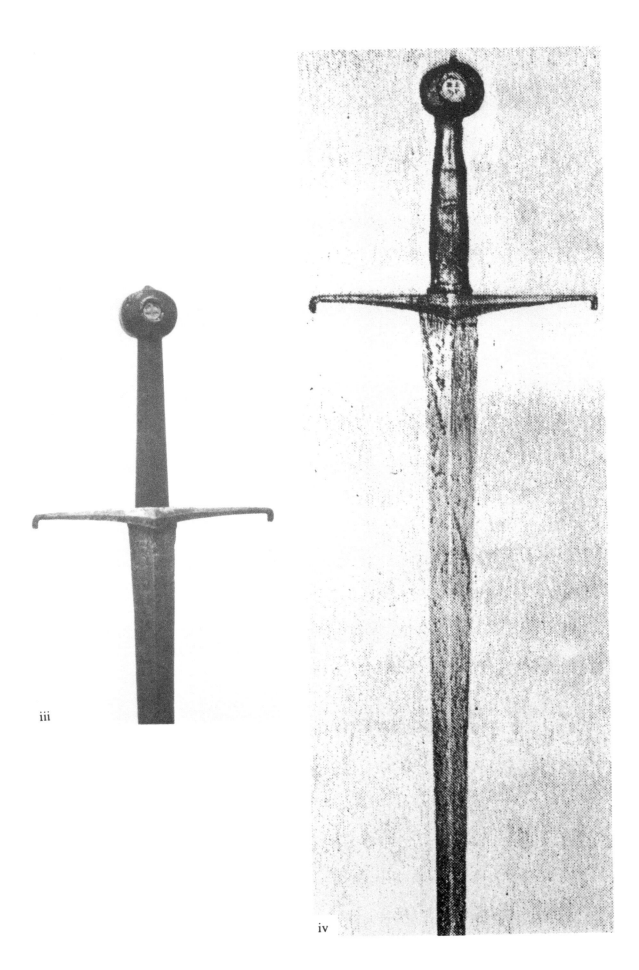

iii

iv

Type XVI-XVIa

It is possible, indeed, it seems inevitable, to suggest that this blade-form developed as a direct offensive answer to the newly-developed reinforced mail armour of the period 1300-1350. It is broad enough, and flat enough in section, to provide an efficient cutting edge, but the lower part below the end of the fuller is nearly always of a stiff flattened-diamond section with a strong median ridge, making it suitable for thrusting. Not all have this ridged lower blade, which makes it very difficult if not sometimes impossible to distinguish whether such a blade is a XVI, or in fact a XIV; No. XVIa.1 in this group is a case in point, its lower blade tapers strongly, though it is flat, but it has a very stout diamond-section reinforced point.

They are quite often shown in art. Sometimes, as in the two shown here at (iii) and (iv), from Italian early 14th century paintings at San Gimignano, they can be matched exactly by survivors – except that they are shown scabbarded. All we have to go on is the long, rather slender, tapering blades and long grips. Compare these two, for instance, with the photograph of the hilt of No. XVI.2 below. A sculptured St. Peter at (v), from a roof-boss in Exeter Cathedral which can be dated to 1328 shows a perfect example of the type, closely matched by No.XVI.3 below.

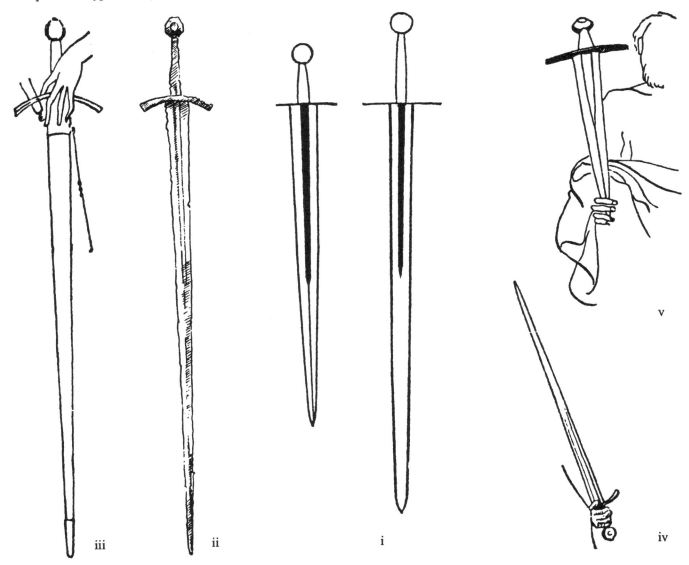

iii   ii   i   v   iv

XVI. 1

Type: XVI
Find-place: London River, off Westminster opposite the Houses of Parliament
Collection: Formerly the old London Museum, now The Royal Armouries IX.13
Blade-length: 27" (68.6 cms)
Pommel-type: 1
Cross-style: A long 7
Date: c.1300-25
Condition: River-found. Excellent some pitting and erosion of the edges near the point and below the cross. Compare this sword with the drawing of the St Peter from the Exeter roof-boss, which was carved before 1328.
Publication: Dufty; Oakeshott, *Catalogue of the Second Park Lane Arms Fair*, London, 1983.

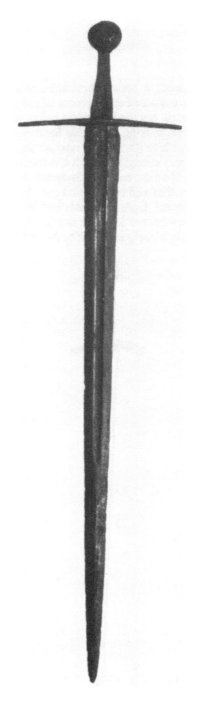

XVI. 2

Type: XVI
Find-place: Unknown
Collection: Royal Armouries, IX.1083 formerly D'Acre Edwards
Blade-length: 32" (81.2 cms) approximately
Pommel-type: J
Cross-style: 2
Date: c.1300-25
Condition: Excavated, almost certainly river-found. Very good though there is a lot of corrosion at the point-end of the blade. The cross is very slightly bent, up one arm and down the other. The metal of the cross is very stout, of square section, and it has always seemed to me when handling this sword that this very shallow reverse curvature couldn't have been made by accident; it must, I think, have been forged that way – though one cannot assume that, in the forging, the bend was deliberate. It is too shallow to have a 'guarding' effect like 16th century vertically recurved quillons; but the process of forging a carefully shaped bar of iron, with a slot in the middle, is a tricky business and an inadvertent bend could very easily occur. There is some distortion to the tang, too.
Publication: Dufty.

XVI. 3

Type: XVI
Find-place: Unknown, but in Denmark
Collection: Nationalmuseet, Copenhagen
Blade-length: 30⅛" (76.5 cms)
Pommel-type: T.1
Cross-style: 6
Date: c.1300-50
Condition: River-found? Excellent. The erosion on the edges of the blade is the result of wear and honing, not corrosion. The fuller bears a neat four-letter inscription inlaid in latten. This inscription is similar to that upon the blade of the big XIIIa in the Burrell Collection in Glasgow, shown here above at XIIIa.10.
There is a sword extremely similar to this – its hilt is identical, though its blade is about 6" longer, in the Museum at Bern (inv. No.840). That one, however, has no inscription.
Publication: Hoffmeyer; Pl.XXXIId.2 p.34 no.1 Oakeshott, *SAC* pl.20b

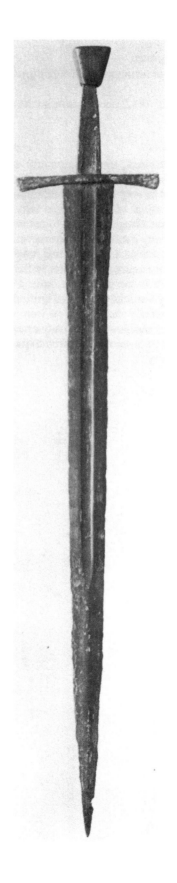

XVI.4

Type: XVI
Find-place: Unknown
Collection: Once my own, then Douglas Ash; then Howard Curtis, now?
Blade-length: 21" (53.4 cms)
Pommel-type: 1
Cross-style: A very sharply curved variant of 1
Date: c.1300-25
Condition: River-found, almost perfect. When I had this little sword, it retained its rich purple-brown patina of Goethite, but Douglas Ash cleaned it off, as can be seen in the photograph. This is an excellent example of the small, efficient, knightly 'Riding Sword'. An identical one is shown on two early 14th century effigies in Germany. (i), of Arnold I Landgraf of Cleve, +1320 in the Stiftskirche at Cleve, and (ii), of one of the hero-figures, c.1308, in the Rathaus at Cologne. Not only are the hilts of the swords on these figures exactly the same as this sword, but the *size* is too, more proof (if any more is needed, which it shouldn't be) that these short swords were not made for boys, or archers etc., but for knights and in this case, great nobles.

Publication: Oakeshott, *Catalogue of the Second Park Lane Arms Fair*, 1983.

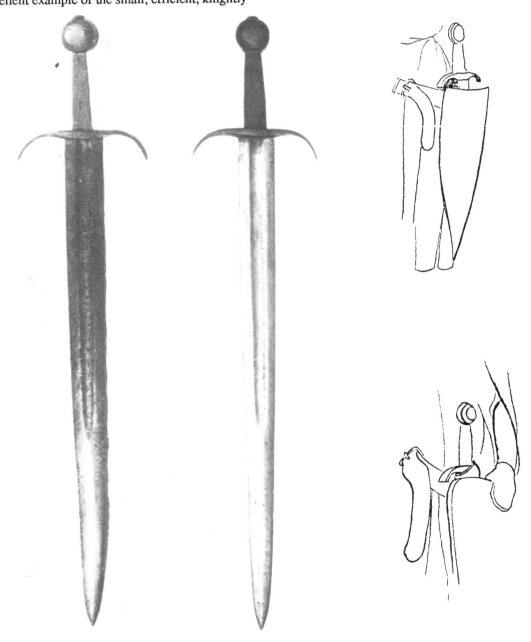

151

XVIa. 1

Type: XVIa
Find-place: London, below foundations of a building
Collection: British Museum, now Royal Armouries
Blade-length: 33" (83.8 cms)
Pommel-type: K
Cross-style: A short Style 11, straight
Date: c.1300-40
Condition: Excavated; but considering that it was found in
more or less dry soil, not river mud, it has very little corrosion.
In 1942 it was almost destroyed, while in the British Museum,
by an incendiary bomb which fell into one of the old Medieval
Galleries. It was bent into a strong s-shape by the heat of the
fire, and its patination turned to an orange-and-red colour.
This is how it was when I first saw it in 1950. It was taken to
the Tower of London armoury workshop in 1974 and restored
to its former shape and colouration.
Publication: Oakeshott, *AOW*; pl.16b Oakeshott, *SAC* pl.28a

This is an exceptionally fine sword. The section of the blade
is very stout, hexagonal, with a deep and well-marked fuller
running just over half-way to the point, which is strongly
reinforced. The stout tang bears a very well-made cutler's or
bladesmith's stamp, a fleur-de-lys within an escutcheon,
placed with the base of the shield towards the pommel. This
also is very well-made, with a neat pyramidical rivet-block.
The short, stubbed cross with clubbed ends is not of a common
variety, so much so that I did not include it in my classification. There is an almost identical sculptured example in Westminster Abbey, on the perfectly preserved effigy of John of
Eltham, who died in 1326, a younger brother of Edward III.
The photograph reproduced here was taken in the British
Museum before the war.

XVIa. 2

Type: XVIa
Find-place: Unknown
Collection: Otto von Kienbusch, now Museum of Art, Philadelphia
Blade-length: ? I assume about 32" (81.4 cms)
Pommel-type: J
Cross-style: 7
Date: c.1300-25
Condition: Excavated. ? River-found. Good. Some deep pitting. I have never seen this sword, nor even a photograph of the whole blade, so I only assume that it is a XVI, not a XII. The shape of the hilt, however, is so closely akin to an undoubted XVI (which I have seen) once in the collection of M. Charles Boissonas in Switzerland, and to those shown in the frescoes by Lippo Memmi in San Gimignano that I believe the assumption that this is a XVI is reasonable. The central boss of the pommel, which doesn't show very clearly in the photograph, is oval, not circular.
Publication: Hayward.

153

XVIa. 3

Type: XVIa
Find-place: Borringholm in Denmark
Collection: Nationalmuseet, Copenhagen
Blade-length: 35 ¾" (91.1 cms)
Pommel-type: A rather exaggerated K
Cross-style: A rather exaggerated 6
Date: c.1300-25
Condition: Excavated (? river found). Very good. There is a good deal of corrosion on the blade, but not much on the hilt. The original grip survives in surprisingly good condition, though the wood core below the cord binding and leather covering has perished a good deal. The most interesting feature is the intact survival of the leather rain-guard.
There is a very similar sword, with a less acutely-tapering blade, in the Oldsaksmuseum in Oslo. (Illustrated in Hoffmeyer, Plate XX.9)
Publication: Hoffmeyer; Pl.20c p.17 no.23; Oakeshott, *SAC* Pl.47

XVIa. 4

Type: XVI
Find-place: Unknown, but in Denmark
Collection: Nationalmuseet, Copenhagen
Blade-length: 31" (78.8 cms)
Pommel-type: 1
Cross-style: J
Date: c.1290-1320
Condition: Excavated (? River found). Very good. The blade is of the same stout, crisp section with a deep fuller as No.XVI.1 above.

XVIa. 5

Type: XVIa
Find-place: ? Germany
Collection: The Royal Armouries. IX.1084. Formerly D'Acre
Edwards
Blade-length: 33" (83.9 cms)
Pommel-type: K
Cross-style: 6
Date: c.1300-25
Condition: Excavated. ? River found. Good, but considerable
erosion of the edges and some deep pitting on the blade. The
grip, of white wood, is modern. The shape of this sword should
be compared with that of No.XVI.1 in this series. The fuller
here is very narrow, but there is a distinct rib in the lower half
of the blade.
Publication: Dufty,

Type XVII

With the coming of this sword-type, we have reached the era of complete plate armour. Though, of course, complete and homogeneous armour would not have been worn in its entirety, or even at all, by all men-at-arms, knights or otherwise. Mail, and occasional reinforcements of plate, or plain leather was often the only defense of the European man-at-arms. All the same, a type of sword had been devised to have some sort of capacity to deal with, at least to dent and hopefully to bore holes in, complete plate armour. These swords which I have classified as Type XVII had always a long hand-and-a-half grip, and a very stout blade of hexagonal section, occasionally with a shallow fuller, and often very heavy and always very rigid and stiff.

The first two swords I show in this section are very familiar to me, and though their blades at least look extremely alike, there is a great difference in weight and balance. The first, XVII.1 is in the Fitzwilliam Museum in Cambridge, where I frequently handle it, and the second, XVII.2, now in the Nationalmuseet in Copenhagen, once hung upon my own wall. The Cambridge one is surprisingly light and responsive in the hand, weighing only just over 2lbs; but the one I had is heavy, even clumsy – a sort of bar of iron, point-heavy and needing a lot of strength to use.

There are many survivors of this type, nearly all of them alike and most not all that handsome. I have shown a few representative examples of a very large class of survivors, those which for some reason seem more interesting (such as those which have long 'ricassos') than the general run of what is on the whole rather a boring type.

XVII. 1

Type: XVII
Find-place: The River Great Ouse at Ely in Cambridgeshire
Collection: The Fitzwilliam Museum, Cambridge
Blade-length: 36" (82 cms)
Pommel-type: T.2
Cross-style: 1, curved
Date: c.1370-1400
Condition: River-found. Almost perfect beneath the smooth, richly dark patina of Goethite. There is no significant pitting in any part. On the tang is stamped a large lombardic letter B and on the blade, in the shallow fuller, is a little dagger-mark inlaid in latten (or, possibly, gold?)
Publication: Redfern, W.B. 'Some Choice Sword-Hilts', *Connoisseur*, 1923; Laking, vol.I; Oakeshott, *AOW*; Oakeshott, *SAC*; Oakeshott, 'Arms and Armour in the Fitzwilliam Museum', *Apollo* 1987.

This is a superb sword, in perfect condition, and is the leading example of what has come to be called the 'Sempach' family of swords, after two which were found in 1898 in the graves of two of the Austrian knights, Friedrich von Tarant and Friedrich von Griffenstein, who fell in the battle fought near Sempach (near Zurich) in 1386. Similar dagger-marks are to be seen (a) on a superb XIIa sword (No. XIIa.2 above) in an English private collection and (b) on the great two-hand sword of Edward III in St. George's Chapel at Windsor. This dates c.1350, and the former from perhaps as early as 1300. Similar, though not identical, dagger-marks appear on the Sempach swords from the abbey of Konigsfield, and on a Type XVIII sword (XVIII.5 below) in an English private collection, and on another sword of the same 'family' found in the lake of Neuchâtel. (XVII.7)

This sword in Cambridge, as familiar to me now in 1989 as if it was in my own collection, is quite surprisingly light, and is beautifully balanced and 'ready' in the hand.

There is a legend, written in horrible white paint, on the side of the blade not shown outward, to the effect that it was found 'in 1845 in the River Cam at Ely'. This is a geographical impossibility. The river at Ely is the Great Ouse; the Cam joins it about 4 miles above Ely, so if it was found in the Cam, it wasn't at Ely; if it was found at Ely, it wasn't in the Cam; but it doesn't matter. The mud of both rivers has the same excellently preservative properties, and a difference of a few miles makes no difference to the sword's excellence. The only difference perhaps is that at Ely the river could, even in the late 14th century, be approached in order to throw a sword in; but where the Cam joins it, in those days it was all marsh and impenetrable scrub land.

It was in a great private collection, owned by an industrialist named Redfern, until it was bought by the Friends of the Fitzwilliam Museum in 1947, and has always before been published as The Redfern Sword. A pity, it should be The Ely Sword, but I supose it is now too well established under its ephemeral collector's name to be altered.

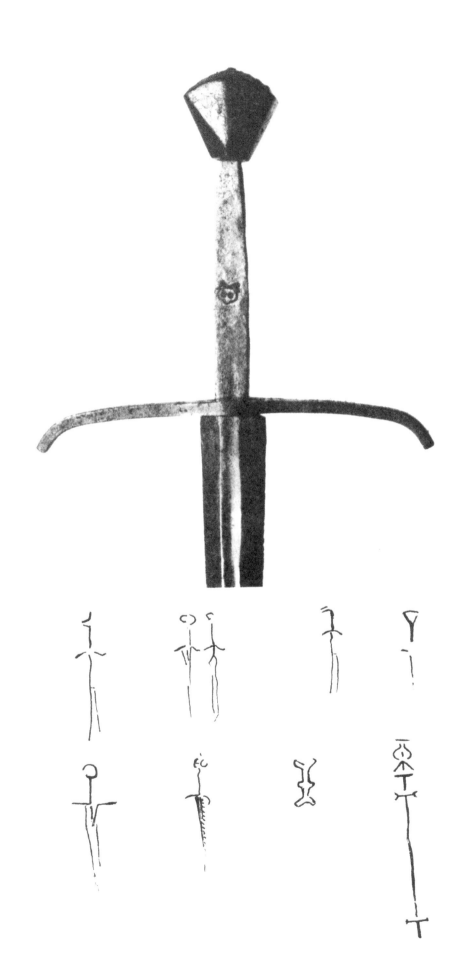

XVII.2

Type: XVII
Find-place: Unknown
Collection: Once my own. Sold to Mr. E.A. Christensen of Copenhagen, now in the Nationalmuseet in that city.
Blade-length: 34¼" (87 cms)
Pommel-type: H.1
Cross-style: 6
Date: c.1360-90
Condition: River-found, by the look of it. Excellent. Very slight pitting here and there. The colour is unusual – purple, with most of the blade an almost peacock blue. There is a mark – a crozier – inlaid in copper in the blade, and a mark in the tang, which looks as if it was cut with a chisel, of double crossed strokes. When I had it, the blade had a considerable bend, in the plane of the blade, as if when it was in the water there was something heavy pressing above it. The Tower of London armoury workshop tried to straighten it cold, but we didn't risk too much pressure. Heat would have done the job, but might have destroyed the gorgeous colour, so I left it as it was. I don't know how it is now.
Publication: Christensen & Hoffmeyer; p.80 n.52; Oakeshott, *AOW*; Oakeshott, *SAC*; Blair, C. No.36

This is a fine sword, whose condition is so like that of the Ely sword. It is a complete contrast as regards its weight and 'feel' in the hand. When I weighed it, after I had bought it in 1952, it was, surprisingly, nearly four pounds. This is very heavy, even for a XVII. It was clumsy, too, the point of balance nearly half-way to the point. The Ely sword only weighs 1.15 kg. (which is 2 lbs) and as I said, feels very lively in the hand.

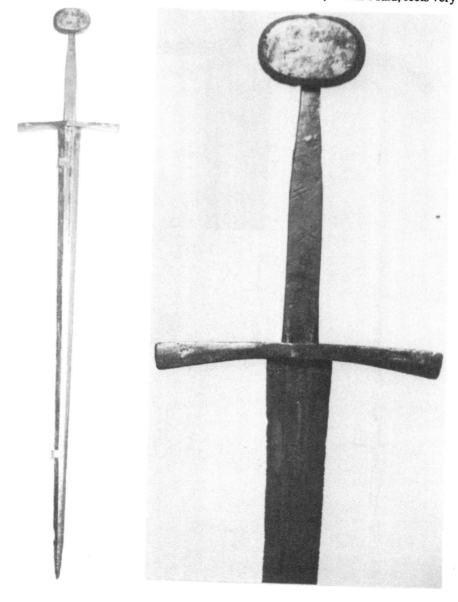

XVII.3

Type: XVII
Find-place: Unknown
Collection: Ex Otto von Kienbusch, now Museum of Art, Philadelphia
Blade-length: I don't know – I would think about 35" (80 cms)
Pommel-type: H.1
Cross-style: 1
Date: c.1360-1400
Condition: Excavated. Not very good. A great deal of pitting.
Publication: Hayward

XVII.4

Type: XVII
Find-place: Unknown
Collection: Ex Otto von Kienbusch. Now Museum of Art,
Philadelphia
Blade-length: At a guess, 36" (82 cms)
Pommel-type: H.2
Cross-style: 1, curved
Date: c.1360-90
Condition: Excavated (? river-found). Good, but considerable
pitting. There is a good mark on the blade, inlaid in copper on
each side and on the tang chisel-marks similar to those on
XVII.2.
Publication: Hayward,

XVII. 5

Type: XVII
Find-place: Unknown
Collection: Formerly Mr. E.A. Christensen; now Nationalmuseet, Copenhagen
Blade-length: 36½" (92.7 cms)
Pommel-type: H.2
Cross-style: 2
Date: c.1380-1420
Condition: Excellent. Indoor (armoury) preservation. There is an Arabic inscription in Nashki script on the blade giving a date of A.D. 1436-7. There is a cross potent inlaid in copper in the pommel. Perhaps the sword of a Templar – though by the probable date of its making, say 1380, the Templars had been destroyed for over 60 years. The grip is a modern replacement.
Publication: Christensen & Hoffmeyer, p.82, no.57; Hoffmeyer, pl.XXe, p.17, no.27; Oakeshott, *SAC* pl.30b

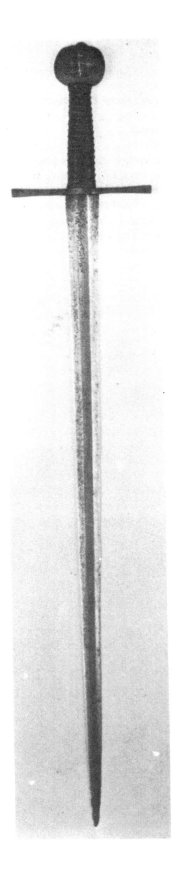

XVII. 6

Type: XVII
Find-place: Unknown
Collection: Formerly Otto von Kienbusch. Now Museum of Art, Philadelphia
Blade-length: I don't know for certain; about 40"
Pommel-type: T.5
Cross-style: 1, curved
Date: c.1380-1425
Condition: Probably river-found, but not certain. Good. Some pitting. Interesting heraldic (personal) mark stamped on tang, an escutcheon with a bordure, a fess and two bezants above and one below: (in chief two bezants a fess and in base one bezant within a bordure). This seems certainly to be a personal blazon, *not* a maker's stamp.
Publication: Hayward,

XVII. 7

Type: XVII
Find-place: The lake at Neuchâtel, Switzerland
Collection: Zurich, Landesmuseum IN 6977
Blade-length: 30" (76.2 cms)
Pommel-type: T.2
Cross-style: 1, curved
Date: c.1360-90
Condition: Water-found, very good with a lot of pitting on the hilt. One of the 'Sempach' family. It bears a little dagger-mark (ii) similar to those on the Konigsfeld swords, and the Ely one.
Publication: Schneider & Stuber; Oakeshott, E. *Catalogue of the Fourth Park Lane Arms Fair*, London, 1987.

XVII. 8

Type: XVII
Find-place: London, under a street.
Collection: British Museum (now lost)
Blade-length: 31½" (80 cms)
Pommel-type: T.4
Cross-style: 1, curved
Date: c.1390-1420
Condition: Was, until 1942, in very good condition. When I saw its remains in 1950, the hilt had been burnt away by the fire in the old Medieval Gallery and the blade was curled round into a circle. These remains are in the Tower of London, but are not (unlike XVIa.1) susceptible to restoration.

XVII. 9

Type: XVII
Find-place: The River Thames, just above London Bridge
Collection: The Royal Armouries. IX.16
Blade-length: 35" (88.9 cms)
Pommel-type: T
Cross-style: 1
Date: c.1375-1400
Condition: Good, though considerably corroded near the point and a good deal of deep pitting all over.
There is a very long 'ricasso' just below the hilt, to enable the sword to be used for effective thrusting play in close combat, when the left hand can be brought forward to grasp the blade below the cross in order to shorten the length of the blade.
Publication: Dufty, Plate 5A; Laking, Vol. I; Blair, C. *EAA* no.34

XVII. 10

Type: XVII
Find-place: Possibly Richard II's Royal Armoury
Collection: The Corporation of the City of Bristol
Blade-length: 38" (96.5 cms)
Pommel-type: T.5 Flat
Cross-style: 1
Date: 1431-2 (perhaps c.1380-1400)
Condition: Perfect; perhaps (being a civic sword) rather over-cleaned).

The hilt is of silver-gilt applied over a core of steel or iron. On the grip is written 'John Wellis of London Groc' and Meyr/to Bristow gave this Swarde Fair. Mercy and Grace and W.Cleve.' Applied to the grip at top and bottom are little silver-gilt escutcheons: at the top the arms of Bristol and at the bottom arms similar to those used by Richard II. These are applied (probably after the sword was made) much in the same way as a modern tourist fixes little shields of arms to his walking-stick. They are put on so that they are the right way up if the sword is held with the point upwards, like a bearing-sword. This it now undoubtedly is, but its general shape and proportions and the 'feel' of it indicate that it was probably a working sword, not a parade one. Claude Blair has suggested that since it bears Richard II's arms, Sir John Wells may have taken an old sword from the Royal Armoury to present to Bristol. In this case, it would date to the last two decades of the 14th century. The form of the cross exactly matches that of the Battle Abbey Sword (1403) now in the Royal Scottish Museum in Edinburgh, so that it seems both hilts were made by the same cutler.
Publication: Blair, C., *EAA* no.44, p.84.

168

XVII. 11

Type: XVII
Find-place: Unknown
Collection: Private
Blade-length: 33" (83.8 cms)
Pommel-type: T.2
Date: c.1375-1400
Condition: Excavated, but excellent. Obviously (like the sword in the Fitzwilliam Museum in Cambridge, No.XVII.1 in this series) a river-find. One of the 'Sempach' family of swords. There is a mark inlaid in latten on the flat of the blade below the hilt.
Publication: Oakeshott, E. *Catalogue of the Fourth Park Lane Arms Fair*, 1987, p.11, Nos. 7 and 7b; Blair, C. *EAA*, No.31.

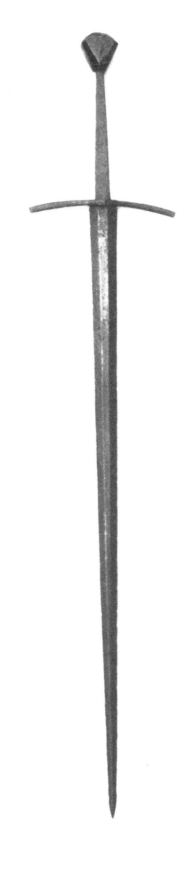

XVII. 12

Type: XVII
Find-place: The River Clyde, Scotland
Collection: The Glasgow Museum & Art Gallery (A.737)
Blade-length;36" (91.4 cms)
Pommel-type: Pommel lacking
Cross-style: A very long variant of 5
Date: c.1380-1420
Condition: Apart from the missing pommel, nearly perfect.
The sword was found by a mechanical digger in dry sand on
the banks of the River Clyde, twelve feet down. The pommel
probably was broken off, unnoticed, by the digger. There is
an overall patination of small pits, but no serious corrosion.
There are fine stamped marks on the blade, a star repeated
three times on each side. The cross is long, of a flat slightly
rounded ribbon section with its long axis on the plane of the
blade. There is a metal rain-guard over the écusson, as in the
Type XVa sword shown here in this series, No.XVa.2. An
exactly similar cross of this rather unusual shape is to be seen
on a sword of the same date in the Museum of the Castel Sant'
Angelo in Rome (No. XIX.9 in this series).

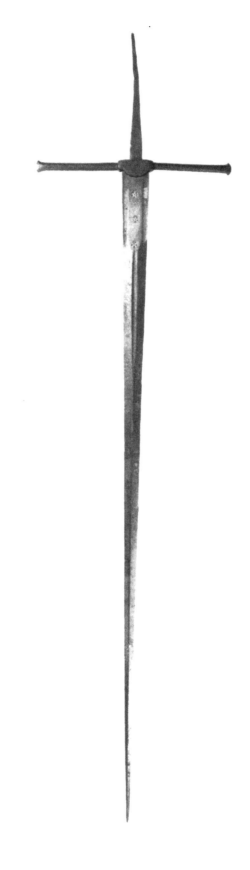

Type XVIII-XVIIIa

This type is the very quintessence of the true, age-old cut and thrust fighting sword; its form and its function goes back to the Middle Bronze Age of c.1000 B.C. Relatively light (its average weight, for its short-hilted version of Type XVIII, is about 2 lbs) with enough breadth at the point of percussion (or as someone in Denmark once put it, the Optimal Striking Point) to deliver a totally effective cut, yet below this the blade tapers sharply to a very acute point, perfectly capable of a very lethal thrust. In nearly every case, too, the section is of a flattened diamond form with a sharp longitudinal mid-rib, making the blade nice and stiff.

This type of blade, in steel not necessarily bronze, goes back into pre-history or very nearly. Many of the fine steel blades of the La Tène culture are of this form, generally about 28" to 30" long and about 2" wide at the hilt (71 cmns to 76 cms, and 5.7 cms). Lying on my table as I write this is a typical Type XVIII blade from a Spanish grave which dates from c.200-150 B.C. – a typical weapon of Hannibal's Spanish cavalry units. In the Nationalmuseet in Copenhagen is a Roman cavalry *spatha*, perhaps a century later, which is also so much a typical XVIII that it might well be taken to date c.1450 A.D. It probably would be, if it came up for sale in one of the great sale-rooms without a reliable provenance attached to it.

It is perhaps curious that the form, obviously so popular in the Celtic and Roman Iron Age, went out of use in favour of the broad, flat slashing blades of Types X to XIV, from c.50 B.C. – A.D.50 until the late 14th century of our era. I firmly believe that it was the forms and developments of defensive armour during those fourteen centuries which determined the form of the sword's blade. Once complete and effective plate armour came into general use, something different was essential, hence Types XV, XVI, XVII and XVIII. Even so, there is a great deal of sound literary evidence in chronicle, poem and prose history – or what, in the case of the incomparable Froissart, was historical novelism – that swords were virtually useless against a fully armoured man-at-arms. The axe, mace, hammer, pick and poll-axe became the favoured knightly weapon. Even so, the sword remained an essential, primary weapon of honour and prestige, and from the late 14th century until the mid-19th, blades of this XVIII and XVIIIa form were the most commonly used. The type lasted perhaps longest in the broadswords of the Scottish Highlanders, the basket-hilted so-called 'Claymore' of the 18th century.

There are 3 sub-types for XVIII (see diagram) because this was so useful and popular a form of sword. XVIIIa denotes a larger XVIII with a longer blade, often with a ⅓ length fuller, and a longer grip, while XVIIIb is a very long-gripped Bastard sword, while XVIIIc is a shorter gripped one.

The word 'Bastard' sword (generally referred to in English contexts as 'hand-and-a-half sword' was applied in the 15th/16th centuries to these long-gripped weapons. This usage is well attested by a remark in a treatise of the 17th century by one Marc de Vulson in his *Vray Theatre d'Honneur*. Describing a duel fought in 1549 before Henry II of France he says of the weapons used 'Deux epées bâtardes, pouvant servir à une main ou à deux' ('two bastard swords able to serve with one hand or with two.')

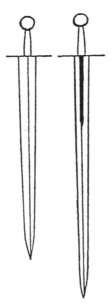

XVIII. 1

Type: XVIII

Find-place: Westminster Abbey, in a chest under a lot of ancient vestments in the S.Triforium

Collection: The Museum, Westminster Abbey

Blade-length: 27" (68.6 cms)

Pommel-type: J.1

Cross-style: 9

Date: Before 1422

Condition: Quite good. This almost certainly hung above the chantry of Henry V until it either fell, or was taken down and stowed away in an old chest under a lot of played-out vestments, in a room in the S.Triforium. It bears the absolutely typical patination of small, even rust-pits under a dark brown covering of old grease and dust, which denotes preservation in a church. The pommel and cross of iron are quite heavily corroded underneath the light gilding which seems to have been added to it at the time of Henry V's funeral in 1422. The crude oak grip, a mere sandwich of roughly cut wood, is I think some sort of rough replacement put on after the original grip had got too rotten to be kept.

Publication: Laking; Mann, James G., *Antiquaries Journal*, 1932; Oakeshott, E., *Connoisseur*, Feb. 1951; Oakeshott, *AOW*; Oakeshott, *SAC*; Tanner, Lawrence, *Antiquaries Journal*, April 1930; Blair, C. *EAA*, No.33

This beautiful, now rather tatty-looking, sword is the very epitome of a fighting weapon. In 1951 I spent a good deal of time with it, for I was allowed to clean it. When I got to it, it was just as it had been taken out of that old chest, and was very dirty. The surface of the blade was fairly clean under the dust and old, hardened grease. The cross and pommel were badly corroded, and a good deal of the ? funerary gilding had flaked off. In the recesses of the pommel, on each side, was a red cross *painted* on to a ground of thin gilt. When I came to clean this, with a bit of cotton wool soaked in methylated spirit, I assumed it was enamel (for even the red cross was hardly visible; in fact, I found that it was only red paint because it began to come off on my cotton wool.

The pommel is very massive, but in fact is not so heavy as its size would suggest, for each of the circular rims which enclose the recesses is made, hollow, of very thin metal, brazed on to a massive iron disc. This I discovered because in one of the rims was quite a big hole, about the size of the head of a panel-pin. It looked like a very odd, deep pit, so I probed it with the prong I keep in my pocket for cleaning out my pipe. It went in to the full depth of the raised rim; so then I tapped both rims (again, with the other end of my pipe-stopper) and found both sides were hollow.

This sword is one of the most beautiful medieval swords to handle I have ever known. It is very light (about 2lbs 3ozs) and balanced like a good fishing-rod. Plain, unadorned and simply austere in form as it is, this is a superb weapon, and despite its plain simplicity one can appreciate that a hard, pratical down-to-earth warrior such as Henry V would use a

sword like this in preference to a more elaborate one. It is an interesting fact, attested by many unquestionable examples, that the swords buried with princes, or hung over their tombs, were always plain, serviceable weapons of first-class quality. A paper on this sword was published in *The Antiquaries Journal* in 1932 by James Mann, stating that it could not have been Henry's V's sword, since it, by its form, clearly belonged to the late 15th century, not to its first quarter. In a reply to this which I published in *The Connoisseur* in 1951, after I had cleaned and handled it I was able to show to everybody's satisfaction – including that of Sir James Mann, as he had by then become – that in fact it was of an early, not a late 15th century type, and that in all probability it was the one once or twice recorded as having been among Henry V's achievements over his tomb. All this 'warlike furniture' – helm, shield and saddle, and since 1951, sword, are displayed in the abbey Museum in the chapel of the Pyx.

I cannot resist adding here a personal anecdote, at the risk of disgusting any scholarly critic who may see this. The day appointed for me to clean the sword happened to be the day of the Memorial Service in the Abbey to Admiral of the Fleet Lord Cunningham of Hyndhope, the great fighting admiral of the second world war. The nave and choir of the Abbey was filled with every conceivable kind of high-ranking service people, from royalty downard; and there was I, alone, up in the triforium of the S.Transept (where, on later ceremonial occasions, television cameras were placed), an ex-Ordinary Telegraphist, with a better view of the whole proceedings than any of the eminent invited guests. I stood up there, holding Henry V's sword, all through that service, looking down upon the proceedings; the final moment, Evening Quarters and the Reveille played upon silver trumpets by musicians of the Royal Marines, was moving enough, stirring enough, by itself; but I heard it with this beautiful sword in my hand, remembering not only my admiral but the hands that had once held the sword.

I have put it first in the sequence of Type XVIII, at the head of a large 'family' of swords, some of which are shown on the following pages, because it is of all the swords I know of this type the finest to handle; this in its own right, as a fighting sword. That it was Henry V's is a bonus.

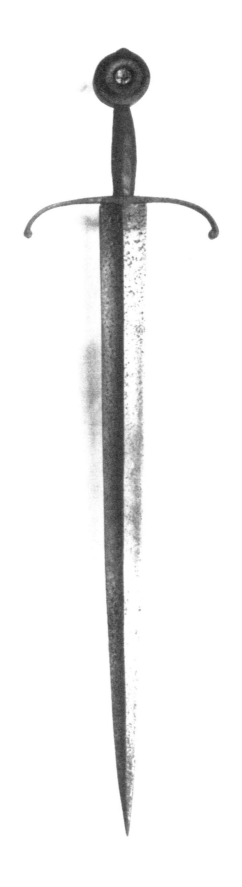

XVIII. 2-3

2. Type: XVIII
   Find-place: Near Nancy in France
   Collection: Private
   Blade-length: 29" (73.7 cms)
   Pommel-type: 1
   Cross-style: 9
   Date: c.1400-25
   Condition: Excellent. Obviously preserved indoors, and cared for. The blade is of an unusual section, a very wide flat hexagon, for this type. In silhouette, very like the Henry V sword.

3. Type: XVIII
   Find-place: Unknown
   Collection: The Royal Armouries
   Blade-length: 32" (81.2 cms)
   Pommel-type: J.1
   Cross-style: 9
   Date: c.1425-50
   Condition: Good. Not excavated. All the indications of preservation in a church. There is a panel of etched floral decoration below the cross on the forte of the blade. This may have been added c.1470-80 to an older sword, but it is not impossible that the sword itself is of this later date. It is noticeable how much more corrosion of the edges there is just below the hilt.

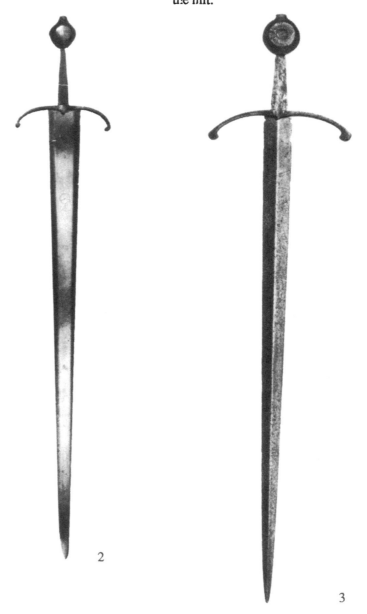

2

3

XVIII. 4

Type: XVIII
Find-place: Unknown
Collection: Once my own, from Gerald Gardiner. Now private
Blade-length: 34" (86.4 cms)
Pommel-type: V
Cross-style: 4
Date: c.1460-70
Condition: Almost perfect. Maybe preserved in a church, but more likely an armoury. The original grip survives, as well as a good deal of the gilding on the iron cross and pommel.
Publication: Oakeshott, *SAC* pl.36b

This is a particularly fine example of a distinctive 'family' of swords, of which I only know at present of three surviving examples – this one, an even better one in the Wallace Collection (see XVIII.4 below) and another, probably having belonged to Ludovico Sforza, Lord of Milan, in the Musée Cluny in Paris. (iii) The sword shown here came up at Sotheby's in 1940, during an air-raid in the London blitz, when sales were held in the basement. Dr Gardiner got it for 35 shillings – in modern money, £1.15p. After Dr Gardiner died in 1955, I bought it – *not* for 35/-.
The photographs, (i) and (ii), show different grips. This is interesting and instructive. The grip shown at (ii) was obviously worn by use; it was of black leather, which had once been red; but it was (I thought) ugly and, anyway, loose. *So I took it off*, cutting delicately with a scalpel down the coarse sewing at the back, below was another, plain, leather covered grip even more worn, of leather which had once been bright green

– you could, when I took the other covering off, see this bright colour at the lower end where it touched the cross. After a few weeks of exposure to the air of my sitting-room, this bright colour merged into the near-black of the rest of this earlier grip-covering. I think it must be admitted that once the outer, rather coarse, cover was taken off, the sword (shown here at (i)) looked a lot better. The exigencies of family responsibility, and a lust to possess another sword, led me to part with it in the early '70s. I don't know where it is now, but whoever has it possesses a very fine late 15th century sword, another classic example of a Type XVIII.

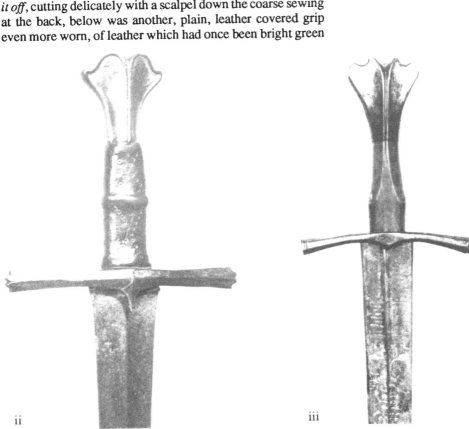

ii   iii   i

175

XVIII. 5

Type: XVIII
Find-place: Unknown, but a church or castle hall
Collection: Once my own, now private
Blade-length: 33 ¾" (85.6 cms)
Pommel-type: 1
Cross-style: A style 6 of octagonal section
Date: c.1290-1330
Condition: Very good. Under a hard patination of red-brown hardened old dust and grease, an overall covering of small rust-pits. The patina is exactly the same as that on the Henry V sword. I cleaned this off all of one side of the blade, leaving it intact on the other. The hilt, covered in the same stuff, I left untouched. The grip is a very crudely-made job of rough deal, made (clearly, like on the Henry V sword, a replacement perhaps put on by – who? a verger, perhaps, or a caretaker, not very long ago). The spaces on the two sides of the sandwich to accommodate the stout tang are very crudely hacked out. Obviously the sword was never dismounted. A few fragments of ancient wood remained in the rectangular hole where the tang passes through the cross. These I have kept. I thought the look of this rather nasty grip would be improved if it were to be bound with cord. This I did. On the blade, just below the cross, is a small incised mark of a dagger, sword, of falchion not very well executed but very like those marks on the Sempach Type XVII swords. (q.v. above). The cross is of a style which, according to works of art, was particularly popular during the 13th century, and hardly at all after. Therefore it is difficult to date this sword. The blade could be as late as 1450, but the hilt couldn't be later than, say, 1320. As it is very plain that the sword has never, certainly not in recent times, been dismounted, I think the whole weapon has to be dated into the years 1290-1320.
Publication: Oakeshott, E. *Catalogue of the Fourth Park Lane Arms Fair*, 1987.

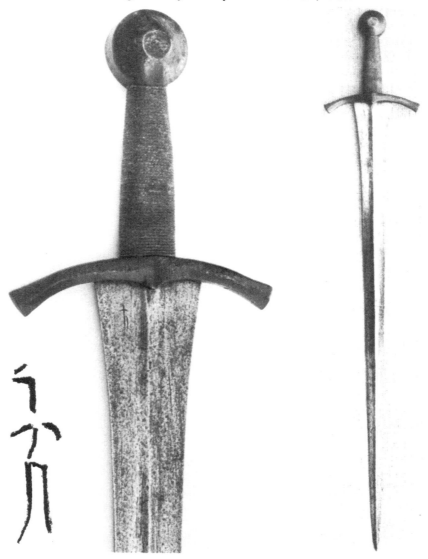

XVIII. 6

Type: XVIII
Find-place: River Dordogne, near Castillon
Collection: The Royal Armouries (on loan)
Blade-length: 27" (68.7 cms)
Pommel-type: J.1
Cross-style: 8
Date: c.1400-40
Condition: River-found. Excellent. Some pitting, one very severe nick in one edge – looks as if got in use, not by corrosion. This is another splendid example of the short 'Riding Sword' which is a very effective cut-and-thrust weapon, *not* made for a boy. This is also a perfect and classic example of a sword of Type XVIII.
Publication: Dufty; Oakeshott, in Stuber & Wetler.

XVIII. 7

Type: XVIII
Find-place: Unknown
Collection: Wallace Collection, London (A.467)
Blade-length: 36⅛" (91.7 cms)
Pommel-type: J.1
Cross-style: 12
Date: c.1475-1500
Condition: Very good. Indoor preservation. The hilt very bright, probably overcleaned. The leather-covered grip is modern. There is a good stamped mark on either side of the blade 9" (23 cms) from the hilt.

It is difficult to date this sword. The Wallace Collection Catalogue puts it into the early 16th century, because of the horizontally recurved cross; but crosses like this are shown in art as early as c.1430, and seem to have been common in the last quarter of the 15th century. So I would suggest a date around 1480. It is of Western European origin, and by its similarity to some hilts shown in drawings by Lucas Cranach of c.1480, may be of German style.

Publication: Mann & Norman; Laking, vol.I.

XVIII. 8

Type: XVIII
Find-place: Unknown
Collection: The Wallace Collection, London. A.466
Blade-length: 34¾" (88.3 cms)
Pommel-type: V
Cross-style: Clubbed and short, Style II
Date: c.1440-60
Condition: Perfect. Carefully preserved in indoor conditions. The pommel is of gilded iron, perfectly preserved; the grip of black horn equally so, but the cross is of copper, more coarsely made than the pommel and the gilding looks different. Some suspicion has recently been cast upon it, the suggestion being that it is a 19th century replacement. There is a mark, inlaid in copper on each side of the blade. This is the second sword in the 'family' referred to under XVIII.4 above.
Publication: Mann & Norman; Seitz, vol.I; Laking, vol.I.

XVIII. 9

Type: XVIII or ? XVIIIa
Find-place: Unknown
Collection: The Royal Armouries. IX.949
Blade-length: 30" (76.2 cms)
Pommel-type: Unclassified – a kind of V
Cross-style: Unclassified, but a writhen form of 2
Date: c.1450-75
Condition: Very good indeed. Obviously preserved with care

in a collection or an armoury since the 15th century. The cross and pommel are of iron gilded. The grip is of reddish-coloured hardwood, with fillets of gilded ? bronze at top, bottom and middle. The curious writhen form of the elements of the hilt foreshadows a fairly common practise in swords of German make during the early 16th century. There is a deeply-stamped mark, unidentified, just below the cross.
Publication: Dufty; Oakeshott, *SAC*

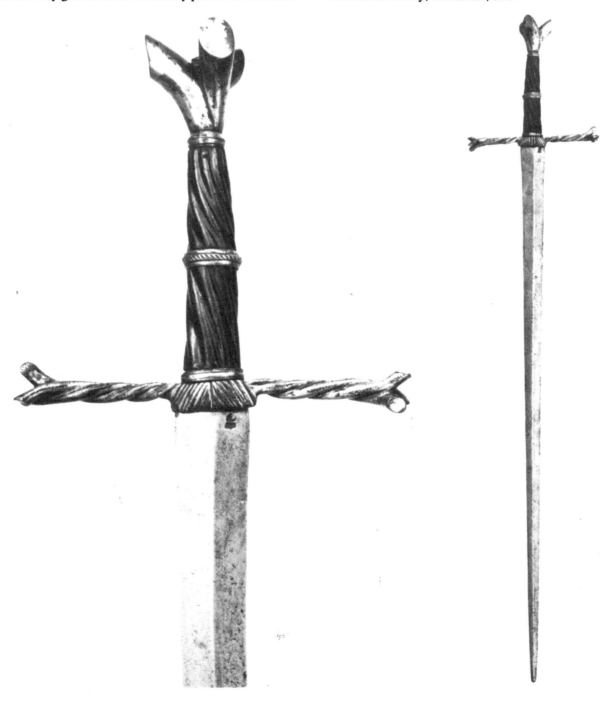

XVIII. 10

Type: XVIII
Find-place: Unknown
Collection: The late Mr E. A. Christensen. Formerly Spitzer.
Now Nationalmuseet, Copenhagen.
Blade-length: 35 3/8'' (90 cms)
Pommel-type: 1
Cross-style: 11
Date: c.1400-50
Condition: Good. Not excavated. A church perhaps? The blade shows a close overall patina of largish pits, but the hilt of gilded bronze is an excellent condition, including the shaped grip of wood bound with fine cord and covered with leather. There is a sword in the Swiss National Museum at Zurich (Inv. No. 6984) which would seem to be from the same workshop, and another similar one in Rome in the Odescalchi Collection (5.35, 196).
Publication: Hoffmeyer; Christensen and Hoffmeyer; Oakeshott, *SAC*

XVIII.11

Type: XVIII
Find-place: Unknown
Collection: Private
Blade-length: 34" (86.6 cms)
Pommel-type: A very highly decorated G
Cross-style: 12
Date: c.1490-1510, Italian
Condition: Near perfect. A little rust-staining on the blade. The pommel is of bronze gilded, with an applied decorative plate of the same in repoussé work, indistinctly signed. The original grip is wood, bound with fine cord and covered with leather, the cross is of iron, lightly cross-hatched and gilded. On the forte of the blade there are faint traces of engraved, or more probably etched, decoration.

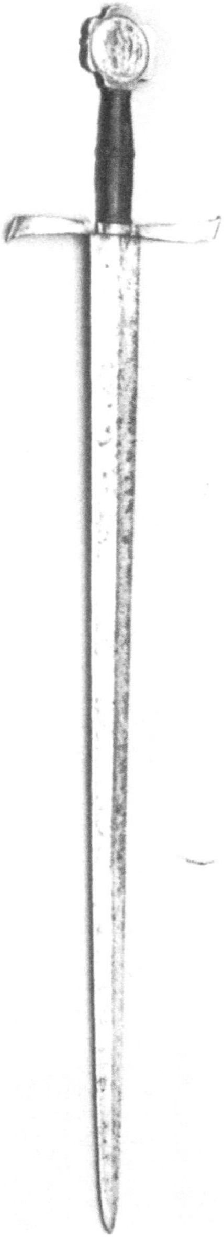

XVIII. 12

Type: XVIII
Find-place: Unknown
Collection: Milan, Museo Poldi Pezzoli, No.440.
Blade-length: 28⅛" (71.4 cms)
Pommel-type: A variant of G.1
Date: c.1480-1500
Condition: Pristine. This has obviously been well cared for. The embellishment of the grip by a series of elegant little steel 'balusters' is, perhaps, a Venetian feature.

There are a few other swords almost identical to this in various collections, all (as far as I know) in the same sort of fine condition. There is one in Naples, (which has a plain grip and a pommel of Type J.1) and a similar one in Madrid, but an extremely similar one was sold by Ineichen Zurich on 5th December 1987 (lot 442).

Publication: Boccia & Coelho No.274; Ineichen, Zurich, *Catalogue of Sale*, 5th December 1987, lot 442; Milan, Museo Poldi Pezzoli, *Catalogue*, 1980, No.440.

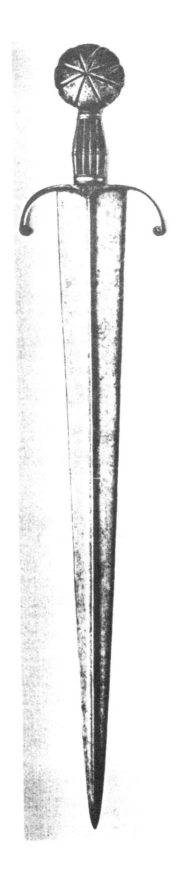

XVIII. 13

Type: XVIII
Find-place: It has probably always been where it is now, more or less.
Collection: Kunsthistorisches Museum, Vienna. A.456W
Blade-length: 27½" (70 cms)
Pommel-type: 1
Date: c.1500
Condition: Pristine.

This sword was made for Philip (The Handsome) Duke of Burgundy, son of Maximilian I and father of the Emperor Charles V. A very splendid example of Type XVIII, its beautiful blade has etched and gilt decoration below the hilt, which is of copper-gilt and ivory. The pommel is of ivory with a central rosette surrounded by a flat concentric circle of gilt bronze, and there are collars of the same at top and bottom of the ivory grip. On the ring on the front of the pommel is an inscription, very cryptic:

AVE/TIMO/RET OR NA TET SA NNA FIT O DA FIT OM AT ERD EY MEM ENT TOMEY.

The ring on the reverse is decorated with an incised leaf-pattern on a hatched ground. The ecusson of the cross and its arms are similarly decorated. At the top of the blade is a most exquisite etched decoration, showing on one side the patron saints of Burgundy, St Andrew and St George, on the other St Romanus and St Michael. The style of the armour worn by these figures is of c.1480-90.

This, in spite of its perfect fighting qualities, is essentially a 'Prunkschwert', a parade sword.

Publication: Gamber, p.29, fig. 22; Oakeshott, *SAC*. pl.35b.

XVIII. 14

Type: XVIII
Find-place: Unknown
Collection: Private
Blade-length: 30½" (77.5 cms)
Pommel-type: J.1. One-sided, octagonal
Cross-style: 12
Date: c.1450-80
Condition: Good. Preserved in an armoury. The original grip survives, a reeded core of wood bound with gilded bronze wire with alternate strands of dark ? steel wire, Turks' heads top and bottom. The pommel of gilded bronze is extremely interesting. On the reverse side it is quite plain, but on the front it conforms with pommel-type J.1. Traces of gilding survive in the recess, and around the raised circular rim there is an incised inscription. This is now almost entirely worn away, but enough remains (filled with gilding) to show that it should be legible under an infra-red light. At one side of the rim is a deep hole, opposite to which is a rectangular slot. Similar slots occur on the rim at 12 o'clock and 6 o'clock. It is, I believe, plain to see that a cross of ? metal was once attached here, pinned by its 3 o'clock arm into the hole, its other arms gripped in the slots. It is reasonable to assume that some form of flat relic, such as a piece of cloth, was held in place by this cross, maybe behind a thin disc of crystal.

The blade has a certain amount of staining, but very few rust-pits. The edges bear signs of severe honing so much so that near to the hilt about ¼" of the edge has been honed away. (cf the sword (no. A500) in the hand of the mounted Gothic armour (A21) in the Wallace collection.

The cross is of plain steel, of a form much in use in central Europe from c.1430 onward.

185

XVIIIa. 1

Type: XVIIIa
Find-place: Unknown
Collection: Formerly in the Wilczec Collection: now ?
Blade-length: About 35" (88.8 cms)
Pommel-type: J
Cross-style: 2
Date: c.1400–40
Condition: Perfect. Obviously preserved in a house or armoury. The original grip of wood, bound with fine cord and covered with leather, survives intact. There is a shield of arms in the pommel, engraved – a lion rampant. On the blade there are two Passau 'Running Wolf' marks, and close up under the cross, a firmly impressed stamp of a daisy or marigold-like mark.
Note: This photograph was taken over half-a-century ago – more like a century – when it was still in Count Wilczec's collection. It doesn't seem to have been seen, or noted anywhere in any publication since then. But it is an absolutely perfect example of this sub-type, and a very beautiful sword into the bargain. It has been suggested that it had belonged to the emperor Albrecht II in 1438/9.
Publication: Wilczec, Count, *Die Erinnerungen eines Waffensammlers*, 1903.

XVIIIa. 2

Type: XVIIIa
Find-place: Unknown
Collection: Formerly D'Acre Edwards, now executors of Sir James Mann on loan to the Royal Armouries.
Blade-length: 33" (83.8 cms)
Pommel-type: T.5 facetted
Cross-style: 4
Date: c.1400-40
Condition: Not very good; it doesn't look as if it was excavated, but I think it must have been. The hilt is in much better condition than the blade, which has a distinct, forge-made bend in it. The wooden grip is modern.
Publication: Dufty; Oakeshott, *SAC*; Seitz, vol.I.

XVIIIa. 3

Type: XVIIIa
Find-place: Unknown
Collection: Unknown. Formerly Spitzer
Blade-length: 30" (76.2) at a guess
Pommel-type: I.1
Cross-style: 8
Date: c.1380-1400
Condition: Very good, though I can't really say much about it. I made this drawing from a photograph in a Sotheby's sale catalogue nearly forty years ago, when I had seen it. It is a beautiful sword, in very well preserved, clean condition with what seemed to be its original, shaped grip. It is illustrated in the catalogue of the Spitzer sale, in the late 19th century. The catalogues of Sotheby sales before about 1940 were destroyed in the air-raids on London in 1940-41, so it can't be looked up. However, it is such a fine example of this type that I have to include it. The assumption must be that it is still in some collection, somewhere.

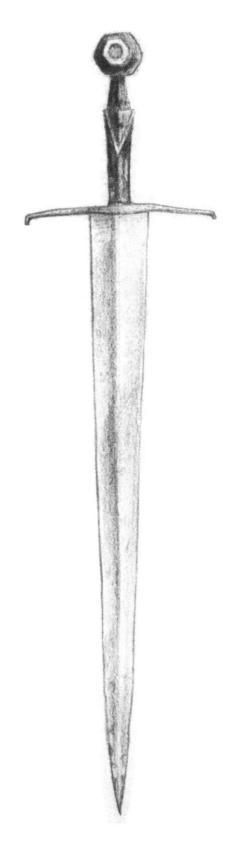

XVIIIa. 4

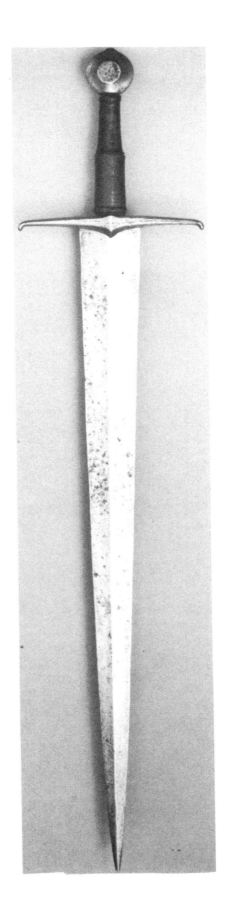

Type: XVIIIa
Find-place: Unknown
Collection: Metropolitan Museum of Art, New York
Blade-length: 31" (78.8 cms)
Pommel-type: I
Cross-style: 8
Date: c.1350-1400
Condition: Perfect. There is just a little staining on the bright
blade, cross and pommel, with an area of shallow pitting in
the middle part of the blade. The original, shaped, grip of wood
bound with fine cord and covered with leather survives. This
is very similar in shape and size, especially the very broad
blade, to the preceding sword, but we have the advantage of
knowing where this one is. Its pommel and grip may not be
quite as handsome, but the cross is of very much finer quality.
Note: In conversation with several present-day craftsmen
who actually make authentic replicas of medieval swords and
armour, using only the tools and methods of working as their
ancient predecessors, I learnt how extremely difficult it is to
forge a decent cross, even of the plainest kind such as Styles
1 and 2. How skilful, then, was the hand that made a Style 8
cross as complex, neat and crisp as this!
Publication: Oakeshott, *SAC*. pl.32, 34
The shape of this hilt would seem to place it firmly in that
'family' shown here at XVa, Nos. 1, 2 and 6, but the very broad
blade differences it from them. It is worthwhile noting here
that, because (perhaps?) it is in such good and carefully-
preserved condition, it must follow that it cannot be earlier
than the 15th century; therefore it is dated c.1400-25 in the
Museum and by Ada Bruhn Hoffmeyer. However, the forms
of pommel and cross are so distinctive of the preceding
half-century, that I feel that it ought to be dated c.1350-1400.
It is a noticeable fact, when you study the work of writers on
arms and armour (who do not specialise in the medieval
world) that any sword of obviously pre-Renaissance type in
good, non-'excavated' condition is automatically dated into
the 15th century. Similarly, any excavated sword in good
condition quite irrespective of its form, or of any internal
evidence such as inlaid inscriptions, is dated to the 14th
century. Only if it has a lobated 'Viking-type' of pommel is it
allowed to date earlier than the 13th century. This of course is
an absurd and fortunately totally outmoded approach. The
reason for it seems to be that, even now in the late 1980s many
'authorities' still get their information about medieval swords
from Sir Guy Laking's monumental work, published in 1921
and compiled a decade earlier. Laking, of course, did not have
the advantage (any more than Rudolf Wegeli did) of the mass
of archaeological and historical evidence regarding medieval
swords which has come to light since the late 1940s. Unfortunately, these monumental (though now exploded) colossi of
the high establishment of pre-Great War date are still too often
regarded as the only true authorities who can be accepted as
having sound knowledge of these arcane matters. Which is a
great misfortune.

XVIIIa. 5

Type: XVIIIa
Find-place: Unknown
Collection: Bayerisches Nationalmuseum, Munich
Blade-length: 36" (91.4 cms)
Pommel-type: J.1
Cross-style: 12
Date: c.1450-80
Condition: As if it had been made yesterday. The long, elegant blade is totally un-stained, and the hilt of gilt-bronze is as new. The long, shapely leather-covered grip is intact, the strong tooling on its surface looking fresh and hardly worn at all. The whole of the leather rain-guard at the lower end of the grip survives. In the recess of the pommel is a gilt-bronze engraved plate showing the virgin and child. Around the rim are the words, in German O MARIA BIT WIR UNS. The back of the pommel is plain.
Publication: This has been published many times in German journals, but in English only Laking, Oakeshott, *SAC*; see also Hoffmeyer, pl.XXIIa. p.22, no.104.

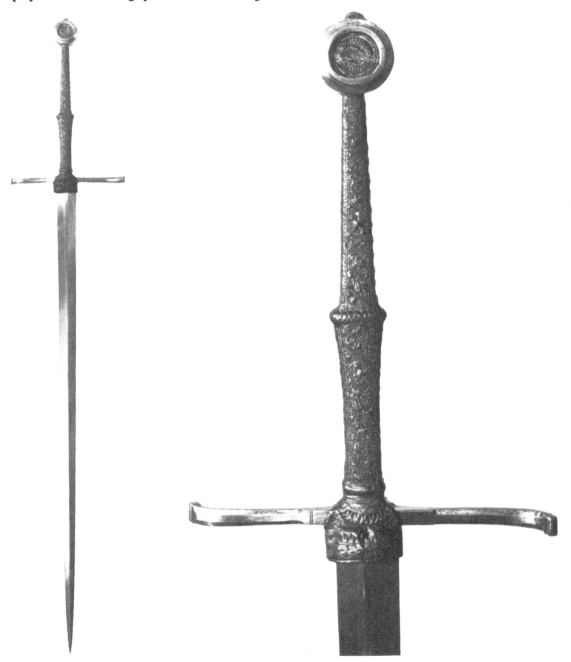

XVIIIa. 6

Type: XVIIIa
Find-place: Bodensee, Switzerland
Collection: Schweizerisches Nationalmuseum, Zurich
LM.8096
Blade-length: 39¾" (101 cm)
Pommel-type: V
Cross-style: 2, with clubbed ends
Date: c.1450-60
Condition: Water-found. Moderate condition, for there is a good deal of quite severe pitting, though this only marks the surface, the elegant pommel and cross are very well preserved.
Publication: Schneider; Oakeshott in Stuber & Wetler

XVIIIa. 7

Type: XVIIIa
Find-place: Unknown
Collection: ? private. Ex. Harold Peterson Collection
Blade-length: 32" (81.3 cms)
Pommel-type: A rounded J, or a flattened R
Cross-style: ? unclassified. Similar to a Style 10, with knobbed ends.
Date: c.1500, + or -20
Condition: Extremely good. If this sword had not been in Peterson's collection, it might have been condemned as a fake. It still might be, but Peterson was a discriminating collector who knew what was what, so it should be given the benefit of any doubt. The grip of wood-cord-leather may be a replacement. The blade is of an unusual and complex shape, having a long ricasso and an extremely sharply-defined mid-rib. I have dated it here at c.1500, but comparing it with representations in art, it could be three-quarters of a century earlier. Or a quarter of a century later. How can one *know*?
Publication: None

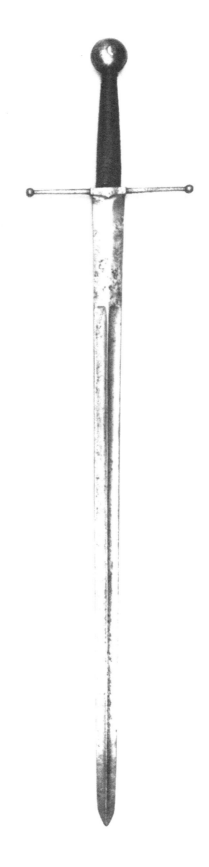

XVIIIa. 8

Type: XVIIIa (a very late example)
Find-place: Unknown
Collection: Private
Blade-length: 42½" (108 cms)
Pommel-type: Unclassified
Cross-style: Unclassified
Date: c.1480-1510
Condition: Excellent. The original grip of wood bound with
fine cord and covered with leather survives, as does much of
the silver plating on the hilt, the grip is really of two-hand
length, though I think it is just a very big bastard sword.
There is a sword in the Schweizerisches Landesmuseum in
Zurich with a very similar complex cross.
(Schneider & Stuber, p.80, No.108, Inv.No. LM16054)

XVIIIa. 9

Type: XVIIIa
Find-place: Unknown
Collection: Ex-Harold Peterson. Now ? private
Blade-length: 35" (89 cms)
Pommel-type: A variant of G
Cross-style: 1
Date: c.1480-1500
Condition: Very good, obviously cared for. The grip may be an old one. The mid-rib of the blade is extremely pronounced, and somehow the middle ridge on the pommel makes a very harmonious whole of the sword.

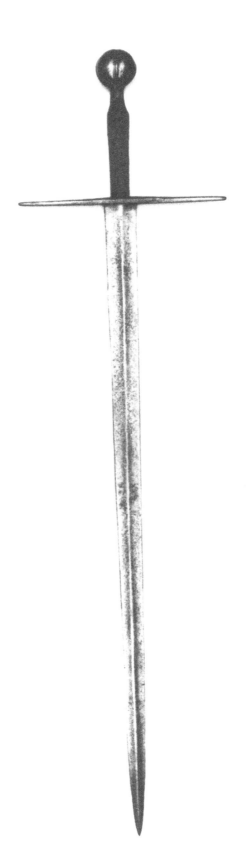

XVIIIa. 10

Type: XVIIIa
Find-place: Schloss Erbach
Collection: Private, ex. Erbach
Blade-length:
Pommel type:
Cross-style: a long 1
Date: c.1480-1500
Condition. Excellent. Preserved until recently in the armoury
of Schloss Erbach. There is a fine mark, an elongated cross
fourché on the blade. The hilt retains not only its original grip
(wood bound with fine cord and covered with thin leather) but
its original colour. The blade, which is only very lightly pitted,
is unusually broad for an XVIIIa.

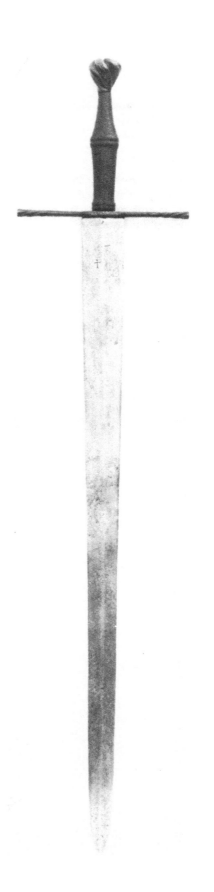

Type XIX

There are a great number of surviving swords of this type, nearly all of them having blades as alike as peas in a pod, and all seeming to have come from the same workshop. Nearly every surviving specimen bears upon it an Arabic inscription in Nashki script, stating that it was deposited in the Hall of Victories in the Arsenal at Alexandria. Most of these were removed to Constantinople by the Turks, at some time between 1517 and 1935! Now most are in the Askeri Museum in Istanbul, but a few escaped and are in European and N. American collections.

The blades of these Type XIX's are of a form which until comparatively recently would have been considered not possibly to date earlier than c.1550, because of their strong, short ricassos and their clean, flat hexagonal section. The ricassos are defined by neatly engraved grooves on each side, coming to a sort of cusp at the lower end against the deep, narrow fuller.

One of these swords which, in addition to a 16th century-looking blade has a single finger-ring below the cross (of style 5), has been published very often, but I have included it here in company with two which as far as I know never have been published. It resides in the Royal Armouries at the Tower of London, and its Arabic inscription gives a date (for its deposition in the Arsenal, not its making) of 1432. There is an almost identical one in Istanbul, with a style 8 cross, and a finger-ring. There are also four others in the Askeri Museum with finger-rings, one with a curious flat oval pommel with a small circular recess in the middle. One which I have shown here, in the Royal Ontario Museum in Toronto, is particularly interesting because *it* bears a date of 1368. This, too, is not the date of its making, which (as an example of a type) can be put back to c. 1350, thus giving a very useful early *terminus post quem* for a very distinctive sword-type.

XIX. 1

Type: XIX
Find-place: Unknown
Collection: Private
Blade-length: 36" (91.4 cms)
Pommel-type: J, recessed
Cross-style: 8
Date: c.1380-1400
Condition: Very nearly perfect. When I saw it in 1986 it had

still a smooth brown 'indoor' patina on it, not having had the oils and dust of the Alexandria Arsenal scrubbed off it. A most elegant, handy, sword, well-balanced though the point-of-balance is toward the point. The shape of these blades, with their gentle taper, is more akin to the old XIIIa blades of the 13th century. This sword is perhaps the supreme example, for elegance, condition and quality, of this type.

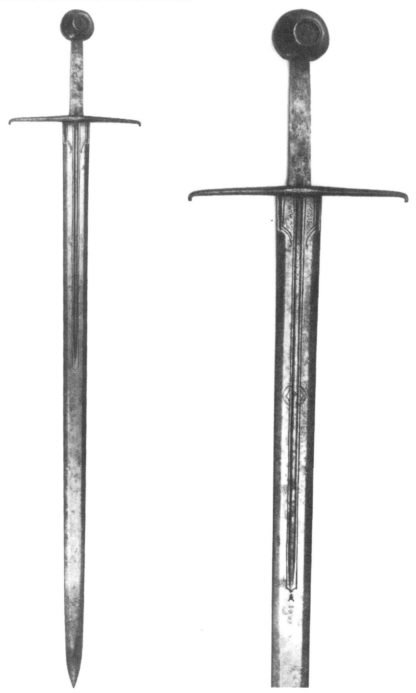

XIX. 2

Type: XIX
Find-place: The Arsenal at Alexandria
Collection: Metropolitan Museum of Art, New York
Blade-length: 35" (88.9 cms)
Pommel-type: A
Cross-style: 5
Date: c.1350-1400
Condition: Very good. The blade is clean, with a few stains.
The hilt is brown. This is either its Arsenal patination or its
'original' colour; or, it is a modern colouration. The grip,
rather crudely bound with a leather thong, is certainly modern.
This was sold at Christies in 1985. Many experts had doubts
as to its authenticity. It looks, and feels, a beautiful, well-bal-
anced, living sword, but the actual style and quality of the
Nashki script of its inscription has caused some concern.

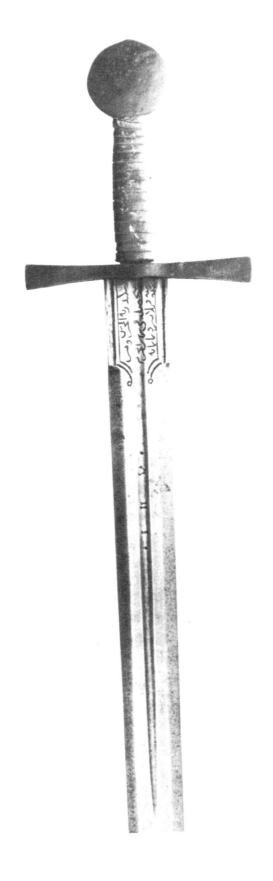

XIX. 3

Type: XIX
Find-place: The Arsenal at Alexandria
Collection: Royal Ontario Museum, Toronto
Blade-length: 32" (81.2 cms)
Pommel-type: T.1
Cross-style: 6
Date: Before 1368
Condition: Very good. The blade has been relatively un-touched, showing some staining and considerable light pitting, the grip is missing. The Arabic inscription gives a date of A.D.1368. The blade can be compared with those of the preceding two swords, showing how much alike they are. It shows also a divergence in the dates of the Arabic inscriptions between the extremes of 1368 and 1437 – all for swords with blades of exactly the same form.
Publication: Oakeshott, *SAC*, pl.39.A.

XIX. 4

Type: XIX
Find-place: The mud of London River, off Bull Wharf, Black-friars.
Collection: The Royal Armouries
Blade-length: 27" (88.6 cms)
Pommel-type: J, recessed
Cross-style: Unclassified previously. Now called Style 12
Date: c.1340-50
Condition: Well-preserved. A few areas of severe pitting below the fine blue-black patina, especially on the pommel. There is a part of the wood (lime-wood?) grip still adhering to the tang. This blade, as you can see, is of exactly the same character as those of the preceding three swords, but it is considerably shorter and broader in proportion. It has of course no Arabic inscription, but is finely marked with a star and a lombardic letter P, and each edge of the ricasso and the fuller is outlined with an inlaid line of latten.
Publication: Oakeshott, E. *Catalogue of the Second Park Lane Arms Fair*, 1986.

XIX. 5

Type: XIX
Find-place: Unknown
Collection: The executors of Sir James Mann, on loan to H.M.
Tower of London A.8-165
Blade-length: 26" (66.1 cms)
Pommel-type: T.3
Date: c.1480-1510
Condition: Good. Not excavated. This is a sword very much
of the same kind as the one shown below, in the Instituto de
Valencia de Don Juan except that the pommel is of a different
style, the cross is straight and there is a rudimentary back-
guard. Also the blade has two narrow fullers divided by a
sharp longitudinal ridge. It is a short sword, sometimes said
to be for the use of a boy, but the grip is of a standard length,
even though the blade is not very long. At the end of the
fullers, there is a neat punched mark of the Biscotto workshop.
Publication: Dufty, Plate 15.c.

XIX. 6

Type: XIX
Find-place: Unknown
Collection: Madrid, Instituto de Valencia de Don Juan
Blade-length: 32" (81.2 cms)
Cross-style: Late, unclassified, complex
Pommel-type: A
Date: c.1460-80
Condition: Very nearly pristine. The original grip, wood covered with brown leather, survives. There is a little very mild pitting scattered over the otherwise undamaged surfaces of the blade. There is only a little wear on the gold damascened decoration (of Hispano-Moresque style) on the pommel and cross. The plain gilding on the arms of the hilt and the two short 'prongs' sticking out in front is worn through in one or two places. there is a lettered inscription on the blade which reads CATHALDO. (ii). This type of hilt – very well developed for its period – is shown very often in art, particularly in the paintings by Nuño Gonçalves of grandees at the court of Alfonso V of Portugal in the period c.1450-65.
Publication: Laking, op.cit. vol.I.; Puricelli-Guerra, Arturo, *Armi in Occidente*, Milano, 1966, No.25. (This shows a beautiful colour photograph of the hilt and upper part of the blade.) Blair, C. *EAA*, No.51.

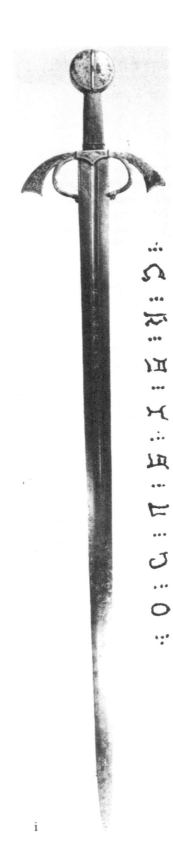

ii

i

XIX. 7

Type: XIX
Find-place: The Arsenal at Alexandria
Collection: The Royal Armouries A.5738/1
Blade-length: 32" (81.2 cms)
Pommel-type: G
Cross-style: 5
Date: c.1400-20
Condition: Very nearly pristine. Having been preserved in the
Arsenal at Alexandria since perhaps a little before the date
engraved in Arabic Nashki script on the blade – 1432. It has
never suffered from exposure, though the pommel under its
black paint or varnish is considerably pitted, as the photograph
XIX.7 (ii) shows. Until restored in the workshop of the Royal
Armouries quite recently, there was a piece of metal broken
off the outside arm of the cross.
Publication: Almost every published work dealing with me-
dieval arms since Laking (op.cit. in 1921) has included this.
The most important however, is D.G. Alexander: 'European
Swords in the Collections at Istanbul', *ZHWK* 1985
Blair, C. *EAA* No.55.

XIX. 8

Type: XIX
Find-place: The River Great Ouse near Ely
Collection: Museum of Archaeology & Anthropology, Downing College, Cambridge
Blade-length: 30" (76.2 cms)
Pommel-type: T.4
Cross-style: 12
Date: c.1400-25
Condition: River-found, fair. There is a lot of pitting all over, except in the fine, well-shaped pommel.

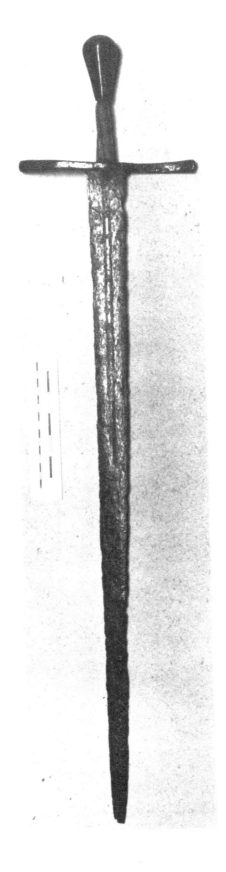

XIX. 9-10

Type: XIX (both swords)
Find-place: Unknown
Collection: Castel Sant Angelo, Rome
Blade-length: c.38" (86 cms)
Pommel-type: (9) T.4 (10) T.5
Cross-style: 11, straight

Date: c.1400-25
Condition: Good. Not excavated? Very hard to tell. Each has a long ricasso at the forte of the blade. This is so that, in close combat, the left hand can be brought forward to grasp the sword's blade below the cross, to shorten it.
Publication: Seitz.

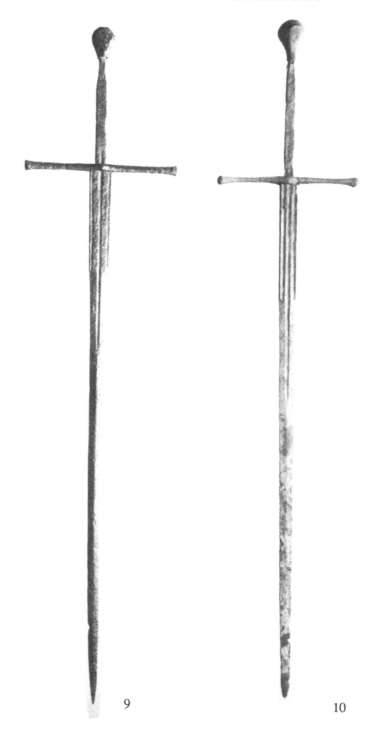

9

10

Type XX-XXa

This type seems to have been more characteristic of the late 15th century than the early 14th, for certainly more surviving examples seem to suggest the later date, but a sword which may be called the archetype can be dated – at least, its characteristically formed blade can – firmly to the early 14th century by the inscriptions and markings engraved upon it.

As in most cases, the type is determined by the form of the blade, and particularly by the arrangement of its fullering. Here it is characterised by a central fuller running over half-way down the blade, flanked by two shorter ones, generally of the same width as the central one, in the upper quarter of the blade's length.

Most survivors of this type are large hand-and-a-half swords, but the archetypical one in question is an enormous bearing sword, shown here at XX.1(i) and XX.1(ii), shows the marks upon it which date it. Another rather later one – a least, the date on it is later, 1427 in Arabic Nashki script – is from the Hall of Victories in the Arsenal at Alexandria. This sword has a hilt quite consistent with a mid-14th century date, a squared 'wheel' pommel of Type K and a straight square-section cross, but the others, as the illustrations which follow demonstrate, have varieties of the 'scent-stopper' pommel and have a distinctly 15th century look about them – i.e. their hilts resemble hilts shown in all forms of art from the 1370s to the end of the 15th century. These will of course be dealt with individually. In previous publications where I presented my typology of medieval swords, I included two other blade-forms in with Type XX, but further study (after all, the typology was originated in 1958!) has made it plain to me that I have to put these other forms into types of their own, XXI and XXII. This will appear in due course.

Type XXa: I felt that it was necessary to differentiate this form of blade from the broader, less acute blades of Type XX; the fullering in this sub-type is the same, but the edges run very sharply to an acute point.

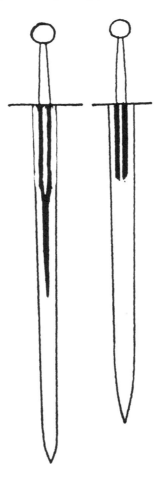

XX. 1

Type: XX
Find-place: Unknown
Collection: Private
Blade-length: 50" (127 cms)
Pommel-type: T
Cross-style: 1
Date: c.1320-40

Condition: Very good. It has obviously been well-cared for. There are a few patches, where there has been very light rusting, scattered over the surfaces of the blade. The grip, wood, with a cord binding covered with leather, seems to be original. The enormous, massive pommel of bright iron has, like the blade, one or two very slight black patches on it.

The very enigmatic marks (see (ii) here) give a very positive date to the early 14th century. The style of the achievements of arms (crested helm and shield) on either side are typical of the period c.1275-1325, as is the style of the letters and the other marks.

Publication: Oakeshott, *SAC*, Plate 40, p.76; Blair, C. *EAA*, No.64.

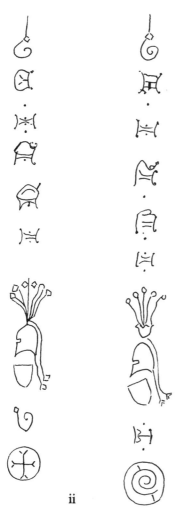

ii

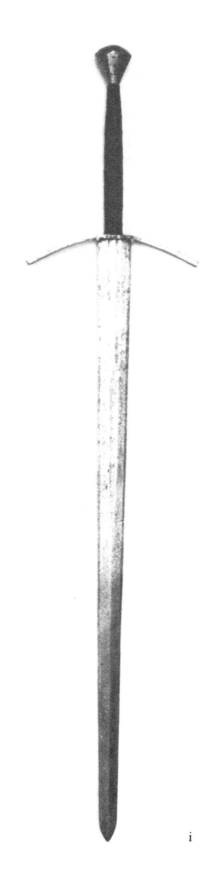

i

XX. 2

Type: XX
Find-place: Unknown
Collection: Kunsthistorisches Museum, Vienna. A.89.W
Blade-length: 42⅛" (107 cms)
Pommel-type: T.1
Cross-style: 1
Date: c.1440-50
Condition: Pristine. This is a two-hand sword, the grip being 15" (38 cms) long. This survives (fine leather over wood) in only slightly worn condition. The lower part, below the central transverse collar, is tooled with diagonal cross-shaped lines. The blade is marked on each side with a shield divided per bend, the Passau wolf-mark, the letters IRI and a bishop's crozier.
Publication: Gamber, 18, p.22; Oakeshott, *SAC*, Plate 40. A.

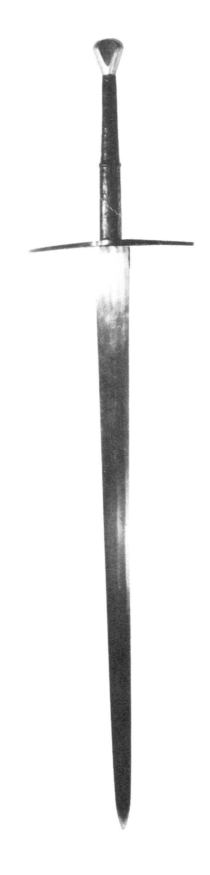

XX. 3

Type: XX
Find-place: Unknown
Collection: Glasgow, The Burrell Collection
Blade-length: 37" (94 cms)
Pommel-type: T
Cross-style: 1
Date: c.1420-50
Condition: Very good. Just a few dark spots on the blade. The grip (thin leather over wood) seems to be original. A big hand-and-a-half sword, quite heavy (about 3lbs) but effectively balanced. Traces of an orb and cross mark about 5" (12.8 cms) down from the hilt.

There is a sword of this type and 'family' in the Castle Museum at Norwich, the twin of this one.

XX. 4

Type: XX
Find-place: Unknown
Collection: Private. Formerly in my own.
Blade-length: 35" (88.9 cms)
Pommel-type: A variant of T
Cross-style: 11, modified
Date: c.1450-75
Condition: Very nearly pristine. The blade is an identical twin with those of this type in Glasgow and Norwich, but the hilt is more elaborate. There are three very deep recesses in the outer face of the pommel, once holding silver or gold statuettes of a holy kind – long since removed. The well-shaped cross is slightly recurved horizontally. The grip (wood bound with fine cord and covered with thin leather) is original. There is a mark of a six pointed star on one side. The point is reinforced. There are the remains of a leather rain-guard at the cross.

Since I wrote this entry, the sword has changed hands again and returned to my care. I have now observed that the form and pattern of the cross is a twin of the cross on the superb sword in Munich (noted above under XVIIIa.5). Both crosses clearly originated in the same atelier, if not made by the same hand. Another interesting point is that the leather covering of the grip, also like that on the Munich hilt, was extended downward over the mid-point of the cross to form a rain-guard. This would have covered this part of the cross, which is clearly seen to be only rather roughly finished, unlike the clean, neat finish of the arms. This is a clear indication that the cutler's shop where the hilt was made also fashioned the grip and rain-guard to fit it.

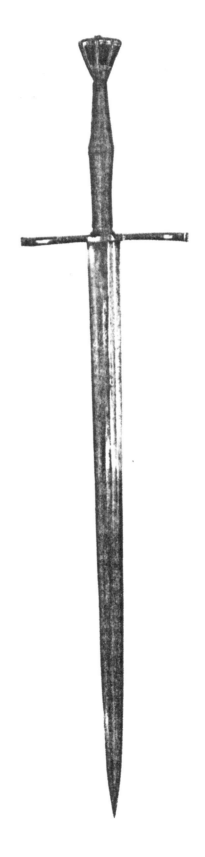

XXa. 1

Type: XX.A
Find-place: Unknown, but obviously an armoury
Collection: Bayerische Nationalmuseum, Munich
Blade-length: ? 34" (86.4 cms)
Pommel-type: T
Cross-style: 1
Date: c.1425-50
Condition: Very nearly pristine. The blade is as fresh as it was made; there are a few pits on the cross and pommel and the original (wood bound with fine cord covered with thin leather) grip is only slightly worn and a little displaced. An absolutely outstanding sword.

The marks on the blade are exceptional, too. There are several conventional latten-inlaid marks (see accompanying sketch) but most interesting is a series of *etched* lettered inscriptions, which look as if they had been added to the blade. They are in Gothic miniscule letters, in a strange mixture of Greek and Latin, placed in eight panels, four on each side. They read:

Side A
+SOTTER+ (Greek for Saviour).
+EMANUEL + /IESUS++NAZARENUS+/+REX JUDEO-RUM+.
Side B
+ALPHA ETO+/+ADONAI+/+TETRAGRAMMA-TON+/+ELOI EL+/

The stamped 'makers' marks on this blade correspond exactly with those on a sword of Type XVa in the Glasgow Museum, shown above at XVa.2.

This is altogether a remarkable sword, and the shape of its hilt shows it to belong to the same 'Family' of swords as the Type XX swords previously shown.

Publication: Wegeli, Rudolf, *Inschriften auf Mittelalterliche Schwertklingen*, Zurich, 1903; Laking, vol.I; Oakeshott, *SAC*, Plates 30A and 31; and most other works treating of medieval arms since the mid-19th century.

ii

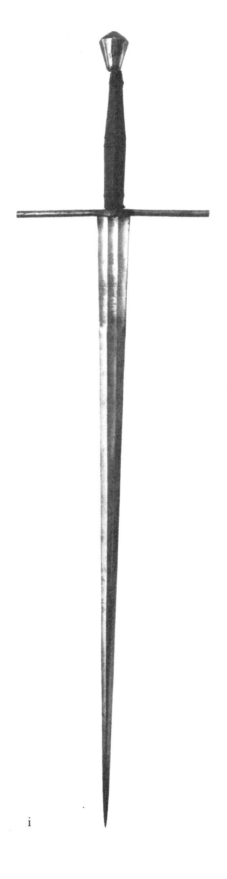

i

XXa. 2

Type: XXa
Find-place: The River Dordogne, near Castillon
Collection: ? Private
Blade-length: 36¼" (92" cms)
Pommel-type: Unclassified
Cross-style: 11, straight
Date: c.1425-50
Condition: Considerable corrosion, and some very wide and
deep nicks on one edge, but none on the other. There are some
remains of the wood of the grip in the lower opening of the
pommel and on each face of the tang. There is also some of
this wood inside the top face of the opening of the cross – i.e.,
the wood of the grip was shaped to fit top and bottom into the
holes in pommel and cross. Like other type XX and XXa
blades, there is a definite 'ricasso' below the hilt. There are
clear traces of a complex pattern in gilt on the upper part of
the blade. These marks (which include a totally indecipherable sequence of letters on each side) are not engraved and
inlaid, but appear to be lightly etched and gilded. The pommel
which is shaped like a more usual Type T.3, pear-shaped, is
mounted with the thin end upwards, instead of downwards to
join the top of the grip. There is another complete sword, the
twin of this with a similar? etched decoration on the blade,
and a fragmentary one, from the same find.
Publication: Oakeshott, in Stuber & Wetler, No.15a (p.19)
and 15 (p.22).

Type XXI-XXII

With these types we come to a point (in the High Renaissance, in cultural terms) when so many varied shapes and sizes of blades, and complexities of hilts, became common that a typology such as this, based upon the outline shape of blades and their section, can go no further. Besides, these two types seem only to have come upon the scene at the very end of the medieval period, and both lasted well into the 16th century.

Type XXI is basically formed upon the type of blade developed in Italy and best known as the Cinquedea – Five Fingers. Not all, however, had the breadth of five fingers at the hilt, nor were they all short like the true Cinquedea. A few were long swords, mounted with the 'typical' and characteristic Cinquedea hilt (like No.XXI.2 here) but most had more conventional sword-hilts, all of which, however, seem to have conformed to a standard pattern – one or other of the variants of the disc pommel (Type H to K) and all with rather short crosses, strongly arched over the blade and with curled-under tips. The exquisite sword made for Cesare Borgia in 1493 is the standard-bearer of this particular 'family' within the type; there are a few others which survive (and, one hopes, more may eventually come to light) but none can match the Borgia one. It is a very worthy adjunct to one of the most exciting and colourful characters of the High Renaissance in Italy. A motto which he adopted 'Fais ce que doit, adveigne qui peut' (Do what you ought, come what may) is a fine sentiment, which by doing always what he ought not, has bought him lasting, probably undeserved, infamy.

Type XXII is not really so handsome a blade-form, but surviving examples are among some of the most lavish parade of swords of the 15th century. Characteristic is a broad, flat blade, the edges tapering in elegant curves to an acute point, and a pair of short, deep and very narrow fullers below the hilt.

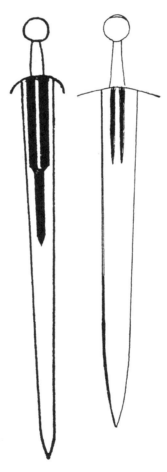

XXI. 1

Type: XX
Find-place: Unrecorded
Collection: Rome, Casa Caetani
Blade-length: 33¼" (84.8 cms)
Pommel-type: G
Cross-style: An extreme form of Style 11
Date: 1493-98

Condition: As new. This sword was made for the notorious Cesare Borgia, at a time when he was Cardinal of Valentino, which puts a date to it of between 1493 (when he got his hat) and 1498, when for reasons of state and politics he relinquished it. It has been published and described so often that it is pointless to describe its purely 'Renaissance' decoration in detail here. Strictly speaking, it is not a medieval sword; but since it is the 'grandfather' of a very distinct family of swords, it has to be included here. Survivors of the family are rare, and fine, but they are seldom seen in art. However, there is an absolutely splendid example on England, on the effigy of Sir Robert Harcourt, K.G., at Stanton Harcourt in Oxfordshire. He died in 1471, and his alabaster effigy – a particularly fine and well-preserved one – was probably made between say 1465 and 1475. I have shown a drawing here at (ii). I spent a long time in that little church making a very careful examination of this alabaster sword, and so I can say that there is no restoration of it, as is so often the case with these alabaster knightly effigies' swords, whose hilts were knocked off and whose daggers – nearly always – were stolen.

The hilt of the Borgia sword is made of gilded bronze with enamel and gold filigree work, and on the ecusson of the cross the words CEAS. BORG. CAR. VALEN.

The upper part of the blade is decorated with etched and gilded designs by Ercole dei Fideli of Ferrara, showing classical scenes celebrating the name of Caesar in the person of the immortal Julius.

Publication: Everywhere. But particularly, in detail, and recently: Boccia and Coelho, Nos. 209-223.

i

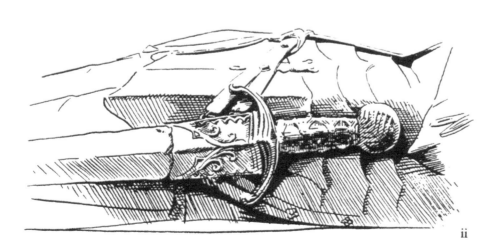

ii

XXI. 2

Type: XXI

Find-place: Unknown

Collection: Formerly de Cosson, Douglas Ash, and myself. Now private.

Blade-length: 32" (81.3 cms)

Pommel-type: There is no true pommel, for it has a pure 'Cinquedea' hilt

Date: c.1480-1500

Condition: Very nearly perfect. The blade is unblemished, but the little filigree rondels in the walrus-ivory grip are modern replacements. There is a very similar sword, in even better condition, in Naples, and the very tatty remains of another, excavated, one in the Fitzwilliam Museum in Cambridge. Both of these have the same kind of bone or ivory hilt as this one.

The Naples one's grip is of ivory, but the cross – the same acutely down-turned form as this, is of plain steel. So is the cross of the one in Cambridge. Here the grip was of ivory or bone, but only fragments of it survive.

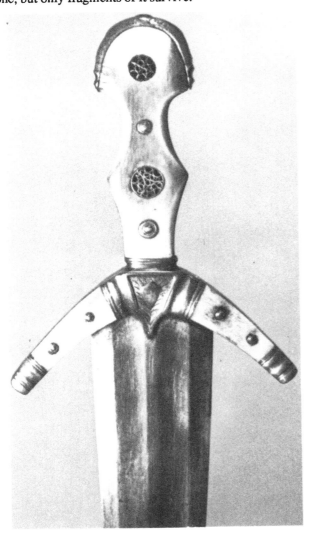

XXI. 3

Type: XXI
Find-place: Unknown
Collection: Private
Blade-length: 30"
Pommel-type: A variant of the spherical Type R
Date: c.1470-90
Condition: Almost perfect. I have never been able to see this sword, and the only photographs I have of it are the one reproduced here (not very good) and a couple of polaroids showing the entire sword. The blade is extremely handsome, of the same general form as XXI.1 here, though its taper is not so acute. The cross is a conventional one of Style 9; the grip is probably original, though very well preserved. The present owner, who sent me the photographs, feels sure that this grip is no modern replacement – and his opinion is one I would not challenge. The pommel, in pristine condition, is a handsome though unusual variant of Type R. There is one of the same variety shown in an Italian painting of a Madonna with saints by Lorenzo di Niccolo Gerini, dated 1404, in the Accademia in Florence.

218

XXII. 1

Type: XXII
Find-place: Schloss Ambras, Austria
Collection: Kunsthistorisches Museum, Vienna
Pommel-type: F
Cross-style: A sort of Style 1
Blade-length: 36" (91.5 cms)
Date: c.1440
Condition: Well-preserved, nearly perfect. This, being a royal parade sword, has been kept in good condition and properly cared for since it was made for Friedrich III when King of the Romans before he became Emperor. The blade is Italian, but the hilt, with its plates of horn on grip and cross and the elaborate 'chappe' or rain-guard is of South German workmanship. The broad, massive blade bears a maker's stamp, a crowned A; and etched and gilded below the hilt are panels of decoration; on one side, between conventional foliage the single-headed black eagle of the Empire on a gold ground, on the other the Austrian 'Bindenschild'.
Publication: Gamber; Boeheim, W. 'Album', vol.I, Plate 7; Oakeshott, *SAC*, Plate 42.A; Laking, vol.I; Blair, C., *EAA, No.45*

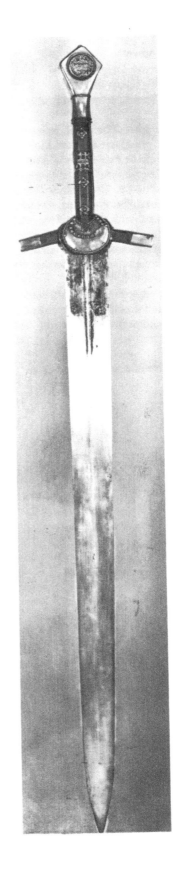

XXII. 2

Type: XXII
Find-place: Unknown
Collection: Once my own. Private
Blade-length: 26" (66 cms)
Pommel-type: There is no pommel, only a 'Cinquedea' hilt
Date: c.1500
Condition: Very good. The blade is superb, with a very fine panel of etched renaissance decoration below the hilt; the strongly arched cross of steel is well-formed and uncorroded, but the plates of the pommel and grip are of dirty brown horn, very crudely fashioned. The arched element of steel on top seems to be original, but the clumsy plates of horn are not in any way consistent with the excellent quality of the metal-work; yet they don't look modern. Maybe the original grip – which would have been of ivory or horn, but beautifully made – in some way became broken, and this crude, 'home-made' replacement was fitted.

There is an extremely similar sword in the Royal Armouries, and another which could be called identical (except that its horn grip is a good one) is in Florence – but its blade is plain, with no etched decoration. It has the same 'sicle' marks, though.

Publication: Oakeshott, *SAC*, Plate 42.c.

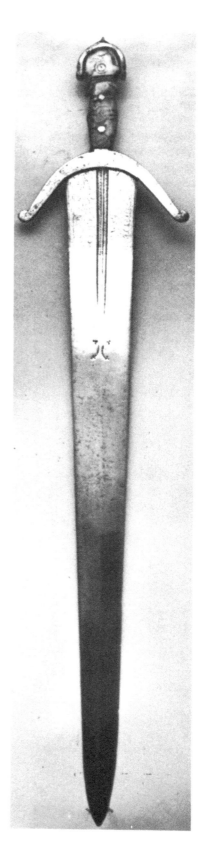

Miscellaneous, Unclassified, and Complex-Hilt Swords

It is inevitable that in formulating a typology it will be found that there are objects which cannot be put into any specific group or category. This is particularly true in the case of swords. From the iron age to the Renaissance, as we have seen, swords can be firmly put into types and families, but after c.1500 (or even 1480) the variations in blade and hilt-forms so proliferated that accurate – even approximate – classification becomes impossible. It has been tried (I have tried it) but always the exceptions outstrip the rules.

In this section I have included first, some swords which are not of any particular type, and a number with complex hilts which, though they date within the medieval period, really belong to that vaguely defined era of 'The Renaissance'. Then there are a number of 'group photographs' swords taken on the same negative. This has the advantage of showing a few diverse swords, exactly and reliably photographed together to the same scale. In one case I have had to put in a drawing, of two swords in the Musée de l'Armée in Paris, which need to be shown to the same scale as one is very large.

Multiple Miscellaneous 1-4

These four swords, three of which have been described in detail above under their types, being taken on the same negative show perfect examples of Types X, XI, XII and XIII and the proportional relationship which each has to the other – and indeed, on average, how the four types generally relate. Three are in the Royal Armouries; (1), (2) and (4) are on loan by the executors of the late Sir James Mann, and (3). once on loan, is now in a private collection. The find-place of two are known – (1) in the River Scheldt and (3) near Cawood in Yorkshire.

(2) in this group is a fine example of a type XI, with a pommel of Type A and a silver-inlaid inscription in the blade of a kind which matches some of the inscriptions in Dr Leppaaho's Finnish Viking swords, firmly dating it c.1100, not the early 13th century as it is labelled.

1   2   3   4

Multiple Miscellaneous 5-8

These four swords are part of the Henderson Bequest in the Fitzwilliam Museum in Cambridge. Here again, all four being on one negative shows the relative proportions of three *Espées de Guerre* of the 12th-13th century and one of the early 14th. They are all typical 'grete swerdes of Almain', 'swords of war' or *grans espés*.

(5) has a fine, deep pommel of Type J with an equal-armed cross incised, and once inlaid with latten or silver, on its central bosses and there are faint traces of a latten inlaid pattern – not an inscription – on one side of the blade, which is in good condition under its dark patina except for a scattering of quite deep pits. The grip is of the late 19th century.

(6) is almost a two-hand sword, for its grip is extremely long in spite of its 'war-sword' length of blade (35⅛" (89.2 cms). It is a heavy weapon, too, just under 4lbs. Its date, c.1280-1310.

(7) with its truly enormous pommel of Type A and its long, rather slender blade is much lighter, and dates probably c.1200-50.

(8) is in spite of its size quite a light and handy weapon for a *grant espée*, and dates perhaps to c.1340-50. The pommel of Type K is unusual in that its central bosses are square, and divided into three strong transverse ridges.

Blade-lengths are as follows:

(5) 35¼" (89.4 cms)
(6) 35⅛" (89.2 cms)
(7) 38⅝" (98.1 cms)
(8) 35⅛" (89.2 cms)

(5) was sold in the Helbing Galleries at Munich in June 1908, lot 53, as also was (7), lot 48.

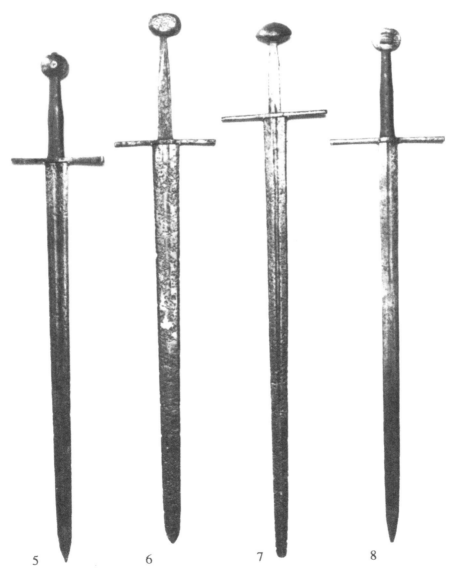

5 6 7 8

Multiple Miscellaneous 9-12

These four swords came up for sale at Sotheby's in 1981, part of a French collection, and I was only able to get this photograph of their hilts, though I examined them all minutely.

(9) Type X, very much pitted, with most of the wood of its scabbard adhering to the back. A very fine big Type A pommel. Now in a private collection.

(10) Type XVII. Condition not bad, excavated and cleaned. A nice pommel of Type 1.

(11) Type XVI. Hard to define, as the blade was very much thinned by corrosion so that the section of its lower part was quite flat. It is quite acutely pointed, so it is probably not a XII, though the edges may have been worn away. The pommel is quite flat, and the grip is a recent replacement. I had this sword in my care for a short time; it is very light and handy, not very long – the blade is 30".

(12) Type XVII. Not a very handsome sword, but a good Type T pommel. It looks as if it had probably been kept in a church.

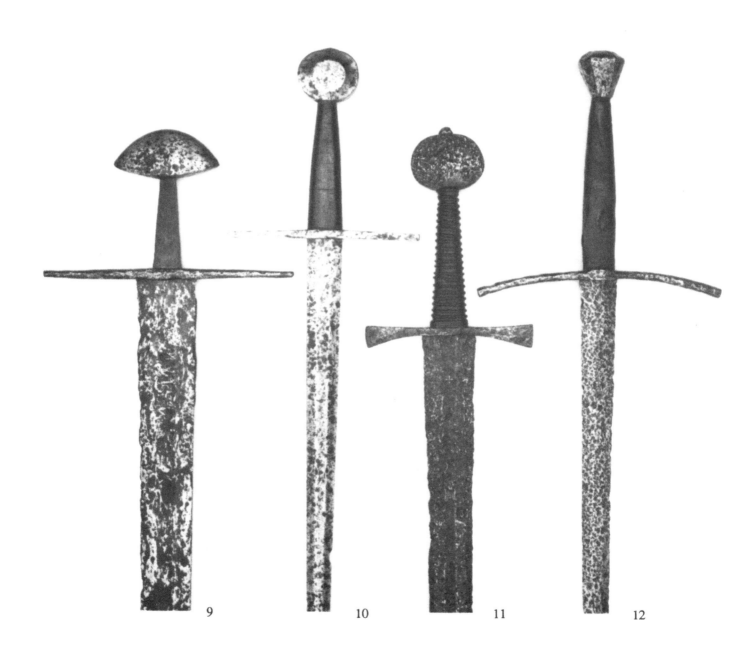

9   10   11   12

Multiple Miscellaneous 13-17

These five swords from the Wallace Collection in London have been published over and over again since the end of the last century, but they are such important examples – well-preserved, too – of their kind that it would be wrong not to include them, and I do so because after all these decades a good print has at last been produced which shows them as they are, not as featureless black silhouettes. Since all five are taken together on one negative, they cannot be slotted into their own types as individuals; there is a vague Type XVIII, an even more vague XVII, an excellent Xa, and another Xa not quite so good, and a fine Viking sword of Petersen's Type K (and my own Type X).

13. Type: XVIII (with no fuller or ridge)
Find-place: Unknown
Collection: The Wallace Collection A464
Blade-length: 31½" (79 cms)
Pommel-type: T1
Cross-style: 1
Date: c.1360-1400
Condition: Good. There are several areas, similar on blade and hilt, of patches (mostly circular) of fairly deep pitting, as if small pebbles had been in the mud which surrounded the sword. There is a mark inlaid in copper on each side of the blade, which has neither fuller nor mid-rib but is of a flat, oval section.

14. Type: XVII
Find-place: Unknown
Collection: Wallace Collection A461
Blade-length: 29⅜" (75.5 cms)
Pommel-type: H1
Cross-style: 1
Date: c.1360-1400
Condition: Quite good in parts, though the lower end of the blade is much corroded. This very stiff, narrow, acutely pointed blade is more like that of a late 15th century *estoc*, or a 16th century rapier. It is purely a thrusting weapon, the blade being very thick and having a very obtusely-angled edge.
Publication: Mann & Norman, p.242, Hoffmeyer, op.cit. Plate XXA

15. Type: XA
Find-place: Once believed to be near Cologne. Now uncertain.
Collection: Wallace Collection A457
Blade-length: 32⅜" (82.2 cms)
Pommel-type: A
Cross-style: 1
Date: c.1050-1120
Condition: Excavated but good. There are just a few deep pits here and there, but most of the surface is very good under the brown patina.

16. Type: XA
Find-place: Unknown
Collection: Wallace Collection A458
Blade-length: 33⅛" (84.7 cms)
Pommel-type: G
Cross-style: 11
Date: c.1150-1200
Condition: Poor. The whole sword is very thin – the pommel is like a biscuit; the cross is flimsy, too, and the blade itself is thin. All this, however, is probably due to the very heavy corrosion which has worn away a great deal of all the surface metal. There are faint traces of silver ornament on pommel and cross.
Publication: Mann & Norman, II P.241, Plate 105; Hoffmeyer, Plate X.f.; Viollet-le-Duc, *Dictionnaire Raisonné du Mobilier Francais*, V, p.376, fig.10.

17. Type: X
Find-place: Probably somewhere in France
Collection: Wallace Collection A456
Blade-length: 30⅛" (76.5 cms)
Pommel-type:
Petersen's Type K. Wheeler's Type IV
Cross-style: not classified
Date: c.850-900
Condition: Good. There is an iron-inlaid inscription in the fuller of the blade, but this has not yet been examined and interpreted. The great interest of this sword lies in the fact that on the underside of the cross are engraved letters, H L I quite clear on the forward arm, and probably (though this is not really clear) T E R on the rear arm. This hilt belongs to a clearly defined group, five with crosses bearing variants of a name. One found in Norway has H L I T E R, one from Kilmainham in Ireland has H A R T O L F R, another from Ballinderry has H I L T I P R E H T and finally one which used to be in the Zueghaus in Berlin has the name twice, H I F I I F R E ? T and H I L T I P R E H T.
Publications: Much has been published about this group as a whole, and the possible interpretation of the names, but the most accessible are as follows:
Laking, I, pp.14-15 and 62 and fig.17; Davidson, p.81 and Plate 11, b and c and figs. 85, 86, 87.

13   14   15   16   17

Multiple Miscellaneous 18-20

This illustration of three swords in the Royal Armouries shows very clearly how small a sword made for a child might be. These are rare – there is one very similar to the one shown here in Copenhagen, which used to be in Mr. E.A. Christensen's collection, and another one in Glasgow. The sword at 18 here has been described above. The blade of 20 is more like a 17th century rapier; its purpose is clearly only for thrusting, and it may perhaps be considered as an early form (it dates c.1350) of the estoc, so popular in the 15th century for fighting over barriers in those duels, often judicial, over barriers called in England 'Justes of the Pees'.

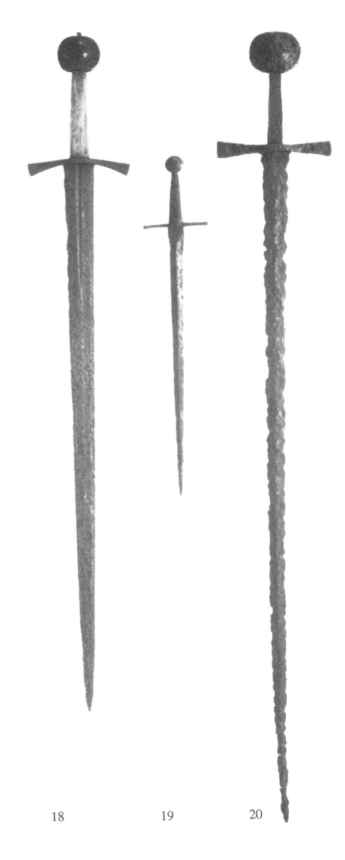

18   19   20

Multiple Miscellaneous 21-22

21. Type: Probably XII
Find-place: Ely, in the Great Ouse
Collection: Museum of Archaeology and Ethnology, Downing College, Cambridge
Pommel-type: A variant of G
Cross-style: Vaguely 1
Blade-length: Only a fragment remains
Date: c.1250
Condition: Bad, except for a beautiful pommel

22. Type: ? Probably X
Find-place: The Great Ouse near Ely

Collection: As 21
Blade-length: Fragmentary
Pommel-type: A variant of H
Cross-style: 6
Date: Could be anything betwen 1075-1300
Condition: Bad, though the hilt is better preserved than the blade.

Both pommels are unusual. There is, however, an exact and dated parallel to the pommel of 21 on a fine grave-effigy of Siegfried von Eppstein, bishop of Mainz, of 1280. The pommel of 22 is one of which I have so far seen no equal.

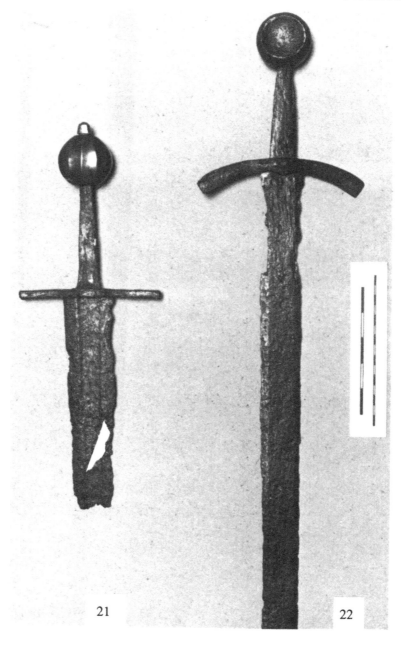

21

22

Multiple Miscellaneous 23-25

3. Type: XI
Find-place: The River Witham at Lincoln
Collection: Lincoln Museum
Blade-length: 33" (83.9 cms)
Pommel-type: 1
Cross-style: 1
Date: c.1100-50
Condition: Quite good. There is a long inscription once inlaid in silver which closely matches one of Dr Leppaaho's Viking grave-finds. (See 23 (ii) below.)

4. Type: XI
Find-place: As above
Collection: " "
Blade-length: 30" (77.5 cms)
Pommel-type: G
Cross-style: 1
Date: c.1100-1150

Condition: Quite good. The rather poor-quality blade has been repaired by a weld in antiquity. There are the remains of an iron-inlaid inscription, now indecipherable.

25. Type: ? XIV
Find-place: As above
Collection: " "
Blade-length: 32" (81.2 cms)
Pommel-type: H
Cross-style: 6
Date: c.1270-1310
Condition: Good. The bronze pommel is very good. No inscriptions. I have called this a XIV, but it is a borderline case between that and Type XII. If a XIV, the date given would be correct; but if a XII, then it could be contemporary with 23 and 24, and so could with them be a relic of the riverside battle of 1141.

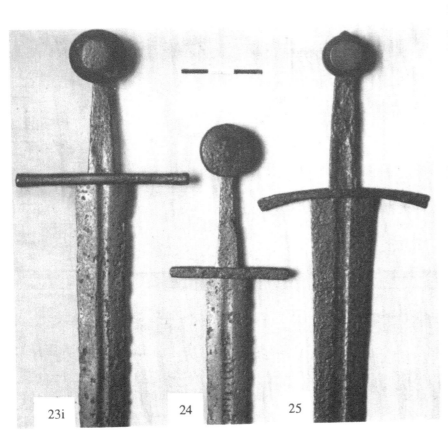

Multiple Miscellaneous 26

Type X
Find-place: unknown
Collection: Musée de l'Armée, Paris
Blade-length: 39"
Pommel-type: 6
Cross-style: 1
Condition: Excellent, probably river-found. This is an enormous sword, and I have drawn it here deliberately alongside the sword of Ramon Berengar III (q.v under XII.4 above) to show its size. Laking illustrates it in Vol.I, saying that the grip (which is of wood covered with silver plate made to emulate a wire binding) is modern, but I am sure it is ancient. In spite of its great size, it is not over-heavy (about 3¾lbs) and is nicely balanced.

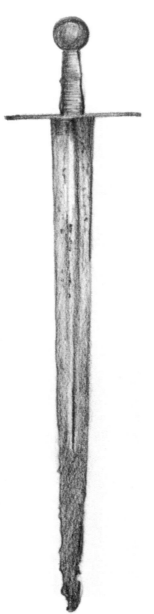

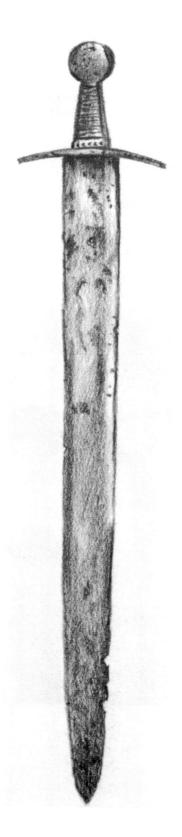

Unclassified 1-3

1. Type: XV
   Find-place: The Dordogne near Castillon
   Collection: Private
   Blade-length: 39¼" (99.5 cms)
   Pommel-type: T2
   Cross-style: II, Straight
   Date: c.1400-50
   Condition: Very good, considering its find-place, with only slight overall pitting.

2. Type: XV
   Find-place: The Dordogne near Castillon
   Collection: Private
   Pommel-type: J1
   Cross-style: 11, straight
   Date: c.1400-50
   Condition: Poor. The blade is terribly eaten away; there is a lot of corrosion on the pommel, but hardly any on the cross. A good example of the curious ways in which corrosion can attack a river-found sword.

3. Type: XVIII
   Find-place: Unknown
   Collection: The Wallace Collection, London A.464
   Pommel-type: T.1
   Cross-style: 1
   Date: c.1400-50 or perhaps 1350-1400?
   Condition: Good, though excavated. The blade is of a rather vague flattened oval section without a mid-rib. There is a nice copper-inlaid mark.
   Publication: Laking, I, pp. 132, 134, fig.164; Hoffmeyer, Plate XXXI.C; Mann & Norman, II, p.243, No. A464.

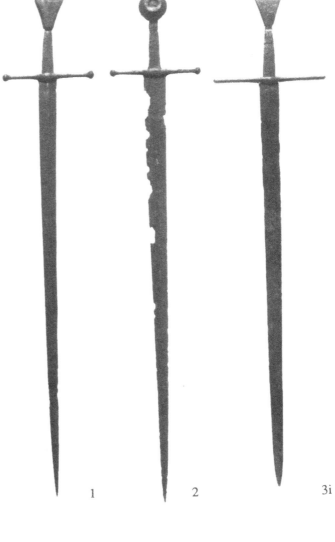

1   2   3i

3ii

231

Unclassified 4

This handy little sword used to be in my care. It might almost be classified as a Type XX, but the blade-section precludes this. It is very flat, with a low central rib which, about 6" (15.3 cms) below the cross turns into a very shallow fuller. The grip is of hard black wood which may be ebony. The sword was photographed for inclusion in a sale catalogue of 1908 by the Helbing Gallery of Munich; at that time there was still about half of the cord binding in place. (Lot 61)

There is a small punched mark on the blade just below the cross, the letters BA. I bought this sword at Sotheby's in 1946 for my uncle, Jeffery Farnol the novelist, and after his death I bought it myself also at Sotheby's. It cost £6 in 1946, £15 in 1954, and I exchanged with Peter Dale Ltd in 1972 for a value of about £250. What is it worth now? I don't know where it is, but presumably in a private collection.

It looks a little like a variety of cinquedea, but is in fact one of those small 'riding swords' so popular in the Middle Ages. The blade is 22" (55.9 cms) long.

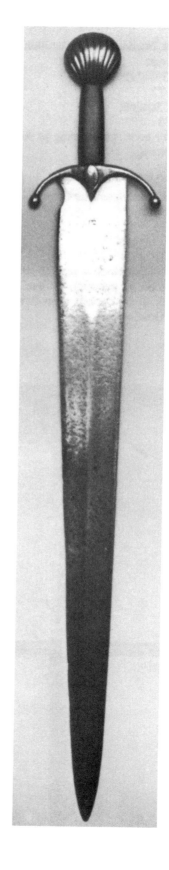

Unclassified 5

This is another 'riding sword' of a totally different shape to the last one. the blade is very light, but quite long (about 28" (71 cms)) of a flat oval section with no fullers or ridge. The cross is much more elegant than the photographs give it credit for. The pommel could be said to be a late survival of a lobated Viking style, but it is more like a flower. The grip shown in the photograph I put on to it, as a sandwich over a flat, broad tang.

I bought it in the saloon bar of The Masons Arms in Vigo Street in London after a meeting of the Arms and Armour Society in 1951. Ten years later it was bought, via Peter Dale Ltd., by the same collector who got the extremely fine and rare late Viking sword shown in this series at XII.11 and dealt with exhaustively here in Appendix B. As far as I know, it remains in that private collection.

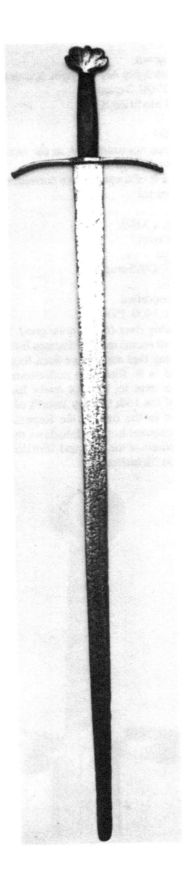

Unclassified 6-7

6. Type: ?XIIIb
   Find-place: Unknown
   Collection: Philadelphia Art Museum. Kienbusch Collection
   Blade-length: 32" (81.2 cms)
   Pommel-type: A modified K
   Cross-style: 2
   Date: c.1400-1500
   Condition: Perhaps not excavated, as the wood-cord-leather grip survives, church preserved, I believe.
   Here the pommel is of a rather more conventional type.
   Publication: Hayward

7. Type: ? Vaguely, a XIII?
   Find-place: Unknown
   Collection: Private
   Blade-length: 30" (77.5 cms)
   Pommel-type: 2
   Cross-style: 12, modified
   Date: Uncertain c.1400-1500
   Condition: Probably river-found, quite good. Dark patina.
   This type of sword seems to be of Eastern European fashion; at least one can say that many have been found in Hungary, for instance, and in E. European collections. The strongly recurved cross is akin to, but not really like the typically Venetian style of the 15th century swords of the mercenary slavonic soldiers in the pay of the Republic. The square pommel with its central boss foreshadows the 'Katzenkopf' (cat's head) pommels of the 17th and 18th century swords of the type known as 'Schiavona'.

Unclassified 8

Type: Unclassified
Find-place: Unknown
Collection: Philadelphia Art Museum, Kienbusch Collection
Blade-length: 29"
Pommel-type: A modified K
Cross-style: Unclassified
Date: c.1400
Condition: Fair, a good deal of pitting under the patina. There are two swords extremely similar to this in the Royal Scottish Museum in Edinburgh, and a particularly fine one in Glasgow; and in a further similar sword is depicted on the churchyard at Kinkell in Aberdeenshire on a grave-slab to Robert de Greenlaw, killed at Harlaw in 1411 (shown here at (ii)). This form of hilt is most positively of Scottish fashion, and is of course of the same general shape as the hilts of the great Twahandswerds, the Claidhamn Mohr of the 16th century.
Publication: Hayward; Oakeshott, *AOW*, Plate 18.

i

ii

Unclassified 9

This is a Bastard sword of a type, form and family which became extremely popular between, say, 1480 and about 1540, in some cases even later. The condition of this one is good, and the fact that some of the thin leather covering of the ancient grip remains, shows how it was made, like a sectional drawing. The photographs don't really show this, which is a pity, for in one's hand there are many interesting (though well enough known and recorded) aspects of the assembling of a sword-hilt.

It is a large (blade length 35" (88.9 cms)) weapon, but nicely balanced and mobile in the hand. There is a certain amount of (indoor) pitting on the blade, but the ironwork of the hilt, originally blued, is hardly pitted at all. It is in a private collection.

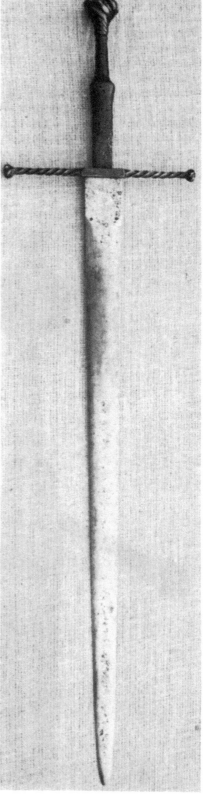

236

Unclassified 10

Type: Vaguely XX
Find-place: The River Bann, Ireland
Collection: The British Museum
Blade-length: (remains of) 29" (73.8 cms)
Pommel-type: Unclassified
Cross-style: Vaguely Style 1
Date: c.1500
Condition: Poor. The point end of the blade is lost, and there is a lot of corrosion except right under the hilt, where there is a ricasso. The tang is of square section and quite narrow, and the disc pommel is hollow; maybe a thin plate on each face has corroded away, but other Scots and Irish swords have pommels which are open on each side to show the tang going through. In this case, it is corrosion, for the other face is still closed. This shows clearly that pommels like this were hollow. The cross is quite an elaborate unit, with a strong iron tube forming the lower part of the grip, which is an integral part of the écusson, which is drawn out downwards in the form of a langet. In its complete condition, this would be a very handsome sword. It is difficult to be certain whether it is of Scottish or Irish origin, for it has characteristics of both national styles.

Unclassified 11

Type: Could be XVIII.A
Find-place: Unknown
Collection: Glasgow Museum and Art Gallery
Blade-length: 16" (40.8 cms)
Pommel-type: W
Cross-style: 3
Date: ? c.1350
Condition: Good. Perhaps river-found
This is one of those very rare tiny little medieval swords made for a boy of perhaps 7 or 8 years old. Unusual too, for the period, is the strong ricasso at the top of the blade. The pommel is matched almost exactly by that on another (though somewhat larger) boy's sword in a private collection in northern England. Another is on a magnificent big Type XIV shown at XIV.5 in this series.

Unclassified 12

Type: ?
Find-place: Unknown
Collection: The Royal Armouries. IX.14.
Blade-length: 39½" (100 cms)
Pommel-type: K
Cross-style: 5
Date: c.1350-75
Condition: Poor. Blade very corroded, but the hilt is better. This is a curious sort of 14th century rapier, perhaps a fore-runner of the popular *estocs* of the next century. A rather ugly sword, very blade-heavy in spite of the massive pommel. There is a very similar sword (No.A461) in the Wallace Collection. Here the blade is much shorter (29⅜", 75.5 cms) but is even narrower, of a flat, rather vague hexagonal section. The pommel is of the same form as this one, but the cross is a thin Style 1.

Unclassified 13

Type: Possibly once a XII
Find-place: In the Rhine
Collection: Museum für Deutsche Geschichte, Berlin
Blade-length: The blade is destroyed
Pommel-type: P
Cross-style: 1
Date: c.1200-1250
Condition: The hilt is quite good, as is the tang, but the blade is completely corroded away. The bronze pommel is interesting, with its incised fleur-de-lys on each side. The fragment of blade remaining reminds one of the comment in *Beowulf* of how the great sword, in the mere cutting off the head of Grendel's mother, melted into 'iron icicles'.
Publication: Mueller and Colling, op.cit., No.20 and p.363.

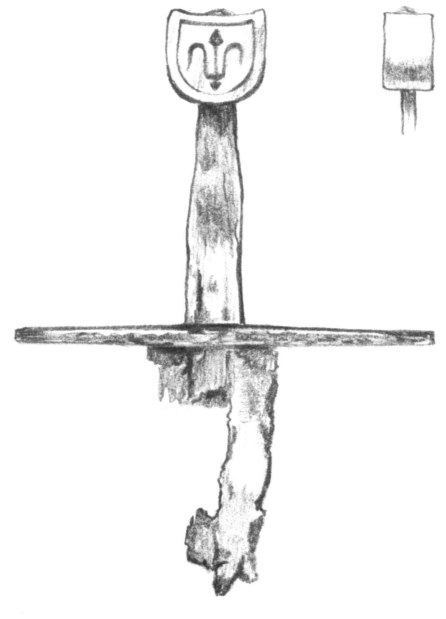

Complex Hilt 1

There are a very great many swords with complex hilts which date within the last years of the 15th century, and so fall within that vaguely-defined period of The Middle Ages – so many that there is no point in showing more than very few. The first here is a very fine weapon, in perfect condition which has a twin in the Victoria and Albert Museum. (Inv.No.M.602-1927) – not, however, quite an identical twin because the pommel, though decorated and lobated in exactly the same way, is of a more oval form, and the guards have only one branch, on the *inside* of the hilt, as if the sword was made for left-handed use. The form of grip, cross and forward ring-guard on both swords are, as near as possible in such a context, identical. They are quite big swords: the blades are 38½" (98 cms) long and the hilts 8¾" (21 cms).

These two have a third 'brother' in Zurich. Here the decoration of incised lines and ridges is slightly different, and the single branch or finger-ring is on the front side of the hilt in the conventional right-handed position. (Schweizerisches Landes museum, Zurich, LM16993.)

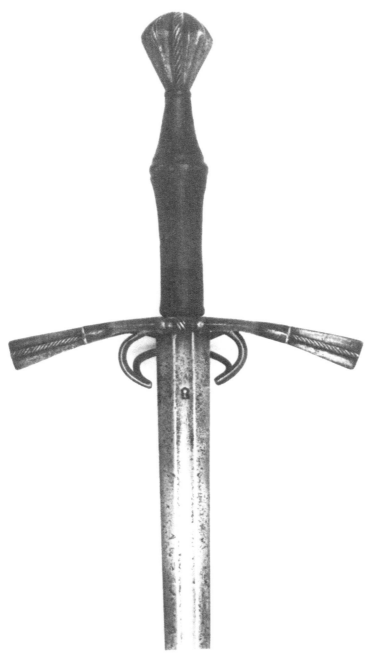

Complex Hilt 2

This rather fuzzy reproduction which was given to me thirty years ago by Claude Blair (who, I believe, took the photograph himself in the museum!) is of a sword of a distinctively Venetian late 15th century style in the Hermitage Museum in Leningrad. There is a group of 17 of these Venetian swords illustrated in *Armi Bianche Italiane* by Boccia and Coelho (Nos.146-164) but this one does not appear with them. Hence, its inclusion here; and also perhaps because I have the print to hand and because it was given me by a friend of great eminence.

Complex Hilt 3

This handsome sword has been classified as of Type XVIII in my *Sword in the Age of Chivalry* (Plate 38), though in my *Archaeology of Weapons* which preceded it I had the sense not to classify it (Plate 20c).

It appeared in both books because it was in my care when I wrote them. I bought it at Sotheby's in 1946 and kept it until 1970 when I exchanged it with the late Eric Valentine for a Viking sword. Since Mr Valentine had it, I believe it has changed hands several times and is now in a private collection. It is in very good condition, the hilt retaining what almost certainly is its original black colouring. The elegant pommel of Type 1 has a rosette on its outer face; the grip, of alternating strands of plain and twisted wires with turk's heads at top and bottom appears to have been on the sword when it was in use, though its style is more of the early 16th century than the date of the sword itself, c.1480. However, since swords very usually had a working life of half a century or so, grips must have been replaced, like scabbards, when they wore out.

There is a fine mark on each side of the blade, made with a punch – a stag trippant within a circle. This same mark was used early in the 17th century by the bladesmith Meves Berns, but here it is in an unmistakeably 15th century blade. Not perhaps surprising, since a stag trippant is a not unusual heraldic charge. Besides, blade-marks seem to have been timeless, since marks on Iron Age swords from la Tène are the same as are found on 16th and 17th century blades as well. This is the very essence of a thrusting sword; the weight is well down the blade, making it seem heavy for a cutting stroke, but in a thrust the weight seems to pull the sword forward and put itself behind the point.

Publication: Blair, C., *EAA*, no.56; Oakeshott, *AOW*; Oakeshott, *SAC*, pl.38.

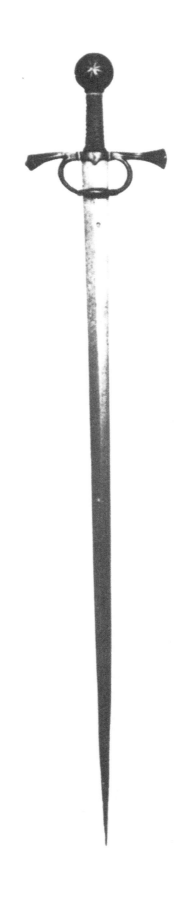

APPENDIX A

The Living Sword: construction of modern replicas of the knightly blade

Tony Mansfield

Preface

My study of the medieval sword owes a great deal to a very many people and institutions. While it is still very much in its infancy, it would never have progressed even as far as it has without their active and ongoing support.

Therefore, I would like to offer my thanks to The Royal Armouries of the Tower of London and David Edge of the Wallace collection for allowing me to take many of their finest pieces from their cases, and study them in sufficient depth to give me a fighting chance of making my own swords have the correct look and feel. To the many blacksmiths and farriers who have been willing to offer knowledge of their skills for my cause; to Chris Bond for giving me my first lessons in forging: to all those unsung heroes in many museums around the country who have dedicated themselves to preserving our heritage and to those almost equally unknown, but far noisier members of the Lion Rampant for their friendship and the opportunity they have given me to see my swords in action and overcome the problems associated with their use.

I would also like to thank some special friends; Mr Ewart Oakeshott for costing me thousands of pounds, infecting me with his boundless enthusiasm for the subject and giving most generously of his time and knowledge; to Miss Paula Senior for her practical input in the making of grips and general forging techniques and especially to both my parents for allowing me to make a great deal of noise and mess in their back garden, their constant support and encouragement and allowing me to bathe afterwards!

Tony Mansfield

Introduction

It is very easy for the modern scholar, in studying the fascinating subject of the art of war and the equally fascinating subject of its instruments, to forget that these instruments were not made for him or her to sit upon and brood over, but to end the life of a fellow human being. What is, to me, the great beauty of many of these instruments serves to blind us further to their ultimate purpose, especially as time draws a kindly veil over the results of their use. The reverence given by all classes of society to what would appear to be a relatively crude chopping instrument seems very hard to justify, especially in the modern view of the medieval sword, which is still regrettably considered by most to be heavy, ugly and unwieldy.

The *purpose* of the weapon has been a primary factor in my own study of the medieval sword. It is quite impossible to make a sword accurately and well without making it suitable for killing, however abhorrent the thought may be to the smith who does it, and my own love for the beauty of my creations is tempered by this one fact. The obvious difficulty of knowing how to balance and grip a sword properly can only be overcome by extensive use of original weapons in a non-live situation; which is, to most, an impossibility. However, the use of blunted weapons in a controlled situation has proven to be an acceptable alternative and personal experience gained on the field of many re-enactments has been invaluable to me.

In this respect, I feel that I can say with some justification that all the swords made by me are truly 'live' blades and I would like to think that by making a functional sword to live on a collector's wall, I have at least contributed to a small extent to increasing our understanding of the primary weapon of the warriors of medieval Europe. The creation of what I would like to think of as the closest possible equivalent of an original blade in pristine condition has, for me, done much to cloak the often badly corroded and largely dead relics seen behind glass walls in the grim dignity which once was theirs.

The material present in the next few pages has been drawn from my own experiences in the production of modern replicas of medieval blades. As such, it is coloured by the very primitive conditions in which I have had to work, and often by the lack of proper tooling and very often knowledge for the particular job in hand. When this has occurred, I have endeavoured not only to present the way in which a particular problem was overcome, but also to show how I would have liked to approach it given the proper tooling, a helping hand or whatever else may have been required.

It is my opinion that most early smiths would have had the same or very similar problems and would have had to make accommodations in much the same way as myself but as knowledge and facilities advanced, better tools would have become available to make possible much that was not previously, and make easier many things which were difficult before.

As a guide to obtaining the correct final form of blade, cross and pommel I have drawn extensively on the work of modern scholars, as well as handling as many original blades as the patience of museums and individuals would allow. This has also

245

offered some chance to determine the correct balance for particular types of blade, although I would say that no two people would have the same blade balanced in the same way, even given similar fighting styles, heights, weights and strengths. I would go even further and say that no two smiths would necessarily make the same type of sword in the same way.

The sword itself was very much more than a simple tool to those who used it, even the most pragmatic of mercenaries, who called their weapons 'Gagnepain' or 'Wynbrod'. It was a symbol of the very ideals of chivalry and one which lived in the hands serving those ideals. From the intensive and often very tiring effort that goes into the production of such a blade, I can only assume that the medieval swordsmith would feel that the weapon he made was more than just another 'job', but the highest expression of his craft which had once been thought to be the work of giants.

Iron and Fire. The tools of the smith

In the manufacture of any weapon, the smith's approach can often determine the degree of success or failure of any weapon he undertakes to make. A careful approach is every bit as important as having the correct skills and starts right from the beginning in the careful selection of materials.

The medieval smith would have had relatively pure wrought iron and high carbon steel as his base materials. The blade would be made from steel and iron forge-welded together in any of a number of clever ways. The proportion of steel to iron in the blade itself would have gone some considerable way to fixing its cost and quality. The cross and pommel would have been made from pure wrought iron, which is far easier to work and more than suitable for these applications, since they were very rarely hit.

The modern smith has to approach locating suitable materials in a slightly different way. Firstly, high carbon steels without additives such as molybdenum or vanadium are just no longer available, and a similar situation applies with wrought iron, unless one is fortunate enough to find a Victorian fence which is being dismantled, or to be on site when an old railway station is being modernised. In addition, forge-welding a tool steel and a mild steel are problematical and would produce a blade which, when tempered, would probably be too brittle for use. Most mild steels appear to be adversely affected by the hardening and tempering process, especially after forging.

In order to function effectively, therefore, the steel used for the blade would have to be both hard and tough, able to take and hold a good edge and to be able to bend to a considerable degree without breaking. Larger swordmaking companies can have special steels made for this purpose, and many choose to do so. The individual, however, has to choose from those steels available to him. Of those, ordinary spring steel has been shown to be much the best.[1] This is a 0.6% carbon/manganese steel used in old style car springs which can be hardened and tempered to produce the correct properties a sword needs to have.

The cross and pommel can use material made to a much less exacting specification, and in the absence of wrought iron, ordinary mild steels of any type can be used to good effect.

The smith's tools were of even greater importance to him than his materials. Often he had a very wide range of hammers, tongs, fullers and punches of which he would make most use of only the few he felt happiest with. Many of these tools were and are best made by the smith for his own use and could be specially modified for a particular application.

The forge and anvil are also of primary importance. A long bed forge is ideal for swordsmithing, since a large proportion of

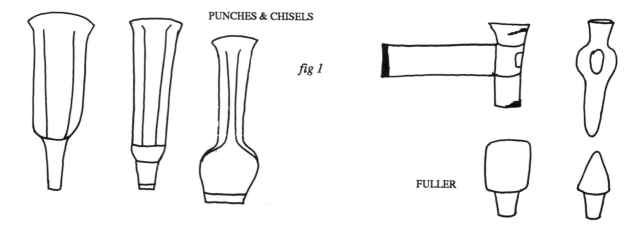

PUNCHES & CHISELS

fig 1

FULLER

---

[1] The full specification of this steel is BS970 Part 1: 1983 EN45 or EN47. EN47 is a slightly better quality version of EN45 which is, regrettably, much harder to obtain.

the blade can be heated at any one 'pass' without having to spend large amounts of time passing the blade through the hot coals and, of course, no forging can be done without a good, flat, anvil with a reasonable selection of stake tools.

A range of different hammers is essential. Heavy forging is done with large hammers with relatively flat surfaces and other hammers of smaller size or cross-section are used to suit a particular application. Punches are used to form holes in both cross and pommel, and fullers are used for precisely that; forming the incorrectly name blood-gutter. (fig.1) It is quite possible that blades of the flattened diamond section were manufactured with special tooling and hammers. This greatly facilitates the forging of the section and makes a form of mass-production possible, at least in theory.

These are only the absolute basics required for forging. Files, grindstones, polishing stones, chisels, knives and acid are only a part of the rest of the tools required to complete the manufacture of a sword, and are equally important in the process of turning a lump of steel into a living blade suitable for the hand fortunate enough to possess it for a time. Their use will also be dealt with here.

Hammer and Hand: the process of forging

In the manufacture of a modern replica, the smith's approach determines the degree of success or failure he has. The first step necessary is to handle the weapon to be replicated in some detail, feel how it moves through the air and make a detailed set of drawings and templates for blade, cross and pommel. If a particular sword is now available for one reason or another, it is equally important to handle similar examples of the same type of weapon so that an accurate guess may be made of the sword's weight, balance and general 'feel'.

This is relatively simple, if time-consuming, process with is absolutely *vital* to the success of the blade. It is all too easy to make a sword from one seen in a case which is too heavy, or improperly balanced or both, an understandable mistake made far too often in the past.

This is perhaps best illustrated by a specific example, one of extreme interest to the writer and a weapon which would be fascinating to the academic, were it still where it was originally laid to rest; i.e. the sword of the Black Prince. This particular weapon resided in Canterbury Cathedral until it disappeared in the Civil War; stolen, as legend has it, by Oliver Cromwell.

With no blade to examine and handle, problems are immediately posed to the smith. Firstly, the blade form has to be decided, and its size and weight determined. Two likely candidates for the blade form exist; Oakeshott's type XV, and his type XVII. Both were popular in the 14th century and are of approximately the right proportions to fit in the scabbard. The former was decided on, purely because it appears to be the more popular of the two blade forms. Sizes could be estimated from the scabbard, which fortunately does survive, and relative proportions of the cross and pommel scaled from the effigy and Stothard's drawing thereof. From this, the blade would appear to be approximately 2" in width, the cross about 7" long and ½" thick at its widest point and the grip about 6⅞" long (fig.2).

Study of other, similar, blades indicates a weight of perhaps just over three pounds and a point of balance 3-4" below the cross. In order to be effective as a thrusting weapon, the blade must be stiff, and therefore of approximately the same thickness along its length, with an acute point which may or may not be reinforced.

Having decided on the form, templates were made of cross, pommel, and blade. For accuracy's sake, these were strictly adhered to, a surprisingly difficult task.

Having selected a suitable flat bar of steel, it is first necessary to round off the corners. If this is not done, the corners will fold over when drawn out, producing a blade which will not function (see figs 3 and 4). Having done this, the blade is then drawn out to the correct length, taking care to keep the thickness as constant as possible down its length. At this stage, the blade should be flat, square, and narrower than the template, to allow for beating in the diamond section. The steel is worked between orange-yellow and low red. Working the steel too hot can cause it to burn, which in turn can cause the migration of relatively large amounts of carbon to the surface, making the steel very brittle, unless normalised afterwards. [2] Working it too cold can 'work harden' the steel. This can, if taken to extremes, produce very fine cracks in the surface of the blade, which obviously weaken it considerably.[3]

During this process, drawing out the steel by hammering the edges of the blade (as shown in fig 5) will tend to twist it in both directions, and great care *must* be taken to straighten it as drawing out takes place. Drawing out also tends to thicken the edges, and these must be kept to the original thickness. It is extremely difficult to do all this with a shaped blade, and much better results are obtained if each bend and twist is corrected as it appears. Essentially then, drawing out a sword consists of placing it at the

2 and 3 The writer has been fortunate enough to see modern fighting weapons break for both these reasons.

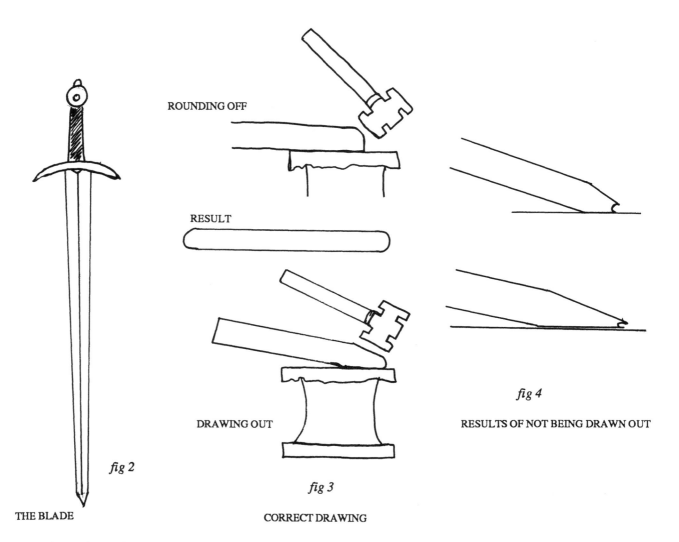

ROUNDING OFF

RESULT

DRAWING OUT

CORRECT DRAWING

fig 3

fig 2

THE BLADE

fig 4

RESULTS OF NOT BEING DRAWN OUT

correct angle on the anvil, hammering one edge, flattening and straightening the resulting twist, turning the sword over and repeating the process for the other side (figs 6 and 7).

This process is repeated for the tang, after forging the blade section. The junction between tang and blade is formed with a special tool, which *must* have a small radius on one corner. If this radius is not put in, a point of stress results on the shoulders of the tang, shortening the working life of a sword considerably. The edges of the tang can then be tidied up with a file, preparatory to burning out the hole in the grip.

At this point, we have a vaguely sword-shaped lump of metal with no edges or point. Formation of the edges is a fairly simple, but time consuming, task. This is done by placing the blade at the correct angle on the anvil and hammering the other side. This process is then repeated for all four sides of the blade, which helps keep the edges even and the blade straight. If one edge is beaten out more than the other, a slight curve in the blade may result. Since the smith almost always works by hand and eye alone, this is actually quite common in blade-making.

Experience shows that the hammering of the diamond is best done on the edge of the anvil and that the blade-section is best done starting from the point and working backward. Again, any resulting bend or twist must be corrected as it appears and care must be taken to work the steel in the correct temperature range. Small hammers are used for the point, replaced with progressively larger hammers as one works up the blade. The point can be reinforced by allowing the steel to thicken slightly during the drawing out process and then beating in the diamond as usual (see fig.8). The worst difficulty encountered in modern forging is selecting a piece of metal that will end up at the correct size when forging is complete. It is usually easier to make a blade slightly too heavy and file it down to size afterwards.

The blade is then thoroughly checked for any bend and twist, which is carefully corrected, and filed prior to the hardening and tempering process. Normally, the fibres of the steel are also packed just prior to hardening and tempering. This masses the fibres of the steel and allows it to hold a better edge. It is done by heating the entire blade until it is barely red when seen in shadow, then hitting the edges smartly with a hammer. If the hammer blows are not kept even along the length of the blade, it will warp in the hardening process, making it necessary to straighten the blade and try again.

The hardening process is apparently very simple. The blade is heated to a good red-orange and then quenched in water and

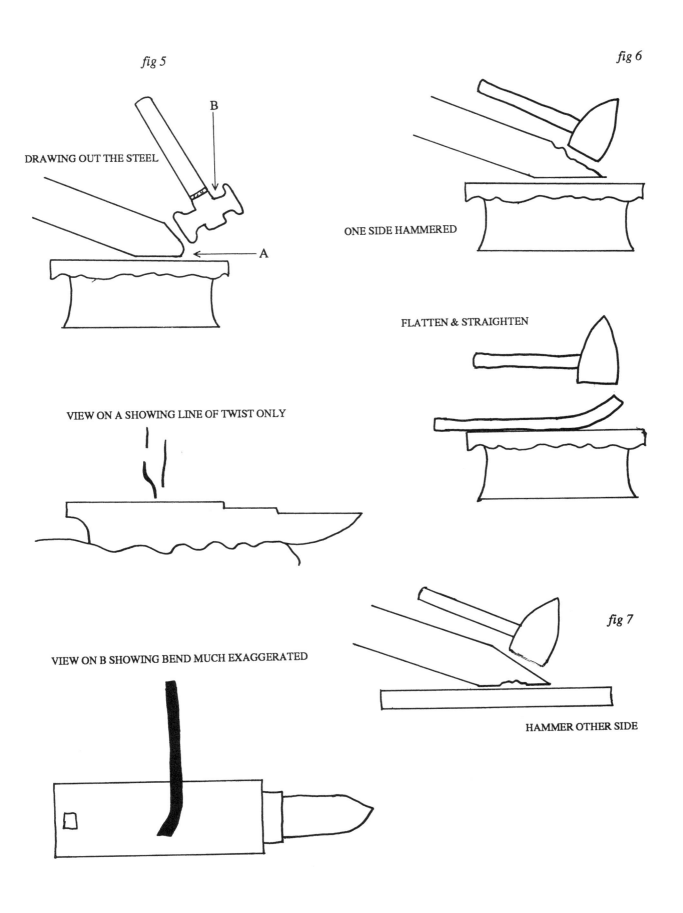

fig 5

fig 6

DRAWING OUT THE STEEL

B

A

ONE SIDE HAMMERED

FLATTEN & STRAIGHTEN

VIEW ON A SHOWING LINE OF TWIST ONLY

fig 7

VIEW ON B SHOWING BEND MUCH EXAGGERATED

HAMMER OTHER SIDE

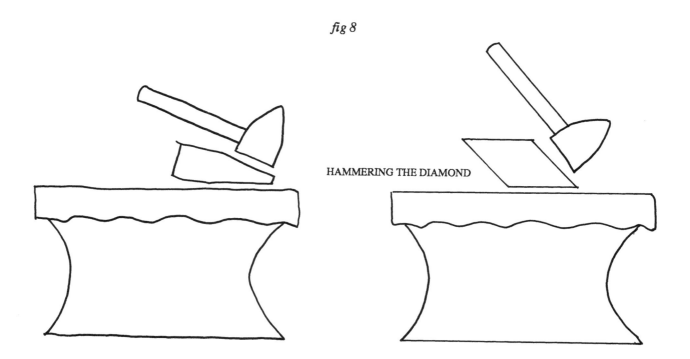

fig 8

HAMMERING THE DIAMOND

oil. While the actual difficulty belies the simplicity of the process, an explanation of why this can occur at all is in order. With a high carbon steel, this produces a very hard and brittle blade which has to be tempered afterwards. Tempering is a controlled softening process which leaves the edges very hard, but produced a flexible core.

The properties of any steel are totally dependant on the iron-carbon ratio and the degree of heat treatment it is given. Heating a piece of steel to different temperatures results in different crystal structures being obtained. At the critical temperature, the crystal lattice of the iron 'opens' and allows the carbon atoms to become integrated with it. This crystal structure is known as *austenite*. If this is cooled very rapidly, another crystal structure known as *martensite* is formed. Martensite holds the carbon atoms in its structure and is the hardest form of steel. Cooling more slowly produces different, softer lattices, some of which are *pearlite, ferrite* and *cementite*. Ideally the smith is trying to produce a blade with a structure known as *tempered martensite*, which has martensite edges, with a ferrite and pearlite body. This can be done in a number of ingenious ways, all of which will work, leaving the method chosen up to the individual smith.

First among these is to heat the blade up to red heat (750-800⑤ C), quench in water or brine and then heat the middle portion to a sub-critical temperature and allow to cool; it is the most common method. Secondly, it is possible to heat the whole blade, but quench only the edges, allowing the rest to cool naturally; this method particularly suits single-edged blades for obvious reasons. Thirdly, the blade can be quenched in oil and allowed to cool to such a degree, that when removed from the quenching medium, the remaining oil is *just* burnt off the surface of the blade. All these methods will produce a working blade, but the author prefers the first two, the first for a two-edged sword, and the second for one with a single edge.

In the hardening process, it is critical that the heat be completely even throughout the blade. If this is not the case, then the blade will twist in tempering, requiring straightening, re-packing and re-hardening. The blade is quenched edge-down, thus preventing the formation of bubbles on the underside, and is moved around in the quenching bath, for the same reason and also to make sure that the medium in which it is being quenched is still cool. If bubbles are allowed to remain on the blades surface, uneven tempering will result which will cause the blade to bend.

Tempering itself can be done in a number of ways. One large swordmaking company uses boiling lead as its tempering medium, which means that the blade does not have to be cleaned before tempering. One swordsmith known by reputation to the writer likes to place his sword on top of his forge, passing it over the coals until a lump of wood begins to smoke when laid on top of it, and the writer prefers to lay red hot bars on the middle of the blade until it turns purple or blue. Blue is best used when flexibility is required i.e. for a slashing blade, and purple give a stiffer blade suitable for thrusting. This process requires that the blade be filed clean first and the presence of several bars of red-hot mild steel. It is greatly facilitated by a helping hand holding one bar in place while the next is heated. This should and does, if correctly done, produce a blade with a hard edge and a soft core.

The blade is then polished. Initially, it is best to remove the scale from forging and hardening with a coarse file, working across the diamond. At this stage, the edges are usually quite thick. This is done to prevent them from cooling too quickly during the hardening process, which would make them extremely brittle. The marks from file or grinder are then removed with a large

250

grinding stone, preferably water- or foot-driven. This process is continued until the edges are just beginning to become sharp. At this stage, the relatively coarse grinding stone is replaced by progressively finer oilstones until a sharp blade with a good finish is produced.

Practical use of sharp swords on inanimate objects has shown that while extremely sharp blades can be produced, these tend to become blunt relatively quickly when used against pieces of plate steel. From this, the writer suspects that the degree of sharpness of a blade would depend upon its purpose, i.e. extremely sharp blades could be used against relatively lightly armoured opponents, and blunter though still sharp weapons would be used against more heavily armoured opponents. Final finishing can be done with fine grades of emery paper, and a very high polish can be put on with used emery soaked in oil. The writer has found that the residue from the sharpening process, when placed on a leather or cloth pad, can also be used to good effect.

After this, the cross and pommel have to be made. While the forging is, in general, much lighter than that of the sword itself, these produce their own problems which have to be overcome. Without a well proportioned cross and pommel, the blade itself can become unwieldy, and while it is possible to make generalizations about weight and balance, the only way that a truly successful combination can be achieved is to liaise quite closely with the eventual user.

In the case of a modern replica, a best estimate has to be made from existing weapons, and this can only be reached by actually handling the weapon to be made, or if this cannot be done, several weapons of approximately similar weight and balance.

In the case of the particular weapon being written about, the sizes were taken off the effigy and a sheet metal template made. The cross was then drawn out using a very similar method to the sword itself, except that all four sides were worked equally. Once drawn out to roughly the correct size, a rectangular hole was put in the cross, by taking it up to red heat and using a cold-chisel to punch the hole. In general, this tends to flatten the middle of the cross, and so this has to be left a little too thick to allow for the effect of the punch. Once just over half way through, the cross is turned over and flattened out and the punching is completed from the other side. This helps to avoid the production of any burr, which would have to be filed away. This operation has to be done with some care, so that the cross remains square and true. If this is not done, it will not sit easily on the blade and would then work loose very quickly, something that swordsmen find very irritating.

After punching, a groove is formed in the base of the cross to accommodate the blade. In a sword of good quality, such as the sword of the Black Prince, it is entirely likely that a tool would be specially made so that this groove would fit the sword blade exactly. After this operation, the cross would be straightened in and then bent to the correct degree around the beak of the anvil. It was, in fact, necessary to make several corrections in order to form the correct curve in the cross. The cross can then be filed, polished and fitted to the blade.

The writer has spent a great deal of time speculating as to a viable method of production of a wheel pommel. In any case, producing one as perfect as that shown of the effigy did prove to be impossible and therefore it was necessary to have one made on a lathe. Under the right circumstances, it would perhaps be possible to extrude a piece of round bar and cut it up with a tool of the right geometry to produce the classic wheel shape. This would need two people to hold the tooling and a very heavy hammer. A recess could be put in the pommel with a flat round punch with a small hole on its face to give it something to centre off, and incidentally provide a key to glue in the insert.

Punching the hole through the pommel is a very time consuming and often difficult task. When the pommel is being punched, it has to be freed by tapping one edge smartly with the hammer (fig 9), which tends to make it slightly elliptical. In addition, punching the pommel at red heat on the anvil tends to squash it and make it oval, something which had to be avoided in this case. The only solution found to this particular problem was to punch it on a large stump, a very smoky task, since the pommel burnt into the wood, but one which kept the ovality down to an acceptable degree. Again, the pommel can then be filed and polished before fitting it to the blade.

In order to put the lion's head into the pommel, the best method would be to make some small round inserts from copper and chisel the lion's head into them. These could then be enamelled and fired, prior to gluing them into the prepared faces on the pommel.

A living blade: the process of assembly

In the process of the manufacture of the blade, it is now necessary to go back some time, to where the blade had just been rough forged. With modern steels, manufacture is greatly eased by forming the hole in the grip before the tempering process, since the temper of the blade would be adversely affected if this were done after.

At this point, a fairly large piece of a suitable wood such as beech is prepared by having a pilot hole burned through it with a piece of red-hot round bar with a point. The tang is then heated to a low red heat and pushed gently through the pilot hole, taking care not to let it become too cool or push it too fast. Either factor could cause the grip to split. The writer has often found it useful to use an oversize piece of wood, which also helps to prevent the grip from splitting. This process does cause a great deal of very acrid smoke, and great care must be taken to keep the hand steady as the tang passes through the wood.

Once pommel and cross are complete, the grip can then be carved with knives and chisels to a suitable size for the hand that is to use it. In this particular case, it was found impossible to twist a wire to emulate that shown on the effigy so a cord was used

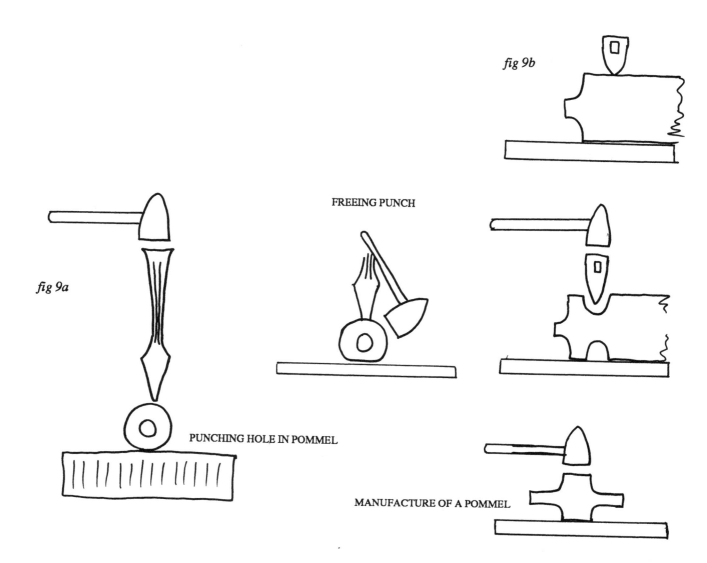

fig 9b

FREEING PUNCH

fig 9a

PUNCHING HOLE IN POMMEL

MANUFACTURE OF A POMMEL

instead. Top and bottom of the cord were secured by placing them in small holes in the grip and holding them in place with a tiny sliver of the same wood.

Cross, grip and pommel can then be fitted to the blade. A tang button is a simple item to place on top of the pommel and the tang can then be riveted over to complete assembly. Riveting the tang is greatly facilitated, at least with modern steels, by the application of a small amount of local heat.

After a final polish, the result is a living blade made for the hand to wield it. While the process was very long, time consuming and intensive, with much of the work done in the freezing cold with no light except that produced by the forge itself, the satisfaction of producing such a blade is unrivalled, a feeling the writer will treasure for the rest of his life.

APPENDIX B

Beati Omnipotensque Angeli Christi
(Blessed and Omnipotent the Angels of Christ)

There are five splendid medieval swords which when considered as a group are important to the advancement of our knowledge of this most interesting (and most neglected) of weapons. Each is an outstanding specimen in its own right; three of them, in state museums, are available for study, but two are in private hands. All except one have been known since the last century, and though two of them have been published several times, never have all five been studied together as a group.

Each sword bears an inscription; four upon the blade and one, the key to the dating of all five, has an inscription in runic characters on the bronze collar which encircled the top of the now missing grip. These runes give a firm date of *c.*1100. The other four swords in this group appear by analogy to fall within the same date range. My purpose here is to consider these five swords, compare the detail and technique of their inscriptions, and reach a conclusion from the evidence such comparison presents.

Foremost for the quality of its gold-inlaid inscription is a sword which was found about forty years ago hanging in a farm kitchen in Northumberland, which suggests that it had a local find-place (Fig.1). It has a short, broad blade and is in excavated condition, but its inscription is a superb piece of medieval art (Fig.2). It is one of those small though eminently serviceable weapons which, though rare, have appeared consistently in archaeological finds that date from the second century A.D. to the eleventh. These little swords are often referred to in Anglo-Saxon and Norse literature, and also appear over and over again in sculpture, monuments and MS paintings from *c.*1275-1500. It has been suggested by those few who have known it that this beautiful little sword was (*a*) a long one broken and repointed recently, (*b*) a sword for a boy or (*c*) a ceremonial weapon. The evidence available points unerringly to the fact that (*a*) is incorrect, (*b*) is extremely unlikely and that (*c*) is untenable because it is a fine 'knightly' fighting sword as will be shown below.

Though the form of this sword is not uncommon,[1] there are only two analogous inscriptions known to me. One of these is on the blade of a sword of the same type as the Northumberland one which was found about a century ago in the defensive ditch of the town of Perleberg in Germany, and it rests now in the Markische Provinzialmuseum.[2] The other is on one side of the blade of a sword (found in the River Ouse near Cawood in Yorkshire) which, once on loan to the Tower of London, is now in private hands[3] (Figs.3 and 4b).

fig. 1　　　　　*a*　　　　　*b*　*fig. 2*

---

1   Oakeshott, Ewart, *The Sword in the Age of Chivalry*, London 1964. This sword is of Type X (Ten) in the typology of medieval swords.

2   Wegeli, Rudolf, *Inschriften auf mittelalterlichen Schwertklingen*, Zürich 1904, p.22, fig.28.

3   Oakeshott, op.cit., plate 3c, where it is wrongly dated the 13th century.

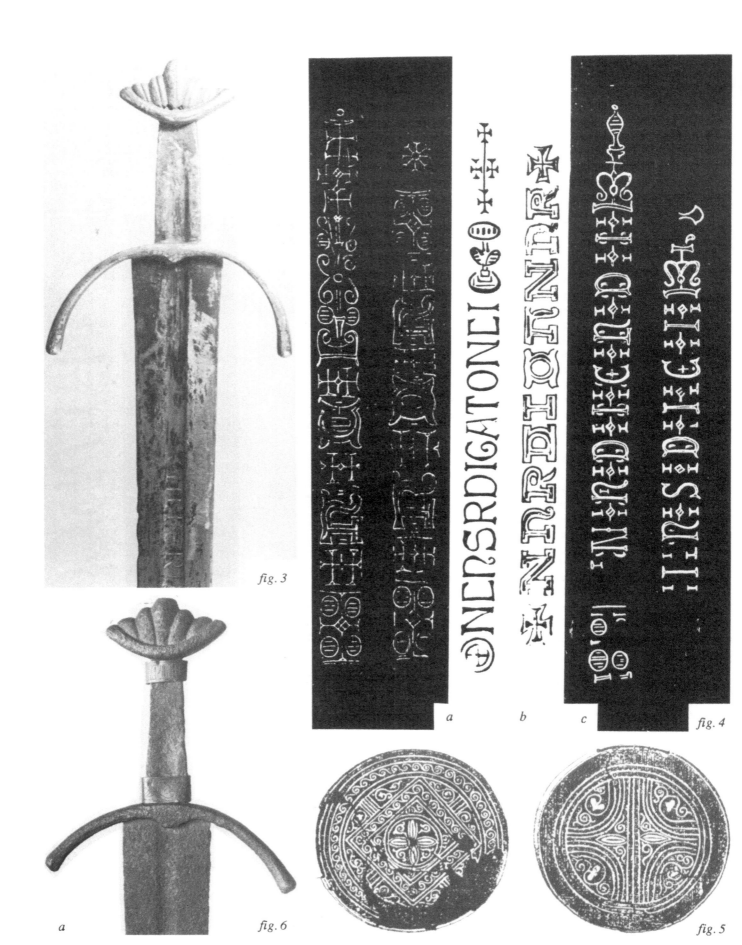

fig. 3

a

b

c

ⲞNENSRDIGATONEI

fig. 4

a

fig. 6

fig. 5

The inscriptions on each side of the Perleberg blade are of exactly the same style, though not the same content (Fig.4a); they are of a like nature, but not identical, with the inscription on the Northumberland sword, but they are so closely akin to the inscription on side (i) of the Cawood sword (Fig.4b) that one is tempted to use (incorrectly) the word 'identical'. We are therefore entitled to believe that all three are so closely related that they must have come from the same atelier, if not from the same hand. Here it should be emphasised that in the early Middle Ages sword-blades were only made in a very few centres of production and that the workshops from which the inscribed blades came were probably very few, so that it is possible to identify not only workshop styles but individual 'handwriting'.

To engrave letters and designs of such delicacy upon a tempered blade preparatory to the application of the inlaying wires of gold or silver or latten was an art which called for great skill on the part of trained calligraphers. Here was no illiterate bladesmith banging red-hot strips of iron into crudely cut, incorrectly arranged letters in an untempered blade (as must have been the case with the iron inlaid inscriptions still very much in use alongside the gold and silver ones), but an artist delicately cutting his inscription into an already tempered blade with a diamond or a burin. It was essential that the blade must have undergone all the finishing processes before the wires were hammered into the engraved lines, or the non-ferrous wires would have melted.

The actual technique of inlaying the fine wires hammered flat into iron sword-furniture is a very ancient one. There is evidence for its use as early as the second century, for among the objects found in the bog-deposit of arms at Nydam in Denmark is a circular disc-shaped chape for a sword-scabbard (Fig.5). The designs are complicated and of a very high aesthetic quality, quite as sophisticated and technically excellent as any of these blade-inscriptions. There are also of course a number of knives and saxes whose blades are inlaid in copper or brass with inscriptions in runic or Latin characters – e.g. the fine Anglo-Saxon knife from Sittingbourne in Kent and the sax from the Thames at Wandsworth, both now in the British Museum. These are much later than the Nydam chape, being of the 10th century.

The Perleberg sword's hilt and blade are of the same type as those of the Northumberland sword (Type X – ten – of the typology worked out in *The Sword in the Age of Chivalry*) but the Cawood one is totally different (Type XII), so different in fact that it has always confidently been dated *c*.1300, by me as well as others. I am asserting now that it is in fact two centuries earlier. Were it not for the fourth sword in this group (Fig.6) such a suggestion might seem absurd; but the runic inscription on the hilt of this sword, datable by the style of the characters and of the legend itself, as well as the circumstances of the conditions under which it was found, give it a firm date of *c*.1100.

Therefore some description of these circumstances and of the runic inscription will be necessary before proceeding to detailed comparisons of the inscriptions on the other four swords.

Fig.6 shows this sword; it was found in 1880 in Norway when a railway cutting was being driven across farmland at Korsoygaden in Hedmark, not far from Oslo, in the Oldsakssammling of which city is a preserved.[4] It was in a stone box or chest, or a cist as archaeologists have called it. It was not a coffin; it was too small, nor were there any remains of cremated bones. Besides the sword there was its scabbard of wood covered with tooled leather, and a round wooden shield with a large metal boss. So far this seems to be the only example of such a find, but we learn from Anglo-Saxon and Norse poems that in Northern Europe from the 7th to 11th centuries the storage, as well as the burial of swords in stone cists was not uncommon. There is a passage for instance in an Anglo-Saxon heroic poem which speaks of a sword hidden in a *Stanfaet*. The literal meaning of *Fat/Faet* is Vessel, or receptacle – the same as the modern word vat, and *Stan* clearly refers to stone. Another word used in similar contexts is *Syncfaet*, treasure-chest.[5]

A parallel word in Old Norse is *Ker*, which suggests a tub or tub-like vessel, and it is used in connection with the storing of swords – so much so that one of the many kennings for a sword is 'Fish of the Ker' and the word is used in the same way as *Faet*. A mythical sword called *Levateinn* in one of the Edda poems is securely hidden in '*the Ker of* Segjarn, secured by nine sure fastenings'. Again in *Gudrunarhvot* we are told that Gudrun chooses helmets and mail-coats for her sons from

fig. 6b

4   Petersen, Jan, *De Norske Vikingesverd*, Oslo 1919; Hoffmeyer, Ada Bruhn, *Middelalderens Tvaeeggede Svaerd*, Copenhagen 1951; and Davidson, Dr. Hilda Ellis, *The Sword in Anglo-Saxon England*, Oxford 1961. Also Oakeshott, op.cit., where it is wrongly dated the 13th century.

5   Ibid., pp.148-9.

such chests in the store-room. The fact that special words were used in Old Norse as well as Anglo-Saxon suggests that a particular kind of stone receptacle was used for arms.

The use of casks for holding swords is borne out by the well-known fact that casks were used for transporting sword-blades from the centres of their production, right up to the end of the 18th century.

There is then an actual *Stanfaet* containing a sword and shield, an archaeological fact which cannot be disputed, and we can compare and check it against that fragment from the Anglo-Saxon poem *Waldere*, where the eponymous hero refers to a sword: '... that other which I possess, hidden in a *Stanfaet*. I know that Theodoric himself intended to send it to Widia, and much treasure along with the sword'.[6]

The reference here to Theodoric and the early date of the poem make it plain that the use of *Stanfaet* in this way goes back at least to the 7th century, the probable date of the poem, if not to the fifth, the actual date of Theodoric. That there was also a shield of undeniably Viking style in the *Stanfaet* at Korsoygaden suggests very powerfully that the sword dates before the 14th century.

All this archaeological and literary evidence of its date however is made purely academic by the runic legend engraved on the bronze *vettrim*. Transliterated, this reads: *Asmundr Gersi Mik–Asleikr a Mik* = Asmund made me. Asleik owns me.

In his definitive work on the Viking sword, Dr Jan Petersen[7] dated this sword at *c*.1050-1100. This dating has been accepted by most authorities on Scandinavian archaeology, but perhaps most significantly to this study of swords by Dr Ada Bruhn Hoffmeyer[8] and Dr Hilda Ellis Davidson.[9] The eminent runologists Eric Moltke and O. Rygh[10] give the runes a rather later date, *c*.1100-1150, but there is nowhere (except in what I erroneously wrote in *The Sword in the Age of Chivalry*) any suggestion that they can be any later than *c*.1150.

We may therefore assign a mean date of *c*.1100 for this sword which must, of course, be for its making, not its using, for very often at this period swords were handed down to several generations of warriors. However, the circumstance of its burial in a stone chest, with a Viking's shield, does indicate that it was in fact enclosed in its *Stanfaet* during the Viking age.

The significance of this sword to this inquiry is of course that its hilt is so very close in the rather unusual forms of cross and pommel to the Cawood one that we cannot evade the conclusion that both were the product of one hilt-making workshop, if not of one individual hilt-maker. Again, one is tempted to make incorrect use of the word 'identical', for the only differences between the two hilts are in minor and unimportant details.

It must therefore be concluded that the Cawood sword dates at latest within the first half of the 12th century, not the 14th. Further evidence for the probability of this date is given by a Viking grave-slab in the church at Ebberston, near Scarborough in Yorkshire[11] (Fig.7). There is almost universal agreement that this grave slab dates within the first half of the 12th century, if not rather earlier. The engraved hilt on this slab is of exactly the same character as both the Korsoygaden and Cawood swords, except that the cross is shorter and it is shown complete with its grip. It indicates that at around 1100 swords of this fashion were in use; and although only two actual examples have survived (from widely separated find-places), there is no reason to believe that the style was in any way unusual in its time.

Because the Cawood sword must now be dated *c*.1100-1150, by analogy the Northumberland and Perleberg swords must be placed within the same date-range because of the close similarities in elements of the inscriptions on all three blades. It is therefore necessary to examine these inscriptions in detail.

First, however, the fifth sword in this group must be considered (Fig.8), for it bears blade inscriptions which have strong affinities with the other three. Not this only, for it has also a motif which appears upon two of the blades unearthed from Viking graves in Southern Finland in the

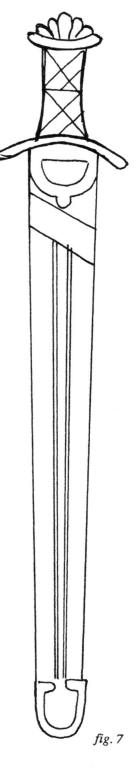

fig. 7

6   Ibid., p.148.

7   Petersen, op.cit.

8   Hoffmeyer, op.cit., vol.1, p.35.

9   Davidson, op.cit., p.80, and Olsen, *Norges Inskrifter Med de Yngere Runer*, Oslo 1941.

10 Davidson, op.cit., p.63 and fig.115. Also Hoffmeyer, op.cit., vol.I, p.35 and vol.II, plate IIIg.

11 Davidson, op.cit., plate XVI, 115 and Hoffmeyer, op.cit., vol.II, plate IIIg.

1950's by Dr Jorma Leppaaho of Helsinki University.[12] This fifth sword, in the Museum für Deutsche Geschichte in Berlin, has thus a strong claim to a date before the mid-12th century. Since it is a long-gripped sword (Type XIIIa) of a kind very typical of north-western European use during the century 1250-1350,[13] to suggest so early a date as the first half of the 12th century is startling and to many experts will seem preposterous. However, the probability exists and must therefore be considered.

Examination of this 'war-swords's' claim to an early date can be done more effectively after detailed comparison between these four inscriptions has been made, and the evidence produced by this examination considered.

If we compare parts of the Northumberland, Cawood and Perleberg inscriptions, (Figs.2b and 4)[14], we are at once struck by certain similarities; the letters in all three, for instance, have a sort of 'shadow' outline surrounding the actual letter, a feature not found on any other blade-inscription known to me. This similarity is emphasised by comparing the Cawood and Perleberg inscriptions, and when the C and the O on the Perleberg blade are compared with the O on the Cawood one, we are faced again with need for the incorrect use of the word 'identical' (Fig.9). Here is the same style, the same *handwriting*, the only difference being in the quality of execution. The Northumberland inscription, inlaid in gold, is of far better quality of drawing and design than the Perleberg one, inlaid in silver, while the Trent one is even less well done. The inlay here is of a grey, dull metal which looks like pewter, and it is interesting that the cross and pommel of the sword were plated with the same metal, of which plentiful traces remain. The Trent inscriptions are unusual too in that each side is totally different in style and content from the other. While side (i) is of the same character as both Perleberg inscriptions, side (ii) is of another kind altogether; though it is interesting to note that it can be matched exactly with one (Fig.4c) on a broken blade in Berlin.[15]

The difference in the quality of both drawing and metal inlay in the three swords suggests that while the Northumberland inscription is the work of a Master, those on the Perleberg and Cawood blades were made by journeymen in the same workshop.

The style and design of the terminal motifs of these inscriptions are striking in the similarity of their concept. They cannot be said to be the same but certain features are common to all three and appear in the large Berlin sword. It is clear that the general style of all of them springs from a common root. In all of them the use of an oval shape filled with a series of short straight lines is found together with a series of multiple crosses. In the Northumberland and Perleberg ones there is a kind of wheel-motif with eight spokes, which appears in the Berlin inscription (Fig.10). The Northumberland and Cawood swords share another motif, the age-old figure of a cross within a circle – in this case concentric circles, three in the Northumberland inscription and two in the Cawood one.

In the case of the big Berlin sword's inscriptions (Fig.11)[16] one of its repeated motifs is of exactly the same style as the motif at the left-hand end of the Perleberg inscription, differing only in minute detail (Fig.12). More significant, however, is the motif in the middle of the B-side inscription on the Berlin sword, for this matches, very closely, a motif which recurs in the Viking blades examined and published by Jorma Leppaaho (Fig.13).[17] So it is plain that this Berlin sword's inscriptions ar of the same character and style not only of the three other swords in this group, but to the Finnish Viking swords as well, all of which cannot be dated later than the first quarter of the 12th century. It is impossible therefore to evade the conclusion that this large *espée de guerre* in Berlin, as well as the Cawood sword, must have been made about two centuries before the date which has hitherto been applied to it.

A further interesting and significant aspect of the central motif on the Berlin blade's inscription is that the terminal of each spiral consists of a tiny, well-drawn beast's head. Many parallels may be found in Viking art. The opposed double spiral, linked but not conjoined, is found on a pendant made

fig. 8

12 Leppaaho, Dr. Jorma, *Späteisenzeitliche Waffen aus Finnland*, Helsinki 1964.

13 Wegeli, op.cit., p.21, fig.24, and Muller, Heinrich and Koller, Hartmut, *Europäische Hieb- und Stichwaffen*, Berlin 1981, pp.116-7, no.25.

14 Wegeli, op.cit., and Oakeshott, op.cit.

15 Wegeli, op.cit., p.26, fig.38.

16 Muller and Koller, op.cit., p.166.

17 Leppaaho, op.cit., plates 22 and 28.

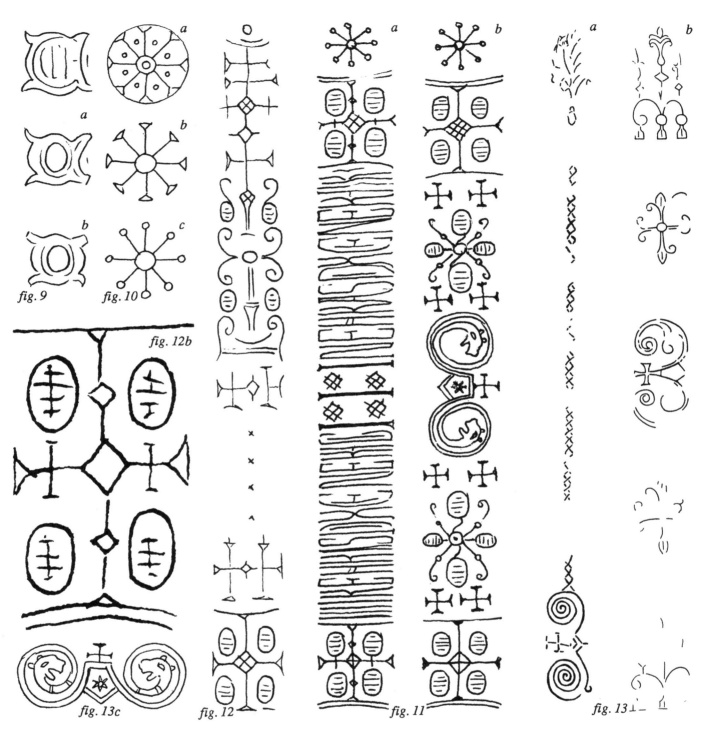

fig. 9

fig. 10

fig. 12b

fig. 13c

fig. 12

fig. 11

fig. 13

in the form of Thor's hammer, from Kalbara in Scania,[18] and again upon the well-known silver-inlaid 9th century axe-head from Mammen in Denmark[19] and the small animal heads are matched by many similar ones upon runestones, churchyard crosses – almost any object decorated in the 'Ringerike' style of the 10th-11th centuries. Perhaps the nearest parallels are from two gilded wind-vanes from Viking ships, the Kallunga vane[20] and the one from Heggin in Norway.[21] Of exactly the same form as the heads

[18]   Davidson, Dr. Hilda Ellis, *Scandinavian Mythology*, London 1980, p.100.

[19]   Ibid., p.71.

[20]   Foote, Peter and Wilson, David, *The Viking Achievement*, London, p.308, fig.55.

[21]   Magnusson, Magnus *Vikings!*, London 1980, p.294.

in the Berlin inscription, but in three dimensions, is the great carved beast's head from the Viking ship-burial at Oseberg.[22] The vanes date from the 10th century, the Oseberg head from the 9th, so it must be clear that the heads, and the linked spiral, on the Berlin war-sword are unlikely to date from the 14th century, even allowing for the longevity of various figures in folk-art.

Convincing as the evidence for the early date of this particular sword is, there must still be doubts in the minds of those experts who have not studied Leppaaho's work and who might wish to adhere to the long-established and respectable dicta of such great authorities of the past as Wendelin Boheim, Rudolf Wegeli, Sir Guy Laking and the Baron de Cosson to mention only a few. Fortunately archaeology, as well as the art and literature of the Viking Age (particularly in Central and Eastern Europe), also shows beyond doubt that swords with long grips, as well as swords with very long blades, were not uncommon from the 2nd century A.D. onwards.

There is an even earlier sword from the Celtic Iron Age (c.500-200 B.C.), found at Orton Meadows, near Peterborough, which has a blade nearly 45in. (140cm.) long. This is in the British Museum.[23] This extremely long blade is damaged, in that 8in. or so from the point it is bent nearly to a right-angle, and the tang is incomplete, so it is not possible to say whether the tang also was long to balance the excessive length of the blade. The length of tang (or grip) is of course crucial to this enquiry, so confirmation for its early use must be sought in art rather than archaeology.

In the Norse literature there are many references to swords with very long blades, as well as to short ones. In the Latin History of Saxo Grammaticus,[24] Book II, writing of events in the 8th century, we find mention of the sword *Laufi* which is said to be 'of wonderful sharpness and unusual length'. Elsewhere the same historian (Book VIII) says that certain followers of Harold of Denmark 'had their bodies covered by little shields and used very long swords'. The opposite picture is given in Half's saga[25] of a band of sword-comrades whose laws commanded '. . . that none of them might have a sword of over an ell long, so that they were forced to get to close quarters'. Likewise in the Saga of Grettir the Strong we read that though he had a fine ancestral sword named *Aettartangi*, which he wore on social occasions, he always preferred a short two-edged sword (its description reminds one of the short Roman *gladius*) for serious fighting.[26]

In the archaeology of the Migration and Viking periods we find both very long and very short bladed swords. There is a sword from Acklam in the museum at Hull which has a blade 39 ½in. (100cm.) long, and a Viking sword in Dublin is only 5cm. shorter[27] (the length of the Berlin blade is about 36in. (92cm.)), but these long swords have grips of normal one-hand length, so do not provide the hard evidence needed. However, there are several swords from the Nydam bog-deposit (c.A.D.300) which do have unusually long grips. In contrast to these very long swords, there are many short ones recorded. In the 6th century Anglo-Saxon cemetery at Sarre in Kent among the long swords two were found whose two-edged blades were only 27in. (69cm.)[28] long, and of course the sword from the Anglo-Saxon royal ship-burial at Sutton Hoo (early 7th century) is only 26in. (66cm.) long; and since the blade is irremovably corroded into its scabbard of fur, wood and leather, the blade itself is some 1½in. (4cm.) shorter.[29]

Such evidence as is available from literature and archaeology, then, provides little that we need for the use of very long grips as distinct from long blades. However, in pictorial art there is enough hard evidence to show clearly that from the 2nd century A.D. until the 12th such long grips were in use. The earliest example is from a carved stone stele from Palmyra in Syria, which shows a sword with a grip of almost two-hand length, while on an Iranian silver bowl of the 4th century is one even longer, and in cave-sculptures in Turkestan dating from the 7th and 8th centuries similar ones are shown.[30] Certainly these are not Western European swords, but they are late Roman ones – all, incidentally, have straight blades. A possible reason for these pictured long-gripped swords from the Near East not being matched by similar representations from the West is not only a matter of the chance survival of the Near Eastern ones: there were no comparable military works of art being made in the West at this time, for in spite of the large numbers of surviving MS illustrations from north-west Europe dating within the same period, hardly any show military features of any kind, and if they do (as in the Utrecht psalter of c.850) such details as sword-hilts are too sketchy to be informative.

One MS at the very end of the period under discussion, the early 12th century, is preserved in the Biblioteca Nacional in Madrid[31]. This is a Byzantine history, written c.1050-75 by Scylitzes, annalist to the Court of Constantinople during the mid-11th century; and illustrated, with very many well-detailed military scenes, about half a century later. A great number of swords and

22   Davidson, op.cit., p.10, and Foote and Wilson, op.cit., plate 22.

23   Oakeshott, op.cit., pp.42-7.

24   *The Latin History of Saxo Grammaticus*, Book II and Book VIII. Also Davidson, *The Sword in Anglo-Saxon England*, p.168.

25   Ibid., p.168.

26   Ibid., p.139.

27   Ibid., p.38

28   Ibid., p.39

29   Bruce-Mitford, Dr. Rupert, *The Sutton Hoo Ship Burial*, London 1972.

30   Hoffmeyer, Dr. Ada Bruhn, Gladius, Tome V, *Military Equipment in the Byzantine Manuscript of Scylitzes in Biblioteca Nacional in Madrid*, Granada 1966, fig.16.

31   Ibid., figs.15, 16.

other weapons of ordinary Western European types are shown, among them at least two swords with long grips. One of these pictured sword-hilts, incidentally, is closely matched by a hand-and-a-half sword in the Schweizerisches Nationalmuseum in Zürich (inv. No. AG2465) which has the same long grip and a flat, boat-shaped pommel. The other is very like the 2nd century one from Palmyra, having a disc-pommel and a grip of full two-hand length (Fig.14). Another 12th century long grip is shown in a wall-painting of *c*.1123 in the church of Santa Maria de Taull in Catalunya. Here the grip is very long, but the blade is of normal length, so it is not intended to be a two-hand sword.[32]

fig. 14

Perhaps the best example of the representation of one of these big swords in use in the mid-12th century is on a fine mosaic icon of St Theodore, at present in the Vatican. Here the soldier-saint is shown with a sword at his side whose blade, in proportion to his leg, would be about 35-36in. (89-92cm.) long, but the grip would be a good 6-7in. (15-18cm.) (Fig.15)[33].

It may be argued that all these long-gripped swords which I have cited are from Byzantium or the Near East. This is true, but during the early Middle Ages the influence of late Roman and Byzantine forms and styles in art and architecture, and of arms as well, was very strong in Western Europe. At the same time we are made aware by Arab and Greek (Byzantine) writers how greatly valued in the Orient were the arms of the West, particularly swords. The Normans of the 11th and 12th centuries, and their Viking forbears before them, were as much at home in the Byzantine, post Roman world as they were in their Northern homelands. The influence of Byzantine art upon Carolingian MS illustration is indisputable, and this influence lasted well into the 12th century – the Bayeux needlework, for instance, is very strongly Byzantine in style and concept; that these influences must have extended to arms and armour was inevitable.

Any analysis in depth of the possible meaning of these inscriptions is beyond the scope of this paper, but it cannot be concluded without at least some passing comment. The inscriptions under discussion here are, as far as our present knowledge goes, incomprehensible cryptograms. In the inscription upon the blade of the Northumberland sword we do at least have a clue: the comma-like mark between the O and the A is a mark of abbreviation for the Latin suffix *que* ('and') so we can assume that the letters are initials of a Latin phrase, probably of a Christian religious nature. A guess might produce, for instance, *Beati Omnipotensque Angeli Christi* – Blessed and Omnipotent the Angels of Christ. Many of these late 11th – early 12th century inscriptions are written out in full, such as Sancta Maria, Benedictus Deus, Deus Meus, Sanctus Petrus to mention only four. Therefore there is a justification to consider these cryptic sequences of letters may be acronyms of a religious kind, phrases taken from the Missal or from the Psalms. However, we cannot altogether rule out the possibility that they stand for phrases or a secular kind in vernacular languages.

Some of the symbols used as terminal decorations on these inscriptions, or indeed as the whole inscription on the obverse of some, like for instance the big Berlin sword, have very close similarity to symbols still used in folk-art; the 'Hex' symbols used today in Pennsylvania, for example, are of the same kind as those on the B inscription on the Berlin blade (Fig.11b). This being so, we cannot altogether rule out the possibility that some of the cryptic sequences of letters may be akin for instance to the hopeful cryptograms which members of the British armed forces put on to the backs of envelopes containing letters home such as SWALK: Sealed With A Loving Kiss. The soldiers, sailors and airmen of other powers did the same. Sentimental and silly, perhaps; but their use was universal. As it was in 1939–45, so may it have been in 1100. We do not know, and until some positive evidence comes to light, ignorance must be our portion. We have to remember that these swords were decorated not for 20th century academic scholars to pore over, but for silly, sentimental, unsophisticated, deeply religious, superstitious and illiterate people who had to rely upon them in the heat of battle. *We* do not know what the inscriptions mean, but we do know that to the men who used the swords there was deep significance, mystery and power in them as well as meaning.

fig. 15

32 Riquer, Marti de, *L'Arnes del Cavaller*, Barcelona 1965, plate 7 opp. p.12.
33 Ziehr, Wilhelm, *The Ancient World from Ur to Mecca*, London 1982, plate 29.

APPENDIX C

The 'Morgarten' Sword

This sword was bought at Sotheby's early in 1938, one of a lot of four. It was thickly covered with deep, brown rust which was not dusty but quite hard. It was among a collection of a Major MacNaghten, of Chew Magna in Somerset. He had bought it, also at Sotheby's, in 1935 where it was catalogued as being from 'a private collection in Austria'. I followed this up, and found that it had come to *that* collection from a church in Austria.

This piece of research was not done at the time when I got the sword in 1938, for I was young and quite inexperienced then; I did it in 1950/51 when, with the Research Laboratory at the British Museum I made the close examination of the sword, a description of which follows.

Being young and inexperienced, I wanted such a fine sword to be clean and shiny, so I set about getting the rust off. This was far more difficult than I had expected, but off it came, only to reveal beneath it a flint-hard black patina. This, of course, should never have been touched, for it was (with the form of the small rust-pits on the surfaces) unassailable evidence of the circumstances under which the sword had been preserved, indoors, in the air, subject to damp particles of dust falling upon well-greased surfaces. However, at that time I knew nothing of such things, so with much labour over a week or two, I got this beautiful patina off, destroyed irreplaceable evidence and, in a sense, ruined the sword. But how it shone!

After the war, I took it to the Wallace Collection to seek the opinion of the Director, Sir James Mann. He pronounced blade, pommel and grip to be ancient (of the early 14th century, he said) but was not very happy about the 'quillons' which he though were rather unusual. This put me on my mettle, and I gladly fell in with his suggestion that I should seek the help of the British Museum.

There, in the research laboratory in 1950 I met Dr Herbert Maryon, a very eminent archaeologist who was at that time piecing together the helmet, shield, harp and drinking-horns from the Sutton Hoo Anglo-Saxon grave-find. Examining the sword, he said that the patination (I told him how I had destroyed the *real* patination) and pit-distribution

i

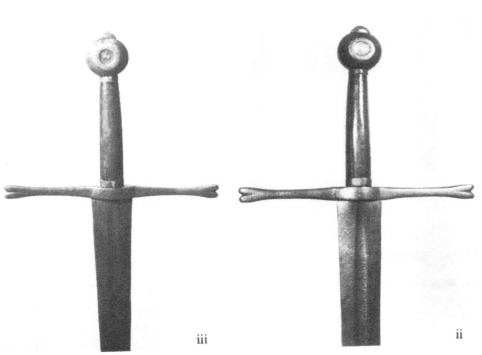

iii
ii

on the 'quillons' was exactly the same as that on the blade, and must have been formed at the same time and by the same atomospheric processes - ergo, the cross ('quillons') was as old as the rest. Dr. Maryon thought the grip was probably of lime-wood, but would need expert biological advice to be certain. He found what he called unmistakeable traces of faint transverse indentations upon the surface of the grip which indicated a cord binding having been pressed hard into the wood by the grip of a hand. He also found, below the lower iron fillet, a fragment of ancient linen, part of the original covering of the grip. Noticing that the wood of the grip was split longitudinally from top to bottom, and was quite loose and clearly only held together by the close-fitting iron fillets at top and bottom, be decided that it would be a very worth-while bit of archaeological study to cut through the wood just below the top fillet with a razor-saw, release the two sections into which the splits had broken the grip, remove them, and see what was inside. This, we did, taking photographs as we went along. I have here included the drawings I made as we uncovered the tang, and a literal reproduction of the notes I made, as well as reproduction of the photographs I took. These are not particularly good, but taken along with the notes they do show what we found.

Examination of the hilt after the grip was removed

1. *The Cross*. This was still firmly wedged by two small slivers of wood driven up from beneath, between the outer edges of the hole in the cross and the tang. It was however possible to move it up about ½". The top of the middle part of the cross, around the opening for the tang, was covered by a black patination under the grip. There were three small iron wedges loose in the grip. These had been driven in on the upper part of the cross to supplement the wooden wedges on the outside. It was clear that these iron wedges had been forced down into the gap between cross and tang by means of a thin flat bar of metal, held sideways and struck with a hammer. The flat top of each wedge showed a deep indentation where the bar had struck, and on the broader sides of the tang were marks – slight dents – probably made by the head of the hammer. These were about ½" above the top of the cross. On one side of the flat upper surface of the cross, below the grip's end, were a series of fairly deep gashes as if the bar driving the wedges in had slipped. All of these marks, on cross, tang and wedges were *below* the flint-hard black patina, and could not have been made recently.

2. *The Tang*. The surface was smoother in its lower ⅓, with a hard patina, but the upper ⅔ were covered with thick, flaky rust, bright dark red at the top, hard and not dusty. The inside of the grip shows that the lower part fitted more closely over the tang, leaving less space for air to get in to cause oxidisation than in the upper part. On one side at the top there is a patch of pale substance. There is also a smear of this on each of the narrow sides of the tang, but none on the other broad side. Was something, now perished, stuck on to the tang, inside the grip? There are a few clamp marks, a series of three short indentations in groups. These indentations are quite straight, about 3mm long and 1mm apart. These also are below the hard patina. Similar marks (identical marks, made obviously by the same clamp) appear on the thick part of the central block of the cross. (These show clearly on photograph iii).

3. *The Pommel*. The under-part of this is roughly hollowed out in an irregular hole below the neatly squared-off boring to take the tang. It is possible to lower the pommel about ⅛", thereby separating it from the rivet-block on top. The flat part of the top of the pommel underneath this block is patinated like the mid-part of the tang, fine-grained red rust, loose on top, above a hard black surface. The under surface of the rivet-block is the same. So is the upper part of it below the rivet, as well as the under part of the rivet itself. It is noticeable that file marks below the patina on the underneath of the pommel where it sits down on top of the grip are made by the same file as marks on the rivet block, and the metal of both parts is the same, and in the same condition - i.e., the pommel has never been disturbed, nor the block replaced. Since the pommel was loose, we wedged it tight by driving three short lengths of shaped match-stick up between pommel and tang.

4. *The Grip*. This was split longitudinally from top to bottom in four places, the splits following the grain of the wood. Two of these splits run from top to bottom, the other two only part of the way. The fillets of iron at top and bottom had been put there to hold it

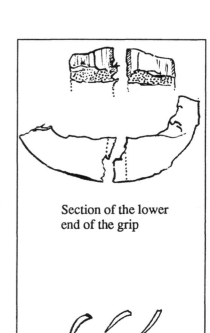

Section of the lower end of the grip

The 3 small iron wedges

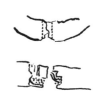

Section of the upper end of the grip

secure, for it seems that the splits were made during the boring-out of the inside of the grip. (Grips made upon a narrow, more or less quare-section tang are bored out first by a long hole being drilled from end to end of the wood, followed by the tang heated red to burn the core of the wood out to more or less the exact shape of the tang). The fillets prevented it from falling apart in use, or being taken apart for examination, so it was decided to cut it laterally just against the lower edge of the upper fillet. Then the first section of the grip was taken off, and a photograph taken before the second part was moved (illus. iv). There was a little piece of white wood (it looked horribly like a matchstick) used as a wedge between the side of the tang and the wood. This is 1^{15}⁄16" long by 3⁄32" wide x 1⁄6", like a long wedge. (This is not a matchstick!).

Then the second, larger half was taken off. There was a similar wedge on the other side of the tang, with a smaller, darker piece put in transversely on each side at the bottom. One of these sections of the grip, has a piece of filling (like plastic wood) in its lower part, under the iron fillet. this is contemporary with the grip; the wood it replaces was clearly burnt away in boring out the core, as a lot of charring is visible round its edges, even on the outside. The inside of this filling is shaped and smoothed to the form of the tang. This was obviously done before the hilt was assembled. It seems that the long vertical splits, in their lower part, were present when the hilt was assembled, for there are small patches of the same filling in them. Dr. Maryon, examining this filling (made of whiting, and gum or mastic) compared it with some similar filling on the Sutton Hoo harp's wood. Both appear to be of exactly the same substance.

At the very top of the grip, under the upper fillet, is a small hole about 1⁄16" wide. This hole, widening and sloping downward, went right through the wood, on one side, to the tang. It is filled with rust; out of it on the inner side of the grip, project two small bent pieces of metal of a flat section, like flat wire. (Could this be the end of a long-destroyed wire binding, under the linen cover of the grip?) There is a smear of the white powdery stuff inside the grip just above this hole, but this comes against the side of the tang *opposite* to the white patch on the tang itself.

Dr Maryon identified the red powdery stuff in this hole as definitely iron rust. He also saw traces (these show faintly in the photograph at v) of an imprint of lacing or sewing, and of a transversely-wound thong.

The splits in the wood are interesting. The edges are discoloured with a reddish-brown stain, which along the outer edges in parts is clotted into quite a thick, hard irregular substance. The photograph shows that about half-way up the grip the sides of these splits are much lighter. Here, the fibres of the wood were not quite separated, and had to be prized apart to get the grip off. The stain looks as if some fluid had oozed into the cracks where they were open. At the top of one crack the stain is fainter but more extensive, filling the whole width of the crack from the extreme top of the grip to about 1" down. This staining is not even; in the lower third of the grip it is patchy, with one or two thick blobs. The stain is only present on one side of the grip.

5. The iron fillets. These are flat strips of iron, the lower one about twice as deep as the upper, bent round and copper-brazed together. The lower one seems to have been joined, before brazing, with a sort of mortice-and-tenon. Both are considerably corroded on their edges. When all the necessary work had been done and notes and photographs made (as well as a small sample of the clotted stain taken off for analysis) the hilt was re-assembled in its original condition. A note, written very small on a folded strip of paper, was put inside stating how and where this opening, examination and re-assembling had taken place.

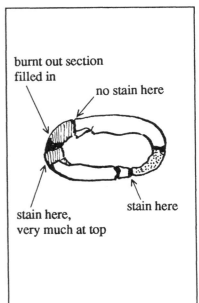

burnt out section filled in

no stain here

stain here, very much at top

stain here

Section and elevation of the lower end of the grip with the filling

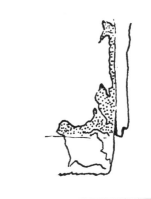

It cannot be a very common experience for a collector to be able to examine so closely the ancient inside of a sword's hilt, certainly not under the auspices of the British Museum with the active participation of so eminent an authority as Dr Maryon. Perhaps the highest moment was when he took the section of grip with the filling in it and actually held it against the filling in the Sutton Hoo harp, to show me how exactly alike the two substances were. I treasured this sword for over thirty years, though I always felt it was rather ugly. Now someone who reads these notes will have it in his own collection, and what I have written here may add to his evaluation of it.

Maybe he will wonder, as I did, what the reddish-brown clotted stain is. when I put this to Dr Maryon, without hesitation he

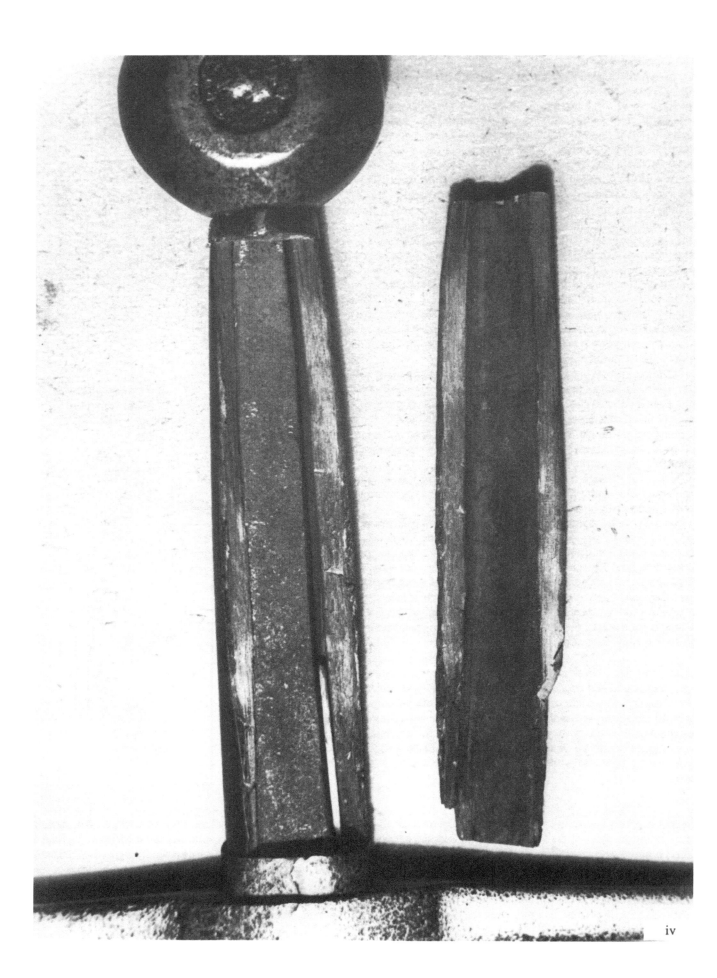

v

said 'Blood, of course'. He added 'That's the most likely thing, anyway. We must get a bit analysed'. Which I did, in the pathological lab. of one of London's hospitals, the answer was cautious. If was definitely not any sort of varnish, or glue, or oil or anything of that kind. It could be blood, but it was so old that analysis of such a small bit could give no more definite a result. So there it is! What, as Dr. Maryon said, is more likely to be ancient blood on the hilt of such a sword?

To substantiate this claim, it is only necessary to quote from a letter written by an officer of the Eniskillens after the charge of the Heavy Brigade (Scots Greys and Eniskillens) at Balaclava in 1855. 'Twice I was unhorsed, and more than once had to grip my sword tighter, the blood streaming down over the hilt, and running up my very sleeve!' What happened to him at Balaclava in the 19th century must have been a common occurrence whenever swords were used in battle.

So it is not unreasonable to suggest certain assumptions: was it hung in that Austrian church over the tomb of one of those desperate knights who fought their way out of the bloody press at Morgarten in 1314? If so, is it not feasible to suggest that the red stain in the grip is indeed blood; good Swiss blood running down the blade and soaking into the grip under the knight's hand? It could be said (it will be said) that this is mere romantic fantasy. But is it? I believe it is no more than a series of reasonable deductions based upon hard, if circumstantial, evidence. We know it came from a church, in Austria; we know it is the kind of sword very popular in S. Germany between c.1280-1350; there are the 92 nicks in the blade, which by the black patination still present under the burred-over edges of those nicks show very clearly that they are not new nicks made by the sword having been used for hedge-cutting; so we can safely assume that at the end of its active life it was used in a desperate situation; we know that the red stain is neither varnish, glue nor paint, but is most likely blood. While it was in my care during those 32 years, I always thought of it as The Morgarten Sword. I still do.

APPENDIX D

A Sword of Edward III

A Sword of Edward III

Type: XVIIIa
Find-place: ?
It came to Paris from Spain in 1893, to England 1899.
Collection: Private
Blade-length: 33½" (86 cms)
Pommel-type: K
Cross-style: 6
Date: After 1348 – say 1350
Condition: Very good. The hilt pristine, except for some hand-wear on the adder-skin cover of the grip. The blade has a patination of red-brown over a surface covered with small shallow rust-pits, of exactly the same appearance as the blade of Henry V's sword (q.v. under XVIII.1 above) in Westminster Abbey.

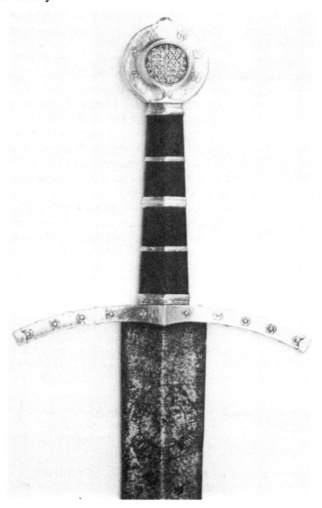

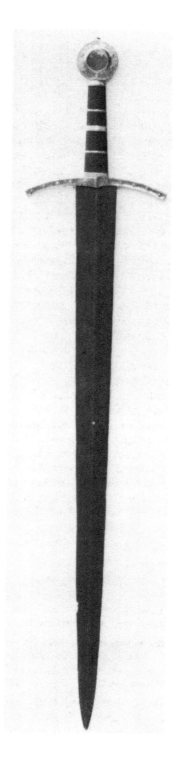

1. A Sword of Edward III

In the preface to this book I made passing reference to the ways in which highly sophisticated scientific examination and analysis of the structure of materials, and the trace-elements in them, can establish the relative antiquity or modernity of works of art. The magnificent sword described in detail below has many times been examined by the old-fashioned visual, aesthetic and archaeological methods, with widely differing opinions being expressed. Now it has been examined by the most up-to-date microscopic and chemical analyses using radioactivation with high-energetic protons and spectrometry of the gamma-radiation emitted by samples of the various metals after post-irradiation chemical pre-treatment. These methods show positively how forgery can be exposed; but they show equally forcefully the opposite, and can re-establish the worth and genuine antiquity of objects which, using the old visual comparative methods, have been by some authorities in the past vigourously though wrongly, condemned. So it is with this sword.

Controversy had bedevilled it ever since it re-appeared in 1895-6 in the showroom of a Paris dealer, whose fame as a faker of medieval metalwork has now for many decades been established beyond question. He was a brilliant fabricator of, in particular, medieval goldsmith's work and enamels. This controversy, often acrimonious and all discreditable, was between those who believed the sword and its companion dagger to be genuine 14th century workmanship, and those who, because (and only because) it was displayed for sale by this well-authenticated faker, Louis Marcy, equally fiercely denounced it.

Its story, from the time of this re-appearance (or, as some would have it, first appearance) is long and complicated and throws doubt upon the integrity, and indeed impugns the honesty, of several respected authorities (all now dead) of the Arms and Armour world, so it may not be told in full. It must however be given here in summary to lead up to the final incontrovertible evidence of scientific examination which shows beyond all reasonable doubt that all the denigration of the past 94 years has been false, and that in no way could such enamels and metals (gold, copper and steel) have been made in the late 19th century.

The following analytical study of the sword has been assembled in the form and in the chronological order in which it has been discussed over this long period, from its first recorded description of 5th December, 1904 until the final denouement of its examination by the Bundesanstalt für Materialprüfung (BAM) of West Berlin, a West German government institution, in 1986. Before giving the detailed accounts of these assessments, however, it will be necessary to relate the 'story' of the sword's wanderings and vicissitudes during these years, in order to strike a proper balance and to set the scene.

The story properly begins with the assessment made in December 1904 by an eminent scholar and antiquarian who for obvious reasons I will only refer to as Mr AH, F.S.A., followed by some vivid (and in one case quite scurrilous) extracts from his correspondence with the Victoria and Albert Museum from 1904 to 1910. After this I will give a brief resumé of the sword's movements with its companion dagger from collector to collector until it came under the hammer at Christie's in 1960 as part of a large collection of medieval swords. This will be followed by the report and assessment I made upon it in 1983 which led up to the final examination by BAM in 1986.

Here then is Mr AH's report, quoted in full:

December 1, 1904

The photographs came from Sir A. Vicars this afternoon. They speak for themselves. But let me specially commend to your notice the dagger of Edward III with the shield of St. George on it. No one save the King had the right to such a badge and I should not be surprised it it dates from the foundation of the Order of the Garter, and is the earliest badge existing of that famous companionship. Would a forger have imagined this!

The chalcedony covering the relic on the pommel of Edward III's dagger is a piece of the same stone as on one side of the pommel of the sword. It is of course only translucent, not transparent. This was to increase the mystery of the objects so enclosed - namely the three fragments of the shroud of the Confessor - not to be seen by every vulgar passing gaze. Would a forger have thought of this! No wonder the De Cossons and the dealers were angry that they missed obtaining these precious relics.

Before AH made this report, and possibly unknown to him, two of the very powerful authorities of the late 19th century, Sir Guy Laking and the Baron de Cosson, visited Louis Marcy's showroom where they found what Laking described as a veritable Aladdin's cave filled with a most splendid assemblage of armour and arms. He described this event in Vol.V of his *Record of Armour and Arms through Seven Ages* (1921). This comment also I give in full (p.143 et seq.)

Our first experience of these forgeries was gained some 15 years ago in Paris when along with a famous German collector, now dead, we were taken to see a small collection of armour and of arms that one of the foremost dealers of the day had been commissioned to sell. It is only fair to this dealer, who is no longer alive, to say that this collection was shown to him with a full belief in the genuiness of its pieces. The splendour of the display was bewildering, indeed it might have been the contents of some Cathedral treasury exposed to view. On the central table of the room in which they were shown were tilting helms purporting to be of the fourteenth and fifteenth centuries, and swords and daggers with historical attributions of about the same epoch, while at the side of the gallery hung a superb half-suit of German Gothic armour.... A morning devoted to the scrutiny of the various pieces sufficed to shake the author's belief in the genuineness of the pieces in the collection, and he suddenly felt convinced that the whole collection was false from beginning to end, but of its kind superlatively deceptive. The clue which helped to unravel the mystery was supplied by one of the helmets, which purported to be a snouted bascinet of the latter part of the fourteenth century. This bascinet, which was beautifully made and bore every appearance of age, was stamped with an armourer's mark, a star within a shield, on the lower part of the visor. Now just such another helmet which turned out to be a clever fabrication, had been offered to and purchased by the author some two years previously, a helmet coated with exactly the same rusting, of the same admirable make, and stamped with the same mark, which, however, was placed low down on the skull-piece. In the same year another bascinet exactly similar was again on the London market. This one was also impressed with an armourer's mark of the same character, a mark appearing on the visor, and placed precisely as in the case of the Paris helmet. It is not difficult to imagine the inference drawn from this discovery. A thorough knowledge of all points of the bascinet helmet which we had, to our misfortune, found to be false helped fairly easily to determine the origin of all the other pieces in this remarkable collection, for on minute inspection they were found to be all of the same make and to be all oxidised by the same means, though in some cases the oxidation was carried to a greater extent than in others. All the pieces, whether sword-blade or defensive plate, all had the same admirable patina of age, all were beautifully made, and in their construction all gave evidence of the maker's genuine knowledge of the true specimens.

Thus Sir Guy Laking. If this statement is examined, it may be found to be exceedingly full of holes; as evidence it is pathetic. He says that a morning - how long is a morning? from 10.00 a.m. perhaps until 12.30 - was given to a minute examination of all the pieces. He has already said that they were numerous. Even if these 2 hours are stretched, that much time would be essential even superficially to examine the 'superb half-suit of German Gothic armour'. How were all these (in some cases) elaborately decorated pieces examined? Visually, probably with a good magnifying glass; there can have been no scientific or technological skill applied; nothing more than the experience, of many years, of a connoisseur. Certainly, as great an expert, as powerful a collector, as experienced a connoisseur of armour and arms as Laking must have a very keen 'nose' for what is right and what is not; but a morning's examination of so many objects of great intrinsic complexity is not enough to convince anybody 85 years later that, as Laking says, *ex cathedra*, that all the pieces were false from beginning to end.

One must concede that perhaps he is on surer ground with the three bascinets he mentions, but even so, one cannot avoid the feeling that the repetition of the same armourer's mark on three similar helmets is more than coincidence, especially since he was so sure that his own one was a fake. One is tempted to think, if he knew all those of Marcy's - all, not just a bascinet - why had he only two years earlier, fallen for a dud? The use of a star as a mark, on sword-blades in particular, was common enough, and in the Odescalchi Collection in Rome (OD536) there is a sword marked with a star within a shield. Is that a fake, too? Besides, when one stops to consider how many bascinets of a universally popular style were made all over Europe for over half a century, it is not unreasonable to assume that one workshop, whose brand-mark was a star within a shield, would have turned out not three bascinets, but in that period more like three thousand. Even so, it is suspicious that as many as three of that hypothetical three thousand should turn up for sale over a period of only two years. Therefore Laking's 'evidence', shaky though it is, might be considered to hold good for Marcy's bascinet; but it has little validity for the other armour and none whatever for the swords.

I have personal experience of only three of the swords which Marcy displayed, one of course being the one under discussion. The other two I have not seen or handled for 30 years, but I am in no doubt (leaving this one, now proved to be authentic) that of the other two one had a genuine 15th century blade, but a very handsome faked hilt; and that the other which until recently was displayed in the Klingenmuseum in Solingen, was fake all through. The blade is clumsy and 'dead' and the hilt is grossly over-decorated, many of its motifs obviously based upon those on the hilt of the Edward III sword, in particular the little rosettes. In the case of the fake these were stamped out (in silver) and soldered on to the surfaces, and are crowded together far too much. It is shown by the x-ray photographs and scientific analysis of the B A M report, that the rosettes on the Edward III hilt are embossed in the actual gold foil covering cross and pommel; the embossed rosettes are supported from beneath (between the iron core and the gold foil) with gold rosettes of exactly the same shape and size.

Laking says that all the pieces showed the same kind of patina on their surfaces, blade and plate alike. This is certainly not so in the case of the sword just mentioned and the Edward III one. The fake has a coarse, even, overall pitting while (as may be seen in the photograph) that on the Edward III blade is very uneven, the pits not being little round holes but irregularly shaped pits of varying depth and size. If the two blades are seen together, it is impossible not be convinced how totally different their surfaces are - not, as in the words of the infallible Sir Guy, that 'all had the same admirable patina of age'. These two certainly did not, therefore doubt must be cast upon the falsity of at least some of the other pieces in that showroom.

Laking also says that some of the swords were carefully made to correspond with entries in English inventories (presumably of the 14-15th centuries, and presumably in the Public Record office in London). One does wonder who could have been the skilled bladesmith, goldsmith, enameller and armourer who had such access to these archives that he could, alone, make objects closely corresponding with various entries. the more it is considered, the more superficial this off-the-cuff condemnation of so long ago seems to be, and the more one has to wonder why it has been so solemnly believed and propagated by generations of experts. He also goes on to say that because of the exposé of Marcy's wares, they now know who made them all; but he does not reveal any names. Perhaps, as has always been assumed ever since, he did mean Louis Marcy?

This conclusion has always been held to be sacrosanct, therefore correct, and since in 1896 there were no scientific means of actually testing the composition of the metal, their decision had been accepted for what it is worth. Therefore for 90 years, on the strength of this analysis and the dubious appearance of one or two other pieces, the whole mass of these objects has been declared to be fake, and anything Marcy is known to have handled is condemned out of hand. Which is absurd. No dealer in his right mind, if he seeks to sell very costly forgeries to experienced connoisseurs, will fail very carefully to include among such forgeries a high proportion of first-class genuine pieces. This is not only obvious common sense, it is well-known and recognised present day practice. Laking and his associates were indeed experienced connoisseurs, but by condemning Marcy's wares *in toto* they showed a very serious failure of common sense, the repercussions of which failure still bedevil the study of arms. In their days it was only necessary to be sufficiently wealthy to amass a great collection to be accredited with infallible expertise to which scholars must defer. It has now been revealed, also, that even comparatively recently serious scholars, as well as such self-appointed authorities, have not been above adding as footnotes to learned articles spurious references to non-existent scholarly publications in order to substantiate opinions they wished to promote. In one extreme case, of which I have personal visual experience, a partly worn-away inscription of a cryptic and unusual kind upon an important item of Renaissance armour was 'improved' by an eminent scholar by added letters in order that his suggested interpretation of its meaning should be made manifest. This was no 19th century restoration, but a mid-20th century falsification. The passage of a few decades upon this doctored lettering begins to show even more clearly where the genuine letters of the inscription fade away and the new ones were added.

Here follow some extracts from Mr AH's letters to the Museum. In the first of these he is more concerned with the sword's companion dagger, but since this also has been subjected to the same test by BAM, his comments are relevant here.

From a letter dated December 15, 1904:-

'...In Edward III's dagger is a very peculiar leaf-shape. Now, if you will look at Stothard's Effigy of William of Hatfield at York, two beautiful etchings, you will see precisely this leaf in the form of a diapered pattern all over the jupon the boy wears; it is a lovely piece of sculpture in alabaster. I have seen it, but it has to be looked for as it is rather out of sight. I happen to know this leaf quite well as I had it reproduced to a large size in ironwork for a church door a long time ago. These two details, and particularly the latter one, are proofs positive to me of the genuine character of the things. No forger could have thought of going to Stothard or York for the latter very rare leaf for his decoration, and I pointed it out to Sir C Robinson...'

This leaf is indeed quite a telling point, but in fairness it must be said that Mr A H had scant appreciation of the care which a forger of Marcy's quality would take to obtain just such a detail. Of course he could have found it in Stothard; and of course he could have gone to York. Whether he would have done so is another matter.

Further extract from the same letter:-

'... Barkentin the goldsmith says no modern workman could put on the gold decorations of these weapons, and they are only a few of the same period that similarly come from Spain. the things are too many to be forgeries, and these details tally too well with historical evidence. It is impossible that a foreign forger could have copies the leopard's face from Canterbury and is he likely to have known of Stothard or - as none of such dealing folk speaks English - how could he have got hold of the information?....'

Here Mr A H shows considerable passion but little sense. To say that it is impossible for a 'foreign forger' to have gone to Canterbury and made a drawing of the leopard's face in the pommel of the Black Prince's sword on his effigy, or on the belt buckle is a piece of absurdly snobbish chauvinism. So it is to say that no dealing folk speak English. Such comments do tend to nullify the reasonably sensible comments which he does make.

The next extract does not deal with the Edward III sword; but I have included it here because it seems that A H's comments in it add to his expressed opinions about some of those so-highly respected wealthy collector 'authorities' of nearly a century ago.

From a letter dated July 29, 1906:-

'I am very sorry some compromise could not be made about the Stibert bequeath, (sic) but I don't know where any things could have been put. Many are out of place, and unappreciated and neglected at the British Museum. Perhaps Read thinks Burgess' things are all forgeries. At the Tower they would have been lost in that overcrowded inadequate space, and probably they would not have been admitted into the Wallace Collection. So they must have been banished to Woolwich Arsenal or forgotten at Whitehall. Moreover no doubt the whole collection is a collection of forgeries, like the Robinson things, for I take it that all the collections I have mentioned are no more genuine than that at Swanage - and I add De Cossons and your things, as well as Minter the auctioneer's and the collection of frauds at Windsor that he has catalogued. All are forgeries we know now! and world famed connoisseurs and students of 50 years work and experience know nothing. Only auctioneers, clerks and ci-devant valets are reliable judges. All this is very sad, but good for the dealers and bad for the serious collectors. I should not wonder if De Cosson now becomes the custodian of the Stibert collection, having I suppose urged its retention in the country of his adoption.'

His reference to a 'ci-devant valet' of course refers to the Baron de Cosson, whose barony was a Papal title which he acquired after he had ceased to be a valet. The Stilbert collection is of course well-known as a major collection of armour and arms in Florence.

From a letter dated August 22nd, 1906. This extract is not relevant, but is revealing:-

'I hear a whisper that 'Charles Hercules Read, Esq., honorary secretary of the Society of Antiquaries' has gone to America and may stay there for good i.e. for his own good. This will make another competitor at Christies against us. I should much like to see the armour at Eastbourne some day. Does Mr Citizen Keasbey work at the subject from books and does he know the right books?'

The 'armour at Eastbourne' was the collection of Henry C Keasbey, an American industrialist of great wealth but little scholarship, though one who has been regarded as an authority on armour and arms. In the next, long extract (which as I have said, is scurrilous) Mr A H gives full rein to his feelings.

From a letter dated January 3rd, 1910:-

'I always wanted to tell you that Keasbey has no authority for condemning Sir Charles' weapons. When he and I went there he would hardly look at them and he certainly did not handle any one item to justify him in saying they were every one of iron. I know every one of them perfectly well and I defy any one to say off hand as K. does that not one was of steel. Many of them are exactly like those in his own collection - several of Sir Charles's came from Laking and I am certain that if they had been in the Eastbourne and not in the Swanage assemblage we should not have heard any doubt expressed as to iron or steel or forgeries or anything else. The close of the matter is they do not belong to Keasbey. I don't believe he thinks anything outside his collection, no matter where it is, to be free from suspicion. He has got forgery on the brain, and he thinks he knows more than anyone else not only about arms, armour, gunlocks, architecture, effigies or anything else. Fancy anybody expounding to me who the Old Lady of Threadneedle Street is! as Keasbey did in the City.

And I assure myself that if there are such a multitude of forgeries, outside the Eastbourne range, in the way of arms and armour then the sooner every one else gives up collecting the better. And if Dillon and De Cosson and Lucas and Keasbey and Read are so cock-sure, and really know who made these things the best thing they can do is announce the name and the site of manufactury and then we shall know how we stand.

They wrap themselves in the mantles of omniscience and people like you and Hope and me are mere donkeys and I suppose the auctioneer belongs to the same crew of infallibles. These heaven-born critics and collectors won't listen to any one who does not agree with them. They envelop the matter in mystery, hints, or garbled statements, or they pour forth a torrent of words and you come away stunned, bewildered and uninformed. They won't meet the case of the Edward III sword and the dagger, and that of the Black Prince. They know little or nothing of the history or of the details of the monumental and Ill.MSS art of that time and they will not discuss the questions with persons like Hope and me who have such detail at our fingers' ends. It is absolutely impossible that any Frenchman making forgeries of Edw III and Black Prince swords and daggers with all their wonderful and precise detail could have carried them out without consulting Hope and me, or either of us. From the multitude of effigies I have measured and drawn to scale and of details full size, I do not want to have them explained to me by tyros like Dillon or Keasbey or the auctioneer. I got beyond that stage before any of them took to antiquities at all. I should not wonder if these miscanes are now denying the things at Swanage in the hope of one day securing them for a small price. I have no doubt there are many doubtful pieces in Keasbey's collection, just as there are at Swanage and in fact in every collection - but these do not condemn the rest.

You remember the buckles and badges and coronal at Swanage? The infallibles condemn them all. They won't examine them, though Cripps stated that the coronal had each piece marked with a Hall Mark - probably the root of Burgundy. They do not possess the things so they shelter their nakedness under the shadow of some nameless forger at or near Paris. We are asked to believe that this man, a Frenchman, doubtless speaking no English, has all our Heraldry, arms armour and details of effigies in Stothard quite at his fingers ends, so that for instance he picked out from the effigy of William of Hatfield at York one of the remarkable leaves which decorate the jupon and put it on the dagger of Edw III that he was forging. This is only one instance - Hope can tell you many others concerning the Heraldic details of this and other royal, weapons, such no foreigner could by any possibility have imagined. He must in such cases have made such blunders as would have exposed him at once.

I am sickened to hear these unfair ignorant comments (?) in which things that are probably all right, and if so priceless, are condemned out of hand by incompetent charlatans.

Yours very sincerely, A.H.'

Perhaps the less that is said about this, the better; but it does take the covers off feelings which at least a few eminent scholars and Fellows of the Society of Antiquaries had for the 'expert' gentlemen named, whose opinions unfortunately have influenced the study of armour and arms in a baneful way for over half a century, while those of real scholars have been unheard. Mr A H had obviously been treated with discourtesy and contumely by men he despised, but clearly he had not hidden his own feelings from them; they may well have retaliated in kind. The whole matter, seen from eighty years on, is distasteful but it is a human story and it sheds some light - possibly much needed - upon the credibility of experts to whose opinions too much weight has been given.

In the early 1920s these things - the Edward III sword and dagger and two other daggers - passed into the collection of Mr D'Acre Kenrick Edwards. It is told that Mr Edwards and Sir Guy Laking were both in the running for appointment as Master of the Armouries at the Tower of London at about this time, but D'Acre Edwards withdrew because he was a member of the Allied Commission for the re-settlement of Germany at the end of the Great War, so Sir Guy took the office. I mention this as an indication of the standing of D'Acre Edwards in the arms and armour world at that time. He, like Mr A H , was never in doubt of the authenticity of the sword and the dagger.

Towards the end of his life Mr Edwards became very friendly with another collector and connoisseur of medieval swords and enamels, Mr J C Pocock. So closely allied did these two become, that Mr Edwards promised that in his will he would leave the Edward III sword and dagger to Mr Pocock. However, at his death in 1959, D'Acre Edwards left no will; nor had he any relatives or friends to be his executors; therefore the Public Trustee was called in to dispose of this very large and important collection. This was first displayed at the showrooms of an estate agent in Lewes, in Sussex; where I had the opportunity of examining the whole collection (over a period of four days). However, since this material was so important, the Public Trustee decided that it should all be sold by one of the great London auction houses; so the collection went to Christie's, where it was sold on April 25, 1961. Mr Pocock was able to obtain the Edward III sword and dagger at a very low price, for of course they had been catalogued as fakes. This is not altogether surprising, because with them there were two other swords from Marcy's hoard which are, undoubtedly, fakes.

Mr Pocock never had any doubts about the genuineness of these pieces; but in March 1966 he was in correspondence with a very high authority, who categorically reiterated his belief that all of this group of weapons were of Marcy's making. Returning to the attack in 1981, he submitted the sword's dagger to limited test, the result of which was totally inconclusive; and since the case had been prejudged for eighty years, he was told that, on purely negative evidence, they must be fakes. In spite of this, he maintained his faith in them, as Mr A H had in the past.

Shortly before his death, Mr Pocock was compelled by illness and circumstance to part with the dagger, soon to be followed by the sword. They passed via a dealer into the hand of their last owner but one, who in turn by force of circumstances was driven to sell them. This time, belief that they were genuinely of 14th century workmanship, and clearly made for Edward III, having become widespread among cognoscenti in high places, they were offered at a figure commensurate with their prestige.

This unfortunately roused the opposition to fresh vigour, and I was brought into the dispute to prepare a detailed report and assessment of the sword - the dagger had by this time been sold (at its asking price) to its present owner. This report is reproduced in full below; and in the end it was perhaps instrumental in persuading the owner of the dagger to acquire the sword as well, particularly as he had already had the dagger tested and proved sound by the Bundesanstalt für Materialprüfung in Berlin.

The sword was submitted to an expert on medieval enamels at the British Museum, who was convinced that the enamelled arms of England in the pommel were genuinely of 14th century making. Then the skin covering of the grip was examined at the British Museum of Natural History and pronounced to be adder skin of very considerable antiquity. In spite of all these opinions (for of course they were only opinions, however soundly based upon expert knowledge) those who denied the weapon's authenticity maintained their negative stance.

In the event the sword was finally bought by the present owner who already possessed the dagger and who was convinced of the sword's authenticity and worth; however, to make sure he very wisely caused it to be tested in every possible way by the Bundesanstalt für Materialprüfung, which tests have shown beyond all reasonable doubt that the sword is not, nor could possibly have been, of late 19th century workmanship.

I give all these reports in full below; my own assessment of 1983 (made, of course, by the old visual, aesthetic and archaeological comparative method) followed by the BAM report in translation, followed by the BAM analytical break-down in the original German.

Thus, by the courageous and responsible action of the present owner, the authenticity of this magnificent royal treasure has at last been established beyond cavil. The doubts can be set at rest, and one of England's national treasures is restored to the light - though not to the country of its origin. But this is irrelevant. The importance is in its total vindication.

2. A Battle-Sword of Edward III (1983)

In this report I shall submit only the evidence shown by the actual physical and aesthetic characteristics of the sword itself. In these I shall apply the experience and knowledge gained by forty years' research almost exclusively devoted to the swords of the European High Middle Ages. This has involved close study of numerous swords and meticulous examination of works of medieval art of all kinds from all parts of Europe.

I shall not describe in detail the forms of each part of the sword, for I assume that this report will be studied with the sword, or photographs of it, to hand, so that its forms will be self-evident. I shall also refer, for convenience, to illustrations, mostly in my own *Sword in the Age of Chivalry* which has more pictures of more medieval swords than any other publication. So if a copy of this is also at hand, it will be helpful. Let me make it clear, however, that the reader should not take too much notice of datings in the text or in some of the captions. It was published nearly twenty years ago, and much of what I wrote in 1963 I have now proved, by new discoveries, to be wrong.

So the sword will be examined entirely on its merits, no account (or no more than is necessary) being taken of the controversial euphoria, condemnation, examination, denigration, defence and rebuttal which has raged around it since 1904. The findings of the reports made recently by Mr Roger Western will be considered and included, as well as the scientific report on the fabrication of the blade made by Dr Allan Williams and the opinion of Mr John Cherry of the British Museum upon the enamelled arms in the pommel. But this report is based solely upon historical, archaeological and aesthetic standards.

This sword is not a ceremonial or parade one. In spite of its richness, the hilt is entirely practical, very restrained in its decoration which is matched by several other swords of the 13th and 14th centuries, which, in spite of royal provenance, and decoration with enamels and/or precious metal, are known to have been, or are at present acknowledged to have been, battle swords.[1] Surviving swords of ceremony or parade, such as that in the Cathedral at Essen (c.1050), that of 'Charlemagne' in the Louvre in Paris, that of the Emperor Friedrich III (c.1440) in the Kunsthistoriches Museum at Vienna, and that of Duke Kristoffer von Bayern (c.1480) in the Schatzkammer at Munich, are all far more elaborately decorated and less practical than the one under discussion. Because of the section and form of the blade it can be regarded as being of my Type XVIIIa.

THE BLADE

1. It has been said that blades of this section belong only to the 15th century, but there is no doubt that they were in use by c.1300. Recent research has shown that in fact they appear in art early in the 12th century and were in fact very common in the Celtic iron Age (c.400 BC - AD 100) and that nearly all Roman short *gladii*, and many long cavalry *spathae*, were of this section. It does not seem to have been used by the Teutonic peoples of the Migration and Viking periods, but reappeared after c.1120. So there is no inherent reason why the blade should be relegated to the late 15th century, as it has been in the past. It has been much used, bearing upon it many signs of wear, honing and combat. It has also, for a considerable period, been well-cared-for and subjected to much rubbing - witness the wear, almost the obliteration, of the engraved or etched?) decoration (q.v. below).

Then it seems after a long period of care to have been somewhat neglected and allowed to rust and get dirty. All the patination caused by this near neglect is *above* the wear on the decoration, so it would appear that, let us say between the time of its making c.1345 to the time of its neglect, c.1688, it was cleaned and polished and cared for as a royal treasure - like the Charlemagne sword in the Louvre - then, after being sent or taken to Spain after 1688 it was kept indoors, in a dry atmosphere, maybe on a wall or maybe in a chest (but not I think wrapped up - where a blade has been wrapped in fabric, fold and crease-marks show as lines of corrosion on the blade). The patination of this blade is exactly like that on the Henry V sword in Westminster Abbey, the sword of Battle Abbey (q.v. below) or the gold and jewelled sword in Essen Cathedral treasury.

From this wear and patination, it is difficult not to deduce these two long periods of wear, first of cleaning and then of neglect. Such neglect would not, of course, affect the materials of the hilt, except the iron below the gold sheathing (q.v. below).

2. *The Marks* There is a bladesmith's mark on one side, very difficult to interpret. A rubbing shows it up rather better than an examination of the mark itself. Like so many of these impressed bladesmiths' stamps, it has been unevenly struck.

---

[1] i.e. the sword of Sancho IV of Castile found in his tomb (+1295): the sword of Can Grande della Scala, Lord of Verona (+1326), found in his tomb; the sword of St. Ferdinand, King of Castile (+1252) in the Real Armeria in Madrid; the so-called Sword of St. Maurice in the Schatzkammer in Vienna (c.1100, with arms c.1200) and the 'Santa Casilda' sword in the Instituto del Conde de Valencia de Don Juan in Madrid.

In many ways it seems to resemble a very well-struck mark on a sword of c.1350 in the Royal Ontario Museum in Toronto. This sword can be dated before 1368, for it bears upon it an Arabic inscription giving that date which says that it was taken during the abortive attempt by Peter of Lusignan, King of Cyprus and Jerusalem, to capture Cairo from the Mamluks in 1365, and was subsequently hung up in the Hall of Victories at Alexandria. Incidentally, the patination on this blade, and many others from the same place which are scattered about in the collections of Europe and America, has exactly the same characteristics as the Edward III sword.

The Garter motto is still mostly visible on one side, but on the other (where it is about 1cm less in diameter) it has been almost worn away. The mark of the portcullis presents a difficulty. Previous scholars who have examined the sword have instantly, without real knowledge of the forms of 14th century blades, assumed that this mark relates to Henry VII - *ipso facto*, the blade is of late 15th - early 16th century date, hence the hilt does not belong (a) to the blade or (b) to the 14th, 15th or 16th centuries but the 19th. Certainly, the portcullis was one of the early Tudor badges, par excellence. But previous to that it has been adopted, c.1400 or before, by the illegitimate son of John of Gaunt, second son of Edward III, and Katharine Swinford. The children of this liaison, which was ultimately legitimised, took the name of Beaufort, and the badge of the Portcullis went with the line. Henry VII's mother, Margaret Beaufort, brought the badge down to the end of the Century, and Henry of Richmond adopted it; and he and Henry VIII used it *ad nauseam*. It is literally plastered all over Henry VII's chapel at Westminster Abbey and even more over King's College Chapel at Cambridge and St. Georges at Windsor; and Henry VIII used it on his gold nobles. But why did Thomas of Beaufort adopt it? Where did he get it from? The need to produce this report quickly has mean that ongoing research into the usage of the portcullis as a charge or a badge before 1400 has not yet brought results, so we must for the present assume one of two things: (1) that the badge did have some significance, personal or national, to Edward III. And it must never be overlooked that he had as much interest in, and emotion about, France (particularly his duchy of Aquitaine) as he had about England. We have to search for possible continental origin for it, as well as an English one. And what about his queen, Philippa of Hainault?[2] and (2) that the marks were indeed added to the blade in Tudor times. This, though not impossible, does seem highly unlikely. What were they added for? If they were added, say in 1485 after Henry VII seized the Plantagenet throne, it is still possible that they could have been subjected to two centuries of cleaning. Two hundred years of rubbing and polishing *might* wear them down as much as three. But if he put his portucllis, why the Garter? *He* had no close personal link with it, as its founder did. One can imagine that Edward was so full of his new Order that he might have embellished everything he could think of with its motto. But this doesn't seem so probable an act of the cold and efficient and totally unromatic Henry VII. Then, could not the portcullis alone have been added by Henry? Hardly likely, since both portcullis and garter seem to have been subjected to the same amount of wear. Both would seem to have been applied to the blade together.

As a point of interest, not really relevant to this inquiry, this blade was made by a left-handed smith. In the forging a sword-blade which is broad and flat, whatever its section is, if the hot blade is held in the tongs in the left hand struck with the hammer in the right, it will develop a twist to the right-hand side - i.e. the plane of the blade twists downward along its length until, at the point, the edge on the right, as it is held outward in the left hand with the flat of the blade at the hilt held parallel to the ground, will be anything from 5 mm to 10 mm lower than the left-hand edge. This will be in reverse if the blade is hammered with the left hand. This observation was made by the actual forging of several new blades (not by me) and the subsequent inspection of many old ones (by me). Forging will often, also produce a quite unwanted but unavoidable bend in the flat of the blade, generally towards the hammer. Many old blades demonstrate this. It is very much harder than one might think to forge a flat blade perfectly straight, or really flat, or really light, either. The quality of the blade under discussion takes on a new dimension in the light of these practical observations; it is, in every way, superb. Its beautiful balance and lightness is quite remarkable.

Comparisons (1). Actual Swords' Blades

(a) Sword of Henry V in Westminster Abbey.
This has the same kind of blade, only about 5" shorter, with a similar section, but its central ridge runs right to the point which is reinforced, whereas the Edward III one peters out about 8" from the point. The colour and patination on each is the same. I cleaned the Henry V one thirty years ago (very carefully) but it has now become very dull and dirty again.
(b) The Sword of Battle Abbey. Royal Scottish Museum, Edinburgh.
A tenure sword, made or assembled during the abbacy of Thomas de Ludlow, 1417. This blade, of a flat diamond section, rather narrow and tapering quite sharply to the point, has like the Edward III sword, seen much use, wear and honing. The patination - it remained in the care of Battle Abbey until towards the end of the last century - is like that on the blade under discussion, evidently quietly gathering dust in the same way.

---

2   The mark is not, in fact, heraldically correct. A heraldic portcullis (viz. Henry VII and the House of Commons) must have a ring at each top corner from which depend chains. These adjuncts are missing here and may be an indication of an early use of the badge.

(c) A sword, c.1375-1425, in the Metropolitan Museum in New York.[3]

This has a blade of the same general form, though it is shorter, broader at the hilt and reinforced at the point; but, though clean and bright, it has the same kind of patination.

(d) A large bearing sword in the collection of Mr R T Gwynn.

This, by reason of marks on the blade, can be dated positively to the early 14th century. It is larger than the Edward III sword, and of a different section (Type XX)[4] but in outline it is the same, and has been preserved under the same conditions as the foregoing. Perhaps its main significance to this inquiry is its close similarity to:

(e) A large war-sword once in the collection of Mr Claude Blair.

This, though also of Type XX, is in silhouette almost exactly like the Edward III sword. Because of its close similarity to the Gwynn bearing sword, it too must be dated within the first half of the 14th century.[5] (There is a third in this group in the Kunsthistorisches Museum in Vienna).

Comparisons (2). Blades Shown in Art

(a) A 'Romance of Alexander' made and illustrated probably in England c.1340 shows very many blades of this kind, or rather, with this ridged section. Some are *epées de guerre*, some shorter arming Swords. The quality of the drawing is excellent and detail is shown very clearly and reliably.

(b) The blade of a sword shown on a sculptured figure in the Rathaus at Cologne, one of the Nine Heroes made c.1310.[6]

(c) The sword, partly drawn from its scabbard, of William Longespée the Younger in his tomb in Salisbury Cathedral has a clear ridged section, c.1290-1310.[7]

(d) The sword on the tomb-effigy of John of Eltham, a younger brother of Edward II who died in 1337. Whereas the section of the Longespée sword has four flat faces, that of John of Eltham has the faces lightly hollowed, like the sword under discussion. There are so many MS illustrations, painting and sculptures dating after c.1350 which show blades of this kind that it would be pointless and tedious to enumerate them. Let it simply be said that in MS pictures of good quality - i.e. well, clearly and accurately drawn - there is little possibility of confusing the delineation of a flat fullered blade with a four-sided ridged one. Compare, for example, the Bodleian 'Romance of Alexander' with the 'Maciejowski Bible' c.1250 in the Pierpoint Morgan Library in New York. Both artists, half a century apart, knew what they were doing and obviously had intimate acquaintance with the war-gear they were illustrating.

THE HILT

This is very distinctively of a kind which was in use between c.1250-1350, give or take a little at each end. Similar hilts are often shown in art (to be discussed below) and there are surviving swords which compare very closely, many of them clearly dateable. Before discussing the hilt as a whole, it may be expedient to comment upon its component parts.

The Pommel

This is of a kind classified in *SAC* as Type K; its usage can be fairly positively pinned down to a period between the decades of 1270 and 1340. It is of iron, sheathed with thick gold which tests have shown to be of a very high and rich quality, to which the depth and glow of the colour attests. The base, against the top of the grip, is most elegantly finished with a small upward-lapping cusp with a quatrefoil rosette at its point. There are six other similar rosettes upon the outer rim of the pommel encircling the inner disc, which is hollowed to contain an enamel of the arms of England and France (Ancient) quarterly within a shield, which is contained within the circular edge by sprays of foliage in gold upon a green ground. The enamel is of champlevé in the manner of Limoges enamels. On the reverse side, as well as the seven gold rosettes, there is inset a disc of transulcent chalcedony beneath which is a ragged, brown fragment of some sort of cloth. It looks like a woollen cloth, for there is a kind of fuzzy nap upon part of it, though because of the opacity of the stone it is difficult to see this. (Comment upon this will follow).

There is a button, in the form of a small, stepped, truncated pyramid to accommodate the rivetted turn-over at the top of the

3   *SAC* Plate 34 (d) A large bearing sword in the collection of Mr R.T. Gwynn.

4   *SAC* p.75

5   *SAC* plate 40

6   Illustrated in Karpa, O. *Zur Chronologie der Kölnischer Plastik in XIV.C.* Cologne, 1933

7   *SAC* p.57, fig.29

tang. This is entirely enclosed within the gold sheathing, but in the x-ray photographs shows up clearly as a separate entity. Mr. Western has commented very cogently upon these tang-buttons: he says, in his report:

> 'The buttons on swords seem to have received no attention from the various authors of books on weapons but perhaps a little more attention should be paid to them. The more delicate ones would be the first thing to be destroyed or lost along with the top of the tang when a sword is dismantled, so their presence is a good sign of the original condition of a sword. Also the size and shape of the button could be of help in dating swords. My studies have led me to conclude that the button had no part in the assembly of a sword prior to c.1260, that early buttons were square and tall say from c.1260-1340 or 50 and that short square buttons were more popular at a later date say from 1325-1400. At a later period coinciding with the introduction of the (scent-stopper) pommel somewhere around 1380 buttons became either globular or flat discs and have remained so.

> Compare the buttons of the following swords:

> *Square Tall Buttons*

> Sir Robert de Bures. d.1302
> Sir Hugh Hastings. d.1347
> Blair, *EAA*, illustration 25 (c.1300) 26 & 29 (early 14th century)
> Swords from the tombs of Filippo dei Desideri d.1315, Cloaccio Beccadelli d.1341
> Sword of the gonfaloniere de giustigia
> Sword of Giovanni de Medici d.1353
> Sword c.1350 (Turin AR G 12)
> Hand-and-a-half sword c.1350 (Brescia MC G 2B)

> *Square but short buttons*

> Ceremonial sword of Fredrick II of Hohenstaufen and of the Emperor Charles IV of Luxembourg known to have been fitted with a new pommel in 1347
> Wallace Collection A460 - 1375
> The sword on the effigy of the Black Prince 1376 or before
> The Battle Abbey sword.

The enamel has been examined by Mr John Cherry of the British and Medieval Department of the British Museum, who can see no reason why it should not be of 14th century date since it is closely akin to enamels made in England - much as those upon the Savernake horn which the Museum acquired recently. It matches these enamels in style, colour, technique; even the damage to each is similar - i.e. when chipped, the actual stuff of the enamel shows the same kind of fracture.

Comment upon the chalcedony overlay on the reverse of the pommel and the relic of cloth beneath it will be made later.

The gold surface on this pommel shows unmistakeable signs of wear, such as might be made over a number of years by the fretting upon it of the wearer's fingers, particularly if the sword was worn at the hip with the arms in the pommel facing outward to the left.

The Pommel: Comparisons

First, comparisons with some surviving swords, starting low and ending high. Only a few significant ones will be given, as there are so many.

1. A Type XVIa sword, found in London, in the Tower armouries, c.1300-25. Here the pommel is quite plain, broad and flat with a raised central boss, with no depressions in it. The button is small, neat and of a true pyramid form. Though this sword is long and looks heavy, it is in fact as light and handy as the Edward III sword. Its cross, incidentally, is exactly paralleled by the cross on the sword on the effigy of John of Eltham in Westminster Abbey.[8]

2. A very similar sword of the same type in the Burrell Collection in Glasgow. Find-place unknown.[9]

3. A large sword of Type XIV in the Metropolitan Museum in New York, c.1300-25. Here the pommel is of much the same form as that in the Edward III sword, a Type K only rather thicker in profile. The rivet-block (button) is very similar in shape. There is an overlaid hollow disc of silver placed over the outer rim which encircles the raised central boss with a latin inscription in

[8] *SAC* plate 28A
[9] *SAC* plate 28C

Gothic miniscule characters. The general form and dimensions of this hilt are very like those of the Edward III sword, though the cross is slightly different.[10] The blade, of course, is quite different.

4. A Type XIV sword in the Oakeshott Collection. This pommel is very like the one in the Burrell Collection (q.v. above, No.2) but is plated - overlaid, rather - with silver, as is the cross, which is also of the same style as the Edward III one.[11]

5. A quite remarkable sword, of Type XIIIa, in the Treasury of Cologne Cathedral, called 'The Sword of St. George'; c.1300-25. The pommel is exceptionally broad, the central disc being wider in proportion than the Edward III one. It is plated with silver-gilt, and the recesses in the central bosses are filled with enamelled devices; on the outside, a sort of heraldic butterfly, in white, purple and yellow enamel on a blue ground, the whole surrounded by a kind of border of little cusped 'architectural' features, hard to describe but very beautiful. The other side shows, similarly surrounded, a feature difficult to interpret. A butterfly with wings folded, perhaps? The top of this pommel has been filed or cut away, to allow a nasty spherical button to be put on top. The grip has been restored, probably in 18th century and quite misunderstood for it tapers upwards toward the pommel, instead of the other way round. It is covered with Morocco leather and loosely bound with silver twisted wire, now considerably displaced. The cross is short, straight, of square section and plated with silver, probably once gilt. The blade is a fine, workmanlike, well-used war blade, broad, flat and fullered for half its length.

This sword (which I have described in detail because it seemed to be necessary) has not been published until this year.[12] If it were to come into the sale room, I believe everyone would at least on first sight, consider the hilt to be a fake. The enamel is particularly garish in colour and the device looks quite improbable. But it seems to have an impeccable provenance and background.

6. The sword of a king of France, c.1300-25, Type XIV. In the Pauilhac Collection in the Musée de l'Armée in Paris. The hilt is almost identical with that of the Edward III sword. The pommel is of the same form, sheathed in gold. The button, rather taller, is enclosed within the gold sheathing. The central bosses are a little smaller in diameter. One holds an enamel: Argent a cross gules. The other, a relic (of dark woolly fabric) behind a piece of ? crystal. Otherwise the pommel is quite plain, without any rosettes or other embellishment. Said to have belonged to 'a King of France' but, in the information at present available here, which king is not indicated. Of all the hilts in existence, this one in every way (see notes below on the cross) is the nearest parallel to the Edward III one.[13]

There was considerable use in decoration of metalwork of quatrefoil rosettes to this period. The effigy of Edward III in Westminster Abbey has a number of them engraved on the broad band across his chest which holds together the two sides of his long cloak; they also appear on the points of the cowters on the Black Prince's effigy in Canterbury Cathedral. However, this motif appears so often in the art of this period in architectural decoration as well as in MSS and figure sculpture that its appearance on these two effigies, so significant to this inquiry, must be regarded as unimportant.

7. The sword of Battle Abbey, Type XVIII, c.1400-20. Royal Scottish Museum, Edinburgh. This is a tenure sword, assembled during the abbacy of Thomas de Ludlow in 1417. The blade is a worn, used war blade, the hilt is of iron overlaid with silver, which over all the surfaces of cross and pommel is decorated with engraved scrolls and sprigs of foliage. In the central recesses of the pommel (Oakeshott, Type J) are enamels showing the arms of Battle Abbey within a shield flanked by the initials T.L., one on each side.

8. A small sword in the Cathedral of Toledo. Type XIIIb, c.1300. Pommel here is similar (Type J) to the Battle Abbey one, also overlaid with silver gilt sheet and enamelled in the central recesses with the arms of Castile and Leon. Probably belonged to one of the sons of Alfonso el Sabio of Castile, one Juan el de Tarifa who was killed in battle in 1319. This has been called a boy's sword (Don Juan was only 19 when he died) but recent research suggests that it is a light riding-sword.

9. The sword given to the City of Lincoln in 1386 by Richard II. The pommel is of a rather oval form of Type J, overlaid with silver-gilt sheathing. The arms of England (England and France (ancient) Quarterly, as in the sword of Edward III) and of the City of Lincoln are engraved on the central bosses on either side. This pommel (and the similarly sheathed cross as well) very distinctly show the same tiny eruptions on the surface of the silver, caused by slag or corrosion in the underlying iron, as does the

---

[10] *SAC* plates 15 and 16

[11] *SAC* plates 19 and 46B

[12] Published and illustrated in Stuber & Wetler

[13] There is a photograph and a very brief note of this in a brochure published a few years ago (1965) as a Supplement to *La Revue Francaise*, 'Le Collection Georges Pauilhac dans la Musée de l'Armée', by Robert-Jean Charles. There are a few other swords which, although they have pommels of a different type to that of the Edward III sword, show similarities of technological construction which are worth noting.

pommel and cross of the Edward III sword. These small blemishes (apparent also on the Pauilhac sword's hilt) are of great significance when compared with those on the Edward III sword. There can be little doubt about the provenance of the Pauilhac sword, and none whatsoever about the Lincoln one.

10. The so-called 'Santa Casilda' sword. Type XII, c.1250-1300, in the collection of the Instituto del Conde de Valencia in Madrid. This was formerly preserved as a treasure in the convent of San Vicente near Logroño. The pommel is quite flat (Type G) of gilded iron. There is a central hollow on each side, filled with enamelled arms which have lost their colour - a Barry Wavy of Four. Round this is an inscription in Lombardic capitals, but this inscription is bordered by a circle, outside and inside, of small punched dots, as in the Edward III pommel.

The Pommel: Comparisons in Art

Again, it will be necessary to select no more than a few examples from the large number of parallels available. Again, the lesser will be taken first, leading up to the more important.
(a) Tomb effigy of Count Ernst von Gleichen in the Cathedral at Erfurt. He died in 1264, but the effigy is probably some years later in date. The pommel shown is of a form almost identical with that of the sword in the Tower armouries referred to above (No.1 in the comparisons with actual swords).
(b) Many of the sculptured figures decorating the Cathedral at Freiburg show these pommels. All date c.1300. Particularly notable is the sword of a soldier in the tympanum over the main doorway, and another on the Easter Sepulchre.[14]
(c) A figure (Godefroy de Bouillon) in the Rathaus in Cologne, c.1310.[15]
(d) The tomb effigies of some of the late 13th - early 14th century Landgeaves of Hesse in the Cathedral at Marburg show pommels of this kind.[16]
(e) The tomb-effigy of Robert d'Artois, + 1317. St. Denis. Here the pommel is extremely clearly shown, as indeed is the whole hilt.
(f) The tomb-effigy of Robert de France, Comte d'Evreux. St. Denis + 1319.
(g) The tomb-effigy of the Black Prince in Canterbury Cathedral, + 1376. Here the pommel is almost exactly the same as the one on his father's sword as to shape and proportions, though the sword itself is of a totally different kind, as typical of the second half of the 14th century as the Edward III one is of the first half.

THE GRIP

This is formed of a core of wood; lime wood was perhaps the most commonly used for this purpose, but the wood of this grip (a little of which shows where the covering is worn) has not been botanically tested. However, its appearance does suggest a close-grained wood like lime. The grip is most elegant, rather flat in section and tapering towards the pommel, both in the plane of the blade and at right angles to it. It is covered with snake-skin, which, examined at the British Museum of Natural History, is said to be that of an adder. The remark that 'it is almost fossilised' cannot and should not be taken literally, for it would take several million years, not six hundred, to fossilise an adder-skin. It was meant in a colloquial way to indicate that it was a very old and well-worn and dried adder skin. It is worn right away, showing the wood core underneath, in two places on the 'outer', i.e. arms, side of the hilt in places where the middle fingers of the right hand would exert great pressure when the sword was in action - it is these fingers that press most hardly upon a sword-grip and do most of the work of holding it. There is another patch higher up which is where the skin of the left hand at the base of the thumb would press and rub if the sword were wielded with both hands. Curiously, this wear indicates that the sword must have been worn with the *relic* side of the pommel facing outward to the left, for if it was drawn from the scabbard with the *arms* side outward, the wear of the fingers of the right hand would have come on the other side of the grip to where it is. This creates something of a puzzle regarding the wear on the gold of the pommel. Further examination and handling of the sword will be needed to clear it up.

The grip is embellished with five fillets of gold; a fairly broad one at the bottom above the cross, a similar one at mid-point and another below the pommel. Between them are two narrower ones. These also show a lot of wear. They are lightly decorated with longitudinal ridges with a light hatched decoration between. This is very similar in style to a sword, now in the Museum of London, which was found in the Thames in 1742 when foundations were being dug for Westminster Bridge. This retains its silver

---

14 Adolf Goldschmidt, *Die Skulpturen von Freiburg und Wechsellburg* illustrates these and many more

15 Karpa, O. *Zur chronologie der Kölnischer Plastik im XIV Jahrhundert*

16 Hamman, R. *Die Elizabethkirche in Marburg*. Vol.II. Die Skulpturen

scabbard mounts, which bear the same kind of decoration as these fillets. It is tempting to suggest the same hand made both. Because of the style of these silver mounts, the Westminster sword can be dated clearly to c.1325-40.[17]

The wood, and the skin covering it, as is the case with most ancient sword-grips, has shrunk slightly so that the fillets Nos. 2, 3 and 4 upwards, are loose. The lower one, No. 2, has left a strong indentation upon the adder-skin, further evidence of the strong grip of a powerful hand.

The shape and section of this grip is most elegant. Very few original grips survive from this period, and most of them are workaday affairs covered with leather or bound with wire; several are shapely but much damaged and no survivor that I know of has this particular section. However, in sculpture there are two particularly fine examples, both are in the Abbey of St. Denis, both are of Princes of France who died in 1317 and one in 1319 and so may have been made by the same sculptor. The first is on the tomb-effigy of Comte Robert d'Artois, + 1317 and, except that it is a short one-hand grip and has no visible fillets (time and people's hands may have rubbed them away) is of exactly the same section as the Edward III sword. Nearby is Robert de France, Comte d'Evreux, whose sword has a grip with the same section. Both of these swords, incidentally are short riding-swords though both men are in full armour; and both have pommels and crosses of the same style as the sword under discussion (q.v. below). There are also effigies in England which have similar grips, but to establish which ones would require a visit to the library of the Society of Antiquaries in London, which, owing to the time factor and the need to make this report quickly, cannot be done at present. However, it can be said with confidence that it is not a very unusual form, for this particular period.

THE CROSS

This is an example of a kind of cross which seems to have been popular particularly during the period between c.1240-1350. (Style 6 in the Oakeshott typology). There are one or two variations on the style, which in its pure form is like the cross on the Santa Casilda sword (q.v. above) where the upper edge may be nearly straight or quite strongly curved, and the lower edge correspondingly more strongly curved, so that the arms of the cross expand at the ends. The cross on the Edward III sword might be regarded as a sub-style, with no widening at the ends.

There are many crosses which have the same silhouette when seen in elevation, but more often than not their section is nearly square, not flat and ribbon-like. (One cannot with justification use the term 'square' for the section of crosses, for only by chance would any be truly, geometrically square). The cross under discussion is slightly hollowed on each of its broader faces, with four quatrefoil rosettes in each face; these are matched by four more on the narrow upper and lower faces. Each tip is neatly finished off with a little cusped cap.

The sheet-gold on the cross displays some of the small irregularities caused by corrosion or slag in the underlying iron similar to those on the pommel, and identical with those upon the hilt of the Richard II sword at Lincoln.

The Cross: Comparisons in Fact

(a) A large hand-and-a-half sword in the Swiss national museum at Zurich, which is considerably earlier than the Edward III sword - c.1200.
(b) Eight others in the same collection, all dating between c.1250-1380.[18]
(c) A Type XIV sword in the Oakeshott collection (q.v. above) plated with silver.
(d) The Santa Casilda Sword.
(e) The Pauilhac 'King of France' sword.
(f) The sword from the tomb of the Emperor Albrecht I, 1308.
(c) and (d) are quite important parallels in this case, for the Santa Casilda sword has the same hollowed faces wherein is an inscription in Lombardic capitals in place of the rosettes of the the Edward III sword, while the Pauilhac one would seem to be by the same hand, it is so closely akin.

---

[17] Oakeshott, op.cit. p.138, fig. 125

[18] These are all illustrated in 'Waffen in Schweizerischen Landesmuseum Griffwaffen 1.' Hugo Schneider and Karl Stuber, Zurich 1981. Nos. 19, 26, 27, 28, 30, 31, 34, 35 and 36.

Again, there are so many that only one or two need to be selected.

(a) A roof-boss in the Angel choir in Lincoln Cathedral[19] c.1280.

(b) The mounted figure on the canopy of the tomb of Edmund, called crouchback, brother of Edward I, in Westminster Abbey, 1296.[20]

(c) A 'Deposition from the Cross' in Lucca Cathedral by Nicolo Pisano, 1258-78.[21]

(d) The tomb-effigy of Robert d'Artois, St. Denis 1317 (fig. 6 herewith).

(e) The tomb-effigy of Robert de France, St. Denis, 1319.

(f) Several of the swords on the hero-figures in the Cologne Rathaus.

(g) Two swords from a 'Maestà' by Lippo Memmi (1317) at San Gimignano.[22]

(h) Several in MSS by Matthew Paris of St.Albans, all c.1250-60.

(j) Several will be found also in the Bodleian 'Romance of Alexander'.

GENERAL REMARKS

In all the foregoing it will have been noticed that no mention has been made as a parallel of one particular very rich sword. I refer to a beautiful weapon now in the Deutschklingenmuseum in Solingen. This was one of Mr D'Acre Kenrick Edwards' prized possessions, sold with the Edward III sword in 1961. In my opinion, it was wrongly dated by Christies in the catalogue of that sale - 'in the style of the late 14th century... the blade 15th century', the latter in italics to show they believed that to be genuine. So it is - of the early 14th century (Type XVI). The hilt should have read '... of the late 13th century'. There are many features in this sword of a similar nature to some on the Edward III one - the little caps at the ends of the cross (though they differ slightly in shape) and the rosettes around the edges of the hexagonal pommel. If one looks at the two side-by-side, as they are shown in the photograph in Christie's catalogue of the sale, the Edward III shows up in comparison as being in excellent taste; beautifully proportioned with the decoration kept to a restrained minimum. The Solingen one, by contrast, is fussy and overdone - far too many rosettes, and the enamelled devices (said to be of the English royal house of Lancaster) seem rather over elaborate, as do the decorations of foliage upon the silver-plated grip.

I have not seen this since I examined it minutely in 1961, but I remember that it felt clumsy in the hand (such a contrast to the Edward III one) and that the colours of the enamels were unconvincing, particularly the green which was - is - of a dark, almost transparent green like créme de menthe. The Solingen Museum have obviously accepted it, but I know that it was very much one of the comparisons which helped to damn the Edward III sword. It may be inferred from the foregoing that I have doubts about the Solingen sword; but I cannot substantiate my misgivings, having only a twenty-year-old memory of it and two good photographs in the Solingen Museum's *Kostbare Blankwaffen* to go on. This sword has to be taken into account in this inquiry, because the doubters will probably cite it as being one of Louis Marcy's fakes, which, having in its decoration several elements parallel with elements in the Edward III hilt, gives great scope for assuming that if Marcy made the one, he must have made the other.[23]

But consider: when a forger seeks to pass forged ten pound notes, he tends to mix them with good ones. In selling his haul of wares from Spain, Marcy's hand would have been greatly strengthened by having amongst them at least one really good genuine 'treasure'.

My conjecture, based as I have said only upon memory, a photograph and the application of Reason, is that, having the Edward III sword, Marcy made the hilt of the Solingen one, giving it Lancastrian heraldry to match the other sword and the two daggers. Made it, and like even the best forgers (Konrad, for instance), overdid it. I don't know. The experts at Solingen must have tested it, and must believe in it. So who am I to condemn it, not having seen and handled it for twenty years? But all the same it will be brought up, and used as evidence against the Edward III sword.

The same remarks (about overdone decoration) apply to the other of the three swords on the left of the photograph in the Christie's catalogue.

The chalcedony stone in the pommel and the relic beneath it present problems which because of a shortage of information must lead away from hard facts somewhat into the realms of speculation. Because of the quality of the sword, and the fragility of the relic, it will not be advisable (though it would be quite easy) to remove the stone and subject the pieces of cloth to a proper

---

[19] Oakeshott, op.cit. p.51, fig.25 (b)

[20] Oakeshott, op.cit. p.46, fig. 21

[21] Oakeshott, op.cit. p.52, fig. 26

[22] Oakeshott, op.cit. p.64, figs. 36 and 37 (see also 38)

[23] Since this report was written in 1983, this sword has now been shown to be, indeed, a fake (1990) blade and all.

examination, which would give positive (or nearly positive) answers to the questions of its substance and its age, because once exposed to the air it might disintegrate. Might, not would. A lot of very ancient fabric has stood up to being knocked about for nine or ten centuries. For instance, in the Muniment Room at Westminster Abbey there are chests containing documents going back to the 12th century, many of them having royal or baronial or episcopal seals appended. These seals are preserved in little bags, neatly fitting them, made out of worn-out and discarded vestments. One of the great seals of Richard I, for instance, is contained in a bag made from a a piece of an 8th century cope. When I handled it, I was not aware of its age until the late Mr. Tanner, librarian and keeper of the Muniments, told me. It looked and felt like a bit of 19th century embroidery. There were many more of the same kind which I saw. So it might seem that the risk to this relic if exposed could be less severe than one would suppose. However, to dismantle it might seem too drastic a course to pursue.

Mr AH, in his letter to the Victoria & Albert Museum of December 1, 1904, says 'The chalcedony covering the relic on the pommel, of Edward III's dagger is a piece of the same stone as on one side of the pommel of the sword.' There is a little vagueness here. Did he mean 'a piece of the same lump of stone' or 'a piece of the same kind of stone'? There is a world of difference between the two meanings. If it is indeed a piece of the same lump of stone (and scientific tests, say in the British Museum of Natural History, might, perhaps show whether it was or not) then whoever put the piece in the pommel of the sword used another fragment of it to cover the relic on the pommel of the dagger. By inference, in that case, the sword and dagger are both right, or they are both fakes. But one piece of chalcedony, cut and shaped in c.1348, would look exactly like another piece cut and shaped in 1890. After all, chalcedony stone was as it were fixed into its present physical state some millions of years ago. Six hundred would have no effect upon it at all, in this time-scale.

Here we come to even more speculation; I have little information, and vague at that. In a telephone conversation with Mr. Pocock on Sunday evening, May 2nd 1982, he said, quite unprompted for we were discussing the sword, 'the dagger's got a bit of the same stone as the sword in the pommel, and a bit of the same cloth underneath it'. Following that, he said he had a letter telling him of the results of tests which had been carried out upon the dagger, and that it was a modern fake. So, if the dagger is a fake, so should the sword be; if it is right, so is the sword.[24]

This presents us with a sort of wandering torpedo which may home in either on the sword, me, or the doubters. But if this sword is a fake, so is the Pauilhac one, and the Richard II City of Lincoln one, and a few others I have cited as parallels.

If, however, we assume that a 14th century piece of chalcedony is of the same physical structure as a 19th century piece (and both would be x-millions years old anyway), there is no need for the piece on the dagger to be assumed to be off the same lump as the piece on the sword. AH suggested that it was, because he wanted it to be. Others said it was, because they wanted it to be for the opposite reason; and Mr. Pocock said it was because he had been told it was by divers experts from 1904 to some time in the 1970s.

What of the relics? The one in the sword shows fairly clearly for the stone above it is wafer thin. The one in the dagger is obscured by a large dome-like piece of translucent stone; one might infer that any ragged fragment of brown cloth put beneath that would look exactly like whatever the beholder want it to look like i.e., it does not necesssarily mean that it must be a piece of the same ancient fabric as the bit in the sword.

The suggestion - no, the positive assertion - made by AH in his letter of 1904 that it is a bit of the Confessor's shroud is quite untenable. How does he know? What is his evidence? None, mere supposition. Actually, since his time a number of princes and prelates have been as it were dug up. Their tombs have been opened and their generally marvellously preserved bodies examined. In no case was such a body wrapped in a shroud. The two 13th century bishops recently uncovered under the floor of York Minster were in full canonicals, complete with crozier and episcopal ring. The body of Fernando de la Cerda, an Infante of Spain who was buried in 1270, and brought into the light of day in 1943 was dressed in the complete everyday court dress of a great noble; these garments, down to his little underpants, were removed and examined and photographed. He also had spurs and a fine, plain sword in its scabbard and a rich belt of gold enamelled with arms, England and Champagne among them. Not a sword-belt, a belt of ceremony. Similar though richer - it included a crown - was the equipment of the body of his elder brother, Sancho IV of Castile. No sign of a shroud. Our King John was taken out of his tomb in Worcester Cathedral in 1742, and found to be dressed exactly as his effigy on the top, sword and all, except that (as he had wished on his deathbed) he wore the cowl of Franciscan friar.

Edward the Confessor was similarly examined by James II, who took his ring away. Again, shortage of time in preparing this prevents me from looking up the record of this. Was there a shroud in 1066, where none was in 1217? No. I don't think it's a shroud of anybody; it looks too fluffy. Part of a robe, saint's or monk's maybe. There were plenty of very revered holy men and women whose garments of rough wool would be precious relics. This must forever remain a matter of speculation.

So too, for the purposes of this report, must the matter of the dagger. The actual form of it is quite consistent with its being genuinely of the mid-14th century. The very restrained elements of decoration on the blade - the St.George's cross in a shield and the little leaf-motif identical with the leaves on the jupon of the effigy of William of Hatfield (a son of Edward III who died in

---

[24] This comment I made before I knew where the dagger is, or that it had been properly tested by BAM and proved to be genuine. The tests show that the stone is not chalcedony, but rock-crystal.

childhood) in York Minster - are consistent with the period and the good taste shown in decorating the sword. The fact that the hilt is of solid gold would be surprising in a fake. Is the gold of the same quality as that on the sword? Is it solid gold? How do we know?[25] If it is, why did Marcy go to the great expense (even in his time) of using solid gold to fake a dagger where gold plating over iron or brass would do just as well? He could have had no idea that things like x-rays and other technological means of testing fakes were going to be invented and employed in half-a-century's time.

I think that to assume that the sword was made specifically for the inauguration of the Order of the Garter in 1348 is to stretch credibility too far. The only evidence for such an assumption is the Garter badges on the blade. I believe, Edward III being the sort of man history shows him to have been, that any sword he might have had made just after that event would have the Garter on it. He might well have put it on all kinds of personal things; of course, there was nothing more intensely personal, or of such high symbolic significance, as his sword to a chivalrous and romantic extrovert upon a pinnacle of power and success. As I said, it's no ceremonial weapon, but an honest, practical, well-used battle-sword of supreme quality, richer than most such weapons of princes which have survived it, maybe. I believe one reason why others have failed to survive, here or in Europe, beyond the 17th century was simply because the richness of their hilts was an irresistable temptation to be turned into cash. It is probably entirely on account of the relic that it was sent or smuggled out to Spain. The fate of supreme armours, for instance. We know, from 17th century records in this country, that the superb parade-armour sent to Henry VIII by Maximilian I was, less than a century after it was made, thrown out in the Tower in 1601 and 'Thrown appon Hepes'. Before the Commonwealth, be it noted.

It is noticeable that no marks - dents, gashes, nicks - such as might be expected to have been caused by the severe combat experience of the blade appear on the cross. There are a few minor indentations on the underside of the cross which have probably been caused by various hard objects having knocked against it in its many travels. This lack of damage, where the blade shows plenty, leads to the questions (i) is not the hilt a 19th century reproduction allied to an old blade and (ii) was not an old used blade put into the hilt of a parade sword? The answer to (i) in my opinion is a flat no. To (ii) I could suggest that this is not at all improbable; but I would add that I have examined the crosses of a very great many medieval swords and found no cut or gash which could have been caused by an opposing blade; nor, curiously, do such scars appear more than extremely rarely upon the hilts of 16th and 17th century swords, even upon the basket guards of Highland broadswords. Of course, these were all iron or steel or bronze guards, not gold ones, so they are mostly hard enough to have received only superficial damage which cleaning and rubbing over two or three or four centuries would wear away. But I believe the answer, particularly in the case of medieval swords which were seldom used for parrying, is that crosses just did not get cut up.

I believe this is a fighting sword. Its richness is consistent with that ebullient monarch's temperament. And anyway, if it is a parade sword, how did the adder-skin on the grip come to be worn right through by usage?

CONCLUSION

Ever since it came out of Spain in 1895, this beautiful sword has been dogged by two enormous disadvantages. One, because of its richness and condition, it was met, and has been met ever since, by that outworn and so often exploded excuse, that it's too good to be true. This, because it has so often been exploded, can be dismissed. The other one cannot - because it was, and has been certified (how?) to have been in the possession of Louis Marcy. This has given it a taint which will take time, effort and an honest and clear demonstration of faith in it to erase. Even so, if this matter is looked at with care and not with a pre-conceived emotional response to the name of Marcy, we may find the taint not to be so poisonous after all. Marcy was a dealer. He also had a skilled workshop in which he made fakes. He must have had craftsmen of many skills - goldsmiths, enamellers, iron workers, bladessmiths, joiners, jewellers. Or is he supposed to have done all this work himself? (But that is by the way). So, he sells works of art, and fabricates them. But the suggestion in all this 80 year-old controversy is that he made everything he sold, which is manifestly absurd. He - even if he was a dim-witted French dealer who had no knowledge of England or the English language, as Mr. AH says he was - would never be so stupid. To make any sort of commercial success of faking, he would have to plant his duds carefully among the good pieces. So in fact if he had this sword, and this dagger, it is by no means essential to assume that they were duds also. Perhaps, somehow, the dagger may hold a key to the problem. Mr. Pocock has that letter to the effect that the dagger has been subjected to tests, which had shown it to be a fake. This is a very serious condemnation and must be taken seriously. But many such tests made several years ago have been by newly-discovered means of examination, proved to be inaccurate. Unless we can see the actual reports by the person who made the tests, and submit the dagger to more up-to-date scrutiny, there will remain much doubt.[26]

The foregoing is merely an expression of my opinion. Informed opinion, I think you will agree, but only an opinion like, so far, everyone else's. Until even more convincing scientific - or supernatural, perhaps - tests have been made, the doubters will continue to doubt. I am not of their company. I believe in it. It is far too convincing, too excellent in all its parts, and in the whole which is greater than the sum of them, to allow me to entertain any shadow of a doubt that it is anything but a sword, and a very precious and cherished one, of Edward III and so, of course, of the Royal House of England.

[25] Now, of course, we do know.

[26] See above

Scientific and Technical Tests on the King Edward III Sword (1986)

Bundesanstalt für Materialprüfung, Berlin

The place of origin and the date of the making of the sword has to be placed during the period 1327-1377 according to its historical setting and associations. Because Northern France was occupied during part of this time (by the English) particularly after the beginning of the Hundred Year's War in 1337, its craftsmanship and technique could be either French or English.

Apart from the purely scientific analysis, which cannot be made without comparison with other contemporaneous work, technical assessment must above all take account of comparative potentialities of material and of craftsmanship. These techniques and materials can be assessed both on a chronological and a geographical basis, as well as by comparison with matters of form and heraldry on hand-made works of art. This report is subdivided into specific investigation of craftsmanship and technical methods of production, the various types of material, the sword's present condition and as far as is necessary in direct association with its historical background.

1. The Blade
2. The Cross
3. The Grip
4. The Pommel
5. Complete assessment of each part using radiography
6. Comparative surveys
7. Analysis of materials

Constant reference will be made to the illustrations.

The Blade

The form of the blade, according to the classification proposed by Ewart Oakeshott in various articles (among others 'A River-Find of 15th Century Swords') a Type XIII war-sword (up to c.1350) but with a blade section making it an average XVIIIa.

The blade is formed in heat, and cold hand-forged to a flat diamond section with the faces slightly hollowed. One cannot detect heat-forging of the steel in its construction. The cutting edges are of a very coarse crystalline formation, now brittle through long, slow corrosion which is demonstrated by the patination of the whole surface of the blade, which because of its homogenous structure has acquired its typical corrosion (illus.1).

With the passage of time the sword must often have been sharpened and cleaned; this is shown by the edges and the surface, particularly in those areas where engraving is present. The obverse, or front face of the sword (indicated by the enamelled plate inserted in the pommel) though now much eroded because of corrosion and friction in cleaning shows the emblem of the order of the Garter, chiselled (or engraved); in the same area there is a similarly worked portcullis as well as a stamped smith's or cutler's mark. The punch for this cannot have been hardened, for its outer edges have been broken (illus. 2 and 3). The Gothic script in the Garter emblem is clearly made by chiselling; this is shown by the sharpness of the edges of the letters, the regularity of their forms, and the right-angled sides of the cuts. Very similar is the chiselling of the squares in the portcullis symbol below the Garter emblem, with their sharp edges and rounded bottoms. The outlines of both emblems are clearly drawn by engraving. Only faint traces of the Garter alone can be discerned on the reverse of the blade, which has been drawn rather smaller. To explain what amounts to the almost complete disappearance of this engraving on the reverse, it is suggested that because it was put on the reverse side of the blade it was not engraved as deeply, or drawn as large, as the one on the 'front' or outward side, and maybe also because the blade had been stored with the reverse side upward, in a position to attract more corrosion; this caused subsequent more vigorous cleaning which has rubbed away much of the engraving.

The transition from the heel of the blade to the tang narrows abruptly to between 4.6mm. The width is reduced from the maximum (at the shoulder) of 615mm down to 23mm over a length of 220.3mm, at 6.7mm wide in an even taper, and is from this distance up to the rivet-head, over a span of 6mm long of rounded section to 4.5mm and up to the rivet-head at 3.2mm wide. The thickness of the tang is reduced from about 4.6mm gently and evenly tapering to 4.3mm to the base of the pommel; and up to the cone of the rivet-head is slightly thicker, almost 5mm through the pommel. The taper to the rivet-head ranges in a span 5mm long from about 4.5mm to 3.5mm, round in section. The rivet-head itself is raised about 1mm and is burred over at right-angles over the (iron) core of the pommel and is partly coated with gold (the gold covering of the pommel) at the edges (illus. 4.i and 4.ii).

The Cross

The core of the cross is of iron (this was ascertained by taking a fine drill-core through the overlaid gold) and is forged into shape. This accounts for irregularities in the overall shape and for the wavy upper surface, because this top surface was not particularly carefully smoothed off after forging by means of filing or a special die-forging technique.

The BAM X-rays show (illus. 5.i and 5.ii) that the hole made to accommodate the tang fits very closely, with a typical indented slot to take the shoulders of the blade which has also been carefully shaped to accommodate the section of the mid-ribs of the blade. This could only have been done when the sword was originally assembled; adaptation of an old blade with a mid-rib and hollowed faces would risk serious damage, and so would not be done.

The shoulders of the blade (or the heel of the blade) is set into the cross to a depth of about 1mm (at the edges) to 3mm (at the mid-rib). Presumably the slot was chiselled out, making a very close fit. This technique of a cross which is not split is characteristic of the period (i.e. the mid-14th century). In this case, it is a matter of smith's work. The slight grooving (on the sides of the arms of the cross) may have been forged, for the underneath is irregularly grooved (i.e. the iron core of the cross show irregularies in the grooving) and the upper and under-sides are slightly arched.

Only gold which is very nearly pure is sufficiently flexible and malleable enough not to fracture under strong tension. Therefore stout gold (foil) of about 0.10 to 0.20mm thick could be pulled round the core of the cross without risk, and could be soldered firmly together on the upper face of the arms of the cross, next to the grip. This joint is clearly visible in illus. 6. Positive soldered joints could not be observed round the rosettes. These upstanding features were beaten out from inside the gold foil, and strengthened by mouldings which were fixed inside the embossings by solder. The joint is partly open.

This decoration by rosettes is difficult to assess. The x-ray photographs of the pommel show that where the rosettes are applied there is a double layer of gold (illus. 7). The main parts of these rosettes however show no joins, as if they were embossed, and strengthened from inside. Their edges too appear to be embossed and not soldered on. If they had been, irregular hard and soft edges would be noticeable.

Apart from the half rosettes set against the caps at the end of the arms of the cross and at the base of the pommel, and also those set on the underneath of the arms of the cross, there is no visible soldering; all the others are obviously supported by punched-out rosettes under the overlying gold foil. The decoration with rosettes cannot be explained otherwise.

The x-ray photographs (illus. 5 and 7) show that there is a double layer of gold, some showing a close joint to the core-material which clearly shows an underlying element. It looks as if in the case of some of the rosettes the foil has been cracked when the rosette was embossed sholwing a thick joint, but this cannot be an indication of soldering. The fillet or collar at the base of the grip is secure, but it is not attached to the wrapping of the cross. Illus. 8 and 9 show soldering joins and traces of solder, particularly on the ridges or fillets soldered on (to the collar at the base of the grip). On the main part of this collar there is a simple pattern of lightly engraved lines of the kind used at this period for enhancing the background of transparent enamels. Any punched decoration here would have caused distortion of the narrow band of metal. Soldered edges and joins appear here clearly and logically, as distinct from the embossed rosettes.

The Grip

In the x-ray photograph at illus. 5.ii the tang shows some distortion and is made slightly irregular by welding. Because of that, the tapering wooden core of the grip has been put on in two halves. It is of relatively soft, light wood, such as lime, and is somewhat shrunken. This wood core is covered with snake-skin, also very dried-out and shrunk, with an overlapping glued joint. There are three gold bands round it, each of the same form. The upper and lower ones are loose, but the middle one is still secure, perhaps glued (illus. 10). These bands have raised fillets soldered on. The middle one has two fillets, and because it is wider is slightly tapered upward. The use of snake-skin was quite common for practical use (probably right-handed) and here it shows hollows made by thumb, index and middle fingers and the edge of the hand. These worn patches are in the correct places anatomically, and the snake skin is merged into the wood surface at the points of pressure. There is no sign of artificial ageing. In the places where the grip of the hand did not press. the skin is almost undamaged except for a little tearing caused by the original stretching and shrinking over the wood.

The Pommel

The collar at the top of the grip is like the one against the cross, formed as a wide band lightly engraved with a double zig-zag decoration between two fillets soldered on (illus. 11 and 12). The flat wedge-shaped element, (where the upper collar embraces the base of the pommel) overlaps the rosette, the central boss of which is worn by friction. The rosette itself seems also to be embossed. On the x-ray photographs of the pommel (illus. 13 and 14) the disc-shaped iron core is shown. The outer rim of this is seen to be convex, or domed, and the typical turn-over of the rivet is domed also.

The pommel also is decorated all over with applied gold foil. The six rosettes on each side are embossed and supported from beneath as on the cross. The outer rim is covered in the same way, also decorated with rosettes with a narrow decorative raised border set in about 2 - 3mm from the rim, decorated with a simple roped pattern (illus. 15). The rivet head is covered too.

The holders for the enamel plate on the front and for the closed reliquary on the reverse, with the chalcedony covering are set into the recesses and secured by a circular soldered frame formed over a thin wire (illus. 16, 17, and 18). The irregular eruptions under the gold coating are definitely formed by corrosion of the underlying iron. Rust increases the volume of the surface, and thus lifts the gold. Illustrations 5 and 14 show in the x-ray photographs the aperture for the tang up to the top of the rivet. This aperture has presumably been chiselled out, cutting to one side from above, and cemented (i.e. coated with some sort of mastic, as in other medieval sword-pommels). A bored-out hole in a casting would present a totally different appearance. Small billets of copper (see the analytical report) were inserted front and back. These are formed with a slight taper (illus. 14 for a view from the side) and have wedged the tang into the over-large opening, otherwise the pommel would wobble and not be secure. The hole for the rivet is clearly visible and the very small but effective rivet-head still partly protrudes from the gold covering, which could only have been applied after the rivet had been burred over to secure the iron pommel. The rivet-head, and the hole it passes through, are of an elongated oval shape. Thus it is clearly shown that this hole has been made by chiselling, cut in and not bored out.

The enamel plate is the same as Limoges champlevé work of the 12th to the 14th centuries. The plate is flat, engraved and enamelled in opaque red and blue. The green enamel at the sides is cloudy, and parts of it are almost translucent - obviously because of insufficient oxide mixing, and overheating. It was finished by polished with some solution and the edges of the metal areas scrived round the outlines (illus. 15 and 16).

In the case of the green enamel, holes and blisters are caused by gas formation in the firing, mostly because of traces of borax and oxide, which has led to subsequent chipping. The red enamel has melted in a relatively fine grain with colour variation towards yellowish, without grained edges and oxide pores. The blue enamel is coarsely pigmented and shows flecks of oxidation and extraneous pigments - white, which indicates an enamel mixture on an already coloured base, like the red enamel. Since the 18th century the base for enamelling has been produced in a different way; this is shown by many examples. The oxidation of the grainy edges and the surface damaged and splintering caused by stress show this enamel to be identical with that of the 14th century, using comparative methods. The oxidation of the edges appears not to have been caused by the iron of the core.

It has been necessary to examine the reliquary unopened. The base shows unworked plain gold. The fabric threads are probably only laid on, held in place by the flat polished chalcedony which only leaves impressions in a few places, probably through the effect of dampness; condensation has build up and discoloured the gold. In illustrations 19 and 20 the woven structure and the discolouration can plainly be seen. Part of the milky appearance of the chalcedony is caused by tarnish on the inside. The inportant thing is the structure of the mineral, which shows the growth-lines in stripes. The traces of grinding and polishing on the chalcedony show straight, flat lines, not curved ones such as would have been produced by a grinding wheel. Probably the stone was simply polished with wood and leather, the earliest method of lapidary workmanship. Also, as far as it is possible to see, the edge is irregular and lacking in strict accuracy, which is typical of work done by hand on an uneven whetstone.

The rivet-head is partly visible, worn on the edges with the overlaid gold masking the joint. The metallurgical structure of the rivet-head is coarse and crystalline, thus very old and undisturbed.

Complete Assessment of the Preceding Section

The fettling (of the hilt), the neat fitting of the blade into the cross, the way in which the tang runs through cross, grip and pommel with its well-fitting tolerances are indicative of practical hand-craftsmanship, as well as comparison with similar pieces shows. The precision with which the pieces fit is technically exact and there are no technological variations in the separate pieces of the hilt. The various areas of wear on prominent points are nowhere articially produced. The outer surface of the gold testifies to frequent hand-wear; the distribution of points of pressure, traces of fine scouring, traces of fine and coarse scratches made in polishing and cleaning have been formed naturally over a long period of time, and are caused by use. The wavy upper (outer?) surface of the cross can be attributed to gradual loosening caused by friction. This only runs in one direction straight towards the outside. The original finish has been affected by use in certain areas. This 'wear' would be uniform all over if caused by articial ageing of the surfaces. The weight-distribution gives the sword a remarkably good balance. The formation of rust in the joints is more pronounced on the reverse side (on which is the reliquary in the pommel) on the slot in the cross and under the gold covering of the pommel, corresponding with deeper corrosion on that side of the blade.

The vague suggestion that weakening or damage to the underside of the cross was caused by battle-wear must be discounted, since swords of such magnificence, though designed to be perfect as fighting weapons, were seldom used in battle conditions. Marks of pressure on the underside of the cross could have been caused by a scabbard. These were generally provided with a metal locket, and maybe the sword was lying stored for a long time in such a scabbard, and condensation may have accumulated inside, while circulation of air kept the outside dry.

Only a few comparable artefacts will be considered without deep examination of art-historical aspects which have been covered very thoroughly in Ewart Oakeshott's report of 1982 in which the blade-type was considered.

From the technical point of view the assembly of the blade and the grip, fitted into a cross not split right through is to be found on several swords of the time. Etched motifs especially on blades and armour first appeared about the middle of the 15th century in accordance with the fashions of the Renaissance to enable decorative ornament to be applied quickly and easily in rich and graphic virtuoso technique. Up to that time, the application of motifs on metal depended upon the use of a burin, or engraving, and sometimes chiselling, on iron. Engraved work always required special skill, especially on iron. Etching became common later and was used with facility since it relied only on technical ability, and etched blades and harnesses were only developed and brought into fashion a hundred years later.

The basic form of the pommel, especially in its hollowed form is not unusual and is found, amongst others, in the Imperial sword of Frederick II, with its later pommel made for Charles IV c.1355 and in a modified form in the 'Sword of St. George' in Cologne which has further developed enamel of a technique from the Rhine area from the first half of the 14th century, and in the sculptured figure of Count Ekkehard of c.1260, and very often in painting, especially Northern French painting of c.1280-c.1420.

Also the rosette motif, imprinted or rather, embossed is found amongst others in the 'Three Kings' shrine in Cologne (1186-1230) and in enamel on the 'Maria' shrine, 1215-1237. An Anglo-Norman reliquary from the end of the 13th century in St. Evremond and an enamelled silver bowl, French of c.1360 in the Louvre in Paris show exactly the embossed rosette motif. Gold plating, and also silver-gilt plating in particularly complex forms and sculptures were a particular technique of the late Middle Ages up to the Gothic period. Very many head-and-arms reliquaries with large surfaces were plated with enormous stress factors; and this was always metal beaten out thin; and not gilding or a similar gold-leaf technique. This masterly craft was never used later; even in Gothic times it was beaten - only much later was it cast.

A sword of a king of France in the Pauilhac collection in the Musée de l'Armée in Paris, dating about 1300-1325 appears to be very similar in the shape of its hilt, technical working of gold plating with a reliquary on one side of the pommel and an enamel plaque on the other side of a similarly shaped pommel.

Still to be considered is the unsolved problem of the origin of this sword of Edward III. It is said that there is no proof that this sword, coming from Spain at the end of the 19th century was ever in the possession of the dealer Louis Marcy. About 1901 the first doubts were expressed about the authenticity of many of Marcy's wares - Marcy, who specialised in *objets d'art* of the later Middle Ages. Many of his wares, on the grounds of stylistic inconsistencies were soon identified as fakes. Their technical quality, however, was remarkable; but comparison of his manufactured pieces with original medieval objects using today's experience and scientific methods makes the distinction obvious. His historical and technical knowledge was limited and confined to what it was possible to make in his time. Until 1920, for example, nothing could have been known about exact empirical analytical processes. Also it was not possible to investigate and analyse the composition of gold, silver, copper and iron. Almost pure gold, as in the case of this sword, would be clearly different from modern gold in its composition, its origin, the method of obtaining it and the purifying and smelting processes used on it, and above all in the trace elements and the matter of platinum content. Decisive also is the temperature range in the composition of the solder, in respect of the cadmium and zinc. Recognisable mixes appear simply in the multiple smelting. So too with the copper; and even if old coins were used, its basic material would be identifiable today. Even a perfect forger at the turn of this century could hardly reckon with these revelations.

In the case of actual craftsmanship the line of demarcation is very difficult to determine, but nearly always stylistic errors can be found which are not compatible with ancient technical methods.

Also, in making such imitations, a very wide knowledge of specific styles is bound to be limited except where a direct copy of an original is made. In the case of this sword, direct acces to an original is unlikely. As an obvious tangible example, one may compare the sword under discussion with two others and two daggers in the illustration from the catalogue of the sale at Christie's on 25th April 1961 (illus. 21). Our Edward III sword, shown in the middle, is described as 'in the style of the late 15th century' with a short visual description. In the same way the two other swords and the daggers are described, little information about these others is available, except for the hearsay opinions that all of them came from the collection offered by Marcy. In the case of the daggers, one is clearly genuine and one clearly false. The expression 'In the style of....' occurs frequently in the catalogue; this is probably due more to uncertainty than to a clear opinion. Only later was the sword on the right given an unqualified 'black mark' as a 19th century fake by the blade museum in Solingen. Only by comparing the qualities of both swords is the difference so strongly apparent, whether it is in the rather primitive neo-classical seeming rosettes and pearled edges, in the engraving, in the curious forms of grip and cross, and the noticeable artificial ageing. It is astonishing that it has been compared with the other, and a common origin assumed. The same consideration applies to the sword on the left.

Also, a supposed relationship of our sword with the dagger on the right is curious; the hitherto accepted argument assumed by the experts that similar stones covered the reliquary, though it is plain that chalcedony covers the sword's and rock-crystal the dagger's. This led to considerable uncertainty which probably damaged the reputation of the objects under consideration.

As for today's probabilities and the acceptance of thorough investigation, no one will be able to deny proveable results, so that now we may be done with old prejudices and the miscarriages of justice.

From the enclosed analytical report from the Bundesanstalt für Materialprüfung (Institute of Material Testing) in Berlin one can see that here is a case of original, natural pure gold, untypical of gold used in the 19th century, and the joints are obviously soldered in antiquity with alloys with a high zinc/tin proportion. The almost entirely pure copper (from the two wedge-plates between the tang and the pommel) corresponds also to natural copper from an ancient source. An order from Limoges (from Louis Guibert's *L'orfèvrerie de Limoges*, 1884 - illus. 5.40) also confirms such working of fine gold. Similar solder recipes are known also from the period - i.e. c.1350.

The micro-section from the edge of the blade confirms its age by its structure.

In fact, there is no hint that this sword was not made at the date assumed for its origin, i.e. from the later 14th century.

PHOTOGRAPHS OF THE
KING EDWARD III SWORD

1

2

3

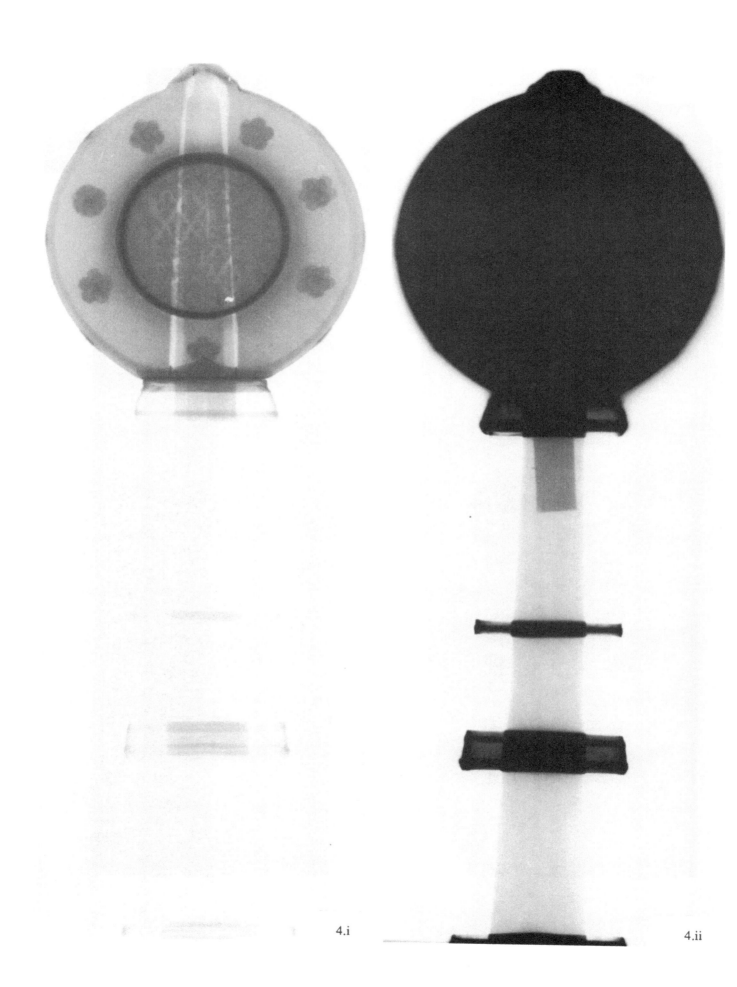

4.i   4.ii

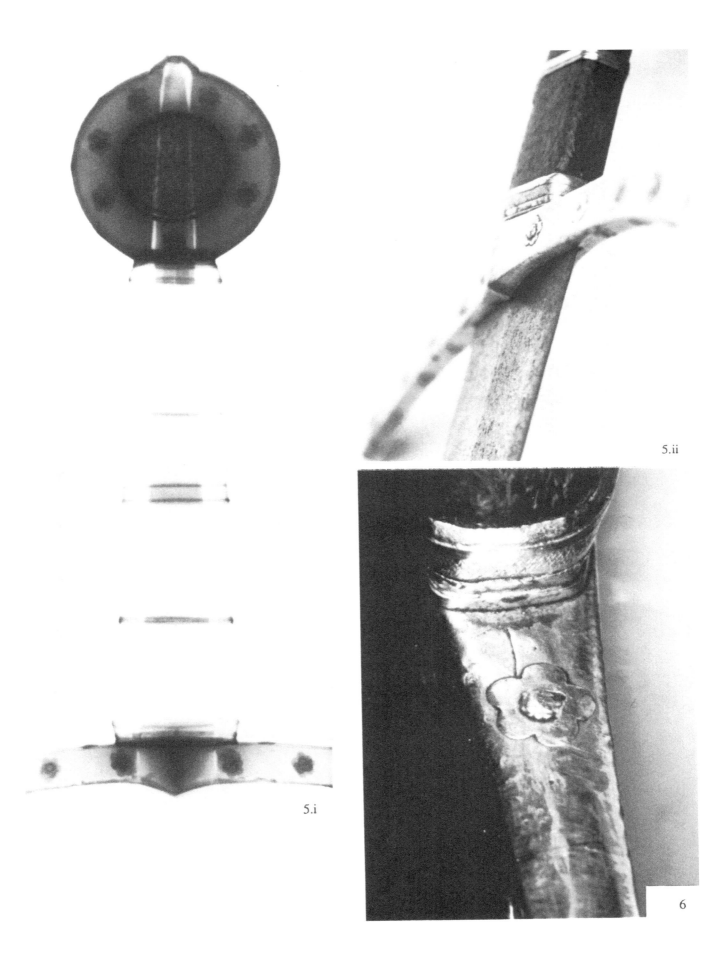

5.ii

5.i

6

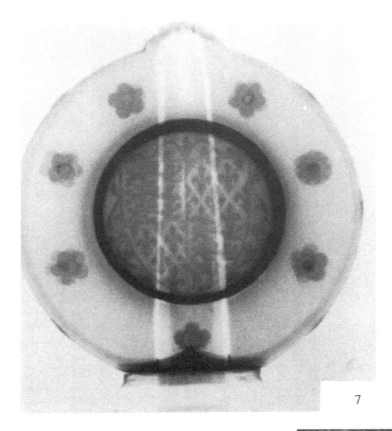

7

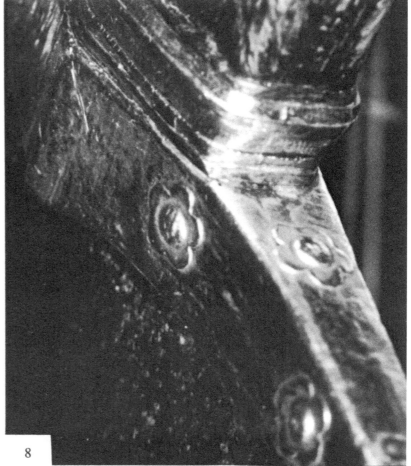

8

9.i

9.ii

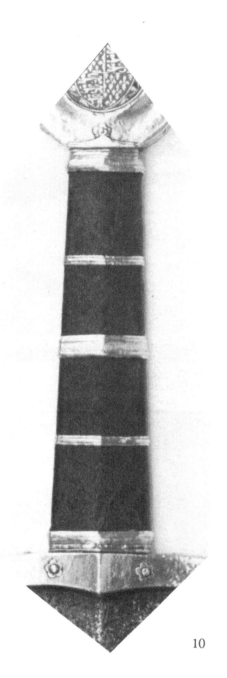

10

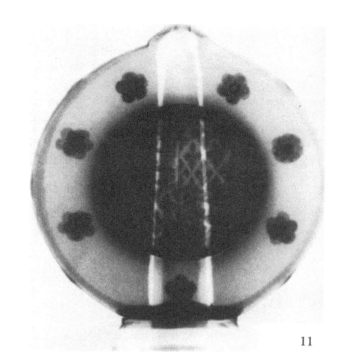

11

12

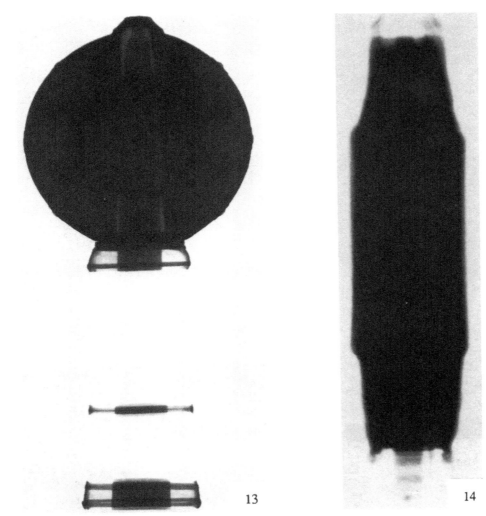

13   14

15

16

17

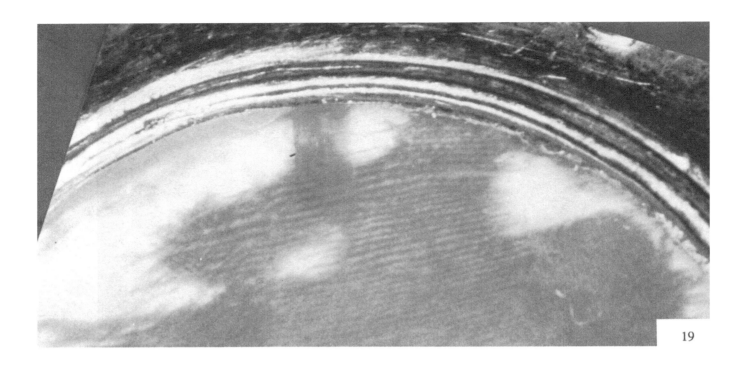

19

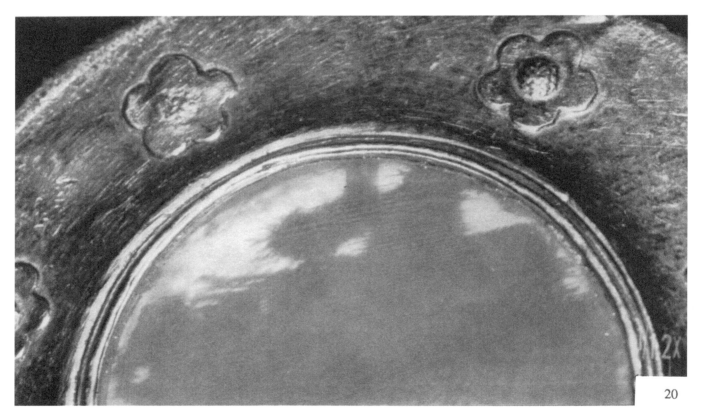

20

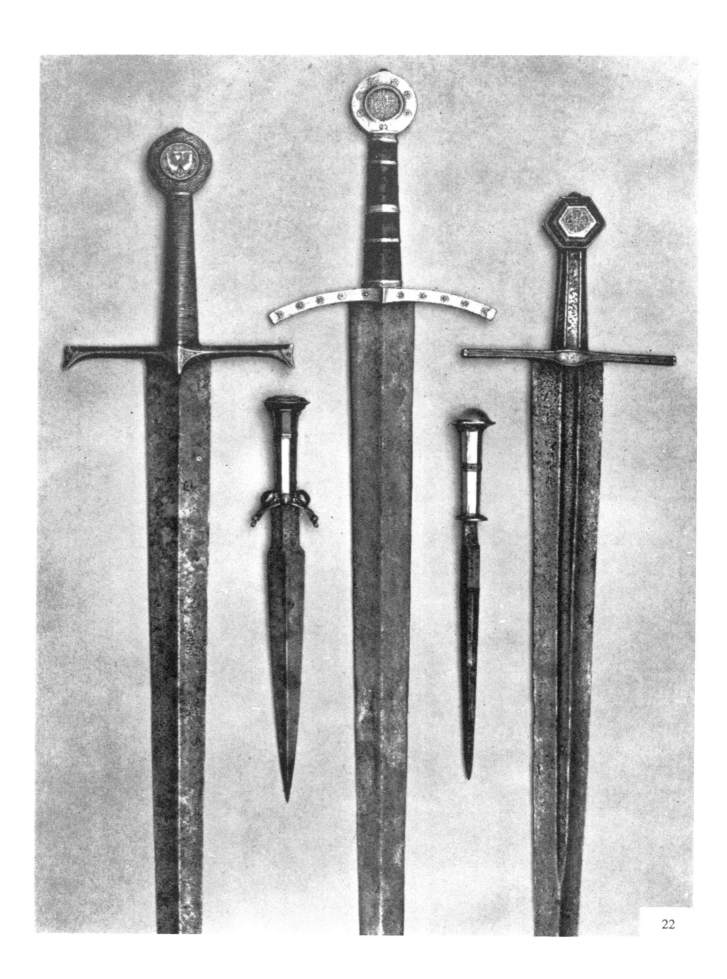

Blatt zum BAM-Prüfungszeugnis 6.3/3666 vom 17.03.1986

Untersuchungsbericht

1. Problemstellung

Gegenstand der Untersuchung ist ein Schwert, dessen Knauf, Griff und Heft mit Gold verziert sind.
Nach Angabe des Auftraggebers stammt das Schwert (Stahlteil) aus dem 14. Jahrhundert. Fraglich ist jedoch, ob die Gold-beschläge ebenfalls aus dieser Zeit stammen oder später angebracht wurden, z.B. in der Renaissance-Zeit, wo aus alten Waffen Schmuckgegenstände hergestellt wurden oder etwa im 19. Jahrhundert, wo durch Fälscherwerkstätten alte Waffen aufgewertet wurden.

2. Probennahme

Da möglicherweise Experten aus der Zusammensetzung des Goldes Schlüsse auf die Herstellungszeit ziehen können, wurden den Goldbeschlägen an 3 Stellen durch Herrn Tauchwitz (im Einverständnis mit dem Auftraggeber) Proben im Milligramm-bere-ich entnommen. Diese Entnahme erfolgte im Beisein von Reg. Dir. Dipl.-Ing. B.F. Schmitt und T.A. Ch. Segebade von der Bundesanstalt für Materialprüfung sowie von 2 Fachhochschulpraktikanten.

Probe 1: Gold vom Goldlot am Heft	Masse 5,45 mg
Probe 2: Gold von der Knaufkapsel	Masse 5,38 mg
Probe 3: Gold vom Goldblech am Heft	Masse 9,22 mg

Röntgenaufnahmen haben gezeigt, daß sich im Bereich zwischen Knauf und Griff beidseitig je 1 Lasche oder Keil befinden, vermutlich aus Metall. Um diese Art des Metalls festzustellen, wurde mit einem feinen Bohrer durch den Griff hindurch ein Bohrspan von diesem Metallstück entnommen.

Probe 4: Metallspan vom Keil	Masse 10,57 mg

3. Analyse der Proben

In den Goldproben sollten die Gehalte folgender Spurenelemente bestimmt werden: Antimon, Blei, Cadmium, Palladium, Platin, Zink und Zinn.
Um diese Elemente im Spurenbereich bestimmen zu können, ist die Abtrennung von der Goldmatrix, gegebenenfalls auch von Silber und Kupfer, falls diese als Legierungsbestandteile vorliegen, erforderlich. Um das Abtrennungsverfahren auf Vollständig-keit und auf Freiheit von Verlusten zu überprüfen, wurde eine Probe 0 hergestellt mit Gold als Matrixmetall und den übrigen Metallen als Spurenverunreinigungen.

3.1 Photonenaktivierung

Die Goldproben 0, 1, 2 und 3 sowie die Metallteilprobe 4 wurden getrennt bestrahlt und jeweils anschließend die chemische Trennung vorgenommen. Bei Probe 0 waren die Gehalte bekannt, bei den Proben 1, 2 und 3 wurde jeweils ein Aliquot der Probe 0 als Referenzmaterial mitbestrahlt. Bei Probe 4 wurde ein Cu-Standard mitbestrahlt.

Bestrahlungsbedingungen: max. Photonenenergie	30 MeV
Elektronenstrom	ca. 100 µA
Bestrahlzeit	600 min

Prinzip

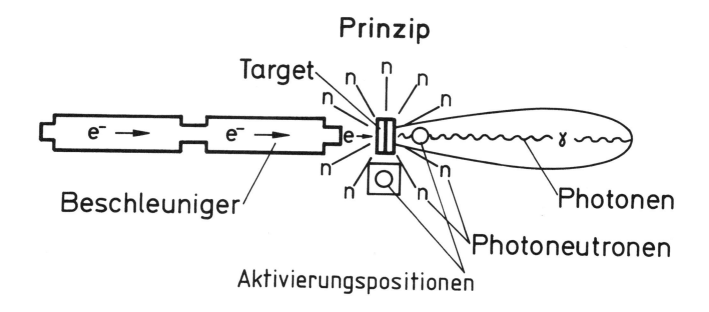

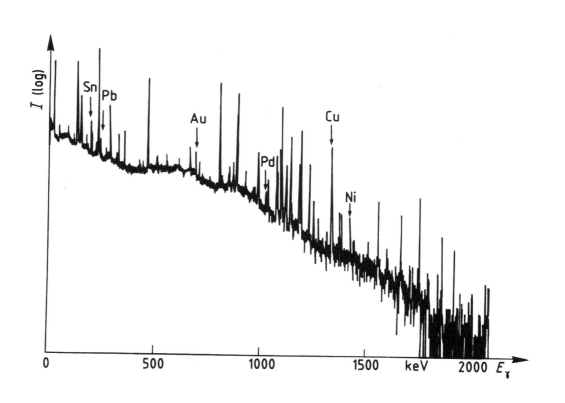

3.2 Abtrennung der Spurenelemente bei den Goldproben

Nach der Aktivierung wurden die Goldproben 1, 2 und 3 in Königswasser gelöst, von den gesuchten Elementen inaktive Trägersalzlösungen zugegeben und Weinsäure zugegeben, um das Ausfallen von Bleisalzen zu verhindern. Die Lösung wurde eingedampft und der Rückstand mit Wasser und Salzsäure aufgenommen. Da Silber nicht in nennenswerter Menge vorlag, fiel kein Silberchlorid aus.

Durch vorsichtige Zugabe von konzentrierter Natriumnitritlösung wurde das Gold ausgefällt. Nach Filtration wird inaktive Goldträgerlösung zum Filtrat gegeben und erneut das Gold mit Natriumnitrit gefällt.

Die restliche Lösung wird eingedampft, mit Cellulosepulver versetzt, getrocknet und zu Pillen verpreßt. Diese Pillen sind, da ihre Geometrie für alle Proben und Standards gleich ist, geeignete Meßpräparate.

3.3 Messung der Proben und des Standards

Für die Messung der γ-Linien wurde ein Koazial-Halbleiter-Detektor, für die weichen γ- und Röntgenlinien ein Planar-Halbleiter-Detektor benutzt.

3.4 Ergebnisse

Die Photonenaktivierungsanalyse erbrachte folgende Ergebnisse:

4. Blatt zum BAM-Prüfungszeugnis 6.3/3666 vom 17.03.1986

	Goldprobe 1 Lot vom Heft	Goldprobe 2 Knauf	Goldprobe 3 Heft	Probe 4 Metallteil
Platin	0,53%	1,06 ± 0,01 %	0,55%	n.b.
Silber	n.b.	n.b.	n.b.	123 µg/g
Zink	53 µg/g	283 ± 20 µg/g	< 50 µg/g	45 µg/g
Palladium	24 µg/g	1300 ± 100 µg/g	47 µg/g	n.b.
Cadmium	< 10 µg/g	74 ± 7 µg/g	< 10 µg/gn.b.	n.b.
Zinn	2,4 µg/g	186 ± 20 µg/g	< 2 µg/g	n.b.
Antimon	0,05 µg/g	88 ± 6 µg/g	< 0,02 µg/g	122 µg/g
Arsen	0,6 µg/g	n.b.	0,23 µg/g	52 µg/g
Blei	470 µg/g	n.b.	551 µg/g	60 µg/g
Matrix Gold	~100%	~100%	~100%	
Kupfer				~100%

Aus den Gehalten an Platin und Spurenelementen läßt sich schließen, daß es sich bei allen 3 Goldproben nicht um neuzeitliches Elektrolytgold handelt. Bei Probe 4 handelt es sich um ein unlegiertes Stück Kupferblech.

4. Bemerkungen:

Umrechnungsfaktoren:

$$1 \text{ µg/g} = 1/10000\%$$
$$\text{bzw. } 10000 \text{ µg/g} = 1\%$$

POSTSCRIPT FOR PEDANTS

I am aware that in the eyes of many who may read this book, and most who may be asked to review it, the inclusion of anecdote must inevitably be assumed to nullify such scholarship as it may contain. Inclusion of anecdote will probably damn the whole work in those eyes; such at least has been the case with all my previous work during the past forty years. So also will the lack, in so many cases, of inventory or accession numbers. Whenever possible these are noted, but because so many of the swords shown were once my own and have now passed from hand to hand in private collections unknown to me – which don't have inventory numbers – I cannot include such essential information. It may also happen that some of the numbers of swords in museums may be incorrect. I have taken numbers from catalogues and/or museum labels, but even so inaccuracies creep in, for museum publications have been known for wrong numbers, like the splendid *European Swords and Daggers in the Tower of London* where wrong numbering is rife.

Each anecdote I have allowed myself is a first-hand comment on my own personal experience of the sword under discussion; only occasionally have I used a second-hand comment and there are none which are not relevant, even interesting or – far worse, *amusing*. Swords are so tightly bound up with everything to do with living human experience, past *and* present, that an attempt to put a little warm flesh on the cold bones of respectable archaeological research may offend the purist, but to the ordinary interested reader, the student and the fighting man for whom all my work has been done, such warmth may help to make a diet of bones a little more appetising. Therefore I make no excuse or apology for my lapses into Anecdotal Chat. I have done what I have done; and I've done it my way.